Toward a General Theory of Action and *The Social System,* Professor Parsons elaborates the major interrelationships between psycho-analytic theory and his functionalist action theory. Part I, Theoretical Perspectives, is an absorbing analysis of the theories of object relations and socialization during the pre-oedipal period. Throughout this section the author departs from Freudian theory on several fundamental points. In Part II, Stages of the Life Cycle, Professor Parsons reflects on the impact of society on the personality in the post-oedipal stage, including his thoughts on the elementary school class as a medium of selection and status differentiation, the situation of the adolescent, and the problems of the aged in our society. The last part of this volume, Health and Illness, begins with a study of social definitions of the statuses and roles of the sick and of the health service personnel who treat them. Professor Parsons then examines the division of labor which should exist between psychiatrist and pastoral counselor in the light of the roles, functions, and training of each. The final piece provides a comprehensive survey of the author's work in the field of medical sociology and a reinterpretation of the present state of health services in our country.

ABOUT THE AUTHOR

Talcott Parsons, the leading figure in American sociology, was formerly Chairman of Harvard University's interdisciplinary Department of Social Relations, where he is Professor of Sociology. He is the major representative of the school of functionalism in American sociological theory. His books, *The Structure of Social Action,* 1949, and *The Social System,* 1951, among others, are recognized as classic statements. Professor Parsons is a steady contributor to academic journals in all areas of behavioral theory.

Social Structure

and Personality

SOCIAL

STRUCTURE

Talcott Parsons

AND

PERSONALITY

The Free Press of Glencoe

COLLIER-MACMILLAN LTD., LONDON

For

ANNE

*A Sensitive and Resourceful
Student of the Problems
of this Book*

Contents

Introduction

THE ESSAYS brought together in this collection go back a little over ten years. At the suggestion of several colleagues, I have included "The Superego and the Theory of Social Systems," which is the oldest of the essays. This article seems to form a generally appropriate point of departure for the lines of thought which run through the whole collection; namely, the problem of theoretical formulation of the relations between the social system and the personality of the individual. These relations are seen not only in cross-sectional terms but also in terms of their bearing on the developmental pattern of the personality through the various phases of the life cycle, and in terms of their relation both to stable adjustments and to the pathologies of illness.[1]

This opening essay sounds the keynote of the author's concern, from his perspective as a sociologist, with the relevance of the psychoanalytic theory of personality for the integration of sociology with psychology, and with particular reference to the problem of the relation between motivation to performance in social roles and the control of that performance through normative mechanisms. Basically this problem, in different ramifications and stages of its development, dominates all five essays in Part One of this collection, entitled *Theoretical Perspectives*. These five papers are presented in the chronological order of their writing, and trace in sequence the

1. An additional reason for including it here is that this essay is no longer available elsewhere in book form. It was originally published in *Psychiatry* (February, 1952) and reprinted as Chapter I of Parsons, Bales, and Shils, *Working Papers in the Theory of Action* (1953), which has been out of print for some time and will not be republished as such.

development of a series of theoretical problems and approaches to
their possible solution.

The first two essays in the present collection were written im-
mediately following the two important publications, *Toward a
General Theory of Action* (with Shils, Tolman, and others) and
The Social System, both of which were published in the fall of 1951;
the first essay, as noted, was included in *Working Papers in the
Theory of Action* (in collaboration with Bales and Shils) in 1953.
This was a period of general theoretical effervescence. My work on
The Social System, profiting directly from collaboration with Shils,
Tolman, and others, and by extensive discussions with Bales, had
opened up what seemed to me to be new perspectives on the relations
between the social system and the personality of the individual.[2]
Chapter 1 was an attempt to reconsider the nature and significance
of Freud's own contribution to the theoretical integration of personality and social system. It took as its point of departure the immense importance of the convergence between Freud and Durkheim
with respect to the internalization of normative culture in the personality of the individual.[3] The essay was thus an attempt to define
further, in their relation to the more technical terms of Freud's own
theory, a set of insights which had been arrived at in the course of
some very general theoretical work. Above all, it presented the first
main statement of what is to me the very important view that the
internalization of culture could not, in Freudian terms, be confined
to the superego, but must also be extended to *all* the structural subsystems of the personality as these were delineated in Freud's later
theory. The culmination of this line of thought will be found in
Chapters 4 and 5 of the present collection, which were written some
five to eight years later.

The second essay on "The Father Symbol" was an attempt to
follow up the ramifications of this general line of thought in another
way, by taking a theme which was obviously central to psychoanaly-

2. These were elaborated in two important chapters of *The Social
System,* namely, Chapter VI on "The Learning of Role-Expectations" or
more briefly on "socialization" of the child, and Chapter VII on "Deviant
Behavior and the Mechanisms of Social Control." There were also important
relations to Chapter IX on "Expressive Symbols and the Social System."

3. On rereading it is evident to me that the contribution of the American social psychologists, Cooley, G. H. Mead, and W. I. Thomas, to this
same development should have been acknowledged there, as it has been in
later publications.

tic theory and approaching the questions of its importance in the cultural and societal areas rather than in the strictly psychological one alone. In an important sense this, like the other essays in Part One, is an expression of the "sociologist's protest" against the biologizing of Freud's theory, which in this instance would contend that the father as symbol was a simple expression of the biological reality of male parenthood. The emphasis was on social structure, and in particular on the significance of the father as the most important point of articulation between the family and the occupational organization of the larger society. Reconsidering this essay, I am struck by the bare mention of the religious usage of the father symbol, as in the concept of "God the Father," and hence by the rich opportunities for further analytical work at this level, which were not exploited.[4]

In terms of content and interest Chapter 3 on the "Incest Taboo" was closely associated with my next major publication, the book written in collaboration with Bales and others, *Family, Socialization and Interaction Process* published in 1955. The perspective of this book was dominated by the conviction that, with very marginal and on the whole minimal exceptions, the nuclear family should be considered as a universal feature of human societies. This view was suggested and confirmed in structural terms by evidence from two main sources, namely the comparative survey carried out by Zelditch (Chapter VI) and the insight that the basic structure of the nuclear family, including above all a coalition between an instrumental and an expressive leader, belonged to a generic type of structure of small groups. This was shown by the development of role differentiation in small groups set up within the laboratory; here the study of Bales and Slater (Chapter V) and previous studies by Bales and his associates (notably Chapter IV of *Working Papers*) provided the main insight.

It then seemed possible to fit Freud's stages of psychosexual development (through the oedipal stage) into an account of the stages of incorporation of the child into this structure of the nuclear family, starting with oral dependency in relation to the mother,

4. Like all the essays included in the present volume, these first two were written for specific occasions. The first, on the superego, was presented in May 1951 to the Psychoanalytic Section of the American Psychiatric Association, whereas the second, on the Father Symbol, was written for the Conference on Science, Philosophy, and Religion and published in their volume, edited by Bryson, Kinkelstein, and MacIver, *Symbols and Values: a Social Study.*

moving on to the "phallic" or "love dependency" phase of early instrumental learning, and into the oedipal crisis in its relation to the internalization of sex-role and the superego. Finally, there was an attempt to give a considerably more circumstantial account of the interaction processes which went on within this structural framework, taking many cues not only from psychoanalytic theory but also from what had come to be known of the phases of process in small groups, and through relation to the work of James Olds (Chapter 4) some of the more strictly psychological mechanisms involved.

The third essay in this collection is an important by-product of this concern with family structure and socialization.[5] The incest taboo had been a focus of attention on the part of social anthropologists for a long time, and it clearly involved all the major concerns of the work on *Family and Socialization.* These included the universality of the nuclear family, the basic constancy of its fundamental role structure—that of the four role-types differentiated on the hierarchical axis of generation—and the qualitative one of sex. It clearly involved the relation of this role structure to the Freudian conception of the stages of psychosexual development and, in turn, the role of eroticism in it. In short it attempted to show how a variety of types of empirical evidence and theoretical analysis which had been recently developing could be brought to bear on a very old, indeed "classic," problem of comparative anthropology.

The last two papers in Part One belong to a somewhat later period.[6] Chapter 4, "Social Structure and the Development of Personality," is more in the nature of a culminating statement of the themes which operated in the first three papers in this collection and in the book on family and socialization, with special reference to their bearing on the relations between psychoanalytic psychology and sociology. It introduces the idea that Freud's concept of "the reality principle," as used in his later theory, referred mainly to what he called "object relations" and hence to the *social* environment of the

5. While serving as visiting Professor of Social Theory at Cambridge, England, I delivered this paper at the London meeting of the British Association of Social Anthropologists in January, 1954.

6. Chapter 4 "Social Structure and the Development of Personality," was originally written as a contribution to a proposed volume in honor of the centenary of Freud's birth, which unfortunately never saw the light. It was published in *Psychiatry,* November, 1958. Chapter 5 was written for a symposium at the meeting of the American Psychosomatic Society in Montreal in 1960, and has not previously been published anywhere.

personality. Second, my interpretation of the concept of identification has accordingly been modified by laying special emphasis on the incorporation of the individual through socialization into the status of membership in collectivities. This perspective seemed to make possible a clearer account of the relations between cathexis and identification. The third closely related innovation was the elaboration of the view that the Freudian conception of internalization could not be confined to the superego; indeed not only was it central to the conception of the ego, as Freud himself made clear, but it must also include the id, as the precipitate of pre-oedipal object relations.

Chapter 5, "Some Reflections on the Problem of Psychosomatic Relationships in Health and Illness," on the other hand, in its main theoretical focus, attempts to open up an essentially new field, in which the earlier psychosocial reference points were rooted, through a concern with the nature of erotic pleasure as Freud had used this concept. That it could not be a phenomenon of "instinct" in the older biopsychological sense, but must be in some sense a generalized mechanism of motivational operation in complex action systems, had already been made clear in the discussion of its place in the incest complex. The conviction of the importance of this view was strongly reinforced from two apparently disparate sources.

One was the return of my interests to problems of larger-scale social systems generally and their economic aspects in particular. In this connection I had become concerned with a more specific analysis than before of the properties of money as a generalized medium facilitating certain modes of social interaction in complex systems— which was eventually documented in the book *Economy and Society* (with Neil J. Smelser), 1956. It seemed that erotic pleasure in the Freudian sense belonged in the same category of phenomena. The other was suggested by the work of my previous associate, James Olds, who had entered the field of study of the neurophysiological mechanisms of behavior, and had established his discovery of the "reward center" in the brain of the rat.[7] Olds' conception of the nature of reward mechanisms which underlay this combination of neurological and behavioral evidence was very close to my own conception both of the way money operates in the case of market systems

7. Cf. Olds, "Self-Stimulation of the Brain," *Science,* March, 1957. For theoretical background see his book, *The Growth and Structure of Motives,* New York, The Free Press of Glencoe, 1956.

and of the way erotic pleasure operates in the socialization process.

Chapter 5 is an attempt to sketch out a conception of the generalized mechanism in this sense as a major feature not only of action systems but also of all living systems. In any case, there seemed to be a continuum from human language and a variety of more specialized mechanisms operating at the macrosocial level, notably money and power in the political sense at one pole,[8] to mechanisms with primary reference to personalities, including affect in the Freudian sense and erotic pleasure, and finally, at the other pole, pleasure at the level of control of the locomotive behavior of the rat.[9] This essay attempts to formulate the idea that a hierarchy of mechanisms of this sort must be involved in the understanding of psychosomatic illness, as phenomena of the "control" of organic processes operating from the level of the personality and the most immediately related layers of the functioning of the organism. Its highly theoretical and speculative nature makes the placing of this essay in Part One, *Theoretical Perspectives,* more appropriate than in Part Three, *Health and Illness.* It points, however, to the problem areas dealt with there.

Part One is perhaps more concerned with personality and social structure whereas, with the transition to Part Two, the emphasis shifts the other way to social structure and personality. In terms of the author's personal concerns this is appropriate, in that none of the essays in either Parts Two or Three was written before 1958, at a time when his interests were quite clearly concentrated in the social system and its cultural boundaries, rather than in the personality system. Nevertheless, the concern with interrelations between social and personal continued to be of prime importance.

It was a major theme of Part One that the rootedness of the personality in the social system of the nuclear family was only part of a larger picture, the rest of which involved the larger-scale structures of complex societies. Furthermore, these larger structures (such as bureaucratic organizations as settings for occupational roles) could not possibly be interpreted as significant primarily because of their direct services to the personality of the individual. The fact that nuclear families in the nature of the case could not function as in-

8. Cf. my paper "On the Concept of Political Power," *Proceedings of the American Philosophical Society,* Vol. 107, No. 3, June, 1963, and also "On the Concept of Influence," *Public Opinion Quarterly,* Spring, 1963.

9. This essay owes a great deal to personal discussions with Dr. Karl Pribram of the Stanford University Medical School.

dependent societies was stressed again and again, notably in Chapter Three on the "Incest Taboo."

The four essays of Part Two take up explicitly some problems of the relation of the personality of the individual to the social structure outside the context of the family, without special reference to problems of malintegration between the two, which is the subject matter of Part Three. The essays in Part Two are appropriately organized in the first instance around the life cycle past the oedipal period, discussion of pre-oedipal phases having been included in Part One.

Any good sociologist would, I think, consider the relation between personality and social structure in the perspective of the life cycle as necessarily including a series of stages of socialization, not excepting the latest phase, the "aging" process. The first three papers of Part Two concern mainly phases of the cycle preceding the assumption of fully adult roles, whereas the fourth concerns the last major phase of the cycle, that of old age.

This leaves an important gap which unfortunately has not been adequately filled in my own work, though more of it is handled in Chapter 8 than in any other in this collection. Two themes which would very much merit attention within this gap are, first, the processes of socialization which are attendant on stages in careers in the occupational world. However important it is for a young man to become independently established in a job, the changes which are likely to occur between that time and the approach of retirement are likely to be profound—the more so the higher level the occupational status.

The other particularly important theme is the socialization process which occurs within the nuclear family, but this time with attention centered on the married couple in relation to each other and to their children. Emphasis is put on such topics as the impact of the first stages of parenthood, especially if it comes some time after marriage, the changes attendant on the growing up of children, and the transitions to the stage of the "empty nest" and to grandparenthood.

This second theme may be said to be a neglected field in a rather general sense; it is dealt with mainly in connection with problems of pathology rather than in a perspective of "normal development." The former theme on the other hand may be said to have been lost between two disciplines. The sociologist tends to deal with occupational roles in the context of their functional significance in employing organizations rather than their place in the total personality system of the individual; whereas the psychologist's attention is not often sharply focused on the structure of social situations.

Chapter 6,[10] "The School Class as a Social System," is a direct extension of the theoretical concerns of the essays in Part One. The primary focus is the drastic structural difference between the family and the school as socializing agencies and the relation of this difference to the importance of universalistic norms in modern society and to the stress on achievement as evaluated by such norms. This, of course, contrasts strikingly with the particularistic and ascriptive emphases of the normative context of socialization within the family.[11]

It is here that a very important extension of the theme of sex-role ascription emerges. Sex-role, the determination of which is deeply involved in the incest taboo, constitutes a basic axis of the *differentiation* of status within the society. In the school, however, children not only are taught but they are differentiated in status in respects which fundamentally influence their life-chances to the extent that the status system itself permits mobility. Perhaps the most important element of the macrosocial context of this analysis was the evidence that the child's school record in *elementary* school was the most important single predictor (especially for boys) of probable future occupational status. The school system thus operates as a critically important *selective* mechanism with respect to the placing of individuals in the social structure as well as a mechanism of socialization in the sense of inducing change in the personality structure of the individual.

This consideration introduces a major complicating dimension for the theoretical treatment of personality and social system as these were considered at the level of Part One; namely, that it is no longer a matter only of the interdependence of ascriptively bound role-expectations and motivations to performance, but also of selection and allocation of persons-in-roles in a ramified role-system. Services of persons become *mobile* resources among which selective choice is possible and conversely the social environment becomes a manifold

10. Occasioned by a request to contribute to a special issue of the *Harvard Educational Review*, Vol. 29, No. 4, Fall, 1959, pp. 292–318, dealing with the social context of education.

11. The analysis presupposes a considered judgment that it is the school, not the child's peer group, which is the *primary* socializing agency.

of alternative opportunities (or hazards) from the point of view of the "status seeking" individual.[12]

Seen in this context, the school class is the primary socializing system for the latency phase of development in our type of society; it takes over from the primary role of the family in the oedipal phase. I think it has been possible to demonstrate the essential differences which enable the school not only to be the agent of internalization of achievement motivation but also to select individuals for future achieved statuses on the basis of differential performance.

The very brief treatment of secondary education in Chapter 6 leads into the subject matter of Chapter 7, "Youth in the Context of American Society."[13] It is an attempt to reconsider the general problem of the place of youth culture in the structure of our society, including the modifications in theory which would need to be made in the light both of social changes and of advances in theoretical insight since previous attempts in this field.[14]

Chapter 8 is placed after the paper on youth because it deals with a rather broader range of problems. It was written in collaboration with Winston White for the volume *Culture and Social Character*[15] which dealt with the work of David Riesman. It takes Riesman's major theme of the relation between character and society and, after outlining our understanding of Riesman's position, sets forth our alternative to it. In order to do this, it was necessary to outline a rather extensive range of topics, starting with our understanding of the main outline of the American value system, and the nature of

12. The above insights owe a great deal to a study of the mobility aspirations and opportunities of high school boys, carried out in collaboration with the late Samuel Stouffer and Florence Kluckhohn. A report of that study, under the editorship of Florence Kluckhohn and the present author is expected soon to be published.

13. This was written for an issue of *Daedalus* (Winter, 1961) which was devoted to problems of youth generally, both in this and in other countries, and in each from various points of view, of which mine was meant to be specifically sociological. Recently published in book form as *Youth, Challenge and Change,* Erik H. Erikson, Ed., New York, Basic Books, 1963.

14. See in particular the essay *Age and Sex in the Social Structure of the United States,* but also the *Kinship System of the United States* and *Sources and Patterns of Aggression in the Western World.* The three are all included in my *Essays in Sociological Theory,* Revised edition, New York, The Free Press of Glencoe, 1954.

15. S. M. Lipset and L. Loewenthal, Eds., New York, The Free Press of Glencoe, 1962.

the processes of structural change in American society which have been occuring—notably differentiation and what we called normative upgrading. We then discussed the major contexts in which the individual is most closely involved with social situations such as occupational roles, education, the family, the adolescent peer group, and the problems of consumption. Our general view is that there has not been the sort of change which Riesman seems to see either in societal values, at the highest level of generality, or in type of dominant character, if he means that through "other direction" the typical individual no longer takes the same kind and degree of personal responsibility for his decisions which his forefathers did. This essay thus attempts to put the whole treatment of the relation of the socialization of the individual to the structure of the society—which runs through Parts One and Two—in the broadest perspective of analysis of the society to be found among these essays.

Chapter 9, "Toward a Healthy Maturity,"[16] finally, extends the analysis to a phase of the life cycle which I had previously dealt with only in the sketchiest way, notably in the old paper on "Age and Sex." Its emphasis on the problem of health thus serves as a transition from Part Two to Part Three, as well as appropriately ending Part Two with the final phase of the life cycle.[17] The problem of health, however, is essentially a point of departure for consideration of the principal alternatives open for defining the social role of the aged in American society, considering both the values of the society and the structural alternatives. The great increase in the proportion of older people is one of the main reference points, as well as the fact that they are on the average in far better states of health than previously. The view presented is that a much more positive mode of utilizing this very important human resource is needed.

The three essays which compose Part Three have in common a bearing on the problems of health and illness. This concern with the

16. It was written as an address to the National Health Forum for a meeting dealing with the relations between aging and health (March, 1960) and was published in the *Journal of Health and Human Behavior,* Fall, 1960.

17. I have, in a working paper on "Death in American Society," attempted to take the final step possible to complete analysis of the life cycle at its terminal stage—a companion piece on birth and attitudes toward it would also be appropriate, though more seems to have been done in this field. A sharply abbreviated version of the paper on death was published in *The American Behavioral Scientist,* May, 1963.

social and psychological context of health and illness the reader familiar with my work will recognize to be an old interest which I have pursued from time to time for many years. Each essay in turn attempts to extend one step further the theoretical treatment of this problem area by integrating previous theory with new empirical and analytical considerations. They all also have in common a belief, carried over from past work, in the great importance of the psychological aspects of health and illness and their intimate connection with the social system. This conviction, of course, provides the thread of continuity with the earlier papers in this volume.

Chapter 10, "Definitions of Health and Illness in the Light of American Values and Social Structure," relative to earlier papers in the field, is above all new in its attempt to relate the role structures involved in illness and its treatment explicitly to the value system, particularly of American society. Hence it tried to build on intervening work on the general topic of the role of values in social systems, and tried to do so in a comparative context, including brief sketches of the differences between the American pattern and those developed in the Soviet Union (largely based on the work of Mark Field) and in Great Britain. This comparison strongly highlights the importance of the activistic element in the American system expressing itself in the valuation of individual achievement and imposing a special obligation on the individual as patient to cooperate actively with health personnel toward the achievement of his own recovery.[18] Among other things, these considerations throw considerable light on the special prominence of psychological interests in American medicine, by contrast with the sharply negative attitudes especially to psychoanalysis in the Soviet Union, and the intermediate attitudes in these respects in Great Britain.[19]

18. Shortly after the completion and publication of this paper, a study by Joseph Ben-David of the Hebrew University, Jerusalem, provided convincing evidence that the "classical" later nineteenth-century German pattern provided a fourth clear-cut type where the patient was treated much more as a passive object of manipulation than in any of the other three cases, a circumstance which has had much to do with the prominence of research in somatic medicine in that tradition and, as Ben-David argues, with the fact that Freud had to pursue his interests outside the main context of German and Austrian university medicine of that time. Cf. Ben-David, "Roles and Innovations in Medicine," *American Journal of Sociology,* 65 (May, 1960), pp. 561–568.

19. This essay was written for and published in the collection edited by E. Gartly Jaco, *Patients, Physicians, and Illness,* New York, The Free Press of Glencoe, 1958.

Chapter 11, "Mental Illness and Spiritual Malaise," is another attempt to consider the role structure and social psychology of health and illness in the United States, but this time, not in relation to those of other societies but rather to a closely related but different set of functions within the same society. This theme is suggested by the rapid rise in recent years of pastoral counseling, particularly in liberal Protestant groups, but also in Jewish and even to some extent in Catholic groups. There has clearly been a problem of distinguishing such counseling from and relating it to psychotherapy.

The essay attempts to clarify these relations within the general context and conceptualization of structural differentiation, which has figured prominently throughout the volume, especially perhaps in Chapter 8. Departing from the early fusion of the contexts of religion, kinship, and health, this essay suggests that the kinship system, on the one hand, and the religious collectivity, on the other, have become progressively more highly differentiated agencies of the social system to the point where they are both "boundary structures": the family mediating between society and the motivational system of the individual personality, and the church mediating between the society and the religious grounding of societal value-commitments on the part of individuals. The emergence of psychiatry as a profession, closely associated with but differentiated from the family, suggests not only that spiritual counseling should be carefully differentiated from psychotherapy—which has not always been the case—but that the minister of religion is not well suited to play the primary role of counselor. As the responsible leader of his congregation as a collectivity, he is in a position more closely analogous to that of the father of a family than to that of a psychiatrist. It would not be surprising to discover the development of a new profession of spiritual counselors whose roles were clearly differentiated from those of the psychiatrist on the one hand and the minister, priest, or rabbi on the other.[20]

The last essay in the volume, "Some Theoretical Considerations Bearing on the Field of Medical Sociology,"[21] seems to provide an

20. The occasion for writing this paper was a symposium on the general topic of *The Ministry and Mental Health*. It was published in the volume bearing that title, edited by Hans Hofmann (New York; Association Press) in 1960.

21. Written for another symposium, this time on the relations between medicine and society, this essay is to appear in a volume edited by Robert N. Wilson and Robert Rapoport.

appropriate close to the present volume because I was asked to take a somewhat autobiographical point of view. Therefore, I went back to the original basis of my interest in the sociology of the professions generally, and medicine in particular, of nearly thirty years ago. This interest concerned the implications of the famous economic doctrine of the "rational pursuit of self-interest" and the fact that its ascendancy as an interpretive principle for modern "capitalistic" society failed to take account of the great and increasing importance of the place of the professions in the structure of that society.

Consideration of medical practice, however, quickly led me into the problems of the motivational complexity of the doctor-patient relationship and the importance for the role-structure of the relation both of the psychological aspects of more ordinary "somatic" illness and of the factors involved in mental and psychosomatic illness, which were then rapidly becoming more widely recognized. It was in this connection that I undertook—on the advice of the late Elton Mayo—an intensive reading of Freud's work. This in turn led to the concern with personality and social structure, in the family as well as in the therapeutic relationship, which in its first phase underlies the material in the essays of Part One, as well as in the book *Family and Socialization.*

Extension of the psychological interests and their theoretical treatment, however, went, as has already been noted, hand in hand with developing an analysis of the place of these phenomena in the structure and processes of the larger society. In this connection a decisive step—mentioned in connection with Chapter 4 in particular —was the insight that both the socialization of the individual personality and the psychological therapy of his illness involved his integration in the solidarity of collectivities in a sense which the traditional individualism of psychological (and of economic) thinking had not made clear.

This last essay concentrates on the implications of this involvement in collectivities for the understanding of medical practice as an institutional pattern: the sense in which doctor and patient, in the nature of the case, constitute a solidary collectivity, and the possible consequences of this for the development of health services.

In a sense, therefore, this final essay marks completion of a cycle in the interests and emphases of my own theoretical work. The starting point lay in problems of the large society, as noted with reference in particular to the problem of capitalism. Exploration of some of the crucial mechanisms by which societies worked led into intensive concern with the personality of the individual, particularly in relation to health and illness and to the process of socialization. The close interdependence of the psychological aspects of these problem areas with the setting of the relevant processes in the structures of a whole variety of social systems, however, led to increasing attention to structural problems on a variety of levels, ranging from the microscopic dyads of mother and child, physician and patient, all the way up to some of the major problems of development of total modern societies seen as a whole.

This book may be taken as its author's strong assertion of a conviction that, though these different phases and levels of the theoretical problem of the relationships of social structure and personality merit distinct treatment for particular purposes, in the larger picture their interdependencies are so intimate that bringing them together in an interpretive synthesis is imperative if a balanced understanding of the complex as a whole is to be attained.

THEORETICAL

PERSPECTIVES

I

The Superego
and the Theory
of Social Systems

IN THE broadest sense, perhaps, the contribution of psycho-analysis to the social sciences has consisted of an enormous deepening and enrichment of our understanding of human motivation. This enrichment has been such a pervasive influence that it would be almost impossible to trace its many ramifications. In the present paper I have chosen to say something about one particular aspect of this influence, that exerted through the psychoanalytic concept of the superego, because of its peculiarly direct relevance to the central theoretical interests of my own social-science discipline, sociological theory. This concept, indeed, forms one of the most important points at which it is possible to establish direct relations between psychoanalysis and sociology, and it is in this connection that I wish to discuss it.

Psychoanalysis, in common with other traditions of psychological thought, has naturally concentrated on the study of the personality

Reprinted from Psychiatry, *Vol. 15, No. 1, February, 1952. The substance of the present paper was read at the meeting of the Psychoanalytic Section of the American Psychiatric Association, Cincinnati, Ohio, May 17, 1951. The theme of the meeting at which it was read was "The Contribution of Psychoanalysis to the Social Sciences."*

of the individual as the focus of its frame of reference. Sociology, on the other hand, has equally naturally been primarily concerned with the patterning of the behavior of a plurality of individuals as constituting what, increasingly, we tend to call a social system. Because of historical differences of perspective and points of departure, the conceptual schemes arrived at from these two starting points have in general not been fully congruent with each other, and this fact has occasioned a good deal of misunderstanding. However, recent theoretical work[1] shows that, in accord with convergent trends of thought, it is possible to bring the main theoretical trends of these disciplines together under a common frame of reference, that which some sociologists have called the "theory of action." It is in the perspective of this attempt at theoretical unification that I wish to approach the analysis of the concept of the superego.

One of the principal reasons for the selection of this concept lies in the fact that it has been, historically, at the center of an actual process of convergence. In part at least, it is precisely because of this fact that Freud's discovery of the internalization of moral values as an essential part of the structure of the personality itself constituted such a crucial landmark in the development of the sciences of human behavior. Though there are several other somewhat similar formulations to be found in the literature of roughly the same period, the formulation most dramatically convergent with Freud's theory of the superego was that of the social role of moral norms made by the French sociologist Emile Durkheim—a theory which has constituted one of the cornerstones of the subsequent development of sociological theory.

Durkheim's insights into this subject slightly antedated those of Freud.[2] Durkheim started from the insight that the individual, as a

1. Cf. Talcott Parsons and Edward A. Shils (eds.), *Toward a General Theory of Action,* Cambridge, Harvard University Press, 1951. Also Talcott Parsons, *The Social System,* New York, The Free Press of Glencoe, 1951.
2. Durkheim's insights were first clearly stated in a paper, "Détermination du Fait moral," published in the *Revue de Métaphysique et de Morale* in 1906, and were much further developed in *Les Formes élémentaires de la Vie religieuse,* his last book (Paris, F. Alcan, 1912).
The earlier paper was reprinted in the volume, *Sociologie et Philosophie,* edited by Charles Bouglé (Paris, F. Alcan, 1929). Its theme is further elaborated in the posthumously published lectures, delivered at the Sorbonne in 1906, which carry the title, *L'Education morale* (Paris, F. Alcan, 1925).
Strongly influenced by Durkheim is the work of the Swiss psychologist, Jean Piaget, who has developed his view on the psychological side. See especially his *The Moral Judgment of the Child* (New York, The Free Press of

member of society, is not wholly free to make his own moral decisions but is in some sense "constrained" to accept the orientations common to the society of which he is a member. He went through a series of attempts at interpretation of the nature of this constraint, coming in the end to concentrate on two primary features of the phenomenon: first, that moral rules "constrain" behavior most fundamentally by moral authority rather than by any external coercion; and, secondly, that the effectiveness of moral authority could not be explained without assuming that, as we would now say, the value patterns were internalized as part of personality. Durkheim, as a result of certain terminological peculiarities which need not be gone into here, tended to identify "society" as such with the system of moral norms. In this very special sense of the term society, it is significant that he set forth the explicit formula that "society exists only in the minds of individuals."

In Durkheim's work there are only suggestions relative to the psychological mechanisms of internalization and the place of internalized moral values in the structure of personality itself. But this does not detract from the massive phenomenon of the convergence of the fundamental insights of Freud and Durkheim, insights not only as to the fundamental importance of moral values in human behavior, but of the internalization of these values. This convergence, from two quite distinct and independent starting points, deserves to be ranked as one of the truly fundamental landmarks of the development of modern social science. It may be likened to the convergence between the results of the experimental study of plant breeding by Mendel and of the microscopic study of cell division—a convergence which resulted in the discovery of the chromosomes as bearers of the genes. Only when the two quite distinct bodies of scientific knowledge could be put together did the modern science of genetics emerge.

The convergence of Freud's and Durkheim's thinking may serve to set the problem of this paper, which is: How can the fundamental phenomenon of the internalization of moral norms be analyzed in such a way as to maximize the generality of implications of the formulation, both for the theory of personality and for the theory of the

Glencoe, 1948). I presume that the psychiatric reader is familiar with the relevant works of Freud. However, two of the most important discussions of the superego are found in *The Ego and the Id* (London, Hogarth Press, 1949) and the *New Introductory Lectures on Psychoanalysis* (New York, Norton, 1933).

social system? For if it is possible to state the essentials of the problem in a sufficiently generalized way, the analysis should prove to be equally relevant in both directions. It should thereby contribute to the integration of the psychoanalytic theory of personality and of the sociological theory of the social system, and thus to the further development of a conceptual scheme which is essentially common to both.

The essential starting point of an attempt to link these two bodies of theory is the analysis of certain fundamental features of the *inter*-action of two or more persons, the process of interaction itself being conceived as a system. Once the essentials of such an interactive system have been made clear, the implications of the analysis can be followed out in *both* directions: the study of the structure and functioning of the personality as a system, in relation to other personalities; and the study of the functioning of the social system as a system. It may be surmised that the difficulty of bringing the two strands of thought together in the past has stemmed from the fact that this analysis has not been carried through; and this has not been done because it has "fallen between two stools." On the one hand, Freud and his followers, by concentrating on the single personality, have failed to consider adequately the implications of the individual's interaction with other personalities *to form a system*. On the other hand, Durkheim and the other sociologists have failed, in their concentration on the social system as a system to consider systematically the implications of the fact that it is the *interaction of personalities* which constitutes the social system with which they have been dealing, and that, therefore, adequate analysis of motivational process in such a system must reckon with the problems of personality. This circumstance would seem to account for the fact that this subject has been so seriously neglected.

It may first be pointed out that two interacting persons must be conceived to be objects to each other in two *primary* respects, and in a third respect which is in a sense derived from the first two. These are (1) cognitive perception and conceptualization, the answer to the question of *what the object is,* and (2) cathexis—attachment or aversion—the answer to the question of *what the object means* in an emotional sense. The third mode by which a person orients himself to an object is by evaluation—the integration of cognitive and cathectic meanings of the object to form a system, including the stability of such a system over time. It may be maintained that no stable relation between two or more objects is possible without all three of these modes of orientation being present for *both* parties to the relationship.[3]

Consideration of the conditions on which such a stable, mutually oriented system of interaction depends leads to the conclusion that on the human level this mutuality of interaction must be mediated and stabilized by a *common culture*—that is, by a commonly shared system of symbols, the meanings of which are understood on both sides with an approximation to agreement. The existence of such symbol systems, especially though not exclusively as involved in language, is common to every known society. However the going symbol systems of the society may have developed in the first place, they are involved in the socialization of every child. It may be presumed that the prominence of common symbol systems is both a consequence and a condition of the extreme plasticity and sensitivity of the human organism, which in turn are essential conditions of its capacity to learn and, concomitantly, to mislearn. These features of the human organism introduce an element of extreme potential instability into the process of human interaction, which requires stabilizing mechanisms if the interactive system, as a system, is to function.

The elements of the common culture have significance with reference to all three of the modes of orientation of action. Some of them are primarily of cognitive significance; others are primarily of cathectic significance, expressive of emotional meanings or affect; and still others are primarily of evaluative significance. Normative regulation for the establishing of standards is characteristic of all of culture; thus there is a right way of symbolizing any orientation of action in any given culture. This is indeed essential to communication itself: the conventions of the language must be observed if there is to be effective communication.

That a person's cathexis of a human object—that is, what the object means to the person emotionally—is contingent on the responsiveness of that object is a fact familiar to psychoanalytic theory. It may be regarded as almost a truism that it is difficult if not impos-

3. Further development of this analytical starting point and of the reasons for assuming it will be found in Parsons and Shils (eds.), *Toward a General Theory of Action, op. cit.* See especially, the "General Statement," and Part II, "Values, Motives, and Systems of Action." The reader may also wish to consult Parsons, *The Social System, op. cit.*

sible in the long run to love without being loved in return. It is more difficult to see that there is an almost direct parallelism in this respect between cathexis and cognition. After all, a person's cathexis of an inanimate object, such as a food object, is not directly dependent on the responsiveness of the object; it is surely anthropomorphism to suggest that a steak likes to be eaten in the same sense in which a hungry man likes to eat the steak. Similarly the cognition of the inanimate object by a person is not directly dependent on the object's reciprocal cognition of the person. But where the object is another person, the two, as ego and alter, constitute an *inter*active system. The question is what, in a cognitive sense, *is* alter from the point of view of ego, and vice versa. Clearly the answer to this question must involve the place—or "status," as sociologists call it—of ego and alter in the structure of the interactive system. Thus when I say a person is my mother, or my friend, or my student, I am characterizing that person as a participant in a system of social interaction in which I also am involved.

Thus not only the cathectic attitudes, but also the cognitive images, of persons relative to each other are functions of their interaction in the system of social relations; in a fundamental sense the same order of relationship applies in both cases.

Thus a social system is a function of the common culture, which not only forms the basis of the intercommunication of its members, but which defines, and so in one sense determines, the relative statuses of its members. There is, within surprisingly broad limits, no intrinsic significance of persons to each other independent of their actual interaction. In so far as these relative statuses are defined and regulated in terms of a common culture, the following apparently paradoxical statement holds true: what persons *are* can only be understood in terms of a set of beliefs and sentiments which define what they *ought to be*. This proposition is true only in a very broad way, but is none the less crucial to the understanding of social systems.

It is in this context that the central significance of moral standards in the common culture of systems of social interaction must be understood. Moral standards constitute, as the focus of the evaluative aspect of the common culture, the core of the stabilizing mechanisms of the system of social interaction. These mechanisms function, moreover, to stabilize not only attitudes—that is, the emotional meanings of persons to each other—but also categorizations—the cognitive definitions of what persons are in a socially significant sense.

If the approach taken above is correct, the place of the superego as part of the structure of the personality must be understood in terms of the relation between personality and the total common culture, by virtue of which a stable system of social interaction on the human levels becomes possible. Freud's insight was profoundly correct when he focused on the element of moral standards. This is, indeed, central and crucial, but it does seem that Freud's view was too narrow. The inescapable conclusion is that not only moral standards, but *all the components of the common culture* are internalized as part of the personality structure. Moral standards, indeed, cannot in this respect be dissociated from the *content* of the orientation patterns which they regulate; as I have pointed out, the content of both cathectic-attitudes and cognitive-status definitions have cultural, hence normative significance. This content is cultural and learned. Neither what the human object *is,* in the most significant respects, nor what it *means* emotionally, can be understood as given independently of the nature of the interactive process itself; and the significance of moral norms themselves very largely relates to this fact.

It would seem that Freud's insight in this field was seriously impeded by the extent to which he thought in terms of a frame of reference relating a personality to its situation or environment without specific reference to the analysis of the social interaction of persons as a system. This perspective, which was overwhelmingly dominant in his day, accounts for two features of his theory. In the first place, the cognitive definition of the object world does not seem to have been problematical to Freud. He subsumed it all under "external reality," in relation to which "ego-functions" constitute a process of adaptation. He failed to take explicitly into account the fact that the frame of reference in terms of which objects are cognized, and therefore adapted to, is cultural and thus cannot be taken for granted as given, but must be internalized as a condition of the development of mature ego-functioning. In this respect it seems to be correct to say that Freud introduced an unreal separation between the superego and the ego—the lines between them are in fact difficult to define in his theory. In the light of the foregoing considerations, the distinction which Freud makes between the superego and the ego—that the former is internalized, by identification, and that the latter seems to consist of responses to external reality rather than of internalized culture—is not tenable. These responses are, to be sure, *learned* responses; but internalization is a very special kind of learning which Freud seemed to confine to the superego.

If this argument raises questions about cognitive function and therefore about the theory of the ego, there are implications, *ipso facto,* for the superego. The essential point seems to be that Freud's view seems to imply that the object, as cognitively significant, is given independently of the actor's internalized culture, and that superego standards are then applied to it. This fails to take account of the extent to which the constitution of the object and its moral appraisal are part and parcel of the *same* fundamental cultural patterns; it gives the superego an appearance of arbitrariness and dissociation from the rest of the personality—particularly from the ego—which is not wholly in accord with the facts.

The second problem of Freud's theory concerns the relation of cathexis or affect to the superego. In a sense, this is the obverse of its relation to cognition. The question here is perhaps analogous to that of the transmission of light in physics: how can the object's cathectic significance be mediated in the absence of direct biological contact? Indeed, embarrassment over this problem may be one source of the stressing of sexuality in Freudian theory, since sexuality generally involves such direct contact.

To Freud, the object tends, even if human, to be an inert something on which a "charge" of cathectic significance has been placed. The process is regarded as expressive of the actor's instincts or libido, but the element of mutuality tends to be treated as accessory and almost arbitrary. This is associated with the fact that, while Freud, especially in his *Interpretation of Dreams,* made an enormous contribution to the theory of expressive or cathectic symbolism, there is a very striking limitation of the extension of this theory. The basis of this may be said to be that Freud tended to confine his consideration of symbolism in the emotional context to its directly expressive functions and failed to go on to develop the analysis of its communicative functions. The dream symbol remained for him the prototype of affective symbolism. It is perhaps largely because of this fact that Freud did not emphasize the common culture aspect of such symbolism, but tended to attempt to trace its origins back to intrinsic meanings which were independent of the interactive process and its common culture. More generally the tenor of the analysis of affect was to emphasize a fundamental isolation of the individual in his lonely struggle with his id.[4]

This whole way of looking at the problem of cathexis seems to have a set of consequences parallel to these outlined above concerning cognition; it tends to dissociate the superego from the sources of affect. This derives from the fact that Freud apparently did not appreciate the presence and significance of a common culture of expressive-affective symbolism and the consequent necessity for thinking of the emotional component of interaction as mediated by this aspect of the common culture. Thus, the aspect of the superego which is concerned with the regulation of emotional reactions must be considered as defining the regulative principles of this interactive system. It is an integral *part* of the symbolism of emotional expression, not something over, above, and apart from it.

The general purport of this criticism is that Freud, with his formulation of the concept of the superego, made only a beginning at an analysis of the role of the common culture in personality. The structure of his theoretical scheme prevented him from seeing the possibilities for extending the same fundamental analysis from the internalization of moral standards—which he applied to the superego —to the internalization of the cognitive frame of reference for interpersonal relations and for the common system of expressive symbolism; and similarly it prevented him from seeing the extent to which these three elements of the common culture are integrated with each other.

This very abstract analysis may become somewhat more understandable if examples are given of what is meant by the cognitive reference or categorization system, and by the system of expressive symbolism, considering both as parts of the internalized common culture.

One of the most striking cases of the first is that of sex categorization—that is, the learning of sex role. Freud speaks of the original "bi-sexuality" of the child. The presumption is that he postulated a constitutionally given duality of orientation. In terms of the present approach, there is at least an alternative hypothesis possible which

4. This view has certainly been modified in subsequent psychoanalytic thinking, but it is the major framework within which Freud introduced the concept of the superego.

should be explored.[5] This hypothesis is that some of the principal facts which Freud interpreted as manifestations of constitutional bisexuality can be explained by the fact that the categorization of human persons—including the actor's categorization of himself taken as a point of reference—into two sexes is not, except in its somatic points of reference, biologically given but, in psychological significance, must be learned by the child. It is fundamental that children of both sexes start life with essentially the same relation to the mother, a fact on which Freud himself rightly laid great stress. It may then be suggested that the process by which the boy learns to differentiate himself in terms of sex from the mother and in this sense "identify" with the father, while the girl learns to identify with the mother, is a learning process. One major part of the process of growing up is the internalization of one's own sex role as a critical part of the self-image. It may well be that this way of looking at the process will have the advantage of making the assumption of constitutional bisexuality at least partly superfluous as an explanation of the individual's sex identification. In any case it has the great advantage of linking the determination of sex categorization directly with the role structure of the social system in a theoretical as well as an empirical sense. Every sociologist will appreciate this since he is familiar with the crucial significance of sex role differentiation and constitution for social structure.

An example of the second role, that of common expressive symbolism, may be found in terms of the process by which a reciprocal love attitude between mother and child is built up. Freud quite rightly, it seems, points to the origin of the child's love attitude as found in his dependency on the mother for the most elementary sources of gratification, such as food, elementary comforts, and safety. Gradually, in the process of interaction, a system of expectations of the continuation and repetition of these gratifications comes to be built up in the child; and these expectations are bound together as a result of the fact that a variety of such gratifications comes from the single source, the mother.

In this process, one may assume that well before the development of language there begins to occur a process of generalization, so that certain acts of the mother are interpreted as *signs* that grati-

5. This is in no way meant to suggest that there is *no* element of constitutional bisexuality, but only that *some* things Freud attributed to it may be explicable on other grounds.

fying performances can be expected—for example, the child becomes able to interpret her approaching footsteps or the tone of her voice. It is suggested that one of the main reasons why the erotic component of the child's relation to the mother is so important lies in the fact that, since bodily contact is an essential aspect of child care, erotic gratifications readily take on a symbolic significance. The erotic element has the extremely important property that it is relatively diffuse, being awakened by any sort of affectionate bodily contact. This diffuseness makes it particularly suitable as a vehicle of symbolic meanings. By this process, then, gradually, there is a transition from the child's focus on erotic stimulation as such, to his focus on the mother's *attitude* which is expressed by the erotically pleasurable stimulation. Only when this transition has taken place can one correctly speak of the child's having become dependent on the *love* of the mother and not merely on the specific pleasures the mother dispenses to him. Only when this level is reached, can the love attitude serve as a motivation to the acceptance of disciplines, since it can then remain stable—even though many specific gratifications which have previously been involved in the relationship are eliminated from it.

The essential point for present purposes is that, in its affective aspect, the child's interaction with the mother is not *only* a process of mutual gratification of needs, but is on the child's part a process of learning of the symbolic significance of a complicated system of acts on the part of the mother—of what they signify about what she feels and of how they are interdependent with and thus in part consequences of his own acts. That is to say, there is developed a complex language of emotional communication between them. Only when the child has learned this language on a relatively complex level, can he be said to have learned to love his mother or to be dependent on her love for him. There is, thus, a transition from "pleasure dependence" to "love dependence." One primary aspect of learning to love and be loved is the internalization of a common culture of expressive symbolism which makes it possible for the child to express *and communicate* his feelings and to understand the mother's feelings toward him.

It would seem that only when a sufficiently developed cognitive reference system and a system of expressive symbolism have been internalized is the foundation laid for the development of a superego; for only then can the child be said to be capable of understanding, in both the cognitive and the emotional senses, the meaning of the prescriptions and prohibitions which are laid upon him. The child must mature to the point where he can begin to play a *responsible* role in a system of social interaction, where he can understand that what people feel is a function of his and their conformity with mutually held standards of conduct. Only when he has become dependent on his mother's love, can he develop meaningful anxiety in that then he might jeopardize his security in that love by not living up to her expectations of being a good boy.

The above considerations have important implications for the nature of the process of identification in so far as that is the principal mechanism by which the superego is acquired. If this analysis is correct, the crucial problem concerns the process of internalization of the common culture, including all three of its major components— the cognitive reference system, the system of expressive symbolism, and the system of moral standards.

In the first place, it would seem to be clear that *only* cultural symbol systems can be internalized. An object can be cathected, cognized, and appraised, but it cannot as such be taken into the personality; the only sense in which the latter terminology is appropriate is in calling attention to the fact that the common culture is indeed part of the personality of the object but it is only an aspect, not the whole of it. Two persons can be said to be identified with each other in so far as they *share* important components of common culture. But since roles in the social system are differentiated, it should be noted that it is always important to specify *what* elements of culture are common.

Secondly, it is important to point out that the learning of the common culture may lead to the assumption either of a role identical with that of the object of identification or of a role differentiated from that object's role. Thus in the case of the boy vis-à-vis his mother, the learning of his sex categorization enables him to understand and accept the fact that with respect to sex he is different from her. The standards of proper behavior for both sexes are shared by the members of both, but their *application* is differentiated. The usage of the term identification has often been ambiguous, since it has been used to imply a likeness both of standards and of application. From the present point of view it is quite correct to speak of a boy learning his sex role by identification with the mother—in that he learns the sex categorization partly from her—and by the fact that he and she belong to different sex categories, which has important implications for *his* behavior. This is different from identification with his father in the sense that he learns that, with respect to sex, he is classed with his father and not with his mother.

Thirdly, there seems to be excellent evidence that while identification cannot mean coming *to be the object,* it is, as internalization of common culture, dependent on *positive cathexis of the object.* The considerations reviewed above give some suggestions as to why this should be true. Internalization of a culture pattern is not merely knowing it as an object of the external world; it is incorporating it into the actual structure of the personality as such. This means that the culture pattern must be integrated with the affective system of the personality.

Culture, however, is a system of generalized symbols and their meanings. In order for the integration with affect, which constitutes internalization, to take place, the individual's own affective organization must achieve levels of generalization of a high order. The principal mechanism by which this is accomplished appears to be through the building up of attachments to other persons—that is, by emotional communication with others so that the individual is sensitized to the *attitudes* of the others, not merely to their specific acts with their intrinsic gratification-deprivation significance. In other words, the process of forming attachments is *in itself* inherently a process of the generalization of affect. But this generalization in turn actually is in one major aspect the process of symbolization of emotional meanings—that is, it is a process of the acquisition of a culture. The intrinsic difficulty of creation of cultural patterns is so great that the child can only acquire complex cultural generalization through interaction with others who already possess it. Cathexis of an object as a focal aspect of identification is then another name for the development of *motivation* for the internalization of cultural patterns, at least for one crucially important phase of this process.

The conditions of socialization of a person are such that the gratifications which derive from his cathexis of objects cannot be secured unless, along with generalization of emotional meanings and their communication, he also develops a cognitive categorization of objects, including himself, and a system of moral norms which regulate the relations between himself and the object (a superego). This way of looking at the process of identification serves perhaps to help clear up a confusing feature of Freud's method of treatment. Freud, it will be remembered, denies that the very young child is capable of object cathexis, and speaks of identification, in contrast with object cathexis, as "the earliest form of emotional tie with an object." He then speaks of identification with the father in the oedipus situation as a reversion to the more "primitive" form of relation to an object.

I would agree that the child's early attachment to the mother and his later cathexis of her are not the same thing. It seems probable that the earliest attachment is, as it were, precultural, while true object cathexis involves the internalization of a cultural symbol system. But it seems extremely doubtful whether the relation to the father in the oedipus situation can be correctly described as a reversion to a presymbolic level. It is impossible to go into this problem fully here; but it may be suggested that the oedipus situation might be better interpreted as the strain imposed on the child by forcing him to take a major further step in growing up, in the process of which the father becomes the focus of his ambivalent feelings precisely because the child dare not jeopardize his love relation to the mother. Although regressive patterns of reaction would be expected under such a strain, these are not the core of the process of identification; however important, they are only secondary phenomena.

If the foregoing account of the internalized content of personality and of the processes of identification points in the right direction, it would seem to imply the necessity for certain modifications of Freud's structural theory of personality. The first point is that it is not only the superego which is internalized—that is, taken over by identification from cathected social objects—but that there are involved other important components which presumably must be included in the ego—namely, the system of cognitive categorizations of the object world and the system of expressive symbolism.

If this is correct, it would seem to necessitate, secondly, an important modification of Freud's conception of the ego. The element of *organization,* which is the essential property of the ego, would then not be derived from the "reality-principle"—that is, from adaptative responses to the external world alone. Instead it would be derived from *two* fundamental sources: the external world as an environment; and the common culture which is acquired from objects of identification. Both are, to be sure, acquired from outside, but the latter component of the ego is, in origin and character, more like the superego than it is like the lessons of experience.

Third, there are similar problems concerning the borderline between the ego and the id. A clue to what may be needed here is given in Freud's own frequent references to what have here been called "expressive symbols," as representatives to the ego of the impulses of the id. It seems to be a necessary implication of the above analysis that these symbolized and symbolically organized emotions are not only representatives *to* the ego; they should also be considered as integral *parts of* the ego. This may be felt to be a relatively radical conclusion—namely, that emotions, or affect on the normal human adult level, should be regarded as a *symbolically generalized* system, that it is never "id-impulse" as such. Affect is not a direct expression of drive-motivation, but involves it only as it is organized and integrated with both the reality experience of the individual and the cultural patterns which he has learned through the processes of identification.

More generally, the view of personality developed in this paper seems to be broadly in line with the recent increasing emphasis in psychoanalytic theory itself on the psychology of the ego, and the problems of its integration and functioning as a system. Freud's structural theory was certainly fundamentally on the right track in that it clearly formulated the three major points of reference of personality theory—the needs of the organism, the external situation, and the patterns of the culture. In view of the intellectual traditions within which Freud's own theoretical development took place, it was in the nature of the case that the cultural element, as he formulated it in the concept of the superego, should have been the last of the three to be developed and the most difficult to fit in.

In the light of the development of the more general theory of action, however, the cultural element must, as I have attempted to show, certainly occupy a very central place. For if the ego and the id in Freud's formulations are taken alone, there is no adequate bridge from the theory of personality to the theoretical analysis of culture and of the social system. The superego provides exactly such a bridge because it is not explicable on any other basis than that of acquisition from other human beings, and through the process of social interaction.

Essentially what this paper has done has been to examine the concept of the superego in the light of the maturing bodies of theory in the fields of culture and of the social system; and it has attempted to follow through the implications of the appearance of the superego in Freud's thinking for the theory of personality itself. The result has been the suggestion of certain modifications in Freud's own theory of personality.[6]

In this sense the paper has contained a good deal of criticism of Freud, which may appear to be out of place in a paper dealing with the contributions of psychoanalysis to social science. It is, however, emphatically not the intent of the author to have this appear as primarily a critical paper. It has been necessary to emphasize the critical aspect at certain points, since the psychiatric or psychoanalytic

6. Perhaps the nature of these modifications will be made clearer to the reader by the following revision of Freud's famous diagram of the personality as a system, which he introduced in *The Ego and the Id., op. cit.,* and which appears in the *New Introductory Lectures, op. cit.,* in revised form. Freud's two versions differ in that only the latter includes the superego. Hence my comparison will be made with this version.

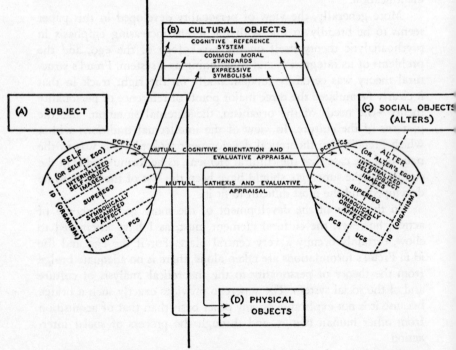

First, in Freud's diagram the superego is placed on one side of the ego. Here it is treated as the focus of the internalized cultural system, and hence put in a central place. Second, my suggested new diagram follows Freud in treating the superego as essentially part of the ego, but extends this conception to include as part of the ego all three components of the internalized

reader is not likely to be adequately familiar with the developments in sociological theory which are so importantly related to the concept of the superego. The essential intent, however, is to contribute to the development of a common foundation for the theoretical analysis of human behavior which can serve to unify all of the sciences which take this as their subject matter. The massive and fundamental fact is that Freud formulated the concept of the superego and fitted it into his general analysis of human motivation. This and the parallel formulations in the field of sociology are the solid foundations on which we must build. I believe it can truthfully be said that we are now in a position to bring the theory of personality and the theory of the social system within essentially the same general conceptual scheme. Freud's contribution of the concept of the superego has been one of the important factors making this possible.

---

culture. Third, a distinction is introduced which Freud does not take account of at all; namely, that between cultural elements as internalized in the personality, and as objects of the situation, as follows:

Cultural Objects	*Internalized Subject and Social Objects*
1. Cognitive reference system	Internalized self-object images
2. Common moral standards	Superego
3. Expressive symbolism	Symbolically organized affect

I think of self as oriented *both* to alter and to the nonsocial situation, which includes both physical and cultural objects. Both orientations include cognition *and* cathexis, and both are subject to evaluative appraisal; but only in the case of alter as an object are these orientations *mutual*.

According to my view, the ego thus includes all three elements of the common culture and repression cuts across all three. Furthermore, there is no reason why large parts of the common culture, repressed or not, should not belong to the unconscious.

It seems to be implied by the position taken here that the integration of personality *as a system* should be regarded as the function of the ego; but, following Freud, it is equally important, as has been said above, that the ego faces three ways, as it were, and is subject to pressures from all three directions—that is, from the individual's own organism (id), from the external situation, and from the internalized symbol systems of the culture.

2

The Father Symbol: AN APPRAISAL IN THE LIGHT OF PSYCHOANALYTIC AND SOCIOLOGICAL THEORY

T HE FIELD of the theory of symbolism, in its relation to the study of values, has many ramifications. One which is of particular interest to the author of this paper, however, is that of the connections between its involvement in sociological theory and in psychoanalysis. The symbolism associated with the father is a particularly interesting field in this connection both because of the prominent part it has played in psychoanalytic theory and because of its sociological relevance to the analysis of the family as a social system and of its place in the wider society. For these reasons the Father Symbol has been selected for special attention in this paper.

This subject presents a favorable opportunity for the analysis of the relations between the two conceptual schemes. The symbolic significance of the father has certainly been central in psychoanalytic theory, at least ever since Freud worked out his analysis of the Oedipus complex, and on the part both of Freud and of his followers

Reprinted from Lyman Bryson, Louis Finkelstein, R. M. MacIver, and Richard McKeon (eds.), Symbols and Values: an Initial Study, *13th Symposium of the Conference on Science, Philosophy, and Religion, New York, Harper & Row, Publishers, 1954. The substance of this paper was read at a meeting of the American Psychological Association in September, 1952, at Washington, D.C.*

it has provided one of the leading themes in almost all attempts to extend the implications of psychoanalysis from the study of the individual personality as such to the sociocultural levels. From the point of view of the sociologist, on the other hand, the father role constitutes one of the obvious keystones of the social structure, not only of the conjugal family but of all kinship systems, and its articulation with the structure of the wider society beyond the kinship group presents sociological problems of the first importance.

The approach taken in this paper will be first, to attempt to place the symbolic significance of the father "figure" or father "role" in the general context of the theory of expressive symbolism in systems of action, and then to attempt to spell out, and to articulate with each other, four different aspects of the significance of this symbol in four different system-references, namely, the developmental phases of personality growth, the adult personality, the family as a social system, and, finally, the large scale society transcending the family, with special reference to our own type of society.

We are here primarily interested in the father, not as a concrete personality or as a concrete role type as such, but as the focus of a symbolic complex. Therefore we must start with certain fundamental considerations about symbols and their place in human action. For our purposes we may define a symbol as an *object*—which may be a physical or social object, event, aspect of a concrete object, or class or complex of any of these—which has acquired *meaning* for one or more actors involving a reference to meaningful entities other than the symbol-object itself. For the object to be a symbol rather than a sign (or signal), this meaning must have acquired a certain level of generalization which we need not attempt to specify here. Thus "my father" as a concrete human person is not as such necessarily a symbol. It is only when some aspect of experience represented by my father comes to "stand for" other aspects of experience associated with other objects and attitudes, that we can speak of the father as a symbol.

We are here interested primarily in the father as what I shall call an "expressive" as distinguished from a cognitive symbol. This is always an aspect of the meaning of any symbolic object, but we will speak of an expressive symbol when this aspect has primacy over the cognitive. A symbol is expressive in this sense in so far as its meaning *has reference* not to other objects as objects but to the motivational state or states of one or more actors; whereas a cognitive symbol has reference to the properties of one or more other situational objects, as objects, and of course other than the symbolic object itself.

The expressive symbol in this sense, or the patterned complex of such symbols is the primary mode of organization of the motivational orientations or attitudes of an actor. It is, indeed the *patterning* of the symbol-meaning *system* as a system which constitutes the principal structure of the orientation system of an actor, and when those of all the actors in a social system are taken into account in their interrelations, of the social system as such.

The relations between the meanings of different particular symbols in such a system may be analyzed either in terms of the structure of the symbolic complex itself, *i.e.,* from a "cultural" point of view, or in terms of the functional interdependence of these and other components in the processes of action and interaction. In the first set of terms, a symbol may belong at any one of several levels of generality, or of specificity. It may further fit into different symbolic complexes according to the type of patterns of generalization and integration by which such complexes are organized. Thus from the point of view of a social system the name of an individual is on a relatively low level of generality because it is tied to him while the concept father can be on a considerably higher level of generality. With respect to the second context, the father symbol may, as we shall see, fit into a complex having to do with rigorous enforcement of stringent rules of conduct, or into one having to do with a generally protective care.

The second set of terms in which symbols can be analyzed concern both the circumstances in which they acquire different types of meaning, and those in which they "function" to influence the processes of action themselves. These will constitute the principal basis for our subsequent analysis.

In general, a sociologist can confidently confirm the central importance which psychoanalytic theory has given to the father symbol, but perhaps can contribute something to the evaluation of the significance of that symbol, particularly of course on the level of the common culture of social systems, but perhaps also to some extent in its place in personality.

Freud was certainly broadly right in emphasizing the place of the father symbol in the socialization of the child, and it is clearly from this set of circumstances that the paramount importance of this symbol derives. But modern sociology has given us considerable resources we can use in defining the context of this importance. The most fundamental set of facts concerns the generality of the occurrence of the human family and the corresponding fact that the main processes particularly of the earlier phases of socialization take place within the family. These facts are of course obvious to common sense, but we can now say a good deal more about their significance than was previously possible.

One obvious probable inference is that this aspect of social organization must be deeply grounded in the biological constitution and conditions of life of the human species. This is undoubtedly correct but does not contradict what is of greater interest to us, namely, that it is equally fundamentally involved with the conditions of development of a human personality and through that with the condition of effective functioning of human society on the cultural levels.

The plasticity of the human organism which makes cultural behavior possible, at the same time necessitates different mechanisms for the orientation and stabilization of behavior than those predominantly operating in the lower organisms; namely, as we now know pretty well, those involved in the internalization of a common culture with a particular reference to the patterned standards of behavior which in a sense are its central core. This common culture *is* the symbol-meaning system with which we are here concerned. Hence the basic structure of the human family, particularly those aspects of it which can be considered to be universal, must have a profound significance for this process.

In spite of the entirely correct emphasis in recent times on "cultural relativity" and with it the variability of kinship systems, there is a fundamental common component in all kinship systems, centering on what is sometimes called the "biological" family, which, however, is certainly far from only biological in significance. This obviously is the "nuclear" group of the two parents and their own children. Sociologically speaking, the core of the family structure is a very special type of three-person group, if only one child be taken into consideration at a time.

This is an acceptable first approximation, but for our purposes it is necessary to distinguish three interpenetrating systems of social interaction which together constitute the strategically important social environment for the process of child development. These consist in three "concentric" circles of the child's social participation, and each in turn becomes of paramount importance in successive phases of his development.

The first of these is the solidary dyadic group formed by the child's early attachment to his mother, the first case of what Freud called "true object cathexis." This is a grouping which, it must be noted, is not originally given with birth, but is built up over a considerable period during which the child gradually develops an orientation to his mother as a "complex object" and himself actively participates in positive interaction with her in showing his love for her, as well as *vice versa*. It is this relationship on which the security is based which is utilized in later phases; it culminates in strategic prominence in the immediate preoedipal phase. In it the father, for the children of both sexes, plays a minimal or at least a secondary role.

Though undoubtedly there are important differences, so long as there is a family system, the fundamental characteristics of this phase and of that into which it leads, are certainly universal; being grounded in the general conditions of socialization within families. This universality depends on the fact that early child care is focused more on the mother than on the father, and correlatively, that on the average the participation of the father in affairs of the social group which transcends the family is greater and strategically more important than is that of the mother.

Under these conditions, which are in a broad sense universal, the little grouping of mother and child is in the nature of the case never independent, but is a subsystem in the first instance of the larger system which is the conjugal family, which in turn is a subsystem of still wider social systems. The father, though by no means alone, stands at the principal point of articulation between his family subsystem and that of the wider society. This is the primary basis of his symbolic significance.

First let us note that in all kinship systems, the marriage bond stands to some extent over against that of mother and child. It antedates it and has a certain structural priority over it which is particularly accentuated in our own kinship system. This means that, within limits, the special exclusive solidarity of mother and child can be maintained only so far as it does not interfere too much with the marriage relationship. Naturally it has a fundamental "niche" so that it is in fact institutionalized in all societies, but there are limits to its claims, and it is the passing of these limits with the process of maturation of the child, biologically and socio-psychologically, which brings on the crisis of the oedipus period.

Freud's own account of the oedipus period from the point of view of the boy, stressed the development of a true object cathexis of the mother on his part which *then* came into conflict with the position of the father. We may here suggest that the object cathexis well antedates the oedipus period, but that it is the pressure exerted by both parents, backed by the general culture to make the boy behave as a "big boy," which means above all to renounce his dependency on his mother, which is the main factor in bringing on the oedipus crisis. Essentially performance capacities have developed which, if they are to grow further, are incompatible with maintenance of the "little boy" dependency ("infantile" does not seem to be a very good word, as it is an age level of four or so which is in question).

These consist in the first instance in actions which gain significance for the family as a collectivity beyond its mother-child sub-system, and are sanctioned by both parents as such. Furthermore in this stage performances begin to be more and more directly and conditionally rewarded; the child is progressively less free to count simply on the security of maternal love regardless of what he does.

The great dilemma in this stage is dependency *versus* the gains of learning to act more independently at a more mature level—for the child to learn to do things for himself, and under expectations of responsibility, as well as with higher levels of skill. It is because of its connection with the dependency problem that the erotic component becomes of strategic significance in the oedipal situation. Infantile and early childhood ("phallic") eroticism play a primary part in the processes of generalization and integration by which the original love-attachment to the mother is built up, but its renunciation at the oedipal stage becomes an imperative of further development because of its fusion with the dependency need, so that by and large to attain the requisite levels of independence and at the same time freely to gratify erotic desires is impossible; hence, what Freud so keenly described as the "latency" period.

It seems to be in this situation that the lower, the "primary" layer of the meaning complex of the father symbol is laid down. It seems to be "normal" though with variations, in all cultures for this oedipal "hump" to be gotten over only with relatively severe strains, and therefore the child's behavior at this stage has many of the characteristics of neurosis which it is a primary function of later family interaction to "cure." The keynote of attitudes toward the father figure is therefore ambivalence. He constitutes the symbolic focus of the pressure from the outside world which is responsible for breaking up the "paradise" of the child's state of blissful security with his mother—even though she is an active collaborator in this break-up there is good reason to believe that the aggression generated in the process tends to be displaced on the father. The father then tends both to personify the "higher" demands or requirements to which the child is being asked to live up, and thus to acquire a high order of respect and authority and, at the same time, he is the primary target of the aggression (and anxiety) generated in the process. This is the aspect of the father as source of the superego on which Freud laid the greatest stress. With reference to it the father tends to mean both that which is respected and to be, on the one hand, emulated, on the other, obeyed, and at the same time an object of anxiety and hatred. In both aspects it should be noted there will be apt to be a certain element of neurotic distortion. Furthermore the special place of the erotic component in the oedipal situation accounts for the sexual tinging of attitudes toward father symbols generally; at the same time envy for their real or alleged sexual privileges and prowess, and the fear of their punishment for ego's sexual wishes or exploits.[1]

This level of ambivalent orientation to the father can be symbolically generalized in a number of respects. This generalization gives us a relatively definite orientation to the father symbol everywhere as the one who must be and, apart from clearly neurotic cases, to some extent genuinely is respected, though he is not the one who *primarily* is loved by the boy at any rate and, in another respect, by the girl. At the same time there is an ambivalent undercurrent in the

1. It may be noted that the general structure of this constellation is closely in accord with that which has been demonstrated to develop in small group interaction (Robert F. Bales, "The Equilibrium Problem in Small Groups," chapter IV, Talcott Parsons, Robert F. Bales, and Edward A. Shils, *Working Papers in the Theory of Action*, New York, The Free Press of Glencoe, 1953). The child may be likened to one of the subordinate members of a small experimental group. Partly by virtue of his low level of participation (*i.e.*, in general family affairs) his primary tie is to the "sociometric star"—his mother. As his participation and hence responsibility increase, however, he must take more and more cognizance of the "task leader" who, with many variations of course, is apt to be the father. He tends both to develop respect for him for his important functions, and to project aggression upon him.

attitudes toward such figures which on occasion may come to the center of the stage. These are the ones who force reluctant compliance and hence sometimes compliance accompanied by a burning sense of injustice. In these respects then the father figure is to a certain extent the prototype of a source of authority. He comes into the individual's most intimate security system and makes disturbing demands. Any individual who is in the analogous position in later life may encounter the basic attitudinal structure which has been built up in connection with this situation.

Even at this level, to say nothing of the one to be discussed next, just what kind of pattern will develop is a function of the kind of father who has in fact been experienced. This is a matter both of variations of personality and of institutional type of father role. Within all these variations there does, however, seem to be a pretty definite common core along the lines just discussed.

Before taking up the next phase of the process a word may be said about the relation to the father on the part of the boy and of the girl. Probably the most important thing to say is that at *this* stage such differences are secondary; it is at the next stage, that in which sex role categorization becomes crucial, that the most important differences emerge. Essentially we may say that this primary oedipal phase has the function of integrating the child into the family as a wider functioning unit than is that of the mother-child pair, and by selective and contingent rewarding and punishing of attempted contributions to family functioning, to bring about internalization of the value-patterns which are common to the family as a system, and of course in general are shared in the wider society. The accent is on *common membership in* the family rather than on differentiation of role within it, beyond of course the always central differentiation between the generations. The girl has just as much an early love relationship with her mother as does the boy, and this must be renounced just as in the case of her brother. The childhood level of dependency is just as unsuitable for either sex beyond a certain point. It is essentially the things which point to the next stage which differentiate the two sexes.

It seems to us that Freud did not sufficiently distinguish the two major aspects of the developmental process in which we are interested, and that this is one primary source of difficulty in the Freudian theory of development. The two are by no means sharply separated in time, but overlap considerably, yet on the whole the one just discussed, the shift from mother-centered to family-centered solidarity, comes earlier than the other, the internalization of sex role categorization. Freud tended to assume that it was such categorization which was not problematical, but only the emotional attitude toward it, the "acceptance" of one's sex role. We will argue that both are highly problematical; that while of course the anatomical differences of the sexes constitute fundamental points of reference for the development of orientations, it is necessary for the child to learn the relevance of these facts to the expectations of behavior which constitute the differentiations of roles of the two sexes.

There is a fundamental double significance of sex role as seen from the point of view of the sociologist. First it is, within the structure of the family, along with age, one of the two primary axes of the role-differentiation of the family itself as a social subsystem. The prototype of sex role differentiation in this connection of course is that of the roles of the two parents, both toward each other and toward their children. Secondly, sex role categorization is the first *universalistic* categorization apart from age which the child encounters and which is of fundamental structural significance to the society as a whole. It is a broad general basis of categorization which does not present the difficulties of learning that, for example, the finer differentiations of performance-capacity do. Sex role thus provides a critically important path of transition from the assumption of differentiated roles *within* the family to that of roles which *transcend* the family and become constitutive of the larger social structure.

It is in this connection that the father becomes the prototype of the quality of "masculinity"; he is the adult male with whom the child of either sex has the closest contact and emotionally the most important relationship. For the boy he provides the most immediate role model of adult masculinity; while for the girl he is the masculine counterpart of her mother's femininity which provides the role model for her.

To a considerable extent it seems to be the common sense of psychology as well as of the general culture, that the more generalized orientation patterns are built up out of highly specific ones, *e.g.,* toward hunger gratification, etc. This undoubtedly is one essential aspect of the problem, but not the most important for present purposes. The process of child development may be treated as in a certain sense an "ontological" recapitulation of the "phylogenic" development of societies. The basic principles governing the processes of development of differentiated and integrated systems of action are, there is cogent reason to believe, the same as those operating in biological developmental and evolutionary processes. One of these is that at the early stages *functional* differentiation is minimal, and is added to only by successive steps according to the principle of increasing specification.

According to this perspective, the two basic phases of child development we are here describing represent two such steps which involve the introduction in the personality structure of the child of what functional analysis of social systems has shown are major pattern-principles of the structure of differentiated social systems. The first is the *quantitative* differentiation of relative strategic functional significance of units in a system which, in the aspect of evaluation, becomes the differentiation of prestige, in that of operative function, of authority. Here in first assuming performance functions in the family as a system, the child learns that by virtue of age he is relegated to a lower status, and the father status symbolizes this central hierarchical principle of system structure. Such a pattern principle, it should be remembered is, at this level of child development, *both highly general and highly concrete.* It is general in that it represents hierarchical differentiation as such without discrimination between the many types and bases of such differentiation which are encountered in complex societies. It is concrete in that it has reference to the experiential situation of the child in the family, and indeed in his particular family. The symbolic content of the pattern system must of course at this stage be derived from this particular nexus of experience.

The second phase or aspect introduces a *qualitative* differentiation of role type, which study of small groups as well as much other evidence, has shown to be of generically central significance to social systems. This is the differentiation between what may be called "instrumental-adaptive" and "expressive-integrative" functional roles, the one being concentrated primarily—though by no means exculsively—on responsibility for the welfare of the system as a system in relation to the exigencies of its situation and the achievement of its goals, the other on the management of the internal motivational tensions of the members and their solidarity with each other to form an integrated group. Though there are many differentiations and qualifications, some of which will be noted later, this is in the broadest respect the *main* axis of the differentiation of sex roles in all societies.[2]

It is probably highly significant for its function in the process of socialization that the family is inherently a very *simply* differentiated system: that age and sex constitute the major axes and the situation is such that differentiation cannot proceed very much farther in terms of the total familial roles of individuals. The significance of this lies in the importance of the generality of the first major differentiations of orientation pattern for the child. From the sociological point of view we may speak of hierarchy and the qualitative differentiation between instrumental-adaptive and expressive-integrative functions as *the* two most fundamental and elementary axes of the functional differentiations of social systems.

In terms of their extension outside the family these two basic modes of differentiation are of quite different significance to the child. While hierarchical differentiation transcending the stages of the life cycle of the individual is fundamental to societies, the particular aspect of it associated with childhood status is destined to be transcended by the mere fact of growing up. One reason then for the great significance of sex categorization is that it is a basis of differentiation of role which will never be transcended but remains indelible for life.

It shares with age hierarchization the property that it is of significance beyond the family circle but, as pointed out, it is only the "precipitate" of hierarchical ordering, not the age factor as such, which for the individual will necessarily remain permanent in defining his own status.

The fact that these two pattern principles both extend beyond the family, is connected with certain problems of the incest taboo which may be briefly mentioned here because of their relevance to the father symbol problem. It is another of Freud's many great contributions to have brought together previous anthropological knowledge of incest taboos and their significance, with the knowledge of the importance of childhood sexuality, or perhaps better eroticism. The primary importance of the latter seems to lie in its role as a vehicle of generalization from specific biologically grounded needs and their gratification to the diffuse love-attachment to the mother and

2. That there should, as Margaret Mead has suggested, sometimes be found a *complete* reversal of the sex roles in this respect is, in view of the feminine functions in child care, it seems to us, doubtful.

the corresponding security-need system. But it is precisely because this erotic attachment must be related to another which is just as fundamental to the family system, that of husband and wife, that it becomes problematical in the course of development. Both the dynamics of this conflict and its constructive use must be analyzed.

The salient features of the process are, since Freud, well known, namely, the temporary repression of the erotic-dependency need system itself in the latency period, and the transfer of erotic object attachment from the intrafamilial mother-object to an extrafamilial heterosexual mate after adolescence. That this process is most intimately connected with that of the extension of the child's reference system outside the family and into the wider society can scarcely be open to doubt. Put in sociological pattern terms, we may suggest that there is an intrinsic connection between erotic attachment and particularism. Therefore the building up on universalistic patterns of orientation, especially the valuation of effective achievement and the acceptance of the disciplines necessary for the development of technical skills, requires emancipation from too deep involvement in erotic attachments. The first step in this process of emancipation, already sketched, operates through bringing the child more into the total family on a responsible level, and forcing him to give way to the erotic priority of the marital relationship over the mother-child relation. The second step, through categorizing him by sex and motivating him to adopt a whole pattern of behavior appropriate to his sex, brings him for the first time much more sharply into a status of equivalence with persons outside his family, *i.e.,* boys and girls of his age level. This of course is greatly accentuated in our society with the experience of school attendance.

It is only when a sufficiently strong character structure, *i.e.,* orientation system, in these other respects has been built up, that erotic attachment is again permitted, but this time *outside* the family of orientation, and with a fundamental alteration of role structure, assuming the parental *role type,* and forming an attachment which will encompass parenthood as well as spousehood. A boy does not become *his* father, does not take over his place, but becomes *a* father in his own new family of procreation. A girl does not take her mother's place with her father and siblings, but becomes a mother and wife. The new, postadolescent role assumption then is a specification of a *more generalized sex role type* which has had to be learned before the specification can occur. One can never by identification with his own father become his father or take his specific role in the family. Phantasies as to the desirability of this are doubtless almost universal among normal boys. But through his father as a role model a boy later learns to become *a* father in another family. Identification therefore means the internalization of a *generalized* role pattern.

It is here that the father as symbol rather than as particular object becomes especially significant. When we speak of the father as a role model or as the prototype of masculinity, we are directly emphasizing his symbolic significance. It is more than the relationship to this particular man which is involved, but it is what this man *means* in a generalized sense. What he means, in turn, must be interpreted in terms of his being an example of a generalized pattern of qualities and behavior. At the beginning of the process the boy experiences his father only as exclusive and particular as an individual. In the course of time he comes to see him as an *example* of the generalized pattern. Only then can he be said to *evaluate* his father as distinguished from *reacting to* him.

The fact of one day coming to be not his father but a father then becomes part of this more complex pattern system which is exemplified by his father, and *ipso facto* by other men. The fact that the father has become a symbol and no longer only an individual opens the door to a further most important development.

There is no such thing as a society without a kinship system. Building on the biological differentiation of the sexes, and bisexual reproduction, but with the crucially important addition of the incest taboo, a kinship system seems to provide the minimum conditions for social life on the *cultural* level, including the socialization of the oncoming generation in the patterns of the culture, in a form which is compatible with the transmission of a stable yet variant ongoing cultural tradition. This is the basis of the overwhelming functional significance of the family in all societies at least until functional equivalents of it appear. But a society which is organized *primarily* about its kinship system is justly called *primitive*—not merely "nonliterate." Certain of the most important potentialities of the higher cultures remain closed to it. And the key to the development of these potentialities lies in the further structural differentiation of the social system which runs concomitantly with the elaboration of the cultural tradition itself.

It is in this connection that sex role is so important because structurally it is the major point of departure for this further differentiation. What is important here, then, is that component of the total sex role which is *not included* in the familial role of the person concerned. Inevitably, then, this component is more prominent and of greater strategic importance in the case of the masculine than of the feminine roles, though of course to varying degrees and in different ways according to the particular social structural type in question.

The child, however, must learn the rudiments of this broader cultural pattern system in the family, in interaction with other family members and most particularly his parents. Therefore it is his father not *qua father, i.e.,* in his intrafamilial role, but as a man with special reference to his role outside the family and to the cultural values he holds with respect to extrafamilial matters, which is the important focus for the child.

It is at this point perhaps that psychoanalytic treatment of the father problem has been least developed. The problem is essentially that of the *analytical breakdown* of the father-image into a variety of components. One essential line of distinction has to do with differentiating those aspects of the actual intrafamilial role of the father which are most essential at different stages of development of the child. The basic distinction we have insisted upon here is that between his role as an authority in breaking up the early mother-dependency and motivating to contributory performance and, on the other hand, his role model function in connection with the assumption of sex role for the boy, and as an ideal of masculinity for the girl. In the latter case authority may be involved quite differently from the former.

This in turn serves as a bridge to the patterning of orientation toward the primary extrafamilial values and roles. The father here becomes a symbol and not just an individual, but it is only in a slightly "equivocal" sense that other men in extrafamilial roles can be spoken of as "father-figures," for example, employers or persons in positions of political authority. The essential problem is that of the relations between their resemblance to the father in either of his two intrafamilial roles, or to him in his more general "personality traits" as most appropriate to his extrafamilial roles.

For our point of departure in tackling this problem we must consider the manner in which the different roles played by the same individual are organized and interpreted. We are in a position now to analyze these in terms of a common set of components, so it is no longer necessary just to say, as most previous sociology has done, that familial roles and, for example, occupational roles are simply different; of course they are, but they are different because they involve the same components in different combinations.

For purposes of illustration we will use the occupational role in our own society because it represents a particularly sharp contrast with *any* intrafamilial role, and because of its very great significance in our type of society.

We may start by pointing out that all occupational roles which approximate the ideal type give primacy to the values of universalism and achievement or performance, the former as contrasted with particularism, the latter with "quality" or ascription.[3]

In both respects kinship presents an antithetical type. We may say then that the common value system of the occupational subsystem of our society is universalism-performance, that of the kinship subsystem is particularism-quality or ascription. How then can they be articulated with each other through the fact that the husband-father role and the occupational role are held by the same person?

The key to this lies in the fact that the *same* value orientation patterns are institutionalized in both role systems, but in *different orders of primacy.* Of the four basic object-categorization or performance-value types (why the two classifications can be identified cannot be gone into here) the order in most occupational roles gives first place to universalism-achievement. Then the order of the other three will differ according to the subtype of role, *i.e.,* according to the functions in the occupational system which the particular role subserves. Thus for a scientist or lawyer universalism-quality will come next, for an executive particularism-achievement, *i.e.,* on the basis of responsibility for the interests of his organization, and for an artist or entertainer particularism-quality in terms of the standards of taste which he exemplifies and interprets or creates.

In the case of the family on the other hand, the paramount value pattern is particularism-quality; it is the maintenance by the family as a collective unit of an appropriate "style" or pattern of life, including of course the treatment of children as part of this. But in this subsystem the father-husband role is differentiated in terms of the

3. For definition and elucidation of these concepts see Talcott Parsons and Edward A. Shils, "Values, Motives and Systems of Action" in *Toward a General Theory of Action,* Cambridge, Harvard University Press, 1951, and Talcott Parsons, *The Social System,* The Free Press of Glencoe, New York, 1951.

primacy *for* this role, *i.e.,* the second place for the family, of the particularistic performance pattern, *i.e.,* of responsibility for the interests of the collectivity *in its relations to the situation,* while the mother-wife role is differentiated in terms of particularism-quality (from her husband's); it is, that is to say, the more direct embodiment of the familial values.

Of course in our society married women take a very large share of responsibility for the practical adaptive affairs of the family. The justification for the above statement lies in the crucial strategic significance for family status and thus welfare of the father's occupational position, both for its direct prestige value—positive or negative—and for the income which is principally derived from it. His concrete occupational role is thus *both* a role *in* the occupational system, *and* a *representative* role in the kinship system. He works, not only for his "firm" but also for his family—and of course himself. His responsibility to his family is thus in the *first* instance discharged by doing well in his occupational role. Probably next to that comes his expressive-integrative function with respect to the family itself, *i.e.,* to his wife and children, and probably last his instrumental-adaptive functions in intrafamilial functions—in our urban middle class family system. In the case of the wife-mother, on the other hand, the expressive-integrative functions come first, the instrumental-adaptive —*i.e.,* housekeeping, shopping, etc., second, and representative roles probably last. This order is shifted toward the upper class levels.

There seem to be two main channels by which this structure of the father's role impinges on the child and becomes of crucial importance to his socialization; both illustrate the extreme importance of generalization and hence symbolization. The first is the recognition accorded in the family to his occupational achievements, above all of course by the mother, but very definitely including his own attitudes toward his role and his success in it, both "intrinsically" from the occupational point of view and in terms of its contribution to the welfare of the family as a whole. The second is the set of concrete interactions of both parents with the child which are congruent in pattern with the father's occupational role, above all the rewarding of small achievements on the part of the child, and punishment of the corresponding small failures. Here the decisive factor is the congruence of pattern so that the child can generalize from these specific events to the extrafamilial situation. The child's own extrafamilial roles in peer group and school early become very significant in this connection, as do the attitudes of the parents toward his behavior in them. This second basic channel acquires a particularly great significance in our kinship system because of the fact that the father's occupational role is typically carried out away from home and, especially in the higher reaches, is often difficult for a child to understand.

In all this it is clear that a crucial place is taken by the inculcation of standards of autonomy in a double sense. The first sense concerns autonomy from dependency on parents; the willingness to take responsibility. The second concerns behavior according to standards which are not measured mainly in terms of family welfare, but of a universalistic character—which therefore are "good" in themselves so far as the family is concerned. The place of these standards will become evident in the sanction system which operates in intrafamilial interaction, as well as in the interpretations of the reasons for these sanctions which are offered to the child.

This completes with one exception the essential considerations which seem necessary to take into account in treating the sociological aspects of the symbolization of the father role. This exception is an analysis of the processes of formation of symbolic complexes in more general terms, which would take us too far afield in the present paper. In this concluding section we shall confine ourselves to bringing together the implications of the main considerations we have reviewed for this problem of symbol formation and that of its functions in personality and social systems.

We have stated above that the main structure of systems of the orientation of action consisted in complexes of symbols and their meanings; this is what we mean by speaking of cultural behavior. When seen in this light, the significance of the father symbol complex derives from the fact that it is one of the principal links between the three phenomena of, first, mature personalities, second, structurally differentiated social systems, and, third, of the fact that the human individual is socialized in the context of that special type of social subsystem, the family. Of all the symbolic complexes centered about familial roles that concerning the father is the one which is most strategically important as linking the earlier familial experience with the role structure of the wider society.

We have found it important to distinguish three main levels in the symbolic complex which centers about the father role which correspond broadly to stages in the socialization process and are closely related to the distinctions between the systems and subsystems of social interaction to which the child must successively be related.

The first of these concerns the core of the oedipal problem in the sense in which Freud himself analyzed it; it is the father as the primary agent of pressure for the child to abandon his early love attachment to the mother, and to renounce both the attendant dependency and the attendant erotic gratifications. On the positive side, this father is also the primary embodiment of what, seen in terms of this reference system, are the higher duties, in the first instance, of a big boy or big girl. The attitudinal structure associated with it is inevitably ambivalent; the child undergoes a temporary neurosis.

The second and third levels or layers concern the child's own sex role assumption; it is here that it is most appropriate to speak of "identification" with the father for the case of the boy.[4]

This sex role assumption, in turn, involves what we may call the intrafamilial and the extrafamilial components. The intrafamilial component involves most intimately the dynamics of the incest taboo, hence the generalization to the assumption of a father role in a new family, not that of his father in the family of orientation; it is a generic father role which is internalized in the boy. As a further differentiation of this element, the third level or layer concerns the extrafamilial component, and merges into the general patterning of the masculine role in the society in question. Its exact content will vary greatly according to the general role structure of the society. We have illustrated by the relation between occupational and familial roles in our own society, and strongly emphasized that in pattern type they are fundamentally different, but that the differences can be analyzed in terms of common structural components.

In all three respects we may speak of father symbols arising so far as the individual generalizes from his experience with his own father to define generic types to which he has special relationships. The first of these three is the most familiar context in which the problem is usually discussed. Unquestionably many individuals generalize in this way from their own father. Thus they may, on the one hand, act toward occupational superiors, political authorities, etc., according to the ambivalent pattern which was appropriate to this classical oedipal situation with nuances appropriate to the particular kinship system. In general, especially perhaps in our society, we may

4. With respect to the concept, identification, and its place in Freud's work see "The Superego and the Theory of Social Systems," Chapter 1 in this volume.

say that the individual who does this in a conspicuous manner is one who has not successfully resolved the oedipal conflicts in his later development.

On the other hand, in many cultural traditions there are prominent symbols which incorporate this fundamental attitudinal complex. Perhaps the most conspicuous and familiar one to us is the Judeo-Christian God in a variety of His aspects of meaning. That *to a greater or less degree* He has been a father symbol is undoubtedly true; the only important point to stress here is how far other aspects of the problem have come into the question. But as the severe enforcer of authority, above all as the prohibitor, perhaps as the One Who has reserved all creativity—which can connote procreation—for Himself, undoubtedly this God has many of the attributes of the classical oedipal father.

Even on this level, however, there is an important question of the relevance of cultural relativity. Judaism and Christianity, seen in comparative religious perspective, are precisely conspicuous for their relative lack of emphasis on female deities which could serve as mother symbols—the cult of Mary in parts of Roman Catholicism being perhaps the principal exception. The primacy of the father symbol in this religious tradition strongly suggests that there is more to it than the reflection of the primary oedipal attitudes; that this has something to do with the strong emphasis in the Western world on types of achievement and rules of conduct which *transcend* the familial situation. God the creator and God the lawgiver are not only more than a father symbol in this primary sense, but are more than a familial symbol in any sense. The power of this symbol has had much to do with transcending the binding of culture to the kinship system as such.[5]

When we come to the second of our phases, the problems of assumption of sex role obviously involve very closely the differentiation of roles from members of the opposite sex and the structuring of attitudes toward them. Here it is not so much the individual's attitudes toward "father figures" as others in roles in some ways resembling that of his own father toward him, that is important, as

5. The apparent paradox involved in these problems may be illustrated by the fact that, while in classical Chinese culture the master religious symbols—Tao, Yang, Yin—clearly are not father symbols, but the social structure is familistically oriented to a far higher degree than ours. It is this kind of problem which a theory of symbolism on the cultural level must work through.

the individual's own attitudes in his own masculine role, in the first instance toward women if he is male, but of course also toward other men. Here psychologically, a primary problem complex concerns the individual's own self-confidence in his own sex role, for we have been given reason to believe that this underlies the successful development of further specifications of role. Here in a sense we run into what might be called father symbolism in reverse; it is not a matter of attitudes toward others as "father figures" but of a person's own attitude toward himself as taking a father role. The ambivalences to be found here should be the obverse of the ambivalences in the "primary" oedipal context. Thus, to take a familiar American example, it may be suggested that the attitude toward women typical of the so-called "wolf" is one of fundamental ambivalence with respect to masculinity, including the assumption of a husband-father role on his own part. The positive side is expressed in the need to impress and gain control over women; the negative side in the inability to accept the normal responsibilities which a socially integrated sexual relationship should involve, and often in the unconscious desire to injure women, by making them commit themselves and then deserting them. It seem probable that such a pattern usually involves an incomplete identification with a stable father figure, perhaps also a component of feminine identification to which the exaggerated and distorted masculinity is a reaction formation. In other words, the wolf may often be latently homosexual.

We are not accustomed to thinking of symbolism in this sphere as "father symbolism" and perhaps we should not call it that. The closeness of the dynamic relation to the symbolism of the first type is, however, clear. On the sociocultural levels we would include here the whole complex of patterns with respect to men's familial roles, and what may be called their protofamilial roles in relation to courtship and extramarital relations to the opposite sex. It is clear that this is a rich field indeed.

The third of our problem areas is the one in which we are least accustomed to thinking of symbolism as related to the father problem at all. We speak of the success pattern and the like. On the whole this attitude is, it seems, correct. But it is highly important that any general theory of the father symbol complex on the sociocultural level should take adequate account of the intimate connections between the father focus as such and the more general complex of symbolization of the masculine role and the attributes associated with it. It seems to be a centrally important implication of the above analysis that the father must be to a boy as to a girl the prototype of adult masculinity.[6]

Hence whatever the major patterns and values attaching to the masculine role in the culture they must be integrated with the symbolization of fatherhood.

This is essentially to say that the father symbol complex cannot be treated as an altogether independent entity. From the point of view of the sociologist it is perhaps the most important single channel through which the value patterns of the culture on the more general level come to be internalized in the process of socialization. If, in one aspect, a great deal of the cultural symbolization is a "projection" of experiences, especially of childhood, undergone in the family situation, it is almost equally the case that the real father is a "projection" *into* the family situation of the major pattern structure of the wider social system. It is perhaps in holding the right balance between these two aspects of the problem that the contributions of the developmental psychologist and of the sociologist to the whole problem can best be integrated with each other.

One final point should be mentioned. As we have noted several times, it was one of Freud's most fundamental contributions to emphasize the ambivalence associated with the father symbol as indeed with the whole oedipal situation. This is of course indicative of emotional strain, of what we have called the universal temporary neurosis of childhood. Hence the father symbolism especially on what we have called the primary level, involves elements of distortion of the reality actually experienced. This appears in various projective forms, in the behavior of the child, and in the adult, for example, in dreams and in other material produced in the course of psychoanalysis.

There is no doubt of the fundamental correctness of the contention of many psychoanalysts that the same components enter into the common symbolism of cultures, and that they do in some sense connote the presence of the types of neurotic strains which are found in patients. The relationship, however, is undoubtedly highly complex

6. It is here that Freud's treatment of the "ego ideal" as distinguished from the superego seems to belong. It seems to us that Freud never satisfactorily worked out the relations of the two and that this is symptomatic of theoretical difficulties Freud had in relating the personality and social system levels of analysis. By making the distinction he was, however, on essentially the track that the above analysis has attempted to follow up.

and needs to be very carefully worked out. We are entirely sure that neurotic conflicts cannot in the nature of the case be evenly distributed throughout a large population. The relation between the cultural symbolism and that of the individual personality cannot be a one-to-one matter.

If, however, we reason carefully in terms of system-references, certain analogies do appear which are at least worth following up. A very tentative one may be hazarded here. Namely, it would, I think, be agreed by most analysts that a personality in whom the father symbol complex as distinguished from the generic masculine role complex was too prominent, was probably on the neurotic side; it is, that is to say, normal to overcome the pattern of oedipal preoccupations. It seems probable that in a social system if there is undue prominence of obvious father symbolization in the cultural tradition analogous conclusions would be justified. The preoccupation with the single leader in modern dictatorships is a case in point.

Two cautions, however, immediately suggest themselves. First, it is very difficult to distinguish the situations of sociocultural ferment in which sheer disorganization is dominant from those in which there is a prominent creative component. Both are apt to exhibit considerable evidence of conflict with the attendant psychological manifestations. What we can legitimately infer then in the first instance is that where such symbolization becomes prominent there is considerable conflict present. Further evidence would be necessary to diagnose the exact character of the conflict and the probabilities of its outcome.

The second caution is as to the obverse phenomenon. We Americans, particularly, take a certain pride in our immunity to authoritarianism, and fundamentally quite rightly. However, in the well known American anti-authoritarian streak it seems almost certain that there is an important component of reaction formation and that there are in fact latent authority and dependency needs which we find it difficult to acknowledge. In other words, if we are to explore analogies of the character suggested here, all of their ramifications should be explored, not only those which are congenial to certain values and attitude types commonly found among members of our profession.

We may close this fragmentary analysis with an expression of hope and confidence. It seems to be unquestionable that the streams of thought of psychoanalysis and of sociological theory have converged to a point where their integration can now prove exceedingly fruitful. There is every prospect that careful and competent research which utilizes the resources available from both sides can produce results of far greater significance than either of them working alone.

3

The Incest Taboo

in Relation to Social Structure

and the Socialization of the Child

AFTER something like a generation in which the attention of anthropologists and sociologists has been focused on the phenomena which differentiate one society from another and the different structures within the same society from each other, in recent years there has been a revival of interest in the problem of what features are common to human societies everywhere and what are the forces operating to maintain these common features. One reason for my present interest in the incest taboo is that it is one of the most notable of these common features. With all the variability of its incidence outside the nuclear family, there is the common core of the prohibition of marriage and in general of sexual relationships between members of a nuclear family except of course the conjugal couple whose marriage establishes it.

In the older discussions the prevailing tendency was to attempt to find a specific "cause" of the taboo, thus instinctive aversion or Westermarck's contention that aversion was acquired through being brought up in the same household. As our empirical information and

Reprinted from The British Journal of Sociology, Vol. V, No. 2, June, 1954. This paper was presented at a meeting of the Association of Social Anthropologists, University College, London, January 10, 1954.

theoretical resources have accumulated, however, it seems less and less likely that this is the most fruitful approach. On the contrary anything so general as the incest taboo seems likely to be a resultant of a constellation of different factors which are deeply involved in the foundations of human societies. Analysis in terms of the balance of forces in the social system rather than of one or two specific "factors" seems much more promising. Furthermore, it seems highly probable that a combination of sociological and psychological considerations is involved; that a theory which attempts to by-pass either of these fields will find itself in difficulties.

The element of constancy clearly focuses in the nuclear family. Perhaps the most recent authoritative survey is that of Murdock,[1] and we have his authority that no society is known where incest between mother-son, father-daughter or full brother-sister is permitted except the few cases of brother-sister marriage in royal families, but never for the bulk of the people. There are a few cases of marriage permitted between half-brother and half-sister, and similar cases of closeness, but only a few. I shall therefore take the nuclear family as my point of departure and attempt to review a few highlights of it as a sub-system of the society. But the nuclear family is, in my opinion, only the focus of the structural problem, not the whole of it. I shall therefore next attempt to link with the relevant considerations about the family, a series of problems about its place in and articulation with the rest of the society. Then, given this wider setting of social structure, I will attempt to analyze some of the relevant problems of psychological mechanism in terms of the characteristics and significance of eroticism in personal relationships and in the personality itself.

I. THE STRUCTURE AND FUNCTIONS OF THE NUCLEAR FAMILY

THE universality of some order of incest taboo is of course directly connected with the fact that the nuclear family is also universal to all known human societies. The minimal criteria of the nuclear family are, I suggest, first that there should be a solidary relationship between mother and child lasting over a period of years and transcending physical care in its significance. Secondly, in her motherhood of this child the woman should have a special relation-

1. Murdock, *Social Structure*, New York, Macmillan, 1949, Chap. 10.

ship to a man *outside her own descent group* who is sociologically the "father" of the child, and that this relationship is the focus of the "legitimacy" of the child, of his referential status in the larger kinship system.[2]

The common sense of social science has tended to see in the universality and constancy of structure of the nuclear family a simple reflection of its biological function and composition; sexual reproduction, the generation difference and the differentiation by sex in the biological sense. While I in no way question the importance of this biological aspect and am in agreement with the view that the human family is an "extension" of a subhuman precultural entity, on the human-cultural levels there is, I am sure, another aspect of the problem of constancy. The two biological bases of differentiation, sex and generation, may be regarded, that is, as "points of reference" of a type of social organization the sociological significance of which is general in the structure of small groups.

Evidence from the experimental laboratory study of small groups[3] has shown first that small groups with no prior institutionalized differentiation of status, differentiate spontaneously on a hierarchical dimension, which I may call "power" in the sense of relative influence on the outcome of processes in the system. This is the case when this differentiation is measured by any one of a variety of possible measures, both from the point of view of the observer and that of participants in group process. We may say there is a differentiation between "leaders" and "followers."

Secondly, there appears a differentiation which cuts across this one, with reference to qualitative *type of function* in the group. The first broad qualitative type of differentiation which appears in this sense is what Bales and I have called that between primarily "instrumental" function in the group and primarily "expressive" function. An instrumental function is one primarily concerned with the relations of the group to the situation external to it, including adaptation to the conditions of that situation and establishment of satisfactory goal relations for the system vis-à-vis the situation. Expressive function on the other hand is concerned primarily with the harmony or

2. It will be noted that I deliberately assume the incest taboo as part of the constitution of the family itself.

3. See R. F. Bales, "The Equilibrium Problem in Small Groups," in Parsons, Bales and Shils, *Working Papers in the Theory of Action,* New York, The Free Press of Glencoe, 1953.

solidarity of the group, the relations internally of the members to each other and their "emotional" states of tension or lack of it in their roles in the group.

Level of differentiation is of course a function of size of the group. By the time we reach a membership of four there can be a typical four-role pattern, differentiated hierarchically into leadership and followership roles, and qualitatively into more instrumental and more expressive roles. I would like to suggest that it is fruitful to treat the nuclear family as a special case of this basically four-role pattern, with generation as the main axis of superior-inferior or leader-follower differentiation, sex the axis of instrumental-expressive differentiation. Obviously the helplessness of the child, particularly in the first years, is the main basis of the former. The universal fact that women are more intimately concerned with early child care than are men (with lactation playing a very fundamental part) is the primary reason why the feminine role, in the family as well as outside, tends to be *more* expressive in this sense than the masculine.[4]

My first point is thus that the nuclear family has certain characteristics common to small groups in general. The effectiveness of its performance of function as a family is, I think, dependent on its having these characteristics. The primary functions I have in mind

4. The best documentation of this generalization available so far is I think a paper by M. Zelditch, Jr., "Role Differentiation in the Nuclear Family," in Parsons, Bales, *et al., Family, Socialization and Interaction Process,* New York, The Free Press of Glencoe, 1955, Chap. VI. Zelditch studied a sample of fifty-five societies and found first an overwhelming preponderance of relative instrumentalism in the father role, second no cases where the available evidence was unequivocal that the mother role in the nuclear family is *more* instrumental than that of the father. The greatest difficulties for this thesis occur in the cases of matrilineal kinship systems where the mother's brother takes over some of the functions of the father in other systems. The weight of Zelditch's evidence, however, suggests that even in these cases the *relative* differentiation on this axis holds, though the span of it is greatly narrowed.

The importance of these four roles for family structure is, I think, emphasized by kinship terminology. I believe it is true that, with all the variation of kinship terminology, there is no known system where these four roles, namely mother, father, brother, sister and, conversely, self, spouse, son, daughter, are not discriminated from each other. Of course frequently incumbents of these roles are classified together with other kin, as father with his brothers. But there is no known system which fails to discriminate the four cardinal roles in the nuclear family from each other. This is to say that generation and sex within the family are universally made bases of discrimination. There is no other set of roles in kinship systems of which this is true.

are a certain significance for maintaining the emotional balances of all members of the family including the adults, and its paramount role as an agency for the socialization of children. The general characteristics I have in mind are three. The first is that it should be a *small* group, especially in its higher status-echelon. Given age-specific death rates as well as birth rates presumably in no society does the effective nuclear family average more than about seven members, and generally fewer. The second characteristic is that the main structural differentiation of the family as a group should be along these two axes, namely that of power or hierarchy and the instrumental-expressive distinction. The third is that *both* the latter should be represented in the "leadership" structure and that there should be a strong "coalition" between them.[5] The fact that the two parents are of opposite sex and that marriage, though with variations, always constitutes an important structural bond of solidarity transcending the parental functions, in a broad way insures this. It should be clear from the above that sex role differentiation in its more generalized sense which impinges on many contexts other than the structure of the nuclear family itself is importantly involved in this structural complex.

But this does not mean that just any kind of small group which met these specifications could perform the functions of the family. It clearly has to be a group which has relatively long duration—a considerable span of years. But it is not indefinite duration. One of its most important characteristics is that the family is a self-liquidating group. On attainment of maturity and marriage the child ceases in the full sense to be a member of his family of orientation; instead he helps in the establishment of a new one. The implications of this basic fact will be briefly discussed in the next section.

Secondly, it must be a group which permits and requires a high level of diffuse affective involvement for its members; though this of course varies with the different roles, being highest for the young child. Clearly no evanescent experimental group could perform the functions of a family. The fact that with few exceptions the nuclear family is the main unit of residence is of critical importance in this connection.

5. The connection between the leadership coalition of the small group and the erotically bound marriage partners was first stated by Bales, "The Equilibrium Problem in Small Groups," in Parsons, Bales and Shils, *op. cit.*, Chap. IV.

Finally, third, I suggest that it is essential to the family that more than in any other grouping in societies, overt erotic attraction and gratification should be given an institutionalized place in its structure. But when we say this is institutionalized we mean that eroticism is not only permitted but carefully regulated; and the incest taboo is merely a very prominent negative aspect of this more general regulation.

This aspect will be more fully discussed in the third section of the paper. But at this point it does seem worth while to summarize the familiar features of the erotic organization of the family. First genital eroticism is both permitted to and expected of the marital pair. Only in certain special religious groups is its justification even in theory confined to the direct procreative function; it is itself a bond and a very important symbol of the solidarity of the marriage pair as responsible for a family. But at the same time—and this fact accentuates this meaning—the marital couple have a monopoly of the right to genital eroticism within the nuclear family, though of course not necessarily outside.

Secondly, pregenital eroticism is positively institutionalized, always in the early mother-child relation, and probably usually to some extent in that of father and child. But clearly it is generally far more important in the case of mother and child.

Third, with probably few exceptions, overt erotic expression except possibly autoeroticism in some cases, is tabooed as between postoedipal children and both parents, and in the relations of the children to each other, except where an older sibling plays a partly parental role to a small child. Finally, no homosexuality is permitted at all within the nuclear family unless we wish to call the attraction between mother and pre-oedipal daughter homosexual. In view of what we know on psychological levels of the erotic potentials of human beings this structure is clearly not one of unrestricted permissiveness, but of a systematic combination of controlled expression and regulatory prohibition. Moreover, in view of the wide variety of human customs in so many respects, its relative uniformity is impressive and deserves to be counted as one of the most important universals of human society.

It would be rash to suggest that the socialization of children could not be carried out except in a group of the specific biological composition of the family, or even without this specific set of erotic relationships. I think, however, that it is fairly safe to contend that the primary socializing agency must be a small group with broadly the sociological characteristics I have suggested, and that even the erotic factor could not vary extremely widely. For example, it could not be completely suppressed, by having all fertilization occur by artificial insemination, and by a careful policy of avoiding arousing any erotic interest on the part of children, or at the other extreme by removing all restrictions on fulfilment of any and all erotic impulses as and when they might be aroused.

II. THE FAMILY AND THE
WIDER SOCIAL STRUCTURE

ONE of the cardinal uniformities of social structure which is most intimately connected with the incest taboo is the fact that nuclear families are *never* found as independent total "societies" on a human cultural level. There is never simply extra-social biological mating outside the family, but the nuclear family is always a unit within a society which contains a plurality of other families, and other types of units; "solidarity" extends over these areas and the other groupings, and even where they are kinship groupings, sociologically they have characteristics very different from those of the nuclear family.

Undoubtedly one of the main characteristics of the more "primitive" societies lies in the fact that a far larger proportion of the total social structure is organized about kinship than is the case with the more "advanced" societies. Indeed there are some where it is difficult to speak of any "statuses" or groups which are not in some important respect kinship statuses and groups. But two main things need to be said. First, though always including nuclear families, the kinship system always also includes groups which differ fundamentally from nuclear families. Secondly, it can, following Leach,[6] probably be said that a kinship system cannot be a completely "closed" system in that features of it always have to be analyzed with reference to economic, political and other considerations which are not peculiar to kinship relations, which do not disappear in social structures which have entirely cast loose from a kinship base.

Whether the groupings which transcend the nuclear family are organized about kinship or not, relative to the family they have in

6. E. R. Leach, *The Structural Implications of Matrilineal Cross-Cousin Marriage,* Royal Anthropological Society, London, 1951.

general—with a few exceptions like friendships—certain characteristics in common. They are groups in which the personal emotional interests of the individual are not so closely bound up as in the family; where the accent is more on impersonal functions of the group. A good kinship case of this type is the lineage as a corporate entity with reference to its political functions. The case of organizations composed primarily of occupational roles in modern society is one where kinship is not prominent. Broadly one may say that in such cases the role or the organization is characterized by primacy of functional responsibility on a social system level, and by relatively severe control of affective spontaneity—by what I have elsewhere[7] called "affective neutrality." These are the structures in which the main functions of direct maintenance and goal-attainment in the society are performed; viz. economic provision, political stabilization and defense, religious expression, etc.

Where the main basis of composition of such groupings rests in kinship, marriage has direct functional significance as a mechanism which establishes important direct ties of interpenetration of memberships between the different elements in the structural network. Under such circumstances marriage cannot be merely a "personal affair" of the parties to it. Where it is difficult to have solidary relationships which do not involve kinship the intermarriage between groups can establish a pattern of such solidarities cross-cutting those based directly or primarily on relationships by descent.

As Fortune was one of the first to emphasize, and Lévi-Strauss has developed further,[8] in this kind of situation it is not so much the prohibition of incest in its negative aspect which is important as the positive obligation to perform functions for the subunit and the larger society by marrying out. Incest is a withdrawal from this obligation to contribute to the formation and maintenance of suprafamilial bonds on which major economic, political and religious functions of the society are dependent.

Where extended kinship groupings have a critical importance in the social structure, it is considerations of this kind which underlie the patterns of extension of the incest taboo beyond the nuclear

7. Cf. Parsons, *The Social System,* New York, The Free Press of Glencoe, 1951, Chap. II.
8. R. F. Fortune, "Incest," in *Encyclopedia of the Social Sciences,* edited by Seligman and Johnson, and Claude Lévi-Strauss, *Les structures élémentaires de la parenté* Paris, Presses Universitaires de France, 1949.

family. Broadly the principles seem to be that intermarriage is forbidden within units which, first, are organized primarily as kinship units, second, have functions in the social system which transcend the personal interests of the members of small family groups, which therefore involve a more impersonal set of disciplines and, third, groups within which, as kinship groups, daily interaction with reference to these interests is relatively close. The lineage and its segments and the male local succession group which Leach discusses, are prototypes of such groups. Illustrating the last criterion it is typical that exogamy often breaks down within the most extensive lineage groups but is maintained within their lower-order segments.[9]

Recent work on kinship seems to indicate that in a very rough way it is possible to construct a series of types in this respect. At one end is the so-called Kariera type which is characterized by symmetrical cross-cousin marriage. This forms a very "tight" form of organization, but is very limited in the range of different kinds of social ties which can be established through it. It makes for a rigid social structure, though probably under certain conditions a relatively stable one.

Lévi-Strauss is probably right that the asymmetrical type of cross-cousin marriage which rests primarily on marriage with the mother's brother's daughter constitutes an important step towards a wider ranging and more flexible set of arrangements as compared both with the Kariera type and with marriage to the father's sister's daughter. It is interesting to note that this is connected with the asymmetry of the structure of the nuclear family itself as that was discussed above. If the masculine role is more instrumental than the feminine in the senses I have discussed, then the men should have more direct and important anchorages in the extended kinship groupings than the women. Then for a woman who has married out of her descent group, the strongest source of support would not be her sister but her brother. This is first because the sister may well have married either into ego's own post-marital group or into another controlled largely by her husband's agnatic kin and second because in the descent group the men have more control in extrafamilial affairs than the women.

The father's brother, on the other hand, is in a status directly similar to that of the father and not complementary to him, while the father's sister belongs to this same agnatic group. Put a little differently an alliance with the mother's brother is the stablest kind

9. For a recent survey, cf. Murdock, *op. cit.*, Chap. X.

of alliance with a distinctly different group and at the same time bolsters the structure of the nuclear family in such a way as to redress the balance resulting from its internal asymmetry by giving the mother external support through a channel independent of her husband.

Lévi-Strauss therefore seems to be right in saying that asymmetrical cross-cousin marriage through the mother's brother's daughter relationship opens up a wider circle which is both stabler and more extensive than any alternative where the kin involved are so close. Leach,[10] however, has made an important additional contribution by showing that on such a basis the kinship system cannot be closed through marriage-exchange relations alone, but that there are several alternative ways in which such a system can work out. Which of them will develop will depend on the economic and political relations of the exchanging kinship units, and hence on the nature and values of the "considerations" which enter into the marriage arrangements other than the exchange of spouses as such.

But all this is compatible in a broad way with Lévi-Strauss' view that this makes women, though in somewhat different ways also men, a kind of symbolic "counters" in a process of exchange. Perhaps I may state it in somewhat different terms by saying that the woman or man, in marrying outside his own descent group, is performing a role-obligation in a social group or collectivity which transcends his own family of orientation, and one to which to some degree his family is subordinated; it is a superordinate unit in the social structure. He is no more free to marry whom he chooses in such a situation than is an industrial worker free within the organization to perform any job-task he chooses regardless of how it fits into the plan for how the total process is to be organized.

It is in this sense that incest would be socially regressive in the sense in which Lévi-Strauss analyses the problem. It would, in an area of the higher integrative structures of the society, constitute giving membership in the lower-level structure priority over that in the higher. It is only on the impossible assumption that families should constitute independent societies and not be segmental units of higher-level organizations, that incest as a regular practice would be socially possible.

These considerations give us the basis for a further generalization concerning the difference between extended exogamous systems and

10. E. R. Leach, *op. cit.*

those found in modern societies. So far as the higher level functions of the society are performed by collectivities the composition of which is determined in kinship terms, there will be a tendency to extend the incest taboo to such collectivities. So far, however, as social function, economic, political and religious, comes to be organized in groups not put together out of kin, the whole issue of exogamy with reference to them will cease to be significant.

There is, however, complete continuity between these two types of cases so far as certain aspects of the social functions of the incest taboo are concerned. We may say that there are two primary inter-connected but independent aspects of this function. In the first place, it is socially important that the nuclear family should not be self-perpetuating and hence that adults should have a personality structure which motivates them to found new and independent nuclear families. Erotic attraction to persons of opposite sex but outside the nuclear family is clearly a mechanism which aids in this But, secondly, it is essential that persons should be capable of assuming roles which contribute to functions which no nuclear family is able to perform, which involve the assumption of non-familial roles. Only if such non-familial roles can be adequately staffed can a society function. I suggest that the critical roles in this class are roles in which erotic interests must be altogether subordinated to other interests.

I thus see the "problem" of the incest taboo in the following setting so far as social structure is concerned. It seems to be clear that human personalities are universally socialized in nuclear families, which are small groups of the special type sketched above. Included in their special characteristics is the role of erotic attraction between their members. The incest taboo operates to "propel" the individual out of the nuclear family, not in one but in two senses. He is propelled into a new nuclear family formed by his marriage. Here the erotic component of his personality is positively made use of. But also he is propelled into non-familial roles, which of course are differentiated by sex and other status-characteristics, but in some sense such roles must be assumed by all adults. This corresponds to the fact that every known society consists in a plurality of nuclear families the duration of which is limited to one generation and also the fact that these families are always relatively low-level units in a social structure the higher-level units of which have different functions in the society, functions which cannot be performed by family groups.[11] It is in this setting that I wish to discuss some of the problems of the psychological characteristics of eroticism and its place in the development of personality.

III. THE PSYCHOLOGICAL CHARACTERISTICS AND FUNCTIONS OF EROTICISM

AFTER all, the most distinctive feature of the incest taboo is the regulation of erotic relationships, within the family and in relation to the establishment of new families. The considerations about social structure which I have advanced therefore need to be supplemented by a discussion of the nature of eroticism and its functions in the development of personality and in the personality of the adult. I shall here put forward a view which has three main emphases. First, eroticism will be held to play a very important part, probably an indispensable one, in the socialization of the child, in taking a raw organism and making a "person" out of it. Second, however, the awakening of erotic interests not only performs functions, it creates problems. There are important psychological reasons why erotic needs seem to be particularly difficult to control. Making use of this instrument of socialization therefore constitutes a kind of "pact with the devil." Once present the question of what is to be done with this force is a serious problem. Finally, third, the view of eroticism I take here will dissociate it considerably from what is ordinarily meant by the "sex instinct" or the instinct of reproduction. Though the interest in genital eroticism of the post-adolescent is undoubtedly genuinely part of the erotic complex, and a very important part, it is only part, and the complex is far broader than such an instinct in two senses. On the one hand its childhood or pregenital aspects are of funda-

11. There are good reasons for believing that there is an intimate connection between the overcoming of the excessive autonomy of the nuclear family and the possibility of a cultural level of social development. In the first place such a group is apparently too small to support an independent language with its minimum of extensity of generalization and communicative range. It is also probable that it is too "ingrown," culturally rather than biologically. One of the important consequences of the incest taboo is to enforce the mixing of family cultures (on the distinctiveness of the cultures of particular households, see J. M. Roberts, *Three Navaho Households*, Peabody Museum Monographs, Cambridge, Mass.). There is an analogy here to the biological functions of sexual reproduction. If, therefore, I may hazard an extremely tentative hypothesis about socio-cultural origins it would be that the earliest *society* had to be a multifamily unit which enforced an incest taboo.

mental importance for our problem and presumably have nothing to do with the reproductive function. Secondly, though there undoubtedly must be a basis in constitutional predisposition, the aspects of eroticism which are important for our purposes involve a very large component which is learned rather than "instinctive" in the usual sense.

I shall rely heavily on Freud for my views of the erotic complex, though I think Freud can be supplemented by some considerations derived from the sociological study of the process of socialization. But after all one of the greatest of Freud's discoveries was the fundamental *importance* of the eroticism of childhood—the fact of its existence was not discovered by Freud, but as so often in the history of science well-known facts excited little interest because nobody knew how to assess their importance. Furthermore, Freud clearly saw the importance of the processes of learning in the development of erotic interests. I may recall his famous statement that "the infant is polymorph perverse." This I interpret to mean that any normal child has the potentiality of developing *any* of the well-known types of erotic orientation, homosexuality, autoeroticism and the perversions as well as what we think of as normal heterosexuality. This can only mean that the latter is in considerable measure the product of the process of socialization, not simply the expression of an instinct.[12]

What, then, are the most important characteristics of eroticism? Erotic interest is, I think, the interest in securing a particular type of organic pleasure, which is in *one* aspect organically specific in a way comparable to the pleasure of hunger-gratification or warmth. But this is only one aspect of it. What is most important about eroticism is, I think, its dual character, the combination of this organic specificity, the possibility of intense pleasure through the stimulation of specific parts of the body, with a *diffuse* spreading into a general sensation of well-being. From stimulation of an erogenous zone then, it is not a very big step to learning that almost any type of bodily contact with the agent can come to be felt as a source of pleasure. I may take a specific example from early childhood. Being fed by the mother is a source not only of hunger-gratification but very early, according to psychoanalytic views, of oral-erotic gratification as well. But from stimulation of this oral-erotic interest there is generalization to pleasurable sensation from any physical contact with the source

12. The best general reference for this aspect of Freud's work is his *Three Contributions to Sexual Theory*.

of the original oral gratification; hence being held and fondled by the mother, is a source of pleasure and a focus of an incipient system of expectations.

Put in psychological terms, erotic gratification is a peculiarly sensitive source of conditioning in the "classical" Pavlovian sense. From desiring the specific stimulation, the child comes to desire diffuse non-specific contact with the object which has served as agent of the original gratification. Eroticism is thus a major, in the earlier stages probably *the* major mechanism for the "generalization of cathexis" by which a diffuse attachment to an object come to be built up.[13]

The great importance of diffuse attachment in this sense to the process of learning has come to be well-recognized. So long as a socializing agent is only a source of specific segmental gratifications, the omission of such gratification will cause the child very rapidly to lose interest in the object. But the process by which the deeper kind of learning[14] is possible involves the building up of need-systems and then their frustration as a preliminary to the learning of new goals and needs.[15] The essential point is that the socializing agent should be in a position to frustrate the child—really seriously—without losing control of him.

Another aspect of the point is that it is by this order of generalization of cathexis that the child is made sensitive to the *attitudes* of the socializing agent, say the mother. This sensitivity to attitude is possible only through transcending the specificity of interest in organic gratifications as such. What matters to the child is whether and how much he feels that his mother "cares." The very fact that erotic gratification is *not* essential to any of the basic physiological needs of the individual organism makes it a suitable vehicle for this generalization.

A further characteristic of eroticism seems to be important in the general situation; it is what underlies my reference above to its arousal constituting in a sense a "pact with the devil." Erotic need, that is,

13. Freud's views on this problem are most fully developed in the late paper, *Hemmung, Symptom und Angst:* English title: *The Problem of Anxiety,* New York, Norton, 1936.
14. Meaning the internalization of cultural values—cf. Parsons, *The Social System, op. cit.,* Chap. VI.
15. This involves what Olds calls the "law of motive growth." See James Olds, *The Growth and Structure of Motives,* Chaps. I and II New York, The Free Press of Glencoe, 1954.

seems to have some of the characteristics of addiction. The erotic interests of childhood cannot be allowed to be dominant in later phases of development, and in normal development are not. But the evidence is that by and large they are not, as the psychologists put it, successfully "extinguished," but rather have to be repressed. From this it comes that the psychoanalysis of any "normal" adult will bring to light "infantile" erotic patterns which are still there, though they have not been allowed overt gratification for many years. The evidence is very clear that normal and pathological differ in this respect only in degree, not in terms of presence or absence.[16] If this general view is correct then the mechanisms for handling such permanently repressed material must be of great importance in the normal adult personality.

Let us look at the matter in more of a sociological perspective. A socializing agent at any given major stage of the process plays a dual role, in *two* systems of social interaction. On the one hand he— or she—participates with the child at the level which is appropriate to the beginning of the phase in question, as in the case of the mother-child love attachment of the immediately pre-oedipal period. On the other hand she—the mother in this case—also participates in the full four-role family system. In disturbing the equilibrium of the former interaction system she acts as an agent of the latter. This act of disturbance constitutes frustration to the child and produces among other things anxiety and aggression. If, on the other hand, there were no positive motivation in his involvement in the relationship other than what he is now denied expression, the attachment would simply break up and no progress could be made, since he is not yet motivated to assume his *new* role in the new and higher level interaction system.

But the specific part of the erotic attachment is a focus of precisely the element of "dependency"—at the relevant level—which has to be overcome if the new level is to be attained. Under the conditions postulated, however, the *diffuse* aspect of the erotic attachment can survive the frustration of the focal specific desire, and it can thus become a main lever by which the child is positively motivated to

16. Eroticism in this respect seems to be a member of a larger class of strong affective interests. Thus the work of Solomon and Wynne ("Traumatic Avoidance Learning: The Principles of Anxiety Conservation and Partial Irreversibility," *Psychological Review*, Vol. 61, No. 6, Nov. 1954) on conditioned anxiety in dogs has shown that a sufficiently acute anxiety is almost impossible to extinguish.

learn a new role which, it must be remembered, involves learning new goals, not merely new instrumental means for the attainment of given goals.

Thus the child's erotic attachment to the mother is the "rope" by which she pulls him up from a lower to a higher level in the hard climb of "growing up." But because the points of attachment of this "rope" remain sensitive, interest in them is not extinguished, there is a permanent channel back into the still operative infantile motivational system. Serious disturbances of the equilibrium of the personality can always re-open these channels. This is what is ordinarily meant by "regression" and early erotic patterns always play a prominent part in regressive tendencies.[17]

There seem to be three stages at which the mother is the primary object of erotic attraction of the child; these are what Freud identified as the Oral, the Anal and the Phallic phases. They correspond to three relatively discontinuous "steps" in the process of learning new levels of personality organization; new goals, and capacities for independent and responsible performance. Each one leaves a residuum of the erotic structures which have been essential in order to make the step, but which if allowed to remain active would interfere with the subsequent steps. Thus there is in all personalities, granting my hypothesis of addiction, a channel through erotic associations, right down into the lowest and most primitive strata of the Id—the most regressive parts of the personality system. These can be reactivated at any time. The connection of this situation with the problem of the probable psychological significance of incest seems to be clear.

From this point of view the problem of incest fits into the larger context of the structuring of erotic motivation in the personality, over time and with reference to choice of objects. The context includes the problem of homosexuality and of the status of the perversions. The goal of socialization—with many variations but in its broad pattern universal—is to establish at least the primacy, if not the complete monopoly over other possibilities, of normal genital erotic attraction which includes choice of object outside the family, and stability of orientation to objects.

Only mother-son incest is as such directly involved in the constellation I have sketched. Here the regressive implications seem very

17. This sociological aspect of the socialization process is much more fully analyzed in Parsons, Bales, *et al.*, *Family, Socialization and Interaction Process, op. cit.*, especially Chaps. IV and VI.

clear. This agrees with psychoanalytic opinion that such incest, where it does appear in our society, is always deeply pathological, on both sides but particularly that of the son.

The case of the daughter vis-à-vis her father is somewhat different. But when she is forced to abandon her primary attachment to her mother, it should be clear that the next available alternative is the father. This is further made "plausible" by the fact that she is taught that it is normal for a female to have a primary attachment to a masculine object, but in this case erotic development of the attachment is blocked. This clearly has to do on one level with the internal equilibrium of the nuclear family as a system. The erotic attachment of the parents to each other is a primary focus and symbol of their coalition as the leadership element of the family as a system. To allow the child who has just been forced out of an erotic attachment to the mother to substitute one with the father would immediately weaken this coalition as a source of generalized pressure to grow up for children of both sexes.

But there is a broader "functional" aspect of the problem. If it is exceedingly important that the boy should find a feminine object outside the family, this is obviously only possible in a generalized way if girls also typically do so. Furthermore, in order to perform her functions as a socializing agent, as mother, it is extremely important that a woman's regressive need systems should not be uncontrolled. Indeed it is probably more important than in the case of the man, because as a mother the woman is going to have to enter into much stronger erotic reciprocities with her young children than is her husband, and at the same time she is in due course going to have to act as the agent of their frustration in these respects. If she is not able to control her own regressive needs, then the mother-child system is likely to get "stuck" on one of the early levels and be unable to take the next step. Indeed such phenomena are prominent in the pathology of family relations in relation to the genesis of mental disorders. Thus the "overprotective" mother, instead of, at the proper time, refusing to reciprocate her child's dependency needs, positively encourages them and thereby makes it more difficult for him to grow up.

Finally, there is the case of the prohibition of brother-sister incest. It seems to me that in the first instance this relates to the symmetry of the nuclear family. Once the oedipal crisis has been passed, the most symmetrical arrangement is that which reserves a monopoly of erotic relations within the family to the married couple. But in a broader context functionally the more important thing is at the relevant time to achieve complete—though temporary—repression of erotic needs for both sexes. Fulfilment of this requirement would be blocked by permissiveness for brother-sister erotic relations.

For childhood eroticism regardless of the sex of the child the original object is the mother. Once this attachment to the mother has ceased to be useful to the development of the personality it tends, I have noted, to be repressed altogether. This means that not only is the original object denied, but those "next in line," that is all other members of the original nuclear family, are tabooed. This in turn, it seems, is an aspect of what I referred to above as the process of self-liquidation of each particular nuclear family.

What Freud called the period of "latency," *i.e.,* from the point of view of overt eroticism, thus seems to be the period in which the individual is above all learning to perform extrafamilial roles. Childhood erotic attachment has played a part in laying the necessary foundations for these processes, but beyond a certain point it becomes a hindrance. Just a word may be said about the first of these steps which seems to have a bearing on the problem of brother-sister attachment.

One of the primary features of the oedipal transition in the course of which the last phase of childhood eroticism is normally repressed is the assumption of sex role, or the first major step in that process. Though the points of reference for the differentiation are unmistakably biologically given, there is strong reason to believe that the role, including the psychological categorization of the self, must be learned to a much greater extent than has ordinarily been appreciated. It seems to be significant that just at this period children begin to be much more independent of their families and to associate particularly with other children. There will be many variations as a function of the structure of extended kinship groups and the nature of residential communities, but it seems to be broadly true that there is a general tendency to segregation of the sexes at this period. The phenomenon so familiar in Western society of the one-sex peer group seems to have a nearly universal counterpart to some extent elsewhere. The turning of primary interests into the channel of relations to friends of the same sex and nearly the same age seems to have a dual significance. On the one hand it reinforces the individual's self-categorization by sex by creating a solidarity transcending the family between persons of the same sex. On the other hand, for the first time the individual becomes a member of a group which both transcends the family and in which he is not in the strongly institutionalized position of being a member of the *inferior* generation class. It is the first major step toward defining himself as clearly *independent* of the authority and help of the parental generation.

Adolescence comes only after a considerable period of this latency-level peer group activity. Along with the fact that the emerging genital erotic interest of adolescence and after involves symmetrical attraction to persons of opposite sex, it is of the first importance that now for the first time erotic attraction is experienced with an object which is broadly an equal, instead of a generation-superior. On both counts there must be a considerable reorganization of the erotic complex in the personality and its relations to the other components before mature erotic attachments become possible. It is a psychiatric commonplace that much of the pathology of marriage relationships and of the erotic interests of adults otherwise, has to do with inadequate solution of these two problems, namely how to form a stable attachment to a single person of opposite sex and how to treat the partner as fundamentally an equal, neither to be dependent on him or her in a childish sense nor, by a mechanism which includes reaction-formation to dependency, to take the parental role and have a compulsive need to dominate.

When all this has taken place the circle is closed by the individual's marriage and parenthood. He has had his erotic ties within the nuclear family of orientation broken. But he has also built up the nonerotic components of his personality structure with the double consequences of building a relatively secure dam against his still-present regressive needs, and building a positive set of motivational capacities for the performance of the nonfamilial roles without which no society could operate. Only when this process has reached a certain stage are the gates to erotic gratification re-opened, but this time in a greatly restructured way and carefully controlled.

Finally, it must not be overlooked that the erotic motivational component of the adult personality is used not only to motivate the marital attachment, but also constructively as itself an instrument of the socialization of the next generation. For it is clear that eroticism is fundamentally a phenomenon of social relationships. Strong erotic motivation is built up in the child only because the mother, and to a lesser degree the father, *enjoys* reciprocal erotic relations with the child. But as in the case of the genital eroticism of marriage, this must be controlled by strong ego and superego structures in the personality, lest the parent be unable to renounce his own need when the time comes.

I expressed agreement above with the view of Fortune and Lévi-Strauss that on the social level incest must be regarded as a regressive phenomenon, a withdrawal from the functions and responsibilities on the performance and fulfilment of which the transfamilial structures of a society rest. The review of the role of eroticism in the development of the personality, which I have just presented, shows a striking parallel. Incestuous wishes constitute the very prototype of regression for the mature person, the path to the reactivation of the primitive layers of his personality structure. But surely this is more than merely a parallel. There is the most intimate causal interdependence. Societies operate only in and through the behavior of persons, and personalities on the human sociocultural level are only possible as participants in systems of socially interactive behavior, as these are related to the needs of human organisms.

I have argued that erotic gratification is an indispensable instrument of the socialization of the human child, of making a personality and a member of society of him. But equally, unrestricted erotic gratification stands directly in the way, both of the maturation of the personality, and of the operation of the society. Indispensable to certain processes of learning, it becomes probably the most serious impediment to further essential stages of maturity. The incest taboo is a universal of human societies. I suggest that this is because it constitutes a main focus of the *regulation* of the erotic factor. The institutionalization of the family provides the organized setting for the positive utilization of the erotic factor, both in socialization and in strengthening the motivation to the assumption of familial responsibility. But the taboo in its negative aspect is a mechanism which prevents this positive use from getting "out of hand," which ensures the self-liquidation of the particular family and the production of personalities by it which are capable of fulfilling the functions of transfamilial roles.

Admittedly, as far as origins are concerned, this is very largely a functional argument and does not solve the problems of how incest taboos came into being. It does, I think, serve to illuminate the manifold ways in which the incest taboo is involved in the functioning of any going society and gives a basis for prediction of the probable consequences of various forms of interference with it or modification of it. It places the problem in the context of analysis of the social system in such a way as also to show the interdependence of social systems with the processes of the personality. Once this level of analysis has been worked out the problem of origins assumes a lesser significance, but also can be approached with better hope of success.

There is one final important point. At the beginning of this paper I referred to the earlier tendency to attempt to find a specific explanation of the incest taboo, and expressed my own belief that an analysis of the interdependence of a number of factors in a system was much more promising. A common counterpart of this specific factor view, is the demand that an explanation in some one simple formula adequately explain all the variations of incidence of the taboo. It seems to me clear that, on the basis of the analysis I have presented, this is an illegitimate and unnessary requirement. I have emphasized that there is a solid common core of incidence, namely centering on the nuclear family. But we know that even this is broken through under *very* exceptional circumstances, namely the brother-sister marriage of a few royal families. This case is not an embarrassment for the kind of theory I have presented. For if the taboo is held to be the resultant of a balance of forces, then it is always possible that the balance should be altered so as to relax it under certain circumstances. As Fortune[18] correctly points out a better test case would be the full legitimation of morganatic marriages in royal families—*i.e.,* as taking the place of politically significant alliances. Essentially the same holds where it is a question of variations of incidence outside the nuclear family. Only a sufficiently full analysis of the conditions of stability of the *particular* social system in question can furnish an adequate answer to the question of why this rather than a different pattern is found in a particular case. But such variations, and the elements of contingency involved in them, do not alter the importance of the massive fundamental facts that no human society is known without an incest taboo, and in no case does the taboo fail, for a society as a whole, to include all the relationships within the nuclear family. It is to the understanding of these massive facts that this analysis has been primarily directed.

18. R. F. Fortune, *op. cit.*

4

Social Structure and the

Development of Personality:

FREUD'S CONTRIBUTION TO THE

INTEGRATION OF PSYCHOLOGY

AND SOCIOLOGY

PERHAPS for reasons connected with the ideological needs of the intellectual classes, the primary emphasis in interpreting Freud's work—at least in the United States—has tended to be on the power of the individual's instinctual needs and the deleterious effects of their frustration. Thus on the recent centenary of Freud's birth there were a number of statements to this effect.[1] The consequence of such a trend is to interpret Freud as a psychologist who brought psychology closer to the biological sciences, and to suggest the relative unimportance of society and culture, except

Reprinted from Psychiatry, *Vol. 21, No. 4, November, 1958, pp. 321–340.*

1. Notable ones were made by Lionel Trilling in *Freud and the Crisis of Our Culture*, Boston, Beacon Press, 1955; and by Alfred Kazin in "The Freudian Revolution Analyzed," *The New York Times Magazine*, May 6, 1956, p. 22. It is perhaps significant that this view is particularly strong in literary circles.

as these constitute agencies of the undesirable frustration of man's instinctual needs.

There is, however, another side to Freud's thinking, which became, I think, progressively more prominent in the course of the complicated evolution of his theoretical scheme, culminating in the works dealing with the structural differentiation of the personality into id, ego, and superego, and in his late treatment of anxiety. This trend concerns two main themes: the *organization* of the personality as a system; and the relation of the individual to his social milieu, especially in the process of personality development. This, in psychoanalytic terminology, is the field of "object-relations"—the most important area of articulation between the psychoanalytic theory of the personality of the individual and the sociological theory of the structure and functioning of social systems.

It is this latter aspect of Freud's thought which will form the subject of this paper.[2] It will be my main thesis that there is in the structure of Freud's own theoretical scheme, a set of propositions which can, with relatively little reinterpretation, be very directly integrated, first, with the sociological analysis of the family as a small-scale social system, and, further, with the problems of the child's transition from membership mainly in his own family to participation in wider circles which are not, in Western societies, mainly organized in terms of kinship. Freud's own contribution here centers chiefly in the earlier stages of socialization, through the Oedipal resolution, but the same principles of analysis can be extended to the later stages.

The most important of Freud's concepts in this respect are

2. This paper belongs in a series of my own writings which have a major concern with the relations between psychoanalytic theory and the theory of social systems. The most important of these are: "Psychoanalysis and the Social Structure," *Psychoanal. Quart.* (1950) 19:371–384, reprinted in *Essays in Sociological Theory* (revised edition), New York, The Free Press of Glencoe, 1954; "The Superego and the Theory of Social Systems," *Psychiatry* (1952) 15:15–25, which appears as Chapter 1 in this book; with Robert F. Bales, *Family, Socialization and Interaction Process,* New York, The Free Press of Glencoe, 1955; "Psychoanalysis and Social Science," in *Twenty Years of Psychoanalysis,* edited by Franz Alexander and Helen Ross, New York, Norton, 1953, pp. 186–215; "The Incest Taboo in Relation to Social Structure and the Socialization of the Child," *British J. Sociology* (1954) 5:101–117, which appears as Chapter 3 in this book; "An approach to Psychological Theory in Terms of the Theory of Action," in *Psychology: A Study of a Science,* Vol. III, edited by Sigmund Koch, New York, McGraw-Hill, 1959.

identification, object-cathexis, internalization or introjection, and the superego. Most attention has been given to the concept of the superego. Although many difficult problems of interpretation cluster about that concept, there is no doubt that it refers to the internalization, to become a constitutive part of the structure of the personality itself, of aspects of the normative culture of the society in which the individual grows up.

Very important clues, on which the present analysis builds, are given by the remarkable convergence between Freud's views on internalization and those developed, independently and at nearly the same time, in sociological quarters, by Emile Durkheim in France and by Charles H. Cooley and George Herbert Mead in the United States. I should regard this convergence as one of the few truly momentous developments of modern social science, comparable perhaps to the convergence between the studies of experimental breeding in the tradition of Mendel and the microscopic studies of cell division from which the conception of the chromosomes as the vehicles of biological heredity developed. The two together produced the modern science of genetics.

In another direction, however, the basic principle on which Freud's conception of the superego was based can be extended, not merely across disciplines to the relations between social structure and personality, but within the personality, to the constitution of its other sectors and structural components. Some have tended to treat the superego as a very special case within the personality, as the only point at which the norms of the culture enter. A major objective of the present paper, however, is to show that the whole logic of Freud's later position implies that the same is true for the structure of the ego also. Indeed it follows from Freud's whole main treatment of the process of socialization—and was, at least at one point, explicitly stated in his writings—that the major structure of the ego is a precipitate of the object-relations which the individual has experienced in the course of his life history.[3] This means that internalization of the sociocultural environment provides the basis, not merely of one specialized component of the human personality, but of what, in the human sense, is its central core. From the standpoint of the main traditions of modern psychology this is a very radical position, so radical that its import has not yet been very widely appreciated.

3. Sigmund Freud, *The Ego and the Id,* London, Hogarth Press, 1935, p. 36. The relevant passage is quoted later in this paper.

The final question inevitably arises as to whether even the id should be completely exempt from this central interpretation of the importance to the theory of personality of object-relations and internalization. In the final section of the paper I shall argue very briefly that the interpretation of the id as a manifestation of "pure instinct" is, in Freud's own terms, untenable. Although of course it is the primary channel of transmission of instinctual energy and more particularized impulses into the personality, it also is structured through internalized object-relations. This time, however, it involves, above all, the residues of the earliest object-relations of the life history of the individual, which have had to be rather drastically reorganized in the course of later life experience.

The analysis to follow is carried out in terms of an explicit theoretical frame of reference which I am accustomed to calling the "theory of action." This is a scheme for the analysis of *behavior* as a system, but broken down in terms of the analytical independence and interpenetration of four major subsystems which it is convenient to call the behavioral organism, the personality, the social system, and the cultural system.[4]

The distinction between, first, the aspects of the system of action centering on the individual and the determinants of his behavior, and, second, the transindividual factors of society and culture, is a very old one, stemming, in one major tradition at least, from the problems of Darwinian biology as applied to human behavior. More recently it has seemed necessary to draw lines within each of the two categories resulting from that distinction—namely, between cultural and social systems, on the one hand, and between organism and personality, on the other.

I shall stress the importance of the latter distinction—between organism and personality—which seems to me to be emergent in Freud's own work.[5] This distinction is, I think, crucial to the under-

4. These have been delineated in a number of places, for example: *Toward a General Theory of Action,* edited by Talcott Parsons and Edward A. Shils, Cambridge, Harvard University Press, 1951. Talcott Parsons, Robert F. Bales, and Edward A. Shils, *Working Papers in the Theory of Action,* New York, The Free Press of Glencoe, 1953. The most recent statements about the four systems are in Talcott Parsons, "An Approach to Psychological Theory in Terms of the Theory of Action," *op. cit.,* and in A. L. Kroeber and Talcott Parsons, "The Concepts of Culture and of Social System," *Amer. Sociological Rev.* (1958) 23:582–583.

5. See Lord Adrian, Review of Ernest Jones, *The Life and Work of Sigmund Freud,* Vol. 1, in *The Observer,* London, November, 1953. This

standing of the place of the theory of instincts in Freud's total psychological theory, and of the role of pleasure and of eroticism. My main emphasis, however, will be on the relations between personality and social system. My view will be that, while the main content of the structure of the personality is derived from social systems and culture through socialization, the personality becomes an independent system through its relations to its own organism and through the uniqueness of its own life experience; it is not a mere epiphenomenon of the structure of the society. There is, however, not merely interdependence between the two, but what I call *interpenetration*. At all stages of the socialization process, from the sociological side the essential concept of *role* designates this area of interpenetration. From the personality side, a corresponding concept of *relational needs* may be used, of which the psychoanalytically central one of the need for love may serve as an example.

THE ORAL STAGE AND THE PROCESS OF IDENTIFICATION

LET me now turn to Freud's theory of object-relations. There are two main approaches to the nature of personality development. One may be illustrated by analogy with the plant. The main characteristics of the mature organism—for example, the number and qualities of wheat grains produced, or the brilliance and shape of the flowers—are predetermined in the genetic constitution of the species. There will, however, be differences in outcome as a function of the favorableness or unfavorableness of the environment. This process of interaction with the environment, however, does not determine the main pattern, but only the degree of excellence with which it "comes out."

The other view sees the genetic constitution as a *nonspecific* base from which the pattern of the adult personality will be evolved,[6]

---

stands in contrast to the interpretation of many other commentators less qualified in biology than Lord Adrian. Compare also the formula that the instinct is the "representative" of the needs of the organism to the "psychic" apparatus.

6. This, for example, is clearly what happens in the learning of intellectual content. This requires "capacity"; but a textbook of algebra, for example, to one not previously trained in the subject is not just a "relatively favorable influence" on the outcome, but the primary source of the content of the learned pattern.

and, as the main pattern-setting components, the *values* of the culture and the *meanings* of social objects experienced in the course of personality development.

These two approaches are not mutually exclusive, although they may be given different relative emphasis. But it is my contention that the main significance of Freud's work for the social sciences consists in the seriousness and the fruitfulness with which he explored the *second* avenue; and, moreover, that the theory of object-relations— while not necessarily more important than the theory of instincts— colors Freud's whole theory of personality, including the theory of instincts.[7]

As noted above, three of Freud's concepts bear most directly on the problem of object-relations—identification, object-cathexis (or object-choice), and internalization or introjection. Freud associated these concepts particularly, although by no means exclusively, with three different levels of the process of socialization. Identification referred in the first instance to the relation established between mother and child in the oral phase. Object-cathexis was used pre-

7. In this connection I am particularly indebted to a paper by John Bowlby, "The Nature of the Child's Tie to its Mother," *The International Journal of Psycho-Analysis,* 1958, Vol. 39, Part V, and to personal discussions with Dr. Bowlby. In terms of relevance to the present context, the most essential point is that there are two main levels in Freud's treatment of the problem of instinct, one of which tended to predominate in his earlier work, the other in the later. The first is closer to the main biological tradition in emphasizing relatively specific inborn patterns of behavior which do not need to be learned. It is a type of mechanism prominently emphasized by current "ethologists" such as Karl Lorenz and Nikolaas Tinbergen. Bowlby emphasizes five such "instinctual responses," as he calls them, which figure prominently in the first year or so of life—namely, sucking, crying, smiling, clinging, and following. The second level concerns the more diffuse "motivational energy" which is particularly involved in Freud's later conception of the id.

The role attributed by Bowlby to the more specific instinctual responses does not seem to me to be incompatible with the general thesis of this paper. That these and other patterns are definitely inborn is not to be doubted. But the higher level of organization of the behavioral system which is thought of as the personality cannot be derived from the organization of these responses without reference to the influence of object-relations in the course of socialization. It has, however, been necessary to revise a number of statements made in an earlier draft of this paper in the light of these considerations. Essentially, the "instinctual responses" may be thought of as a set of mechanisms of behavior which operate at a level intermediate between the metabolic needs of the organism, on which Freud himself and many later psychoanalysts have laid such great emphasis, and the higher-order mechanisms of control of behavior through internalized objects.

ponderantly to characterize the relation of mother and child in the phase between the oral and the Oedipal; while internalization or introjection referred mainly to the establishment of the superego in the Oedipal phase. It will be my thesis that each of these concepts, in different ways, designates an aspect of the integration of the personality in a social system, an integration which is characterized by a particular process of *learning* in a particular context of object-relations.

Therefore, I suggest, first, that Freud tended to confuse the genetic and the analytical uses of these concepts, and, second, that for the general purposes of the theory of personality, the analytical meaning of them is more important than the genetic.[8]

I shall now attempt to sketch these processes, mainly in my own terms, although with continual references to Freud, in order to establish a basis for clarifying some theoretical implications of Freud's treatment of them.

Freud, in common with many other writers, maintained that the starting point for what I would call the process of socialization was the action of persons responsible for child care—in the first instance, the mother—as agents for the gratification of organic needs.[9] Of such needs, in the earliest phases that for nutrition is paramount. In addition, the mother is the primary object for gratification of a series of instinctual responses at the behavioral level.[10]

The psychological importance of this physiological dependence on a human agent is partly a consequence of the "satisfaction" of the inborn needs. But there are also physiological mechanisms by which this satisfaction becomes a *reward*.[11] In order for it to acquire

8. There is a notable parallel in this respect between Freud and Durkheim. Although the empirical subject-matters of their concern are miles apart, Durkheim, in his treatment of the relations of mechanical and organic solidarity, particularly in his *The Division of Labor in Society*, (New York, The Free Press of Glencoe, 1947) tended to treat them as associated with stages in the evolution of social systems, but also tried to put them in the context of an analytical theory of social systems. See my paper, "Durkheim's Contribution to the Theory of the Integration of Social Systems," in *Emile Durkheim, 1858–1917. A Collection of Essays with Translations and a Bibliography,* edited by Kurt Wolff, Columbus, The Ohio State University Press, 1960.

9. The thesis is perhaps most clearly stated in *The Problem of Anxiety*, New York, Norton, 1936.

10. Bowlby, *op. cit.*

11. In this connection I am particularly indebted to the work of James Olds, who strongly emphasizes the independence of pleasure-reward mecha-

this meaning, the child must learn that instinctual gratifications are in some sense contingent *both* on the action of the mother *and* on that of the child. For example, it seems to be established that there is an inborn sucking response, but the child early learns to suckle better than he is equipped to do by sheer "instinct." He learns how to move his lips, what posture is best, when to exert effort, when to relax, and so on, for the amount of milk he gets and the ease with which he gets it are contingent to an appreciable degree on his own goal-oriented action.[12] This holds even apart from any influence he may exert on when and under what circumstances the breast or bottle will be presented to him.

On the mother's side also, feeding a baby is by no means purely instinctive but involves elements of skill and "intentional"—not necessarily conscious—regulation. She tries to "get him" to nurse properly, by her manner of holding him, by her sensitivity to his "need to rest," and by her judgment as to how far to "force" him and when he has "had enough." In addition, she is the primary agent of imposition of any sort of schedule on the feeding, and she determines the "picking up" and the "setting down" of the baby and the way he is dressed, covered, bathed, cleaned, and so on.

Thus even at this very elementary level, the relations between mother and infant constitute a genuine process of *social interaction*, of which "care" in the sense of sheer attending to physiological needs, is clearly only one component. The child, from the beginning, is to some degree an active agent who "tries" to do things and—increasingly with time—is rewarded or punished according to his "success" in doing them. The mother, on her side, actively manipulates the situation in which this learning takes place. However genuine the process of interaction as such, she is in the overwhelmingly predominant position of power, controlling the timing of feeding and other acts of care—indeed, the whole setting of the experience of being cared for. The child develops an attachment to her as an object in such a way that the *organization* of the emerging motivational system is a function, not simply of his own inde-

---

nisms from the instinctual needs, frustration of which is closely associated with pain and other compulsive mechanisms. See James Olds, "Self-Stimulation of the Brain," *Science* (1958) 127:315.

12. See Roy R. Grinker, *Psychosomatic Research,* New York, Norton, 1953.

pendently given needs, but of the way in which her responses to these needs have themselves been organized.[13]

Thus the infant in the first few weeks if not days, of life comes to be integrated into a social system. Relatively definite expectations of his behavior are built up, not only in the predictive sense, but in the normative sense. He nurses "well" or "badly"; he cries only when he "should" and is quiet the rest of the time, or he cries "when there isn't any good reason." Inevitably, the behavior of adults takes on the character of rewarding him for what *they* feel to be "good" behavior and punishing him—including omitting reward—for what they feel to be "bad" behavior, and otherwise manipulating sanctions in relation to him.

From the point of view of the infant, there are two particularly crucial aspects of his situation which present cognitive problems to him. The first is the problem of "understanding" the conditions on which his gratifications and frustrations depend—the cues, or conditional stimuli, which indicate the consequences for him, of acting in a given way. The psychology of learning shows that a high level of "rationality" or "higher mental process" is not required for significant learning to take place, if the situation is structured so that certain modes of action consistently produce rewards, while others do not. The second problem presented to him is the focus of *organization* of this system of cues. This is not simply the question of what specific cues indicate probable gratification or deprivation of specific needs, but rather, of what more general *formula* of action can serve to improve the chances of generalized gratification.

Here again, it is not necessary to assume any rationalistic hypotheses. If the pattern of sanctions imposed is *consistent* over a range of more specific actions, it may be assumed, on learning theory grounds, that there will be generalization from the more specific items to the *pattern*.[14] Thus, where the child "tries" to nurse properly

13. Part, however, of the mother's position of power vis-à-vis the child is not a matter of sheer freedom of action on her part, but is determined by third parties involved in the relationship. For instance, the father may not participate very actively in early child care, but the fact that the mother lives with him in a common household greatly affects her treatment of her child. There may also be older siblings. Then, of course, this family is part of a larger society which imposes both relational constraints and a set of values which, among many other things, provide certain norms for what is considered *proper* treatment of infants.

14. The presumption is that the generalized pleasure mechanism plays a crucial part in this learning process and that this is, as will be noted below, a primary reason for the importance of childhood eroticism.

in the sense of "cooperating" with the mother, he is more likely to be gratified. This is perhaps to say that she presents prominently displayed cues and supplementary rewards. It is not a very long step from this level to thinking of the organized pattern of sanctions in terms of the *intentions* of the mother. The significance of this step derives from the fact that there is generally a *single* primary agent of early child care,[15] and that in a variety of significant respects the actions of this agent come to be *contingent* on what the child does. In these circumstances, the learning of the *meaning* of a cue is, I think, synonymous with the imputation of intention to the agent.

The concept of intention as here used involves two central components. The first is the *contingency* of what alter (the agent of care) does on what ego (the child) has done or is expected to do, so that alter's action may be treated as a sanction in relation to ego's action. The second is the component of *generalization*. There exist not merely discrete, disconnected sanctions, but a pattern of relatively systematic and organized sanctions which eventually leads to the learning of a complementary pattern of responses, which is also organized and generalized. In its relation to discrete, particularized acts on either side of the interaction process, the pattern of the sanction system acquires the character of a set of values or norms which define the relation between acceptable, rewarded behavior on the one hand, and unacceptable, nonrewarded, or punished behavior on the other.

Because of the immense inequality of the power relationship, the most important change brought about by this early phase of the process of interaction is the change in the personality of the child, although there is presumably a secondary one in the mother. The primary change in the child is the introduction into his personality, as a behavior system, of a new level of *organization*. In his orientation to the external world, it is a new level of capacity for organized behavior, for successfully attaining his goals and for coping with a variable situation. Internally, it is a new level of organization of his motivational or instinctual impulses or needs which, in one of its aspects, introduces a system of *control over* these impulses, but in another provides a pattern for their utilization in the interest of the newly learned goals and interests. In Freud's famous metaphor, this

15. This proposition needs qualification for certain types of variability in the structure of social situations, such as kinship systems.

new organization derived from contact with objects—the ego—was likened to a rider on the impulse system, the id, a horse which may ordinarily do the rider's bidding, but on occasion may be difficult or impossible to control.[16]

The essential point here is that this system of internal control over the child's own instinctual or impulse system has become established through a generalized pattern of sanctions imposed by the mother, so that the child learns to respond, not simply to specific proffered rewards, but to "intentions," and thereby learns to "conform" to her wishes or expectations. In so doing he has learned a new *generalized goal,* which is no longer simply to gratify his constitutionally given instinctual needs, especially for food, but to "please" his mother. It is the attainment of this new level of organization, including a new goal, which I think Freud primarily designated as *identification.* This is a mode of *organization* of the ego with reference to its *relation* to a social object. One can clearly say that, at the same time, it is learning to act in conformity with a set of norms.

To sum up the main characteristics of this learning process, its basis is the establishment of a determinate set of relations between a set of inborn mechanisms of the organism, on both metabolic and behavioral levels, and a set of stimuli from the environment. There are particularities, of organic and instinctual gratification and of practices of care, but equally on both sides there is *generalization.* There is reason to believe that, on the side of the learning infant, the most important vehicle of generalization is the pleasure mechanism,[17] which must not be confused with sheer organic or instinctual gratifications in the particularized sense; whereas it is quite clear that on the environmental side it is the *patterning* of the system of sanctions which constitutes the element of generalization.

The *correspondence* of these two patterns of generalization is the essential basis of the beginning of a new motivational structure, which can be called the ego. This new structure, in its external, environment-oriented process—which may be called "goal-gratification"

16. Freud, *New Introductory Lectures on Psychoanalysis,* New York, Norton, 1933, p. 108. It goes without saying that in terms of "motivational force" the id is "stronger" than the ego, as a horse is far stronger than its human rider. The ego, however, is not an energy system but a "cybernetic" type of *control* system. For this function relatively little energy is needed.

17. For some purposes it may well be necessary to distinguish different kinds of pleasure, for instance, erotic pleasure may be a special type.

—concerns the relation of the child to a social object outside himself. In its internal, organism-oriented process, it concerns his relation to a generalized neurological mechanism by which a plurality of gratification is organized to produce—perhaps to maximize—what has come to be called pleasure.

In Freud's view, it is fundamental that the external situation and the internal physiological system are to an important degree independent of each other. This is the basis of Freud's contention that the pleasure principle and the reality principle must be treated as analytically independent. At the same time, their integration is the most fundamental condition of the functioning of a personality as a system at this nodal point of articulation between the organism at one of its boundaries and the external world at another.

Freud's commonest formula for instinctual impulse—governed by the pleasure principle—is that it is the "representative" of the needs of the organism to the psychic apparatus—the ego, as he referred to it in his later work.[18] This formula seems to be acceptable in the present terms. The point further to emphasize is that the most crucial part of "reality" even at the oral level is *social;* it is the mother as a social object, acting in a role in a system of social interaction. While one aspect of reality is nonsocial—that is, milk as food-object —it is the *agency* of the mother as the source of the milk which organizes the learning process. It is in terms of generalization that the social qualities of the significant object become crucial.

I should now like to look at the structure of this aspect of the mother-child system. The step to identification implies that the child's "interest" in the mother is, after a time, no longer exhausted by the fact that she acts as an instrumentality of discrete organically or instinctually significant goal-gratifications—food, clinging, and so on. *She, as role-person,* becomes on a higher level a meaningful object. Inevitably, in the learning process, the meaning of the mother as object must be established *through generalization from* gratification—and deprivation—experiences on nonsocial levels. But once this meaning has become established, then in a sense the tables are turned; the discrete, instinctually significant gratifications and deprivations become *symbols* of the intentions or attitudes of the mother. Food then is no longer sought only because it produces

18. In somewhat different and more strictly theoretical terms one might say that it constitutes an *input* from the organism to the personality system.

specific organic pleasure; and—perhaps just as important—it is no longer rejected simply because of alimentary discomfort. More generally, a primary—indeed *the* primary—goal of the developing personality comes to be to secure the favorable attitude of the mother or, as it is often called, her love. Specific gratifications on lower levels, then, have become part of an organization on a wider level, and their primary meaning derives from their relation to the paramount goal of securing or maximizing love. Indeed, I think it a legitimate interpretation of Freud to say that only when the *need for love* has been established as the paramount *goal* of the personality can a genuine ego be present. This need, then, in an important sense comes to control the ontogenetically older goal-needs of the organism, including, eventually, that for pleasure. There must be provision for the adequate gratification of the latter, but, at the same time, each must take its place in an organized system of gratifications.

What, now, of the internal aspect at the level of oral generalization? Undoubtedly one of Freud's greatest discoveries was that of the significance of childhood eroticism and its beginnings in the oral stages of development. I have suggested that the integration of external and internal references, of reality principle and pleasure principle, is the most important single condition of attainment of an organized ego. Although Freud was not able to spell out the physiological character of childhood eroticism very far, I think it can be regarded as, essentially, a built-in physiological mechanism of the *generalization* of internal reward, which matches the generalization of external goal-gratification. Erotic pleasure seems to be essentially a diffuse, generalized "feeling" of organic well-being which is not attached to any one discrete, instinctual need-fulfillment. When one is hungry, eating produces gastric pleasure; when one is cold, being warmed produces another specific feeling of pleasure. But erotic pleasure is not, as such, dependent on *any one* of these or *any specific combination* of them. The mouth is, Freud held, an erogenous zone; thus oral stimulation through sucking is one important, specific source of this more generalized erotic pleasure. Yet oral stimulation produces a pleasure which is *independent* of that produced by the ingestion of food; and, moreover, this pleasure is capable of generalization to a higher level. Organically, the main manifestation of oral eroticism seems to be the capacity for pleasure in diffuse bodily contact, which is connected by generalization with stimulation of the mouth,[19] so that being held, fondled, and so on produce pleasure as a fundamental type of generalized reward.

Thus certain capacities of the organism operate as mechanisms which facilitate the generalization of cathexis, and hence of goals, from the goal-objects which immediately gratify particularized needs, to the *agent* of these gratifications, this agent coming to be treated as an organized system of sanctioning behavior. Eroticism, whatever the physiological processes involved,[20] is a mechanism of internal reward by which fixation on the more specific instinctual gratifications is overcome in favor of pleasure in the diffuse and generalized relationship to a nurturing social object.

I have suggested that this establishment of an organized ego in the personality through a pattern of sanctions designates essentially what Freud meant by identification. Several of Freud's own formulations of the concept stress the striving to be *like* the object. This emphasis requires elucidation and some qualification. Only in a very qualified sense can one say that an infant learns to be like his mother. Rather, he learns to play a social role *in interaction* with her; his behavior—hence his motivation—is organized according to a generalized pattern of norms which define shared and internalized meanings of the acts occurring on both sides. Together, that is, mother and child come to constitute a *collectivity* in a strict sociological sense. But this does not mean that the two members of the collectivity are alike, in the sense that they play identical roles; on the contrary, their roles are sharply differentiated, as are the norms which define the respective expectations. Thus I should like to speak of identification as the process by which a person comes to be inducted into membership in a collectivity through learning to play a role complementary to those of other members in accord with the pattern of values governing the collectivity. The new member comes to be *like* the others with respect to their common membership status and to the psychological implications of this—above all, the common values thereby internalized. Psychologically, the essential point is

19. It may be that a special connection is thus established between the independent instinctual responses of sucking and clinging. Such a connection between discrete gratifications would imply a generalized medium analogous to money in social systems. It is as such a medium that I conceive pleasure. See, for example, Olds, *op. cit.*

20. Olds' work implies that these processes operate at the level of the central nervous system, not of the "erogenous" peripheral areas alone. *Op. cit.*

that the process of ego development takes place through the learning of social roles in collectivity structures. Through this process, in some sense, the normative patterns of the collectivity in which a person learns to interact become part of his own personality and define *its* organization.[21] At the same time, however, by internalizing the reciprocal role-interaction pattern he lays the foundation of capacity to assume alter's role as well as his own.

OBJECT-CHOICE AND INTERNALIZATION

THE other two of Freud's basic concepts in this area are object-choice, or cathexis, and internalization, or what is sometimes called by Freud's translators introjection.[22] I have emphasized that for the infant the mother is a *social* object and becomes the most important part of "reality"—that is, of the environment external to him. But although he comes to be profoundly "attached" to her—that is, to "cathect" her as an object—he can scarcely be said to have chosen her. Object-choice is an act of the ego, and the neonate does not yet have an ego. He can be rejected by the mother, but he can neither choose nor reject her at first.

In the phase of primary identification, the infant is learning a role in, and the values of, a collectivity. There is, of course, an essential element of spontaneity or autonomy in response to the actions of alter. Yet the motivation of action in conformity with the expectations of the new role is still, for a time, directly dependent on the sanctions appropriate to the learning process; ego is able to fulfill alter's expectations in anticipation of reward. But now the capacity develops to implement autonomously the newly learned values in the absence of the accustomed rewards—as Freud clearly recognizes when he speaks of identification as having fully taken place only when the object has been renounced or lost.[23]

I spoke of the process of learning a role vis-à-vis the mother[24]

21. Freud clearly recognized the duality of being both like and unlike the object in speaking of the boy's identification with the father, and the girl's with her mother in the Oedipal period. See *The Ego and the Id, op. cit.,* pp. 44–45.

22. The German term used by Freud is *Introjektion.*

23. *The Ego and the Id, op. cit.*

·24. Throughout this discussion I speak of the mother as the primary object of cathexis. More strictly, one should refer to a generalized parent, since before the Oedipal transition the category of sex has presumably not yet been fully internalized, nor the agency-roles of the two parents fully discriminated.

as involving at least *two levels* of generalization and organization. The pattern of sanctions imposed by the mother incorporates and expresses the *higher* of these two levels. The consequence of successful identification is to develop the capacity to implement this higher pattern level in one's autonomous behavior, and not merely in response to the expected rewards of another. This capacity is perhaps the most important respect in which the child has through identification come to be like the mother.

If, however, action in accordance with the newly acquired value-pattern is to be reality-directed, it must establish goals in relation to objects. Here the object-world is not to be treated merely as given, taking over the care of the helpless infant. Instead, the new ego actively "tries out" its capacity for organized behavior in its object-environment. Object-choice, in Freud's sense, is the "spontaneous" investment of libido by the ego in seeking attachment to an object in the external world.

Typically, at the first stage of this process, the object "chosen" is the mother, who was the primary agent of care in the oral phase. But it is a mother who comes to play a different *role* vis-à-vis her child. She shifts from rewarding his conformity with the minimum expectations of being a "good child" to rewarding his attempts to perform above that minimum. The emphasis of his role shifts, in turn, from ascription to achievement. The minimum base is taken for granted, but beyond that his rewards depend far more heavily on *how well* he performs.

In one sense this shift involves a turning of the tables. If the *diffuse* attitude of the mother toward her child in the oral phase could be called love, then one may say that now, by his identification, the child has become capable of displaying and acting upon a similar attitude—that he can love an object, normally his mother.

If the child's need to love and have this love reciprocated is strongly attached to an object, then this object gains a very strong point of leverage for motivating him to new levels of achievement. This is because the mother can not only dispense specific rewards for specific performances, but she can treat these as *symbols* of her acceptance of the attachment of the child to her as a love-object—that is, of her reciprocation of his love.

The period when the love-attachment to the mother is paramount is the period of learning the basic *skills* of action—walking, which is, in a sense, the foundation of all the motor skills, and talking, which is the foundation of skills in communication. Object-choice, then, is the motivational foundation of that aspect of socialization in which basic performance patterns are learned. The diffuse attachment to the object of cathexis is the basis for the motivational meaning of the more specific rewards for specific performances.

It is worth while here to note the double reference of *meaning*. In speaking of the process by which identification is established, I discussed the organized pattern of sanctions as establishing the generalized meaning of the specific acts of the child and the mother. Now, in speaking of the process of achievement-learning, I refer to the diffuse love-attachment as the basis for the primary meaning of particular rewards—and of course of ego's own acts of performance in relation to these rewards. This, essentially, is what I mean by the internalization of a value-pattern—that it comes to define meanings for the personality system as such. The first set of meanings is organized about the sanctions applied to the child, the second about a set of performances he has spontaneously tried out and learned successfully to complete.

Freud's concept of object-cathexis designates the primary basis on which *one* type of process of differentiation in the structure of the personality takes place.[25] The starting point for this process is the "internalized mother" established through the previous identification. But from this base comes to be differentiated an autonomous subsystem of the personality oriented to active manipulation of the object-world. The dependency component of the personality then becomes the restructured residue of the internalized mother, which gives a more diffuse and generalized *motivational* meaning to the specific acts and rewards involved in the exercise of motor and communication skills. On the other hand, the "self," or the ego in a more differentiated sense than at the oral level, is the part which assumes the role of autonomous initiative in the performance process.

The great increases in performance capacity which occur in this pre-Oedipal love-attachment period lead to an immense widening of the child's range of contacts with the world in which he lives. He is continually engaged in trying out new motor skills and in learning

25. I have analyzed this elsewhere at considerably greater length. See Parsons and Bales, *Family, Socialization and Interaction Process, op. cit.,* especially Ch. 2. This book may be used for general reference, although in a few respects my views have changed since its writing.

about his world, both by direct observation and by insistent questioning through the newly learned medium of language.

In relation to the infant, the mother played a role which was to a very important degree determined by her other roles—those of wife, of mother of older siblings of the infant, and of member of the household as a system, as well as her various extrafamilial roles. One may presume that these other involvements appeared mainly, from the point of view of the infant, as restrictions on her exclusive devotion to him. But with his growing mobility and communication, the other persons to whom his mother is related become more and more clearly defined objects. These other persons, typically his father and his siblings—including, perhaps, by now a younger sibling—form the primary focus of this new structuring of the situation in which he acts and learns.

Thus a new phase in the processes of identification emerges, focused on the assumption of membership in the child's total nuclear family of orientation. This is a far more complex process than the original identification with the mother, since it involves at least three such identifications which are interdependent but also partially independent—namely, identification with the family as a collectivity, identification in terms of sex, and identification by generation.

What is required at this stage is the child's internalization of a *higher level* of generality of organization. In his relation with his mother, he has already learned the fundamentals of reciprocal role-behavior in a *dyadic* relationship, the simplest type of social system. But the circumstances of this early socalization have stacked the cards in favor of dependency, and so the problem of *independence training* is now, in the pre-Oedipal period, a focal one. The fundamental question is the balance between dependency and autonomy, the ranges within which the child can take independent initiative and those within which he must give way to the wishes and sanctions of his role-partner.

With the Oedipal period the child begins to have a plurality of dyadic relations—with his mother, father, sister, brother; and these, in turn, must be organized into a higher-order system, the family as a whole. It is in this context that Freud most prominently raises the problems of the superego and its place in the personality. Just as he treats identification with the mother as producing an internalized base from which object-choices are made, so he speaks of the superego as providing, for the latency period and later, the internal surrogate of the *parental function* as it operated in the control of the pre-Oedipal child.[26]

The situation of the primitive mother-identification was sociologically very simple, because the child was primarily related to a single person as object; the essential points were that it was a social object, and that mother and child together formed a collectivity. Now the situation has become much more complex, but nevertheless the same basic principles obtain. What Freud refers to as the parental function may be interpreted to mean a function of the family as a system, and moreover to include the functions of *both* parents as the leadership coalition of the family. Seen in these terms, *the family* is an object with which the child identifies, and through this identification he becomes a full-fledged member of that family; he and its other members come to constitute a collectivity which, if not new, is at least, through his altered status and the adjustments made by other members, a changed one.

The superego, then, is primarily the *higher-order* normative pattern governing the behavior of the different members in their different roles in the family as a system. This pattern is first impressed upon the child through the sanctions applied to his behavior— through the rewards and punishments which, although administered by different members of the family in different ways, presumably have a certain coherence as a system, deriving mainly from the coordinated leadership roles of the parents. Therefore, a new element of organization is introduced into the personality by this process of identification, an organization on a higher level of generality and complexity than before, giving the child new goals and values.

The child through this process comes to be "like" the object of his identification in the same essential sense, and with the same qualifications, as he earlier came to be like his mother. He has acquired a pattern of orientation which he holds in common with the other, more socialized, members of his family. When this pattern has been internalized, he can act, in relation to the extrafamilial world, in terms of that pattern without reference to the earlier system of sanctions. In the same sense in which the oral mother became a lost object, so the latency child's family of orientation eventually becomes a lost object—a process normally completed in late adolescence.

Within the family, the child's role has become far more complex than it was earlier; he has as many subroles as there are dyadic

26. See *New Introductory Lectures, op. cit.,* p. 91.

relations to other family members. But from the point of view of the wider society he plays *one* role—that defined by his age-status as latency-period child of his family, and by his sex.[27]

SEX ROLE, EROTICISM, AND THE INCEST TABOO

ONE aspect of the greater complexity of the new system of identifications and object-relations is the fact that the child cannot identify indiscriminately with all the available objects of his nuclear family. Two of the subsidiary identifications within the family, by sex and by generation, are to become structurally constitutive for his status in the wider society, and these are cross-cutting. It is essential to the understanding of the differential impact of the Oedipal situation on the sexes that for the boy the tie to his mother—the original object of identification and of subsequent object-cathexis—is not included in either of these new identifications; whereas for the girl the tie to the mother is included in the identification by sex.

Hence the girl can, in relation to her mother, repeat on a higher level the infantile identification, and can to a degree take over the mother's role as an apprentice in the household and in doll-play. She is, however, precluded from taking over the mother's role in relation to the father by her categorization as belonging to the child generation.

The boy, on the other hand, must break radically with his earlier identification pattern; he cannot turn an object-cathexis into an identification except on the familial level, which has to be shared with the other members. He is blocked by the importance of the sex categorization from identifying with the mother in intrafamilial function, and he is blocked by the generation categorization from taking a role like the father's in relation to her. Moreover, the father is a more difficult object of identification, because so much of his role is played outside the household. While the boy's subjection to his father's authority has often been considered the central factor in explaining the boy's ambivalent attitudes toward the father, it is only one component in a larger complex; the other considerations I have mentioned are perhaps equally important. The authority

27. See Robert K. Merton, "The Role Set," *British J. Sociology* (1957) 8:106–120, for an excellent discussion of the complexity of role-constellations.

factor does, however, gain significance from the fact that at the Oedipal period the child begins to have much more important relations outside his family; in a sense, the father is the primary representative of the family to the outside society, and of the latter to the family.

Another important feature of the complexity in the Oedipal period is that the ascribed identification is *selective*—except for the over-all familial identification—among the members of the family. In particular, the very important possibility of the child's object-choice of the parent of opposite sex, and vice versa, is *excluded* from the main formal identification structure and relegated to the status of "secondary" or informal attachments; and such an attachment, if it becomes too strong, can be both disruptive of the family as a system and a distorting factor in the personality development of the child.

This relates to two fundamental and interrelated sociological problems in which Freud took a considerable interest but on which further light can now be thrown—the roles of the sexes, and the incest taboo. Freud is clear and insistent about the existence of what he calls constitutional bisexuality, and hence about the fact that the motivational structure of sex role is importantly influenced by object-relations in the course of the person's life history. One can extend the argument by noting that the learned aspect of sex role provides an essential condition for the maintenance of the family as an integral part of the social structure, and hence of its functions in the socialization of the child.

The feminine role is primarily focused on the maternal function. The crux of this is, through the *combination* of instrumental child care and love, to provide a suitable object for the child's earliest identification, and subsequently for the child's autonomous object-cathexis. The agent of these functions must be anchored in an organizational unit of the larger society, otherwise the leverage for socialization beyond the earliest stage would not be adequate.

The masculine role, on the other hand, is not primarily focused on socialization, but on the performance of function in the wider society—economic, political, or otherwise. If boys are to achieve in this arena, they must make the proper set of transitions between the intrafamilial context of early socialization and the larger societal context. The coalition of the *two* parents in the family leadership structure is the main sociological mechanism which makes this possible.[28] Clearly, also, the relation of girls to their fathers, and hence to men in general, is just as important as that of boys to their mothers in balancing these forces as they are involved in the functioning of human society.

Consideration of the incest taboo brings up again the problem of the role of eroticism in the socialization process. Throughout the stages of this process so far considered—the oral stage, the stage of first object-choice, and the Oedipal stage—the main principle operating is the internalization, through successive identifications, of social object-systems and cultural patterns of the organization of behavior on progressively higher levels of complexity and generalization. These new identifications lead to new object-choices and new definitions of goals in relation to these objects.

I have suggested that at the oral level eroticism is primarily significant as a vehicle for the generalization of reward in its internal, physiological aspect. Apparently there is a duality of levels of the object-relation to the mother corresponding to the duality of hedonistic rewards—that is, rewards in the form of stimulation of erogenous zones and in the form of a general sense of well-being. It is this correspondence that makes oral eroticism so important. I am not competent to follow the subsequent course on a physiological level, but I would like to suggest that, with a difference, there is probably a repetition of this pattern in the "phallic" stage. The essential point here is the erotization of the genital organs, which is presumably partly instinctive and partly learned, either through masturbatory activities or through some kind of adult stimulation, or both.

This is the period during which the differentiation of personalities by sex role first becomes of critical significance. The genital organs are clearly, in the prepubertal period, the primary anatomical differentiae by sex. Hence they are particularly appropriate as *symbols* of sex-identification. The erotic gratification attained through genital stimulation then becomes a type of internal pleasure which can become directly associated with learning to act *in the role* of a member of the appropriate sex group. The diffuse sense of bodily well-being, which is the critical feature of erotic gratification in its generalized

28. See R. F. Bales, "The Equilibrium Problem in Small Groups," in Parsons, Bales, and Shils, *Working Papers in the Theory of Action, op. cit.,* pp. 111–163.

aspect, may then come to be associated with proper fulfillment of the expectations of sex role.

These considerations seem to be essential as background for the discussion of the incest taboo. In the period of identification with the mother, eroticism operated through affectionate physical contact with the object—through the stimulation of erogenous zones and through the induction of a diffuse sense of bodily well-being. The object was a single person, and the physical contact with her—being caressed or fondled—becomes the prototype of erotic gratification on the more generalized level.

In the Oedipal period, however, the significant object for identification is not an individual, but a collectivity, and tender physical contact with a complex collectivity is clearly not possible; thus eroticism cannot serve as a socialization mechanism as it did in the pre-Oedipal period. Indeed, the necessity to achieve a fundamental identification without the help of this internal reward may constitute one of the main sources of strain in this stage. This, more than the punishing aspects of paternal authority, may be why the superego stands out as being peculiarily impersonal and in some respects threatening.

From the point of view of the process of socialization, the incest taboo functions primarily as a mechanism by which the child is both forced and enabled to internalize value systems of a *higher order* than those which could be exclusively embodied in a dyadic two-person relation or in a social system as simple and diffuse as the nuclear family. The tendency of erotic relations is to reinforce solidarity *à deux,* to give the single person as object priority over the larger collectivity or system of collectivities in which the dyad is embedded. If the child is to internalize these higher-order value-systems, he must learn, in the requisite contexts, to do without the crutch of erotic gratification.

From the point of view of the society as a system, the incest taboo has another order of functional significance which is closely linked with the above. It serves to maintain a diversity of cultural patterns on the lowest level of internalization in personalities; thus the combination of these patterns takes place on a higher level of generality, where there is not so strong a tendency to "reduce" them to a less general common denominator. In other words, the incest taboo insures that new families of procreation will be set up by persons socialized in two distinct families of orientation. The culture internalized in the early stages by the children of the new family will then have a dual origin, and will in certain respects constitute a new variant a little different from either of the parental ones, as they are from each other. The argument is not that the crossing of familial cultures reduces them to greater uniformity; on the contrary, by *preserving variability* at the lower levels of generality, it prevents the establishment of a uniformity which might lessen the pressure to achieve higher levels of generality capable of including *all* the variable versions as instances.

Another aspect of the problem, which ties these two together, is the bearing of the incest taboo on the internal structure of the nuclear family. The erotic relation of the parents to each other is a primary focus of their solidarity. Its exclusiveness—even in comparison with the mother's relation to the small child—tends to symbolize their solidarity vis-à-vis third persons. As the child becomes more active and develops higher capacities for performance, there is a strong pressure for him to develop or reinforce erotic relationships to his parents, to both of them in different ways. The developing importance of sex as an ascribed focus of status then makes for attachment to the parent of opposite sex, thereby implicitly challenging the parent of the same sex. But the erotic solidarity of the parents tends to lead to rejection of the child's advances in this direction, so that his *primary* new identification is forced into the mold of member of the family as a whole, and into his sex and generation roles within it. The parent's erotic solidarity thereby forces him to a higher level of value-internalization than that governing *any* dyadic relation within the family and prepares him, in his latency period and in subsequent orientations outside his family, to internalize still higher-level patterns of value.

These considerations alone do not adequately account for the brother-sister aspect of the incest taboo. While this is the weakest of the three taboos within the nuclear family, it is none the less very strong. I suggest that this version of the taboo is internalized, at least in part, by emphasis on *generation* as an institutionalized status-component. The main focus of the prohibition of erotic relations to the Oedipal child is on his *age* status. He is too old for infantile erotic gratifications, and too young for adult. He must be classed with the parent of the same sex with respect to sex, but he cannot presume to the adult privilege of genital eroticism. The identifications with the family as a whole and by sex create a configuration in his environment which leaves no place for an erotic relation to a sibling of the opposite sex—indeed, for any overt erotic relation at all. Closely related is the fact that two siblings who have both internalized the same "generalized parent" have substantially less psychological protection against dependency than if, as is the case with the unrelated partners, their parental figures are independent of each other. Finally, the one-sex peer group is, for the latency child, the primary heir of the earlier security-base in the family of orientation. Brother-sister incestuous needs would cut across this basis of solidarity.

More generally, in one major aspect the significance of the Oedipal transition lies in the fact that the child reaches a level of internalized values and a complex structure of identifications which enable him to dispense with erotic rewards as a primary mechanism of further socialization. The basic difference betweeen the pre-Oedipal stages within the family and the post-Oedipal stages mainly without it is that, in the former, identification and object-choice involve an erotic attachment to a primary personal object, whereas later they do not. This shift is, as I have suggested, essential if the internalization of social value systems on high levels of generality is to be achieved.[29]

At the same time, the immediately pre-Oedipal attachment of erotic significance to sex-role, and the symbolization of this by the awakening of genital eroticism at the phallic level, has laid the foundations for the formation later by the individual, through his marriage, of a new family in which he will play conjugal and parental roles. But the erotic need, thus restructured, is allowed expression only in the context of an adult personality in which the higher-level value-patterns have had an opportunity to develop and consolidate their position. It is only through this nonerotic component of the parent's personality structure that he has a sufficiently strong superego and a sufficiently mature ego to be able to serve as a model for identification for his children, and that hence socialization beyond the stages of early childhood becomes possible.

In the light of these considerations Freud's famous view about the sexual genesis of all the neuroses may perhaps be interpreted in a sense acceptable in current sociopsychological terms. The most im-

29. The taboo on homosexuality is dynamically closely related to that on incest. It applies, however, mainly to emancipation from the latency-period one-sex peer group, not from the family of orientation. Homosexuality would be the most tempting latency-period form of eroticism.

portant point is that the personality structure, as a precipitate of previous identifications and of lost objects, develops by a process of *differentiation* from the earliest and simplest identification with the mother. Both this early relationship of identification and the succeeding object-choice relationship contain in their motivation an essential erotic component. Without the element of erotic attachment, sufficient motivational leverage could not have existed to bring about the learning processes involved in the identification and in the performance learning later based upon it. Moreover, the evidence is that the erotic needs thus built up are never extinguished, but remain permanent parts of the personality structure.

The reason why neuroses, like other disturbances of personality functioning, involve important regressive components is essentially that the more generalized *motivational* structures—as distinguished from social values, where the order of generality is the reverse—are laid down in early childhood. Regression to deep enough levels, then, will always involve motivational structures in which erotic needs from an essential component. Hence is a neurosis which pervades the personality as a whole, an erotic component will always be present, not to say prominent, and by the same token, there will of necessity be a prominent component of erotic disturbance in its etiology.

This is not at all to say that all motivation is, in the last analysis, sexual. It is rather to say that, on the genetically earliest and hence in one sense most fundamental levels, the sexual—or better, erotic —element is always prominently involved, both symptomatically and etiologically. But this does not in any way contradict the importance of the capacity to develop and operate motivational structures which are *not* primarily oriented to erotic gratifications, but rather to impersonal or "affectively neutral" patterns of behavior. This occurs by the process which Freud usually refers to as sublimation.[30]

POST-OEDIPAL OBJECT-RELATIONS

FREUD treated the relation between the Oedipal and latency periods as essentially parallel with that between the earlier oral and object-choice periods. The Oedipal period involves an identification process through which the "parental function" is internalized to form

30. Freud's own analysis of this process is, in my opinion, considerably less satisfactory than his analysis of the earlier ones.

the superego. The identification, I have argued, must be interpreted to refer to membership in the nuclear family as a collectivity, and within that, to the child's own sex and generation roles. But once this process of identification has been completed, the child can turn to a new process of object-choice, this time in relationships primarily outside his family of orientation. What may be called his dependency base still remains inside that family: he lives with his parents and siblings, and they remain responsible for his subsistence and for a general protective function toward him; moreover, his place in the community is still defined primarily by his family membership.

But from this base, which is analogous to his identification with his mother at the earlier period, he ventures out to establish important relations outside the family. In a differentiated society of the modern Western type, this occurs typically in two overlapping contexts—the school, in which his formal education begins, and the informal peer group, usually composed of age-mates of his own sex. There are two particularly prominent features of these new object-relations: None of them is overtly erotic in content or tone—hence Freud's concept of latency; and the pattern of relationship is, for the first time, not ascribed in advance. Age and sex status are ascribed, but the level of performance and the rewards for it which are accessible to the child are not, either in the school or in the display of various kinds of prowess in his relations with his peers. He is exposed, within the limits permitted in the community, to open competition with his age-peers, from which a significant structuring of the social groups will emerge, independent of the structure of the families from which the competitors come.[31]

This structuring seems to revolve about two axes. The first, achievements which can be evaluated by universalistic standards, has as its prototype the mastery of the intellectual content of the school curriculum, but other things, such as athletic prowess, fall into the same category. It is certainly of significance that the foundations of the skills involved in intellectual function are laid down in the latency period—notably the use of *written* language and the skills of abstract reasoning, as Piaget has so fully shown.[32]

31. For a discussion of the sociological significance of this transition, see S. N. Eisenstadt, *From Generation to Generation,* New York, The Free Press of Glencoe, 1956, especially Chs. 1 and 3.

32. See Barbel Inhelder and Jean Piaget, *The Growth of Logical Thinking from Childhood to Adolesence,* New York, Basic Books, 1958.

The second axis is the establishment of position in more-or-less organized groups where status is not ascribed in advance. The focus here is on the assumption of such roles as leadership and followership, and of primarily task-oriented or primarily integrative roles in relation to one's fellows. The contexts in which this learning takes place range from the school class itself, under the direct supervision of the teacher, to wholly informal peer activities entirely removed from adult participation.

It is a striking fact, perhaps particularly striking in the United States with its tradition of coeducation in the schoolroom, that in the latency period the peer group is overwhelmingly a *one*-sex peer group. The child is here "practicing" his sex role in isolation from the opposite sex. When this isolation begins to break down and cross-sex relations assume a prominent place, this is in itself a sign of the approach of adolescence. With this a further differentiation begins to take place, into, first, a sphere in which erotic interests are revived—which leads into marriage and eventually the establishment of a family of procreation; and, second, a sphere of organizations and associations in which the direct expression of erotic interests remains tabooed.[33] The essential point is the discrimination of the contexts in which erotic interests are treated as appropriate from those in which they are not. Their appropriateness is clearly confined to a single role-complex within a much larger context, most of which is treated as nonerotic.

It is my principal thesis that, in the analysis of object-relations, there is complete continuity in the basic conceptual framework appropriate to identification in the oral stage, and object-choice in the post-oral stage, on the one hand; and the latency period and adolescent socialization, on the other hand. The learning of roles in school and peer group occurs through the mechanisms of object-choice, motivated by prior identifications; but, in the first instance, collectivities rather than persons are clearly the most significant objects. Then—just as within the nuclear family significant new dyadic relations besides that with the mother develop—significant new dyads form in school and peer groups, with the teacher and with particular age-mates. But the significance of these dyads must be understood

33. Same-sex friendship seems to occupy an intermediate position between these two types. See footnote 30.

within the context of the new collectivity structures in which the child is learning to play a role, or a complex of roles.

Similarly, this later process of object-choice leads to a new set of identifications, which involve the collectivity-types outside his family in which the child acquires memberships and roles. As in the case of the mother-child dyad and of the nuclear family, he internalizes the values of these collectivities as part of the process of identification with them and assumption of a role in them. The differences lie in the greater diversity of memberships the child acquires, the higher level of generality of the values he internalizes, and the absence of erotic rewards in the learning process. The direct involvement of such rewards is no longer necessary, because of the more highly differentiated and organized personality structure which the post-Oedipal child brings to his object-relations; in fact, the regressive associations of erotic experience would militate against his attaining the higher disciplines which are now needed.

By the completion of the major phase of adolescence, the normal child has presumably achieved, outside the family of orientation, identification with four main types of collectivity, and has hence internalized their values and become capable of pursuing the goals appropriate to them independent of the detailed pattern of sanctions which have operated during the internalization process. These are: (1) the subsociety of his age-peers as a whole, embodying the values of the so-called youth culture; (2) the school, which is the prototype of the organization dedicated to the achievement of a specified goal through disciplined performance; (3) the peer-association, the prototype of collective organization to satisfy and adjust mutual interests; and (4) the newly emerging cross-sex dyad, the prototype of the sole adult relationship in which erotic factors are allowed an overt part.

These identifications form the main basis in personality structure on which adult role-participations are built. Through at least one further major step of generalization of value-level, participation in the youth culture leads to participation in the values of the society as a whole. Participation in the school leads to the adult occupational role, with its responsibility for independent choice of vocation, a productive contribution, and self-support. The peer-association identification leads to roles of cooperative memberships in a variety of associations, of which the role of citizen in a democratic society is perhaps the most important. Finally the dating pattern of adolescence leads to marriage and to the assumption of parental responsibilities.[34]

I emphasize this continuity from the objects of identification in childhood to the role and collectivity structure of the adult society in order to bring out what is to me the central point of the whole analysis. This is that Freud's theory of object-relations is essentially an analysis of the relation of the individual to the *structure of the society* in which he lives. Freud analyzed this relation from the point of view of the individual rather than from the point of view of the structure of the social systems concerned. His perspective also was primarily developmental in the psychological sense; sociologically stated, he was mainly concerned with the processes by which the individual comes to acquire membership in social collectivities, to learn to play roles in them, and to internalize their values, and he was most interested in the identifications entered into in early childhood.

But throughout the course of personality development, identification, object-choice, and internalization are processes of relating the individual to and integrating him in the social system, and, through it, the culture. Since these processes are a relational matter, eventually technical analysis has to be applied to both sets of relata, as well as to the relationship itself. Had Freud lived long enough to enter more deeply into the technical analysis of the object-systems to which the individual becomes related, he would inevitably have had to become, in part, a sociologist, for the structure of these object-systems is—not merely is influenced by—the structure of the society itself. Essentially, Freud's theory of object-relations is a theory of the relation of the individual personality to the social system. It is a primary meeting ground of the two disciplines of psychology and sociology.

CONCLUSION

IN the introductory section of this paper, I suggested that if the individual's object-relations in the course of his life history are as important as they seem to be, then the significance of internalized social objects and culture cannot, as some psychoanalysts have

34. These two paragraphs constitute the barest sketch; some tentative further steps of such an analysis will be found in chapters 6, 7, and 9 of this volume.

tended to assume, be confined mainly to the content of the superego. On the contrary, it must permeate the whole personality system, for, with all Freud's emphasis on differentiation within the personality, he consistently treated it as an integrated whole.

In certain respects the ego should provide the test case of this hypothesis. Indeed, the increasing attention of Freud himself in his later years to problems of ego psychology, an area which has been considerably further explored by such authors as Heinz Hartmann and Ernst Kris, seems to be closely related to his increasing attention to the field of object-relations. At the same time, I do not think that the id should be exempt from the logic of this development.

First, however, let me say something about the ego. Since the ego is the primary location of interchange between the personality and the outside world of reality, and since the most important aspect of reality itself is social, the conclusion is inescapable that the ego is "socially structured." It is a particularly welcome confirmation of this hypothesis—much of which has been worked out from a sociological point of view—to find that Freud himself explicitly recognized it. The most striking passage I have found deserves to be quoted at length:

When it happens that a person has to give up a sexual object, there quite often ensues a modification in his ego which can only be described as a reinstatement of the object within the ego, as it occurs in melancholia; the exact nature of this substitution is as yet unknown to us. It may be that by undertaking this introjection, which is a kind of regression to the mechanism of the oral phase, the ego makes it easier for an object to be given up or renders that process possible. It may even be that this identification is the sole condition under which the id can give up its objects. At any rate the process, especially in the early phases of development, is a very frequent one, and *it points to the conclusion that the character of the ego is a precipitate of abandoned object-cathexes* and that it contains a record of past object-choices.[35]

I think it can, then, quite safely be said that object-cathexes and identifications do not, in Freud's own mature view, simply "influence" the development of the ego, in the sense in which temperature or moisture influences the growth of a plant, but that the structure

35. *The Ego and the Id, op. cit.,* p. 36. The italics are mine. The relation of this passage to Freud's late view of the role of anxiety (*The Problem of Anxiety, op. cit.*), as concerned primarily with the fear of object-loss, is clear.

of the object-relations a person has experienced is directly *constitutive* of the structure of the ego itself.

If it can be said of the ego that it is a precipitate of abandoned object-cathexes, there does not seem to be any serious doubt that the superego is primarily social and cultural in origin. Indeed, this has been clearly recognized by psychoanalysts ever since the introduction of the concept by Freud. Freud's formula that the superego represents the parental function is to my mind the most adequate one. He also quite explicitly refers to it as the focus of "that higher nature" representing the "moral, spiritual side of human nature,"[36] which we have taken into ourselves from our parents.

The role of the id is focal to the issue with which the present discussion started—namely, the relative importance of "instinctive" as compared with cultural, social, and other "environmental" influences in the motivation of personality. The concept of the id in Freud's later work is, of course, one primary heir, although by no means the only one, of such concepts as the unconscious, the primary process, and the libido in his earlier work. Furthermore, in the enthusiasm of discovery, Freud tended to contrast the id as sharply as possible with the ego, which seemed to be the closest, of all the components of the personality, to traditionally rationalistic common sense—as, for instance, when he spoke of the id as entirely lacking in organization.[37]

Against the tendency to highlight the conflicts between the ego and id must be set the view implied in the metaphor of the horse and rider, the conception of the ego as a system of control. Furthermore, the id is treated at many points in specific relation to the pleasure principle, and I have suggested various reasons for assuming that pleasure is an organizing mechanism which integrates diverse motives at lower levels of organization.

A still further consideration which points in this direction is the progressive increase in the generality which Freud attributed to the basic instinctual urges, ending up with only a single underlying duality. This is not inconsistent with Bowlby's views of the importance, in more specialized contexts, of various more particularized instinctual responses.[38] But it does imply that, from a very early phase of development, the basic *organization* of the motivational system

36. *The Ego and the Id, op. cit.,* pp. 46–47.
37. For example, *New Introductory Lectures, op cit.,* p. 103.
38. Bowlby, *op. cit.*

cannot be derived from instinctual sources, but must come from identifications and internalized objects.

It is my own view that the distinction between instinctual and
learned components of the motivational system cannot legitimately
be identified with that between the id, on the one hand, and the ego
and superego on the other. Rather, the categories of instinctual and
learned components cut across the id, the ego, and the superego. The
id, like the other subsystems, is organized about its experience in
object-relations. It differs, however, in two fundamental respects
from the other subsystems. First, it is oriented, as the other two are
not, to the person's own organism as object. This seems to me to be
the essential significance of the pleasure principle as the governing
principle of the id. Secondly, however, the object-cathexes which are
constitutive of the structure of the id are predominantly those of the
earlier phases of the process of socialization, so that in any internal
conflicts involving the problem of regression, id-drives represent the
regressive side of the conflict.

However true it may be that advancing beyond certain early
levels of development requires transcending the fixation on these
early cathexes, and however much the mature personality must
control them through ego and superego mechanisms, it still remains
true that these are particular cases of identification and internalization of objects—not the leading example of motivation in their
absence.

Thus it seems to me that the general principles of object-relations
through identification, object-cathexis, and internalization must be
extended to the *whole* psychoanalytic theory of personality. Indeed,
this is the position Freud eventually, in all essential respects, came to,
even though he had not ironed out all of the inconsistencies in his
treatment of these matters, nor reconciled many of his earlier statements with his later ones.

There are two particular virtues of this position. First, it formu-
lates psychoanalytic theory in such terms that direct and detailed
articulation with the theory of social systems is enormously facilitated.
This is of the first importance to the theory of the motivation of social
behavior and hence, in my opinion, is an essential prerequisite of the
advance of sociology in certain connections. But at the same time
there are reciprocal benefits for psychoanalysis—for example, this
formulation suggests ways in which personality theory must take

account of variations in the structure of the social system on which it impinges.

On a more general level, however, this view should do much to relieve psychoanalytic theory of involvement in a false dilemma in its use of the categories of heredity and environment. As general biology is showing with increasing clarity, it is not a question of whether or how much one or the other factor influences outcomes—in this instance, in the field of behavior. The trend is strongly away from a "predominant-factor" explanation of the phenomena of life, toward a more analytical one. Analytically conceived variables are, except for limiting cases, always *all* important. The salient technical problems concern their clear definition and the working out of their intricate modes of *interrelationship* with each other. This paper has, in this respect, been meant as a contribution to what I conceive to be the major trend of psychoanalytic theory in this same direction.

5

Some Reflections on the Problem of Psychosomatic Relationships in Health and Illness

WHATEVER else they may be, health and illness are conceptions which are built into the institutionalized role-structure of societies; this has perhaps become a commonplace, but is nevertheless a convenient starting point. There is a wealth of evidence of this, with much of which most readers are familiar. One crucial point is the variability of the boundaries between health and illness and hence between illness and other forms of deviance, from society to society and within the same society over time.

Perhaps illness can best be conceived of as the impairment of the individual's capacity for effective performance of social roles and of those tasks which are organized subject to role-expectations. Capacity thus thought of must be treated as relative to a conception of "normal" developmental stage and pattern, and to ability as a factor of potentiality either given in the genes or learned through educa-

Presented at the meeting of the American Psychosomatic Society, Montreal, March 27, 1960.

tion and training. Thus the "mentally retarded" child is not normally thought of as ill. His situation is also clearly distinguished from opportunity factors by being ascribed to the individual person, not the situation in which he is placed, however much situational factors may play etiological or therapeutic roles with reference to illness. Finally, illness—as impairment of capacity—must be distinguished from states of inadequate motivational commitment to performance. The sick person is incapacitated, not because he doesn't "want" to perform, but in some sense because he is unable to, however difficult it may be to draw the line—as psychiatrists well know.

The primary characteristics of illness as a social role, I have formulated[1] as follows: (1) It is a partially and conditionally legitimated state in which others are expected to treat the sick person with compassion, support, and help; but it is not to be evaluated as in itself a "good thing"; (2) It is the basis of a series of legitimized exemptions from the fulfillment of normal expectations, in work, family obligations, and even in showing consideration and good temper toward others; (3) Through the conception of incapacity the individual is not held responsible for his state, in the sense that he could be expected to become well through "pulling himself together" by an act of will, and (4) It has a definitely ascribed goal of action which is given priority over other goals, namely to "get well." The patient himself is expected both to seek competent technical help and to cooperate actively with therapeutic personnel in getting well.

In certain limiting cases, such as natural catastrophes, role-expectations similar to those involved in the concept of illness are applied to people in situations in the etiology and maintenance of which they cannot be presumed to have any significant motivationally meaningful participation. The older conception of illness tended to treat it in just this way, but the combination of the increased importance of interest in mental and psychosomatic illnesses—including the many cases where both aspects are intertwined—have made such a view untenable. I shall of course proceed on the assumption that mental illness is not an epiphenomenon of physiological and biochemical processes, but rather involves an analytically independent level of organization by which the functioning individual can be incapacitated. If this is the case, it is not difficult for the sociologist

1. Cf. "Definitions of Health and Illness in the Light of American Values and Social Structure," which appears as Chapter 10 in this volume.

to show certain main ways in which this "personality system," as I like to call it, is linked with the role structure of the social system. Although it is not in any technical sense a sociological problem, as the one just mentioned is, the same general analytical logic can be used to link the psychological and somatic-physiological aspects of the individual's functioning as personality and as organism.

The basic conception is that "behavior" is subject to a graded hierarchical system of control mechanisms in the cybernetic-information theory sense, and that this system constitutes a continuous series extending from the highest level of the cultural and the social system, through the personality and the higher-order organic systems, to organs, tissues, and cells, and indeed even to subsystems of cells. On the "visible" cultural, social, and hence psychological levels, the basic processes of control are what we ordinarily call processes of communication. They operate through the media of signs and symbols, the most generalized human symbol-system being that of language. For symbols to be effective there must be standardized "codes," in terms of which their meanings are "known," these are general systems of "patterns" and "norms." There must be communicators capable of sending messages in these codes, and receivers capable of understanding or "decoding" them. At each end of the relationship the "meaning" of the symbols and their combinations must articulate, in definite ways, with the structure of the systems in question, e.g., personalities in roles.

A good place to begin substantive discussion is the conception of psychotherapy. This obviously is both a *social* situation (therapist and patient constitute a social system) and a process of communication, in that the therapist does *nothing* but talk and, of course, regulate the conditions of communication. What we call illness is hence, under some conditions subject to influence by verbal communication—if psychotherapy ever "works." This indisputable fact implies, to my mind, two fundamental sets of assumptions.

The first is a set of congruences between the structure of the personality system of the patient and the structure of the social system *constituted by* therapist and patient. This congruence was perhaps first brought to technical awareness and formulation by Freud's idea of transference and its role in therapy. But for the patient to "project" his internalized conceptions of earlier significant objects onto the therapist—and in this context, for the therapist's communications to have significant effect on the relevant aspects of the personality structure of the patient involved in his illness—it seems to be necessary to assume that these aspects of structure are congruent with current, though specialized, social relationships and, what is the second set of assumptions, that the relationships in the patient's life history in fact genetically derive from social or object-relations of the past. This of course is a fundamental tenet of psycho-analytic theory. It seems to me that it implies that the main structure of the personality as a system at the psychological rather than the organic level consists in internalized systems of "social objects" which essentially are "precipitates of" the social relationship systems of the decisive periods of the individual's socialization.[2]

The system of internalized objects provides the primary link in the hierarchy of control between the social system and the personality. Therapy is a *social* process and in certain respects a specialized mechanism of "social control," but it is also a means of controlling personalities through activating certain potentialities of the internalized social objects of which they are composed. Its specialized character as a mechanism of social control consists in the accessibility of the individual through it to types of influence which cannot be exerted in the course of "ordinary" social interaction, such as those of the ordinary educational procedures, or of ordinary interaction in the family.

Next, it will perhaps be best to discuss briefly a relation at the social level itself between two essential elements of a control system, without any reference to illness. Language is presumably the most generalized and basic symbolic medium of social communication. There are, however, not only importantly specialized uses of language but also more specialized media which, by their very specificity, are particularly well suited to illustrate my point. The most striking of these is money which, in a modern society, mediates a vast network of relationships. Money is most definitely a medium of communication. "Dollars" and even the gold which allegedly "backs" them are strictly symbols. A payment is a message and the only immediate physical consequence is an entry on some account book. Like other symbols, however, those of money have powerful realistic

2. I have set forth this position most fully in "Social Structure and the Development of Personality," which appears as Chapter 4 in this volume. It seems to me, on the basis of the evidence cited there, that Freud himself steadily moved in this direction as his theoretical scheme matured.

effects. They create and absolve from obligations of the most serious character.

A monetary system, however, can operate as an effective medium of exchange in a stable system only under certain definable conditions. Among the most important ones are what people in my profession call the institutionalized norms which govern markets. The most fundamental of these is the institution of contract. This consists of a set of rules which not only permits but also facilitates the making of agreements by private parties. These rules also regulate those agreements, by endowing some of them with legally enforceable consequences, by defining various limits within which agreements are permissible, the bearing of consequences on the interests of third parties and the like. The institution of property, which is another complex of rules governing the relations of persons and collectivities to valued objects, is also essential to a monetary system. The most important characteristic of a set of institutional norms in this sense is that they are, in general, not alterable as part of the particular transactions mediated by money. You can acquire money from and transfer it to others, and you can do the same with other objects of property rights, but you cannot at will alter the institution of property. Where such alteration occurs it is by special procedures which are not ordinary contractual transactions.

It is my suggestion that there is a comparable set of relationships within the structure of the personality of the individual. I have the impression that what is called cognitive process for the personality is, in general, closely analogous to linguistic communication for the social system. There is, however, one particular more specialized mechanism which plays a central part in personality and which seems to be analogous to money in the social system—namely pleasure.

The analogy seems to me to be strengthened by a fact about money that I have not yet mentioned to which there seems to be a close parallel in the case of pleasure. Money not only mediates transactions between units of the social system but also regulates in particular, though not exclusively, the process of physical production—that is, the adaptive relations of the society to the physical environment. There is an important sense in which the significance of monetary regulation seems to have been generalized from physical production to other contexts.

The analogy in this respect lies in the fact that pleasure seems above all to be an access-regulator of personality to the performance-capacities of the physical organism. It is a medium which, if not symbolic in the cultural sense, has properties which are in the strict and legitimate sense analogous to those of symbolic media at the cultural level.[3] What pleasure does is to mobilize organic energies in the interest of integrated patterns of behavior, and beyond that to serve as a primary mechanism of learning in that it imparts motivational meaning to new patterns of behavior. At the human level, I take it that the most important of these new patterns are the ones referred to above as organized, in terms of internalized object systems. My hypothesis is, therefore, that pleasure constitutes the principal link in the hierarchy of control systems between the aspects of personality structure which are organized about internalized social objects and the control of the physical capacities of the organism which are most important for behavior, including, of course, such cases as the physical processes of speech and symbolic behavior.

It is interesting that Freud in talking about the libido often spoke of an "economic" aspect. Though, so far as I know, he was completely innocent of any knowledge of technical economics, I think there was a fundamental correctness in this usage, because of the analogy I have suggested, that pleasure is to the "economy" of behavioral energy as money is to that of societal economic "production."

In speaking of money I have suggested that a monetary system can operate effectively only within a framework of institutionalized norms. The same should clearly hold for a pleasure system, and I do not think we have far to look for the primary analogy in human personality. It clearly seems to be the superego, which is a set of internalized standards, deriving in Freud's formula, from "parental function" in the family. I have not yet had the opportunity to pursue the analogy in detail, but I think it likely that first the superego must be considered to be a structurally differentiated system, not an undifferentiated entity, and second, that the principles on which its structure operates will be found to be directly analogous, making allowance of course for the different systems in which they operate,

3. In this discussion of pleasure I am basing myself above all on the point of view represented by James Olds (cf. "Self Stimulation of the Brain," *Science,* March, 1957). I am not fully clear about the relation between the relatively generalized sense in which Olds speaks of pleasure and the specificity of erotic pleasure as this concept is used by Freud. They seem to refer to two different levels of organization, the latter being predominantly if not specifically human and therefore protocultural if not actually cultural.

to the complex of institutionalized norms governing economic process in the social economy, notably through markets.

The analogy also seems to me to hold with respect to the relation between the two. Pleasure, that is to say, can "circulate" in serving to motivate particular acts and classes of acts. Any attempt to alter the norms laid down as part of the superego is, however, a different matter. This involves a structural reorganization of the personality system.

I would follow the later Freud in believing that the superego in this context stands between the pleasure system, or the id, and the mature ego, which above all is oriented *outward* to the management of ongoing social interaction. One of Freud's most fundamental, though not very explicit, insights was that the prototype of "reality" —in the sense of the reality principle—is *social* reality, *i.e.*, object-relations.

For reasons such as this I think it can be suggested that the conception of mental health should focus on the *integrity* of the superego (*i.e.*, a superego "adequate" to the individual's life situation) in its function of control over the underlying pleasure system. It constitutes a set of structures which cannot be changed, except through special procedures, without serious disorganization. If subject to sufficiently severe pressures, short of major structural change, there will be manifestations of disorganization at the various points in the total system where controls are less rigid than those imposed by superego structures. There are two main directions in which sufficient "give" may be expected to be possible; namely (1) "outward" in the normally ego-controlled behavioral area which, as I have noted, is in the first instance social, and (2) "inward," which means in the direction of the functioning organism.

Before entering into these alternatives, a little more needs to be said about the pleasure mechanism itself. One of its most important properties is, as Olds points out, that the pleasure mechanism is not self-limiting, and if not adequately controlled can get "out of hand." This is one of the properties which first suggested the analogy with money because uncontrolled "pleasure-seeking" is analogous to monetary inflation. It is quite clear that inflation cannot be controlled by isolated units of an economy, but that the problem focuses at the system level in such fields as central banking, credit systems, and governmental finance.

Second, with reference to organic structure, the primary anatomical focus of the pleasure mechanism is not in particular organs, but in the brain; Olds' work, and that of others, seems to have made this quite certain. Attachment to particular organs such as the erogenous zones must be a special case of significance in particular contexts, not the general case. This circumstance greatly strengthens the suggestion that pleasure is a *symbol*-like mechanism, not an organic "need" in the usual sense, and certainly not in a metabolic sense. Its function is control, not nutrition or anything like it.

Third, there is the special relation to learning which I have noted. In this connection pleasure may be likened to the *capital* function of money, in providing funds for investment, facilitating the development of new productive capacity, etc. New increments of pleasure may be said to be the main facilitating factor in motivating new learning (*i.e.,* the "reward" factor). But there must also be another category of input which constitutes a restructuring of the personality. This I assume to be the object-systems which derive from the social environment. This is analogous to the "new patterns of organization" which must be developed in the process of economic growth through the factor called "organization" by economists.

Returning again to the social definition of illness and health, it seemed legitimate to consider mental illness as a set of maladjustments, defined in terms of the individual's incapacity in the above sense, in his relations to the *social* situation. It is thus conceived as a form of impairment of capacity for social functioning, without specific reference to somatic impairments. Somatic illness, on the other hand, is in social terms to be defined as impairment at the *task* level, that is, incapacity to carry out the bodily operations which are necessary in the performance of social roles—of course incapacity as here conceived includes situations in which it is possible for the individual to perform, but this would be done at an important risk to his future health.[4]

The above distinction between mental and somatic illness broadly coincides with that between the outward and the inward directions of the propagation of disturbance from control by the internalized superego. The suggestion, then, is that the superego constitutes a kind of "watershed" between the two primary "reference systems" of the personality. In approaching the problem of suggesting how "psychic" disturbances can be propagated into the organism, a little

4. This distinction between the role and task levels in its relation to the two kinds of illness, is developed in Chapter 10.

more needs to be said about the superego in relation to the pleasure system which I have suggested it controls in the normative sense.

The structure concerned seems to be the one built up through the socialization process down through the oedipal period. Resting on organically given—in that sense "instinctual"—bases, it consists essentially of internalized object-systems, the motivational significance of which has been built up through "investment" of libido, *i.e.*, their becoming motivated in terms of the "pleasure principle." When, through change in the social situation of the individual, these have become "lost objects," their maintenance as motivational systems becomes independent of situational sanctions emanating from the original objects of cathexis. If they remain effective in a motivational sense, this can only mean that they stimulate each other through internal processes of communication. It is this system of pre-oedipal internalized objects which, together with its instinctual bases, is governed by the pleasure principle which, in my interpretation, constitutes Freud's id, as this conception crystallized in his later thinking. The system of normative regulation to which it is subject in turn then constitutes the superego.[5]

The oedipal superego, as the "dam" between the id and the ego, is the result of the completion of the primarily intrafamilial stage of socialization and is the foundation of capacity to begin to function, first in the school, in roles which have been cast loose, to a greater or lesser degree, from childhood dependencies on the parents. It is the internal personality counterpart of the boundary between society and personality.

The central frame of reference of economic theory is that of supply and demand. It turns out that this is essentially the same conceptual scheme—in the sense that they are both special cases of the same more general one—as the "law of effect" of classical learning theory.[6] I suggest that pleasure always operates on the "demand" side of this relationship. As in the case of the economic analysis of markets, deficits of production may result from disturbances originat-

5. This whole subject-matter is replete with ambiguities. Here I refer to the superego as that aspect of internalized values which culminates in the internalized parental function. It is most important to recognize that internalization of values does not stop at this phase of socialization. Whether or not the term superego is to be used to designate later accretions to the internalized value system as well is a question I cannot enter into here.

6. This view was stated in Talcott Parsons and Neil J. Smelser, *Economy and Society*, New York, The Free Press of Glencoe, 1956, Chap. 1.

ing on either side. My very broad suggestion is that the direction of "psychic" influence on somatic processes is one of disturbance of the flow of pleasure stimulus to somatic performance, while the somatic sources of illness are those which arise on the "supply" side of processes in what I am here calling the pleasure system. It seems likely that such concepts as anxiety, guilt, and shame can be translated into terms which admit of interpretation as different ways in which the flow of pleasure-reward, in relation to various somatic functions, can be conceived as diminished or blocked.

These presumably are to be related to superego controls and in some kind of relation to disturbances of ego functioning. Surely there must be many variegated phenomena and mechanisms in this area. Thus, again in terms of the societal analogy, there is a great difference between the inhibiting effect of direct prohibitions and of "anomic" areas of indeterminacy in the definition of expectations—as well as conflicts between incompatible normative expectations.

Turning to the supply side, if I may continue to pursue the analogy, distinctions need to be made between three kinds of functioning which can be interfered from the pleasure side—including over- as well as under-stimulation as modes of "interference." Alexander, among others, makes a distinction between the behavioral and the "vegetative" aspects of the organism. The former concerns the somatic mechanisms which implement the principal "purposive" mechanisms in relation to the external world. Included here would be the functions of perception and motor implementation, and, of course, symbolic behavior. These are the mechanisms normally under "conscious" or "preconscious" control. They certainly include internalized skills and the like, but presumably they have an indirect rather than a direct relation to the id system. Hysterical paralysis, as a simple unconscious "prohibition," is perhaps the prototypical psychosomatic phenomenon in this area.

What Alexander calls the vegetative system concerns the functions primarily involved in the homeostatic control of the metabolic processes, which are essential conditions of the behavioral mechanisms, but neither identical with them nor controlled in the same ways. This has apparently been the main field of the concern with psychosomatic phenomena, perhaps the best known case being that of peptic ulcers. Here, so far as I understand what has gone on, an important recent set of findings concerns the independence of factors on the "supply" side of the relationship, in that pepsin secretion does not seem to be a function of psychic states in the same sense as that of hydrochloric acid.

If we presume that on its organic side the pleasure system centers in particular parts of the brain then, I gather from people much more qualified than I,[7] in a broad way the kinds of neural mechanisms by which disturbances can be propagated from these centers to either the control of external-behavioral mechanisms or of the visceral processes are coming to be relatively well known. Particularly in the latter case, of course, hormonal as well as neural mechanisms in general are involved. This side of the problem, however, is entirely outside my field of competence; it is the point at which another category of experts must take over.

There is a third problem area where the analogy between the economic and the pleasure systems seems to be so striking that a few words about it are in order. Because of my greater competence there, I may start at the economic end. In its relation to "consuming households" a differentiated economy is involved in a double interchange. On the one hand it produces "goods and services" for consumption which are "paid for" by money. Without the mediation of money, high specialization in production and extensive markets would not be possible. But on the other hand, producing units, *i.e.,* "firms," receive labor services from households, which in turn are paid for by money wages; this is putting it in the conventional terminology of economic theory. It is essential that the households to which most outputs of goods are sold are not the same households as those from which a typical firm draws most of its labor supply. Clearly it is money wages which is the primary source of the income from which households pay for consumers' goods. It is the monetary balances of this system as a whole which define the equilibrium of Keynes' famous system.

In sociological terms, the essential component of labor may be said to be "motivational commitment to role-performance." It may be considered as an "energy" category. Unemployment may be said to be a state of incomplete utilization of available productive energy. It need not derive from "unwillingness to work" but rather from maladjustments at the monetary level, *e.g.,* "oversaving."

It is very suggestive that libido or some such concept may be a category analogous to labor commitment; it is energy originating in the organism which is suitable and available for motivating action-

7. Particularly Dr. Karl Pribram (personal discussion).

commitments in social roles. The diversity of the role-situations in which an individual is placed, however, and the instability and independent variability of these situations, means that there must be some generalized mechanism or mechanisms of control between the particular motivational commitment and the "pool" of available energy. It seems too natural an inference to miss that pleasure is such a mechanism, or a constellation of them. This is to say there may be general states of "withdrawal of cathexis" which are closely analogous to the famous Keynesian "voluntary unemployment."

There seem to be no general grounds on which such withdrawals (and the converse overinvestments) need to be confined to either the external or the internal context of reference. In the external context, perhaps this is an aspect of the familiar depressive states. In the internal reference it may well have to do with depressions of the "will to live," or to recover, which are familiar to medicine, but which somehow cannot be pinned down to specific pathological states of specific mechanisms or organs.[8]

Considerations of this order seem to be closely related to the concept of "strain" as Selye has developed that for the organic level.[9] At the personality level, then, the general conceptions of "conflict" which have been so widely held seem to be related. Finally, sociologists have been operating with a concept of strain in helping to explain such phenomena as ideological selection and distortion.[10] It seems to me that there is a fundamental similarity in the mode of conceptualization at all three levels. Perhaps in one main aspect it may be stated that the conception of a system of control implies that there are important resistances to control and that the successful operation of the mechanisms is therefore problematical.

Two further main conceptions seem to be needed in order to complete the picture, both of which are very familiar. One of these is that there are thresholds beyond which "strain," or some such factor, will lead to a breakthrough of control and the setting up of a pathological process involving some kind of "vicious circle." Any complex living system of course has many different mechanisms

8. Cf. Curt P. Richter, "On the Phenomenon of Sudden Death in Animals and Man," in Charles Frederich Reed, Alexander and Tomkins, Eds., *Psychopathology, a Source Book,* Cambridge, Harvard University Press, 1958.

9. Cf. paper in Reed *et al., op. cit.*

10. For one example of its use cf. Francis X. Sutton, Harris, Kaysen and Tobin, *The American Business Creed,* Cambridge, Harvard University Press, 1956.

of control at many levels, so a state of being "out of control" at one level very generally activates "defenses" at the next higher levels, which in turn of course may or may not be successful in the particular case. There is, hence, an essential relativity in this conception; what is a pathological vicious circle at the lower levels may be a malintegration which puts strain on the mechanisms of control at the higher levels.

The second main conception is best exemplified by that of regression as used in psychoanalytic theory. This is to say something like the proposition that, when the higher-level controls are subject to sufficient strain, the phenomena which "break through" into pathological form are, in content, components of the lower-level systems which are "asserting themselves" independently of their normal controls. In some way or other, however, this assertion is likely to lead to consequences which are inappropriate or maladaptive, relative to the exigencies under which the system operates. Hence, the immediate gain of release of tension or strain is likely to be made at the expense of building up strains in the longer run; indeed it is this which justifies calling it pathological.[11]

From the viewpoint of the ego-functions of the personality the pleasure system, the id, is clearly a lower-level system. Breakthrough of the controls to which it is normally subject is therefore a main feature of psychopathology. Its assertion, in conflict with these normal controls, is also "regressive" in that it constitutes behavior to some degree appropriate to childhood situations but inappropriate in adult social interaction. From the point of view of the social system then, much psychologically "normal" ego-functional behavior may be socially pathological. One aspect of this is the problem of "self-interest" seen in relation to the needs for "social control." It is not necessary to assume that the self-interested person who acts contrary to social interests is mentally ill. It does, however, seem to be correct to say that certain categories of what in this sense is self-interested behavior are socially regressive in the present sense.

An important consideration in this present connection is the problem of order. The higher-level system always imposes order on an actually and even more potentially "chaotic" lower-level system. One of the best-known cases of this is the relation between ego and id in

11. Among many sources on this point cf. Harold G. Wolff, "The Mind-Body Relationship," in L. Bryson (ed.), An Outline of Man's Knowledge of the Modern World, New York, McGraw-Hill, 1960.

Freud's later theory. To Freud, the id was "chaotic," precisely because in the structure of the personality it was the lower-level system which, in the interest of functioning vis-á-vis reality, had to be adequately controlled.

It is, however, a main inference from the present analysis that this must be a relative difference. My suggestion has been that the pleasure principle is itself a mechanism of control—a way of imposing order on still lower-level processes and "needs" of the living system which is the human individual. These needs, it has been suggested, are those concerned with the physical aspects of the organism, which again is far from being a simple matter of a single level, but is itself a complex hierarchically organized system.

To sum up, health in the most general terms may be thought of as the state of the individual as a whole, psychologically and somatically considered, from the point of view of the adequacy of the control systems which bear on his capacities, in the sense discussed above. Illness, conversely, is a more or less serious breakdown of these controls resulting in incapacities. Since social role performance is the primary field of functioning of the individual, the higher-level conception of capacity must be defined relative to this.

The individual in this sense is, however, a complex unit with above all two analytically distinguishable "layers" seen in terms of the hierarchy of control. He is a "personality" seen in the perspective of his membership in the society and his cultural involvements and commitments. He is an "organism" seen in the perspective of his biochemical and physiological constitution and his involvement with the physical environment. These two "aspects" are clearly distinguishable only analytically, but the distinction is nonetheless vital precisely because it is one in terms of hierarchy of control.

In this perspective, I suggest, the pleasure system plays a particularly strategic role in that it seems to be, as a mechanism of control, the principal link between the two layers. It is above all the set of mechanisms by which the energy and the operative potentials of the organism can be effectively mobilized in the interest of the values and goals of the personality. It is my tentative view that *all* the primary aspects of the problem of health can be defined in terms of the various levels of factors impinging on the pleasure system.

In presenting this point of view I have used intellectual tactics which have probably raised eyebrows to a very high level. In general, of course, the argument of this paper is "speculative." It refers at various points to what I feel to be established empirical generalizations. But the main line of the analysis is quite clearly not established by "hard" empirical research. Furthermore it makes very explicit use of an elaborate analogy. It is an analogy the two elements of which are drawn from fields not usually thought of as having any useful mutual relevance at all; namely, economics and the psychophysiological borderline.[12]

This seems to me, however, to be a use of the concept analogy in a constructive sense; namely, a process in living systems where function is similar but mechanisms are different. Quite clearly money and pleasure as mechanisms are quite different; they belong in different systems. But this does not preclude that, with due allowance for the difference of systems, their functions are similar; I think I have presented considerable evidence that they are, and the matter is capable of substantially further development even in our present state of knowledge.

Beyond this, however, money and pleasure are connected in that there is complete continuity in the sense of hierarchy of control and of other factors, between the cultural, social, psychological, and organic levels. It seems to me that the ultimate justification of my analogy must rest on the establishment of this continuity. The science of living systems is ultimately one science, not an aggregate of unrelated sciences.

To anyone with only a bowing acquaintance with the range of the subject-matter it cannot but be very striking that at so many different levels, mechanisms which have certain common characteristics seem to be in the center of attention, notably "circulating media" which control various processes, but are not as such "resources" which are consumed in the course of the processes they control. Thus, from the bottom up, we have enzymes and coenzymes, hormones, such neurological mechanisms as pleasure, and probably cognition, at the psychological levels "affect," and at socio-cultural levels, language, money, and power. Certainly relations between the properties of these mechanisms cannot be purely adventitious.

12. My own preoccupation with this analogy has a long history. It goes back to discussions with James Olds a number of years ago. A much earlier and less-developed version was presented at the International Psychological Congress in Brussels in the summer of 1957, in a meeting in which Clyde Kluckhohn, James Olds, and Karl W. Pribram participated. A very brief resumé is printed in the proceedings of the Congress.

PART
Two

STAGES OF

THE LIFE CYCLE

6

The School Class as a Social System: SOME OF ITS FUNCTIONS IN AMERICAN SOCIETY

THIS essay will attempt to outline, if only sketchily, an analysis of the elementary and secondary school class as a social system, and the relation of its structure to its primary functions in the society as an agency of socialization and allocation. While it is important that the school class is normally part of the larger organization of a school, the class rather than the whole school will be the unit of analysis here, for it is recognized both by the school system and by the individual pupil as the place where the "business" of formal education actually takes place. In elementary schools, pupils of one grade are typically placed in a single "class" under one main teacher, but in the secondary school, and sometimes in the upper elementary grades, the pupil works on different subjects under different teachers; here the complex of classes participated in by the same pupil is the significant unit for our purposes.

Reprinted from the Harvard Educational Review, *Vol. 29, No. 4, 1959, pp. 297–318. I am indebted to Mrs. Carolyn Cooper for research assistance in the relevant literature and for editorial work on the first draft of this paper.*

THE PROBLEM: SOCIALIZATION
AND SELECTION

OUR main interest, then, is in a dual problem: first of how the school class functions to internalize in its pupils both the commitments and capacities for successful performance of their future adult roles, and second of how it functions to allocate these human resources within the role-structure of the adult society. The primary ways in which these two problems are interrelated will provide our main points of reference.

First, from the functional point of view the school class can be treated as an agency of socialization. That is to say, it is an agency through which individual personalities are trained to be motivationally and technically adequate to the performance of adult roles. It is not the sole such agency; the family, informal "peer groups," churches, and sundry voluntary organizations all play a part, as does actual on-the-job training. But, in the period extending from entry into first grade until entry into the labor force or marriage, the school class may be regarded as the focal socializing agency.

The socialization function may be summed up as the development in individuals of the commitments and capacities which are essential prerequisites of their future role-performance. Commitments may be broken down in turn into two components: commitment to the implementation of the broad *values* of society, and commitment to the performance of a specific type of role within the *structure* of society. Thus a person in a relatively humble occupation may be a "solid citizen" in the sense of commitment to honest work in that occupation, without an intensive and sophisticated concern with the implementation of society's higher-level values. Or conversely, someone else might object to the anchorage of the feminine role in marriage and the family on the grounds that such anchorage keeps society's total talent resources from being distributed equitably to business, government, and so on. Capacities can also be broken down into two components, the first being competence or the skill to perform the tasks involved in the individual's roles, and the second being "role-responsibility" or the capacity to live up to other people's expectations of the interpersonal behavior appropriate to these roles. Thus a mechanic as well as a doctor needs to have not only the basic "skills of his trade," but also the ability to behave responsibly toward those people with whom he is brought into contact in his work.

While on the one hand, the school class may be regarded as a primary agency by which these different components of commitments and capacities are generated, on the other hand, it is, from the point of view of the society, an agency of "manpower" allocation. It is well known that in American society there is a very high, and probably increasing, correlation between one's status level in the society and one's level of educational attainment. Both social status and educational level are obviously related to the occupational status which is attained. Now, as a result of the general process of both educational and occupational upgrading, completion of high school is increasingly coming to be the norm for minimum satisfactory educational attainment, and the most significant line for future occupational status has come to be drawn between members of an age-cohort who do and do not go to college.

We are interested, then, in what it is about the school class in our society that determines the distinction between the contingents of the age-cohort which do and do not go to college. Because of a tradition of localism and a rather pragmatic pluralism, there is apparently considerable variety among school systems of various cities and states. Although the situation in metropolitan Boston probably represents a more highly structured pattern than in many other parts of the country, it is probably not so extreme as to be misleading in its main features. There, though of course actual entry into college does not come until after graduation from high school, the main dividing line is between those who are and are not enrolled in the college preparatory course in high school; there is only a small amount of shifting either way after about the ninth grade when the decision is normally made. Furthermore, the evidence seems to be that by far the most important criterion of selection is the record of school performance in elementary school. These records are evaluated by teachers and principals, and there are few cases of entering the college preparatory course against their advice. It is therefore not stretching the evidence too far to say broadly that the primary selective process occurs through differential school performance in elementary school, and that the "seal" is put on it in junior high school.[1]

The evidence also is that the selective process is genuinely assorta-

1. The principal source for these statements is a still unpublished study of social mobility among boys in ten public high schools in the Boston metropolitan area, conducted by Samuel A. Stouffer, Florence R. Kluckhohn, and the present author.

tive. As in virtually all comparable processes, ascriptive as well as achieved factors influence the outcome. In this case, the ascriptive factor is the socio-economic status of the child's family, and the factor underlying his opportunity for achievement is his individual ability. In the study of 3,348 Boston high school boys on which these generalizations are based, each of these factors was quite highly correlated with planning college. For example, the percentages planning college, by father's occupation, were: 12 per cent for semi-skilled and unskilled, 19 per cent for skilled, 26 per cent for minor white collar, 52 per cent for middle white collar, and 80 per cent for major white collar. Likewise, intentions varied by ability (as measured by IQ), namely, 11 per cent for the lowest quintile, 17 per cent for the next, 24 per cent for the middle, 30 per cent for the next to the top, and 52 per cent for the highest. It should be noted also that within any ability quintile, the relationship of plans to father's occupation is seen. For example, within the very important top quintile in ability as measured, the range in college intentions was from 29 per cent for sons of laborers to 89 per cent for sons of major white collar persons.[2]

The essential points here seem to be that there is a relatively uniform criterion of selection operating to differentiate between the college and the non-college contingents, and that for a very important part of the cohort the operation of this criterion is not a "put-up job"—it is not simply a way of affirming a previously determined ascriptive status. To be sure, the high-status, high-ability boy is very likely indeed to go to college, and the low-status, low-ability boy is very unlikely to go. But the "cross-pressured" group for whom these two factors do not coincide[3] is of considerable importance.

2. See table from this study in J. A. Kahl, *The American Class Structure*, New York, Rinehart & Co., 1953, p. 283. Data from a nationwide sample of high school students, published by the Educational Testing Service, show similar patterns of relationships. For example, the ETS study shows variation, by father's occupation, in proportion of high school seniors planning college, of from 35 per cent to 80 per cent for boys and 27 per cent to 79 per cent for girls. (From *Background Factors Related to College Plans and College Enrollment among High School Students*, Princeton, N.J., Educational Testing Service, 1957.)
3. There seem to be two main reasons why the high-status, low-ability group is not so important as its obverse. The first is that in a society of expanding educational and occupational opportunity the general trend is one of upgrading, and the social pressures to downward mobility are not as great as they would otherwise be. The second is that there are cushioning mechanisms which tend to protect the high status boy who has difficulty

Considerations like these lead me to conclude that the main process of differentiation (which from another point of view is selection) that occurs during elementary school takes place on a single main axis of *achievement*. Broadly, moreover, the differentiation leads up through high school to a bifurcation into college-goers and non-college-goers.

To assess the significance of this pattern, let us look at its place in the socialization of the individual. Entering the system of formal education is the child's first major step out of primary involvement in his family of orientation. Within the family certain foundations of his motivational system have been laid down. But the only characteristic fundamental to later roles which has clearly been "determined" and psychologically stamped in by that time is sex role. The post-oedipal child enters the system of formal education clearly categorized as boy or girl, but beyond that his *role* is not yet differentiated. The process of selection, by which persons will select and be selected for categories of roles, is yet to take place.

On grounds which cannot be gone into here, it may be said that the most important single predispositional factor with which the child enters the school is his level of *independence*. By this is meant his level of self-sufficiency relative to guidance by adults, his capacity to take responsibility and to make his own decisions in coping with new and varying situations. This, like his sex role, he has as a function of his experience in the family.

The family is a collectivity within which the basic status-structure is ascribed in terms of biological position, that is, by generation, sex, and age. There are inevitably differences of performance relative to these, and they are rewarded and punished in ways that contribute to differential character formation. But these differences are not given the sanction of institutionalized social status. The school is the first socializing agency in the child's experience which institutionalizes a differentiation of status on nonbiological bases. Moreover, this is not an ascribed but an achieved status; it is the status "earned" by differential performance of the tasks set by the teacher, who is acting as an agent of the community's school system. Let us look at the structure of this situation.

"making the grade." He may be sent to a college with low academic standards, he may go to schools where the line between ability levels is not rigorously drawn, etc.

THE STRUCTURE OF THE ELEMENTARY
SCHOOL CLASS

IN accord with the generally wide variability of American institutions, and of course the basically local control of school systems, there is considerable variability of school situations, but broadly they have a single relatively well-marked framework.[4] Particularly in the primary part of the elementary grades, *i.e.,* the first three grades, the basic pattern includes one main teacher for the class, who teaches all subjects and who is in charge of the class generally. Sometimes this early, and frequently in later grades, other teachers are brought in for a few special subjects, particularly gym, music, and art, but this does not alter the central position of the main teacher. This teacher is usually a woman.[5] The class is with this one teacher for the school year, but usually no longer.

The class, then, is composed of about 25 age-peers of both sexes drawn from a relatively small geographical area—the neighborhood. Except for sex in certain respects, there is initially no formal basis for differentiation of status within the school class. The main structural differentiation develops gradually, on the single main axis indicated above as achievement. That the differentiation should occur on a single main axis is ensured by four primary features of the situation. The first is the initial equalization of the "contestants' " status by age and by "family background," the neighborhood being typically much more homogeneous than is the whole society. The second circumstance is the imposition of a common set of tasks which is, compared to most other task-areas, strikingly undifferentiated. The school situation is far more like a race in this respect than most role-performance situations. Third, there is the sharp polarization between the pupils in their initial equality and the *single* teacher who is an adult and "represents" the adult world. And fourth, there is a relatively systematic process of evaluation of the pupils' performances. From the point of view of a pupil, this evaluation, particularly

4. This discussion refers to public schools. Only about 13 per cent of all elementary and secondary school pupils attend non-public schools, with this proportion ranging from about 22 per cent in the Northeast to about 6 per cent in the South. U.S. Office of Education, *Biennial Survey of Education in the United States, 1954–1956,* Washington, U.S. Government Printing Office, 1959, Chap. ii, "Statistics of State School Systems, 1955–56," Table 44, p. 114.

5. In 1955–56, 13 per cent of the public elementary school instructional staff in the United States were men. *Ibid.,* p. 7.

(though not exclusively) in the form of report card marks, constitutes reward and/or punishment for past performance; from the
viewpoint of the school system acting as an allocating agency, it
is a basis of *selection* for future status in society.

Two important sets of qualifications need to be kept in mind in
interpreting this structural pattern, but I think these do not destroy
the significance of its main outline. The first qualification is for variations in the formal organization and procedures of the school class
itself. Here the most important kind of variation is that between
relatively "traditional" schools and relatively "progressive" schools.
The more traditional schools put more emphasis on discrete units of
subject-matter, whereas the progressive type allows more "indirect"
teaching through "projects" and broader topical interests where more
than one bird can be killed with a stone. In progressive schools
there is more emphasis on groups of pupils working together, compared to the traditional direct relation of the individual pupil to the
teacher. This is related to the progressive emphasis on co-operation
among the pupils rather than direct competition, to greater permissiveness as opposed to strictness of discipline, and to a de-emphasis
on formal marking.[6] In some schools one of these components will
be more prominent, and in others, another. That it is, however, an
important range of variation is clear. It has to do, I think, very
largely with the independence-dependence training which is so
important to early socialization in the family. My broad interpretation is that those people who emphasize independence training will
tend to be those who favor relatively progressive education. The
relation of support for progressive education to relatively high socio-
economic status and to "intellectual" interests and the like is well
known. There is no contradiction between these emphases both on
independence and on co-operation and group solidarity among pupils.
In the first instance this is because the main focus of the independence
problem at these ages is vis-à-vis adults. However, it can also be said
that the peer group, which here is built into the school class, is an
indirect field of expression of dependency needs, displaced from
adults.

The second set of qualifications concerns the "informal" aspects of
the school class, which are always somewhat at variance with the

6. This summary of some contrasts between traditional and progressive
patterns is derived from general reading in the literature rather than any
single authoritative account.

formal expectations. For instance, the formal pattern of nondifferentiation between the sexes may be modified informally, for the very salience of the one-sex peer group at this age period means that there is bound to be considerable implicit recognition of it— for example, in the form of teachers' encouraging group competition between boys and girls. Still, the fact of coeducation and the attempt to treat both sexes alike in all the crucial formal respects remain the most important. Another problem raised by informal organization is the question of how far teachers can and do treat pupils particularistically in violation of the universalistic expectations of the school. When compared with other types of formal organizations, however, I think the extent of this discrepancy in elementary schools is seen to be not unusual. The school class is structured so that opportunity for particularistic treatment is severely limited. Because there are so many more children in a school class than in a family and they are concentrated in a much narrower age range, the teacher has much less chance than does a parent to grant particularistic favors.

Bearing in mind these two sets of qualifications, it is still fair, I think, to conclude that the major characteristics of the elementary school class in this country are such as have been outlined. It should be especially emphasized that more or less progressive schools, even with their relative lack of emphasis on formal marking, do not constitute a separate pattern, but rather a variant tendency within the same pattern. A progressive teacher, like any other, will form opinions about the different merits of her pupils relative to the values and goals of the class and will communicate these evaluations to them, informally if not formally. It is my impression that the extremer cases of playing down relative evaluation are confined to those upper-status schools where going to a "good" college is so fully taken for granted that for practical purposes it is an ascribed status. In other words, in interpreting these facts the selective function of the school class should be kept continually in the forefront of attention. Quite clearly its importance has not been decreasing; rather the contrary.

THE NATURE OF SCHOOL ACHIEVEMENT

WHAT, now, of the content of the "achievement" expected of elementary school children? Perhaps the best broad characterization which can be given is that it involves the types of performance which are, on the one hand, appropriate to the school situation and, on the other hand, are felt by adults to be important in themselves. This vague and somewhat circular characterization may, as was mentioned earlier, be broken down into two main components. One of these is the more purely "cognitive" learning of information, skills, and frames of reference associated with empirical knowledge and technological mastery. The *written* language and the early phases of mathematical thinking are clearly vital; they involve cognitive skills at altogether new levels of generality and abstraction compared to those commanded by the pre-school child. With these basic skills goes assimilation of much factual information about the world.

The second main component is what may broadly be called a "moral" one. In earlier generations of schooling this was known as "deportment." Somewhat more generally it might be called responsible citizenship in the school community. Such things as respect for the teacher, consideration and co-operativeness in relation to fellow-pupils, and good "work-habits" are the fundamentals, leading on to capacity for "leadership" and "initiative."

The striking fact about this achievement content is that in the elementary grades these two primary components are not clearly differentiated from each other. Rather, the pupil is evaluated in diffusely general terms; a *good* pupil is defined in terms of a fusion of the cognitive and the moral components, in which varying weight is given to one or the other. Broadly speaking, then, we may say that the "high achievers" of the elementary school are both the "bright" pupils, who catch on easily to their more strictly intellectual tasks, and the more "responsible" pupils, who "behave well" and on whom the teacher can "count" in her difficult problems of managing the class. One indication that this is the case is the fact that in elementary school the purely intellectual tasks are relatively easy for the pupil of high intellectual ability. In many such cases, it can be presumed that the primary challenge to the pupil is not to his intellectual, but to his "moral," capacities. On the whole, the progressive movement seems to have leaned in the direction of giving enhanced emphasis to this component, suggesting that of the two, it has tended to become the more problematical.[7]

7. This account of the two components of elementary school achievement and their relation summarizes impressions gained from the literature, rather than being based on the opinions of particular authorities. I have the

The essential point, then, seems to be that the elementary school, regarded in the light of its socialization function, is an agency which differentiates the school class broadly along a single continuum of achievement, the content of which is relative excellence in living up to the expectations imposed by the teacher as an agent of the adult society. The criteria of this achievement are, generally speaking, undifferentiated into the cognitive or technical component and the moral or "social" component. But with respect to its bearing on societal values, it is broadly a differentiation of *levels* of capacity to act in accord with these values. Though the relation is far from neatly uniform, this differentiation underlies the processes of selection for levels of status and role in the adult society.

Next, a few words should be said about the out-of-school context in which this process goes on. Besides the school class, there are clearly two primary social structures in which the child participates: the family and the child's informal "peer group."

FAMILY AND PEER GROUP IN RELATION
TO THE SCHOOL CLASS

THE school age child, of course, continues to live in the parental household and to be highly dependent, emotionally as well as instrumentally, on his parents. But he is now spending several hours a day away from home, subject to a discipline and a reward system which are essentially independent of that administered by the parents. Moreover, the range of this independence gradually increases. As he grows older, he is permitted to range further territorially with neither parental nor school supervision, and to do an increasing range of things. He often gets an allowance for personal spending and begins to earn some money of his own. Generally, however, the emotional problem of dependence-independence continues to be a very salient one through this period, frequently with manifestations by the child of compulsive independence.

Concomitantly with this, the area for association with age-peers without detailed adult supervision expands. These associations are tied to the family, on the one hand, in that the home and yards of

---

impression that achievement in this sense corresponds closely to what is meant by the term as used by McClelland and his associates. Cf. D. C. McClelland *et al., The Achievement Motive,* New York, Appleton-Century-Crofts, Inc., 1953.

children who are neighbors and the adjacent streets serve as locations for their activities; and to the school, on the other hand, in that play periods and going to and from school provide occasions for informal association, even though organized extracurricular activities are introduced only later. Ways of bringing some of this activity under another sort of adult supervision are found in such organizations as the boy and girl scouts.

Two sociological characters of peer groups at this age are particularly striking. One is the fluidity of their boundaries, with individual children drifting into and out of associations. This element of "voluntary association" contrasts strikingly with the child's ascribed membership in the family and the school class, over which he has no control. The second characteristic is the peer group's sharp segregation by sex. To a striking degree this is enforced by the children themselves rather than by adults.

The psychological functions of peer association are suggested by these two characteristics. On the one hand, the peer group may be regarded as a field for the exercise of independence from adult control; hence it is not surprising that it is often a focus of behavior which goes beyond independence from adults to the range of adult-*disapproved* behavior; when this happens, it is the seed bed from which the extremists go over into delinquency. But another very important function is to provide the child a source of non-adult approval and acceptance. These depend on "technical" and "moral" criteria as diffuse as those required in the school situation. On the one hand, the peer group is a field for acquiring and displaying various types of "prowess"; for boys this is especially the physical prowess which may later ripen into athletic achievement. On the other hand, it is a matter of gaining acceptance from desirable peers as "belonging" in the group, which later ripens into the conception of the popular teen-ager, the "right guy." Thus the adult parents are augmented by age-peers as a source of rewards for performance and of security in acceptance.

The importance of the peer group for socialization in our type of society should be clear. The motivational foundations of character are inevitably first laid down through identification with parents, who are generation-superiors, and the generation difference is a type example of a hierarchical status difference. But an immense part of the individual's adult role performance will have to be in association with status-equals or near-equals. In this situation it is important to have a reorganization of the motivational structure so that the original dominance of the hierarchical axis is modified to strengthen the egalitarian components. The peer group plays a prominent part in this process.

Sex segregation of latency period peer groups may be regarded as a process of reinforcement of sex-role identification. Through intensive association with sex-peers and involvement in sex-typed activities, they strongly reinforce belongingness with other members of the same sex and contrast with the opposite sex. This is the more important because in the coeducational school a set of forces operates which specifically plays down sex-role differentiation.

It is notable that the latency period sex-role pattern, instead of institutionalizing relations to members of the opposite sex, is characterized by an avoidance of such relations, which only in adolescence gives way to dating. This avoidance is clearly associated with the process of reorganization of the erotic components of motivational structure. The pre-oedipal objects of erotic attachment were both intra-familial and generation-superior. In both respects there must be a fundamental shift by the time the child reaches adulthood. I would suggest that one of the main functions of the avoidance pattern is to help cope with the psychological difficulty of overcoming the earlier incestuous attachments, and hence to prepare the child for assuming an attachment to an age-mate of opposite sex later.

Seen in this perspective, the socialization function of the school class assumes a particular significance. The socialization functions of the family by this time are relatively residual, though their importance should not be underestimated. But the school remains adult-controlled and, moreover, induces basically the same kind of identification as was induced by the family in the child's pre-oedipal stage. This is to say that the learning of achievement-motivation is, psychologically speaking, a process of identification with the teacher, of doing well in school in order to please the teacher (often backed by the parents) in the same sense in which a pre-oedipal child learns new skills in order to please his mother.

In this connection I maintain that what is internalized through the process of identification is a reciprocal pattern of role-relationships.[8] Unless there is a drastic failure of internalization altogether, not just one, but both sides of the interaction will be internalized.

8. On the identification process in the family see Chapter 4 in this volume, "Social Structure and the Development of Personality."

There will, however, be an emphasis on one or the other, so that some children will more nearly identify with the socializing agent, and others will more nearly identify with the opposite role. Thus, in the pre-oedipal stage, the "independent" child has identified more with the parent, and the "dependent" one with the child-role vis-à-vis the parent.

In school the teacher is institutionally defined as superior to any pupil in knowledge of curriculum subject-matter and in responsibility as a good citizen of the school. In so far as the school class tends to be bifurcated (and of course the dichotomization is far from absolute), it will broadly be on the basis, on the one hand, of identification with the teacher, or acceptance of her role as a model; and, on the other hand, of identification with the pupil peer group. This bifurcation of the class on the basis of identification with teacher or with peer group so strikingly corresponds with the bifurcation into college-goers and non-college-goers that it would be hard to avoid the hypothesis that this structural dichotomization in the school system is the primary source of the selective dichotomization. Of course in detail the relationship is blurred, but certainly not more so than in a great many other fields of comparable analytical complexity.

These considerations suggest an interpretation of some features of the elementary teacher role in American society. The first major step in socialization, beyond that in the family, takes place in the elementary school, so it seems reasonable to expect that the teacher-figure should be characterized by a combination of similarities to and differences from parental figures. The teacher, then, is an adult, characterized by the generalized superiority, which a parent also has, of adult status relative to children. She is not, however, ascriptively related to her pupils, but is performing an occupational role—a role, however, in which the recipients of her services are tightly bound in solidarity to her and to each other. Furthermore, compared to a parent's, her responsibility to them is much more universalistic, this being reinforced, as we saw, by the size of the class; it is also much more oriented to performance rather than to solicitude for the emotional "needs" of the children. She is not entitled to suppress the distinction between high and low achievers, just because not being able to be included among the high group would be too hard on little Johnny—however much tendencies in this direction appear as deviant patterns. A mother, on the other hand, must give *first* priority to the needs of her child, regardless of his capacities to achieve.

It is also significant for the parallel of the elementary school class with the family that the teacher is normally a woman. As background it should be noted that in most European systems until recently, and often today in our private parochial and non-sectarian schools, the sexes have been segregated and each sex group has been taught by teachers of their own sex. Given coeducation, however, the woman teacher represents continuity with the role of the mother. Precisely the lack of differentiation in the elementary school "curriculum" between the components of subject-matter competence and social responsibility fits in with the greater diffuseness of the feminine role.

But at the same time, it is essential that the teacher is not a mother to her pupils, but must insist on universalistic norms and the differential reward of achievement. Above all she must be the agent of bringing about and legitimizing a differentiation of the school class on an achievement axis. This aspect of her role is furthered by the fact that in American society the feminine role is less confined to the familial context than in most other societies, but joins the masculine in occupational and associational concerns, though still with a greater relative emphasis on the family. Through identification with their teacher, children of both sexes learn that the category "woman" is not co-extensive with "mother" (and future wife), but that the feminine role-personality is more complex than that.

In this connection it may well be that there is a relation to the once-controversial issue of the marriage of women teachers. If the differentiation between what may be called the maternal and the occupational components of the feminine role is incomplete and insecure, confusion between them may be avoided by insuring that both are not performed by the same persons. The "old maid" teacher of American tradition may thus be thought of as having renounced the maternal role in favor of the occupational.[9] Recently, however, the highly affective concern over the issue of married women's teaching has conspicuously abated, and their actual participation has greatly increased. It may be suggested that this change is associated with a change in the feminine role, the most conspicuous feature of which is the general social sanctioning of participation of women in the labor force, not only prior to marriage, but also after marriage. This

9. It is worth noting that the Catholic parochial school system is in line with the more general older American tradition, in that the typical teacher is a nun. The only difference in this respect is the sharp religious symbolization of the difference between mother and teacher.

I should interpret as a process of structural differentiation in that the same category of persons is permitted and even expected to engage in a more complex set of role-functions than before.

The process of identification with the teacher which has been postulated here is furthered by the fact that in the elementary grades the child typically has one teacher, just as in the pre-oedipal period he had one parent, the mother, who was the focus of his object-relations. The continuity between the two phases is also favored by the fact that the teacher, like the mother, is a woman. But, if she acted only like a mother, there would be no genuine reorganization of the pupil's personality system. This reorganization is furthered by the features of the teacher role which differentiate it from the maternal. One further point is that while a child has one main teacher in each grade, he will usually have a new teacher when he progresses to the next higher grade. He is thus accustomed to the fact that teachers are, unlike mothers, "interchangeable" in a certain sense. The school year is long enough to form an important relationship to a particular teacher, but not long enough for a highly particularistic attachment to crystallize. More than in the parent-child relationship, in school the child must internalize his relation to the teacher's *role* rather than her particular personality; this is a major step in the internalization of universalistic patterns.

SOCIALIZATION AND SELECTION IN THE ELEMENTARY SCHOOL

TO conclude this discussion of the elementary school class, something should be said about the fundamental conditions underlying the process which is, as we have seen, simultaneously (1) an emancipation of the child from primary emotional attachment to his family, (2) an internalization of a level of societal values and norms that is a step higher than those he can learn in his family alone, (3) a differentiation of the school class in terms both of actual achievement and of differential *valuation* of achievement, and (4) from society's point of view, a selection and allocation of its human resources relative to the adult role system.[10]

Probably the most fundamental condition underlying this process

10. The following summary is adapted from T. Parsons, R. F. Bales, *et al., Family, Socialization and Interaction Process,* New York, The Free Press of Glencoe, 1955, esp. Chap. IV.

is the sharing of common values by the two adult agencies involved —the family and the school. In this case the core is the shared valuation of *achievement*. It includes, above all, recognition that it is fair to give differential rewards for different levels of achievement, so long as there has been fair access to opportunity, and fair that these rewards lead on to higher-order opportunities for the successful. There is thus a basic sense in which the elementary school class is an embodiment of the fundamental American value of equality of opportunity, in that it places value *both* on initial equality and on differential achievement.

As a second condition, however, the rigor of this valuational pattern must be tempered by allowance for the difficulties and needs of the young child. Here the quasi-motherliness of the woman teacher plays an important part. Through her the school system, assisted by other agencies, attempts to minimize the insecurity resulting from the pressures to learn, by providing a certain amount of emotional support defined in terms of what is due to a child of a given age level. In this respect, however, the role of the school is relatively small. The underlying foundation of support is given in the home, and as we have seen, an important supplement to it can be provided by the informal peer associations of the child. It may be suggested that the development of extreme patterns of alienation from the school is often related to inadequate support in these respects.

Third, there must be a process of selective rewarding of valued performance. Here the teacher is clearly the primary agent, though the more progressive modes of education attempt to enlist classmates more systematically than in the traditional pattern. This is the process that is the direct source of intra-class differentiation along the achievement axis.

The final condition is that this initial differentiation tends to bring about a status system in the class, in which not only the immediate results of school work, but a whole series of influences, converge to consolidate different expectations which may be thought of as the children's "levels of aspiration." Generally some differentiation of friendship groups along this line occurs, though it is important that it is by no means complete, and that children are sensitive to the attitudes not only of their own friends, but of others.

Within this general discussion of processes and conditions, it is important to distinguish, as I have attempted to do all along, the socialization of the individual from the selective allocation of contingents to future roles. For the individual, the old familial identification is broken up (the family of orientation becomes, in Freudian terms, a "lost object") and a new identification is gradually built up, providing the first-order structure of the child's identity apart from his originally ascribed identity as son or daughter of the "Joneses." He both transcends his familial identification in favor of a more independent one and comes to occupy a differentiated status within the new system. His personal status is inevitably a direct function of the position he achieves, primarily in the formal school class and secondarily in the informal peer group structure. In spite of the sense in which achievement-ranking takes place along a continuum, I have put forward reasons to suggest that, with respect to this status, there is an important differentiation into two broad, relatively distinct levels, and that his position on one or the other enters into the individual's definition of his own identity. To an important degree this process of differentiation is independent of the socio-economic status of his family in the community, which to the child is a prior ascribed status.

When we look at the same system as a selective mechanism from the societal point of view, some further considerations become important. First, it may be noted that the valuation of achievement and its sharing by family and school not only provides the appropriate values for internalization by individuals, but also performs a crucial integrative function for the system. Differentiation of the class among the achievement axis is inevitably a source of strain, because it confers higher rewards and privileges on one contingent than on another within the same system. This common valuation helps make possible the acceptance of the crucial differentiation, especially by the losers in the competition. Here it is an essential point that this *common* value on achievement is shared by units with different statuses in the system. It cuts across the differentiation of families by socio-economic status. It is necessary that there be realistic opportunity and that the teacher can be relied on to implement it by being "fair" and rewarding achievement by whoever shows capacity for it. The fact is crucial that the distribution of abilities, though correlated with family status, clearly does not coincide with it. There can then be a genuine selective process within a set of "rules of the game."

This commitment to common values is not, however, the sole integrative mechanism counteracting the strain imposed by differentiation. Not only does the individual pupil enjoy familial support,

but teachers also like and indeed "respect" pupils on bases independent of achievement-status, and peer-group friendship lines, though
correlated with position on the achievement scale, again by no means
coincide with it, but cross-cut it. Thus there are cross-cutting lines of
solidarity which mitigate the strains generated by rewarding achievement differentially.[11]

It is only *within* this framework of institutionalized solidarity
that the crucial selective process goes on through selective rewarding
and the consolidation of its results into a status-differentiation within
the school class. We have called special attention to the impact of
the selective process on the children of relatively high ability but
low family status. Precisely in this group, but pervading school
classes generally, is another parallel to what was found in the studies
of voting behavior.[12] In the voting studies it was found that the
"shifters"—those voters who were transferring their allegiance from
one major party to the other—tended, on the one hand, to be the
"cross-pressured" people, who had multiple status characteristics and
group allegiances which predisposed them simultaneously to vote
in opposite directions. The analogy in the school class is clearly to
the children for whom ability and family status do not coincide. On
the other hand, it was precisely in this group of cross-pressured voters
that political "indifference" was most conspicuous. Non-voting was
particularly prevalent in this group, as was a generally cool emotional
tone toward a campaign. The suggestion is that some of the pupil

11. In this, as in several other respects, there is a parallel to other
important allocative processes in the society. A striking example is the
voting process by which political support is allocated between party candidates. Here, the strain arises from the fact that one candidate and his party
will come to enjoy all the perquisites—above all the power—of office, while
the other will be excluded for the time being from these. This strain is
mitigated, on the one hand, by the common commitment to constitutional procedure, and, on the other hand, by the fact that the nonpolitcal bases of social
solidarity, which figure so prominently as determinants of voting behavior,
still cut across party lines. The average person is, in various of his roles,
associated with people whose political preference is different from his own;
he therefore could not regard the opposite party as composed of unmitigated scoundrels without introducing a rift within the groups to which
he is attached. This feature of the electorate's structure is brought out
strongly in B. R. Berelson, P. F. Lazarsfeld and W. N. McPhee, *Voting,*
Chicago, University of Chicago Press, 1954. The conceptual analysis of it is
developed in my own paper, " 'Voting' and the Equilibrium of the American Political System" in E. Burdick and A. J. Brodbeck (eds.), *American
Voting Behavior,* New York, The Free Press of Glencoe, 1959.
   12. *Ibid.*

"indifference" to school performance may have a similar origin. This is clearly a complex phenomenon and cannot be further analyzed here. But rather than suggesting, as is usual on common sense grounds, that indifference to school work represents an "alienation" from cultural and intellectual values, I would suggest exactly the opposite: that an important component of such indifference, including in extreme cases overt revolt against school discipline, is connected with the fact that the stakes, as in politics, are very high indeed. Those pupils who are exposed to contradictory pressures are likely to be ambivalent; at the same time, the personal stakes for them are higher than for the others, because what happens in school may make much more of a difference for their futures than for the others, in whom ability and family status point to the same expectations for the future. In particular for the upwardly mobile pupils, too much emphasis on school success would pointedly suggest "burning their bridges" of association with their families and status peers. This phenomenon seems to operate even in elementary school, although it grows somewhat more conspicuous later. In general I think that an important part of the anti-intellectualism in American youth culture stems from the *importance* of the selective process through the educational system rather than the opposite.

One further major point should be made in this analysis. As we have noted, the general trend of American society has been toward a rapid upgrading in the educational status of the population. This means that, relative to past expectations, with each generation there is increased pressure to educational achievement, often associated with parents' occupational ambitions for their children.[13] To a sociologist this is a more or less classical situation of anomic strain, and the youth-culture ideology which plays down intellectual interests and school performance seems to fit in this context. The orientation of the youth culture is, in the nature of the case, ambivalent, but for the reasons suggested, the anti-intellectual side of the ambivalence tends to be overtly stressed. One of the reasons for the dominance of the anti-school side of the ideology is that is provides a means of protest against adults, who are at the opposite pole in the socialization situation. In certain respects one would expect that the trend toward greater emphasis on independence, which we have associated

13. J. A. Kahl, "Educational and Occupational Aspirations of 'Common Man' Boys," *Harvard Educational Review,* XXIII (Summer, 1953), pp. 186–203.

with progressive education, would accentuate the strain in this area and hence the tendency to decry adult expectations. The whole problem should be subjected to a thorough analysis in the light of what we know about ideologies more generally.

The same general considerations are relevant to the much-discussed problem of juvenile delinquency. Both the general upgrading process and the pressure to enhanced independence should be expected to increase strain on the lower, most marginal groups. The analysis of this paper has been concerned with the line between college and non-college contingents; there is, however, another line between those who achieve solid non-college educational status and those for whom adaptation to educational expectations at *any* level is difficult. As the acceptable minimum of educational qualification rises, persons near and below the margin will tend to be pushed into an attitude of repudiation of these expectations. Truancy and delinquency are ways of expressing this repudiation. Thus the very *improvement* of educational standards in the society at large may well be a major factor in the failure of the educational process for a growing number at the lower end of the status and ability distribution. It should therefore not be too easily assumed that delinquency is a symptom of a *general* failure of the educational process.

DIFFERENTIATION AND SELECTION IN THE SECONDARY SCHOOL

IT will not be possible to discuss the secondary school phase of education in nearly as much detail as has been done for the elementary school phase, but it is worthwhile to sketch its main outline in order to place the above analysis in a wider context. Very broadly we may say that the elementary school phase is concerned with the internalization in children of motivation to achievement, and the selection of persons on the basis of differential capacity for achievement. The focus is on the *level* of capacity. In the secondary school phase, on the other hand, the focus is on the differentiation of *qualitative types* of achievement. As in the elementary school, this differentiation cross-cuts sex role. I should also maintain that it cross-cuts the levels of achievement which have been differentiated out in the elementary phase.

In approaching the question of the types of capacity differentiated, it should be kept in mind that secondary school is the principal springboard from which lower-status persons will enter the labor force, whereas those achieving higher status will continue their formal education in college, and some of them beyond. Hence for the lower-status pupils the important line of differentiation should be the one which will lead into broadly different categories of jobs; for the higher-status pupils the differentiation will lead to broadly different roles in college.

My suggestion is that this differentiation separates those two components of achievement which we labelled "cognitive" and "moral" in discussing the elementary phase. Those relatively high in "cognitive" achievement will fit better in specific-function, more or less technical roles; those relatively high in "moral" achievement will tend toward diffuser, more "socially" or "humanly" oriented roles. In jobs not requiring college training, the one category may be thought of as comprising the more impersonal and technical occupations, such as "operatives," mechanics, or clerical workers; the other, as occupations where "human relations" are prominent, such as salesmen and agents of various sorts. At the college level, the differentiation certainly relates to concern, on the one hand, with the specifically intellectual curricular work of college and, on the other hand, with various types of diffuser responsibility in human relations, such as leadership roles in student government and extracurricular activities. Again, candidates for post-graduate professional training will probably be drawn mainly from the first of these two groups.

In the structure of the school, there appears to be a gradual transition from the earliest grades through high school, with the changes timed differently in different school systems. The structure emphasized in the first part of this discussion is most clearly marked in the first three "primary" grades. With progression to the higher grades, there is greater frequency of plural teachers, though very generally still a single main teacher. In the sixth grade and sometimes in the fifth, a man as main teacher, though uncommon, is by no means unheard of. With junior high school, however, the shift of pattern becomes more marked, and still more in senior high.

By that time the pupil has several different teachers of both sexes[14] teaching him different subjects, which are more or less formally organized into different courses—college preparatory and

14. Men make up about half (49 per cent) of the public secondary school instructional staff. *Biennial Survey of Education in the United States, 1954–56, op. cit.,* Chap. ii, p. 7.

others. Furthermore, with the choice of "elective" subjects, the members of the class in one subject no longer need be exactly the same as in another, so the pupil is much more systematically exposed to association with different people, both adults and age-peers, in different contexts. Moreover, the school he attends is likely to be substantially larger than was his elementary school, and to draw from a wider geographical area. Hence the child is exposed to a wider range of statuses than before, being thrown in with more age-peers whom he does not encounter in his neighborhood; it is less likely that his parents will know the parents of any given child with whom he associates. It is thus my impression that the transitions to junior high and senior high school are apt to mean a considerable reshuffling of friendships. Another conspicous difference between the elementary and secondary levels is the great increase in high school of organized extra-curricular activities. Now, for the first time, organized athletics become important, as do a variety of clubs and associations which are school-sponsored and supervised to varying degrees.

Two particularly important shifts in the patterning of youth culture occur in this period. One, of course, is the emergence of more positive cross-sex relationships outside the classroom, through dances, dating, and the like. The other is the much sharper prestige-stratification of informal peer groupings, with indeed an element of snobbery which often exceeds that of the adult community in which the school exists.[15] Here it is important that though there is a broad correspondence between the prestige of friendship groups and the family status of their members, this, like the achievement order of the elementary school, is by no means a simple "mirroring" of the community stratification scale, for a considerable number of lower-status children get accepted into groups including members with higher family status than themselves. This stratified youth system operates as a genuine assortative mechanism; it does not simply reinforce ascribed status.

The prominence of this youth culture in the American secondary school is, in comparison with other societies, one of the hallmarks of the American educational system; it is much less prominent in most European systems. It may be said to constitute a kind of structural fusion between the school class and the peer-group structure of the elementary period. It seems clear that what I have called the

15. See, for instance, C. W. Gordon, *The Social System of the High School: A Study in the Sociology of Adolescence,* New York, The Free Press of Glencoe, 1957.

"human relations" oriented contingent of the secondary school pupils are more active and prominent in extracurricular activities, and that this is one of the main foci of their differentiation from the more impersonally- and technically-oriented contingent. The personal qualities figuring most prominently in the human relations contingent can perhaps be summed up as the qualities that make for "popularity." I suggest that, from the point of view of the secondary school's selective function, the youth culture helps to differentiate between types of personalities which will, by and large, play different kinds of roles as adults.

The stratification of youth groups has, as noted, a selective function; it is a bridge between the achievement order and the adult stratification system of the community. But it also has another function. It is a focus of prestige which exists along side of, and is to a degree independent of, the achievement order focussing on school work as such. The attainment of prestige in the informal youth group is itself a form of valued achievement. Hence, among those individuals destined for higher status in society, one can discern two broad types: those whose school work is more or less outstanding and whose informal prestige is relatively satisfactory; and vice versa, those whose informal prestige is outstanding, and school performance satisfactory. Falling below certain minima in either respect would jeopardize the child's claim to belong in the upper group.[16] It is an important point here that those clearly headed for college belong to peer groups which, while often depreciative of intensive concern with studies, also take for granted and reinforce a level of scholastic attainment which is necessary for admission to a good college. Pressure will be put on the individual who tends to fall below such a standard.

In discussing the elementary school level it will be remembered that we emphasized that the peer group served as an object of emotional dependency displaced from the family. In relation to the pressure for school achievement, therefore, it served at least partially as an expression of the lower-order motivational system *out* of which the child was in process of being socialized. On its own level, similar things can be said of the adolescent youth culture; it is in part an expression of regressive motivations. This is true of the emphasis on

16. M. W. Riley, J. W. Riley, Jr., and M. E. Moore, "Adolescent Values and the Riesman Typology" in S. M. Lipset and L. Lowenthal (eds.), *Culture and Social Character*, New York, The Free Press of Glencoe, 1961.

athletics despite its lack of relevance to adult roles, of the "homo-sexual" undertones of much intensive same-sex friendship, and of a certain "irresponsibility" in attitudes toward the opposite sex—*e.g.*, the exploitative element in the attitudes of boys toward girls. This, however, is by no means the whole story. The youth culture is also a field for practicing the assumption of higher-order responsibilities, for conducting delicate human relations without immediate super-vision and learning to accept the consequences. In this connection it is clearly of particular importance to the contingent we have spoken of as specializing in "human relations."

We can, perhaps, distinguish three different levels of crystalliza-tion of these youth-culture patterns. The middle one is that which may be considered age-appropriate without clear status-differentia-tion. The two keynotes here seem to be "being a good fellow" in the sense of general friendliness and being ready to take responsibility in informal social situations where something needs to be done. Above this, we may speak of the higher level of "outstanding" popularity and qualities of "leadership" of the person who is turned to where unusual responsibilities are required. And below the middle level are the youth patterns bordering on delinquency, withdrawal, and generally unacceptable behavior. Only this last level is clearly "re-gressive" relative to expectations of appropriate behavior for the age-grade. In judging these levels, however, allowance should be made for a good many nuances. Most adolescents do a certain amount of experimenting with the borderline of the unacceptable patterns; that they should do so is to be expected in view of the pressure toward independence from adults, and of the "collusion" which can be ex-pected in the reciprocal stimulation of age-peers. The question is whether this regressive behavior comes to be confirmed into a major pattern for the personality as a whole. Seen in this perspective, it seems legitimate to maintain that the middle and the higher patterns indicated are the major ones, and that only a minority of adolescents comes to be confirmed in a truly unacceptable pattern of living. This minority may well be a relatively constant proportion of the age cohort, but apart from situations of special social disorganization, the available evidence does not suggest that it has been a progres-sively growing one in recent years.

The patterning of cross-sex relations in the youth culture clearly foreshadows future marriage and family formation. That it figures so prominently in school is related to the fact that in our society the element of ascription, including direct parental influence, in the choice of a marriage partner is strongly minimized. For the girl, it has the very important significance of reminding her that her adult status is going to be very much concerned with marriage and a family. This basic expectation for the girl stands in a certain tension to the school's curricular coeducation with its relative lack of differentiation by sex. But the extent to which the feminine role in American society continues to be anchored in marriage and the family should not be allowed to obscure the importance of coeducation. In the first place, the contribution of women in various extra-familial occupations and in community affairs has been rapidly increasing, and certainly higher levels of education have served as a prerequisite to this contribution. At the same time, it is highly important that the woman's familial role should not be regarded as drastically segregated from the cultural concerns of the society as a whole. The educated woman has important functions *as wife and mother,* particularly as an influence on her children in backing the schools and impressing on them the importance of education. It is, I think, broadly true that the immediate responsibility of women for family management has been increasing, though I am very skeptical of the alleged "abdication" of the American male. But precisely in the context of women's increased family responsibility, the influence of the mother both as agent of socialization and as role model is a crucial one. This influence should be evaluated in the light of the general upgrading process. It is very doubtful whether, apart from any other considerations, the motivational prerequisites of the general process could be sustained without sufficiently high education of the women who, as mothers, influence their children.

CONCLUSION

WITH the general cultural upgrading process in American society which has been going on for more than a century, the educational system has come to play an increasingly vital role. That this should be the case is, in my opinion, a consequence of the general trend to structural differentiation in the society. Relatively speaking, the school is a specialized agency. That it should increasingly have become the principal channel of selection as well as agency of socialization is in line with what one would expect in an increasingly differentiated and progressively more upgraded society. The legend of the "self-made man" has an element of nostalgic romanticism and is destined to become increasingly mythical, if by it is meant not just mobility from humble origins to high status, which does indeed continue to occur, but that the high status was attained through the "school of hard knocks" without the aid of formal education.

The structure of the public school system and the analysis of the ways in which it contributes both to the socialization of individuals and to their allocation to roles in society is, I feel, of vital concern to all students of American society. Notwithstanding the variegated elements in the situation, I think it has been possible to sketch out a few major structural patterns of the public school system and at least to suggest some ways in which they serve these important functions. What could be presented in this paper is the merest outline of such an analysis. It is, however, hoped that it has been carried far enough to suggest a field of vital mutual interest for social scientists on the one hand and those concerned with the actual operation of the schools on the other.

7

Youth in the Context of
American Society

THE passage of time has recently been symbolized by the
fact that we have elected the first President of the United
States to be born in the twentieth century—indeed, well inside it. It
is perhaps equally relevant to remark that we have recently entered
an era in which a substantial proportion of current youth (rather
than children) will experience a major part of their active lives in
the twenty-first century. Thus a sixteen-year-old of today will be
only fifty-five at the coming turn of the century.

It is possible that the twentieth century will be characterized by
future historians as one of the centuries of turmoil and transition—
in the modern history of the West, perhaps most analogous to the
seventeenth. It is also likely, however, that it will be judged as one
of the great creative centuries, in which major stages of the process
of building a new society and a new culture, will have occurred. The
tremendous developments in the sciences and in the technologies
deriving from them, the quite new levels of industrialization, and
the spread of the industrial pattern from its places of origin, together
with the long series of "emancipations" (e.g., women's suffrage and
the rapid decline of colonialism) will presumably figure prominently
among its achievements. At the same time, it clearly has been and
will probably continue to be a century of turmoil, not one of the

Reprinted from Daedalus, *Journal of the American Academy of Arts and Sciences, Vol. 91, No. 1, Winter, 1962.*

placid enjoyment of prior accomplishment, but of challenge and danger. It is in this broad perspective that I should like to sketch some of the problems of American youth, as the heirs of the next phase of our future, with both its opportunities and its difficulties.

In the course of this century, the United States has emerged at the forefront of the line of general development, not only because of its wealth and political power but also—more importantly in the present context—because it displays the type of social organization that belongs to the future. Since during the same period and only a little behind our own stage of progress a somewhat differing and competing version has also emerged in the Communist societies, it is not surprising that there is high tension at both political and ideological levels. Obviously, the meaning of American society presents a world-wide problem, not least to its own citizens and in turn to its younger ones: since they have the longest future ahead of them, they have the most at stake.

SOME SALIENT CHARACTERISTICS OF AMERICAN SOCIETY

BEFORE we take up the specific situation of youth, it will be best to sketch a few of the main features of our society and the ideological discussions about them, with special reference to their effect on youth. The structural characteristic usually emphasized is industrialism. It is certainly true that the United States has developed industrial organization and productivity farther than any other society in history. Not only has it done this on a massive scale, both as regards population and area, but it has also attained by far the highest levels of per-capita productivity yet known. The salience of industrialism in turn emphasizes the economic aspects of social structure: a high evaluation of productivity, the free enterprise system, with the private, profit-oriented business firm as a conspicuous unit of organization, and with private consumption prominent in the disposal of the products of industry. This last feature includes both the high levels of current family income and what may be called the "capitalization" of households through the spread of home ownership, the development of consumer durable goods, and the like.

It would be misleading, however, to overstress this economic aspect. Economic development itself depends on many noneconomic conditions, and economic and noneconomic aspects are subtly interwoven in many ways. The same period (roughly, the present century) which has seen the enormous growth of industrial productivity has also seen a very large relative, as well as absolute, growth in the organization and functions of government. The largest growth of all, of course, is in the armed services, but by no means only there. State and local governments have also expanded. Another prominent development has been that of the legal system, which is interstitial between governmental and nongovernmental sectors of society. I mean here not only legislation and the functioning of courts of law but also the private legal profession, with professional lawyers employed in government in various capacities.

A consideration of the legal profession leads to one of the learned professions in general, the educational organizations in which men are trained, and the cultural systems that form the basis of their competence. The most important development has been the growth of the sciences and their application, not only in industry and the military field but also in many others, notably, that of health. Though they are behind their physical and biological sister disciplines, the sciences dealing with human behavior in society have made very great advances, to an altogether new level. To take only the cruder indices, they have grown enormously in the numbers of trained personnel, in the volume of publications, in the amount of research funds devoted to their pursuit, and the like. All this would not have been possible without a vast expansion of the educational system, relatively greatest at the highest levels. By any quantitative standard, the American population today is by far the most highly educated of any large society known to history—and it is rapidly becoming more so.

Furthermore, this has become in the first instance a society of large organizations, though the tenacious survival of small units (in agriculture, but more broadly in retail trade and various other fields) is a striking fact. (It is important to note that the large organization has many features that are independent of whether it operates in private industry, in government, or in the private nonprofit sector.) It is also a highly urbanized society. Less than ten per cent of its labor force is engaged in agriculture, and more than half the population lives in metropolitan areas, urban communities that are rapidly expanding and changing their character.

It is also a society with a great mobility as to persons, place of residence, and social and economic status. It is a society that within about eighty years has assimilated a tremendous number of immigrants, who, though overwhelmingly European in origin, came from a great diversity of national, cultural, and religious backgrounds. Their descendants have increasingly become full Americans, and increasingly widely dispersed in the social structure, including its higher reaches. After all, the current President of the United States is the grandson of Irish immigrants and the first Catholic to occupy that office.

Overriding all these features is the fact that this is a rapidly developing society. There are good reasons for supposing that rapid change is generally a source of unsettlement and confusion, particularly accentuated perhaps if the change is not guided by a set of sharply defined master symbols that tell just what the change is about. The American process of change is of this type; but we can also say that it is not a state of nearly random confusion but in the main is a coherently directional process. Since it is not centrally directed or symbolized, however, it is particularly important to understand its main pattern.

There has been the obvious aspect of growth that is expressed in sheer scale, such as the size of the population, the magnitude and complexity of organization. At the more specifically social levels, however, I should like to stress certain features of the process that may help to make the situation of American youth (as well as other phenomena of our time) more understandable. On the one hand, at the level of the predominant pattern, our value system has remained relatively stable. On the other hand, relative to the value system, there has been a complex process of change, of which structural differentiation is perhaps the most important single feature. It is associated, however, with various others, which I shall call "extending inclusiveness," "normative upgrading," and "an increasing conceptualization of value patterns on the general level." These are all technical terms which, if they are not to be regarded as sociological jargon, need to be elucidated.

Values generally are patterned conceptions of the qualities of meaning of the objects of human experiences; by virtue of these qualities, the objects are considered desirable for the evaluating persons. Among such objects is the type of society considered to be good, not only in some abstract sense but also for "our kind of people" as members of it. The value patterns that play a part in controlling action in a society are in the first instance the conceptions of the good type of society to which the members of that society are committed. Such a pattern exists at a very high level of generality, without any specification of functions, or any level of internal differentiation, or particularities of situation.

In my own work it has proved useful to formulate the dominant American value pattern at this very general level as one of *instrumental activism*. Its cultural grounding lies in moral and (eventually) religious orientations, which in turn derive directly from Puritan traditions. The relevance of the pattern extends through all three of the religious, moral, and societal levels, as well as to others that cannot be detailed here. It is most important to keep them distinct, in particular the difference between the moral and the societal levels.

In its religious aspect, instrumental activism is based on the pattern Max Weber called "inner-worldly asceticism," the conception of man's role as an instrument of the divine will in building a kingdom of God on earth. Through a series of steps, both in internal cultural development and in institutionalization (which cannot be detailed here), this has produced a conception of the human condition in which the individual is committed to maximal effort in the interest of valued *achievement* under a system of normative order. This system is in the first instance moral, but also, at the societal level, it is embodied in legal norms. Achievement is conceived in "rational" terms, which include the maximal objective understanding of the empirical conditions of action, as well as the faithful adherence to normative commitments. It is of great importance that, once institutionalized, the fulfillment of such a value pattern need not be motivated by an explicit recognition of its religious groundings.

One way of describing the pattern in its moral aspects is to say that it is fundamentally individualistic. It tends to maximize the desirability of autonomy and responsibility in the individual. Yet this is an institutionalized individualism, in that it is normatively controlled at the moral level in two ways. First, it is premised on the conception of human existence as serving ends or functions beyond those of physical longevity, or health, or the satisfaction of the psychological needs of the personality apart from these value commitments. In a sense, it is the building of the "good life," not only for the particular individual but also for all mankind—a life that is accounted as desirable, not merely desired. This includes commitment to a good society. Second, to implement these moral premises, it is necessary for the autonomous and responsible achievements of the individual to be regulated by a normative order—at this level, a moral law that defines the relations of various contributions and the patterns of distributive justice.

The society, then, has a dual meaning, from this moral point of view. On the one hand, it is perhaps the primary field in which valued achievement is possible for the individual. In so far as it facilitates such achievements, the society is a good one. On the other hand, the building of the good society (that is, its progressive improvement) is the primary goal of valued action—along with such cultural developments as are intimately involved in social progress, such as science. To the individual, therefore, the most important goal to which he can orient himself is a contribution to the good society.

The value pattern I am outlining is activistic, therefore, in that it is oriented toward control or mastery of the human condition, as judged by moral standards. It is not a doctrine of passive adjustment to conditions, but one of active adaptation. On the other hand, it is instrumental with reference to the source of moral legitimation, in the sense that human achievement is not conceived as an end in itself but as a means to goals beyond the process and its immediate outcome.

This value pattern implies that the society is meant to be a developing, evolving entity. It is meant to develop in the direction of progressive "improvement." But this development is to be through the autonomous initiative and achievements of its units—in the last analysis, individual persons. It is therefore a society which places heavy responsibilities (in the form of expectations) on its individual members. At the same time, it subjects them to two very crucial sets of limitations which have an important bearing on the problem of youth.

One of these concerns the "moralism" of the value system—the fact that individualism is bound within a strongly emphasized framework of normative order. The achievement, the success, of the individual must ideally be in accord with the rules, above all, with those which guarantee opportunity to all, and which keep the system in line with its remoter values. Of course, the more complex the society, the greater the difficulty of defining the requisite norms, a difficulty which is greatly compounded by rapid change. Furthermore, in the interest of effectiveness, achievement must often be in the context of the collective organization, thus further limiting autonomy.

The second and for present purposes an even more crucial limitation is that it is in the nature of such a system that it is not characterized by a single, simple, paramount goal for the society as a system. The values legitimize a *direction* of change, not a terminal state. Furthermore, only in the most general sense is this direction "officially" defined, with respect to such famous formulae as liberty, democracy, general welfare, and distributive justice. The individual is left with a great deal of responsibility, not only for achieving *within* the institutionalized normative order, but for his own interpretation of its meaning and of his obligations in and to it.

Space forbids detailing the ramifications of this value system. Instead, it is necessary to my analysis to outline briefly the main features of the process of social change mentioned above. The suggestion is that the main pattern of values has been and probably will continue to be stable, but that the structure of the society, including its subsystem values at lower levels, has in the nature of the case been involved in a rapid and far-reaching process of change. This centers on the process of differentiation, but very importantly it also involves what we have referred to as inclusion, upgrading, and increasing generalization. I shall confine my discussion here to the structure of the society, though this in turn is intimately connected with problems concerned with the personality of the individual, including his personal values.

Differentiation refers to the process by which simple structures are divided into functionally differing components, these components becoming relatively independent of one another, and then recombined into more complex structures in which the functions of the differentiated units are complementary. A key example in the development of industrial society everywhere is the differentiation, at the collectivity level, of the unit of economic production from the kinship household. Obviously, in peasant economies, production is carried out by and in the household. The development of employing organizations which are structurally distinct from any household is the key new structural element. This clearly means a loss of function to the old undifferentiated unit, but also a gain in autonomy, though this in turn involves a new dependency, because the household can no longer be self-subsistent. The classical formula is that the productive services of certain members (usually the adult males) have been alienated from the organization directly responsible for subsistence and thus lost to the household, which then depends on money income from occupational earnings and in turn on the markets for consumers' goods.

These losses, however, are not without their compensations: the gain in the productivity of the economy and in the standard of living of the household. This familiar paradigm has to be generalized so as to divest it of its exclusively economic features and show it as the primary characterization of a very general process of social change. First, it is essential to point out that it always operates simultaneously in both collectivities and individual roles. Thus, in the example just given, a new type of productive organization which is not a household or (on more complex levels) even a family farm has to be developed. The local community no longer consists only of farm households but also of nonproducing households and productive units—*e.g.*, firms. Then the same individual (the head of the household) has a dual role as head of the family and as employee in a producing unit (the case of the individual entrepreneur is a somewhat special one).

By the extension of inclusiveness, I mean that, once a step of differentiation has been established, there is a tendency to extend the new pattern to increasing proportions of the relevant population of units. In the illustrative case, the overwhelming tendency that has operated for well over a century has been to reduce the proportion of households which are even in part economically self-sufficient, in the sense of a family farm, in favor of those whose members are gainfully employed outside the household. This is a principal aspect of the spread of industrialization and urbanization. The same logic applies to newly established educational standards, *e.g.*, the expectation that a secondary-school education will be normal for the whole age cohort.

Normative upgrading means a type of change in the normative order, to which the operation of units, both individual and collective, is subject. It is a shift from the prescription of rules by a special class or unit in a special situation to more generalized norms having to do with more inclusive classes of units in wider ranges of situations. Thus the law that specifies that a railway engine must be equipped with a steam whistle to give warning at crossings has by court interpretation been generalized to include any effective warning signal (since oil-burning locomotives are not equipped with steam).[1] But in a sense parallel to that in which differentiation leads to alienation from the older unit, normative upgrading means that the unit is left with a problem, since the rules no longer give such concretely unequivocal guidance to what is expected. If the rule is general enough, its application to a particular situation requires interpretation. Such upgrading, we contend, is a necessary concomitant of the process of differentiation.

When we speak of norms, we mean rules applying to particular categories of units in a system, operating in particular types of situations. For example, individual adults may not be employed under conditions which infringe on certain basic freedoms of the individual. The repercussions of a step in differentiation, however, cannot be confined to this level; they must also involve some part of the value system; this is to say, the functions of the differentiated categories of units, which are now different from one another, must not only be regulated but also legitimized. To use our example again, it cannot be true that the whole duty of the fathers of families is to gain subsistence for their households through making the household itself productive, but it becomes legitimate to support the household by earning a money income through work for an outside employer and among other things to be absent from the household many hours a week. At the collectivity level, therefore, a business that is not the direct support of a household (such as farming) must be a legitimate way of life—that is, the unit that employs labor for such purposes, without itself being a household, must be legitimate. This requires defining the values in terms sufficiently general to include both the old and the new way of life.

The values must therefore legitimize a structural complex by which economic production and the consumption needs of households are met simultaneously—that is, both the labor markets and the markets for consumers' goods. For example, this structural complex is of focal importance in the modern (as distinguished from medieval) urban community. The value attitude that regards the rural or the handicraft way of life as morally superior to the modern urban and—if you will—industrial way (a common attitude in the Western world of today) is an example of the failure of the adequate

1. Willard Hurst, *Law and Social Process in United States History,* Ann Arbor, University of Michigan Press, 1960, Ch. 2.

value generalization that is an essential part of institutionalizing the process of structural change.

To sum up, we may state that both the nature of the American value pattern and the nature of the process of change going on in the society make for considerable difficulties in the personal adjustment of individuals. On the one hand, our type of activism, with its individualistic emphases, puts a heavy responsibility for autonomous achievement on the individual. On the other hand, it subjects him to important limitations: he must not only be regulated by norms and the necessity of working cooperatively, in collective contexts; he must also interpret his own responsibilities and the rules to which he is subject. Beyond that, ours is a society which in the nature of its values cannot have a single clear-cut societal goal which can be dramatically symbolized. The individual is relegated to contributions which are relatively specialized, and it is not always easy to see their bearing on the larger whole. Furthermore, the general erosion of traditional culture and symbols, which is inseparable from a scientific age, makes inadequate many of the old formulae once used to give meaning and legitimation to our values and achievements. This is perhaps true in particular of the older religious grounding of our values.

Not unrelated to these considerations is the very fact of the *relative* success of the society in developing in relation to its values. Not only is there a high general standard of living, which, it should be remembered, means the availability of facilities for *whatever* uses are valued; *e.g.,* increased income may allow for attending prize fights or symphony concerts—a not inconsiderable amount has been going into the latter channel. There is certainly a much better standard of minimum welfare and general distributive justice now than in our past. However much remains to be done, and it is clearly considerable, it is no longer possible to contend that poverty, misery, preventable illness, etc., are the primary lot of the average American. Indeed, the accent has shifted to our duty to the less favored portions of the world. Furthermore, for the average individual, it is probable that opportunity is more widely open than in any large-scale society in history to secure education, access to historically validated cultural goods, and the like. But perhaps it can be seen that, in the light of this all too brief analysis, the great problem has come to be, what to do with all these advantages—not, as has so often been true, how to avoid the worst disasters and take a few modest little steps forward.[2] To be sure, there is a very real danger of the collapse of all civilization through nuclear war; but somehow that danger fails to deter people from making significant investments in the future, not only for themselves as individuals, but also for the society as a whole.

THE POSITION OF AMERICAN YOUTH

IT is in this broad picture of the American social structure and its development that I should like to consider the position of American youth. Contrary to prevalent views that mainly stress the rising standard of living and the allegedly indulgent and easy life, I think it is legitimate to infer that the general trend of development of the society has been and will continue to be one which, by and large, puts greater rather than diminished demands on its average individual citizen—with some conspicuous exceptions. He must operate in more complex situations than before. He attempts to do many things his predecessors never attempted, that indeed were beyond their capacities. To succeed in what he attempts, he has to exercise progressively higher levels of competence and responsibility. These inferences seem to me inescapable when full account of the nature of the society and its main trends of development is taken.

If capacities and relevant opportunities developed as rapidly as do demands, it would follow that life on the average would be neither more nor less difficult. There seems reason to believe that, if anything, demands have tended somewhat to outrun the development of capacities—especially those for orienting to normatively complex situations—and in some respects even opportunities, and that this is a major source of the current unrest and malaise. My broad contention, taking due account of the process of change just outlined, is that this society, however, is one that is relatively well organized and integrated with reference to its major values and its major trends of development. If those values are intact and are by and large shared by the younger generation (there seems to be every indication that they are), then it ought to be a society in which they can look forward to a good life. In so far as their mood is one of

2. To sociologists, the frustrating aspects of a favorable situation in this sense may be summed up under the concept of "relative deprivation." See Robert K. Merton and Paul Lazarsfeld, *Continuities in Social Research: Studies in the Scope and Method of "The American Soldier,"* New York, The Free Press of Glencoe, 1950.

bewilderment, frustration, or whatever, one should look for relatively specific sources of difficulty rather than to a generalized malintegration of the society as a whole.

It may be well to set the tone of the following analysis by an example of the ways in which current common sense can often misinterpret phenomena that raise distressing problems. American society, of course, is known for its high divorce rate. Until the peak following World War II, moreover, the trend was upward throughout the century, though since then it has appreciably declined. This divorce rate has widely been interpreted as an index of the "disintegration of the family" and, more importantly, of the levels of moral responsibility of married persons.

That it results in increased numbers of broken families is of course true, though the seriousness of this is mitigated by the fact that most divorces occur between childless couples and that most divorced persons remarry, a large proportion stably. In any case, the proportion of the population of marriageable age that is married and living with their spouses is now the highest it has been in the history of the census.

The main point, however, is that this point of view fails to take into account the increased strain put on the marriage relationship in the modern situation. In effect, it says, since an increased proportion fail in a difficult task relative to those who previously failed in an easier task, this increased rate of failures is an index of a declining level of responsibility; seen in this light, this interpretation is palpably absurd, but if the underlying situation is not analyzed, it is plausible.

The increased difficulty of the task has two main aspects. One is the increased differentiation of the nuclear family from other structures in which it was formerly embedded, notably the farm and other household or family enterprises from which economic support was derived. This differentiation deprives the family and the marriage relationship within it of certain bases of structural support. This is clearly related to the component of freedom mentioned above; the freedom of choice of marriage partners is clearly related to the spread of the view that really serious incompatibility may justify breaking the marriage tie.

The other factor is the enhanced level of expectations in functioning outside the family for both adults and children. For adults, particularly men, the central obligation concerns the levels of responsibility and competence required by their jobs; for children, these requirements of growing up in a more complex and competitive world, going farther in education, and undertaking substantially more autonomous responsibility along the way impose greater demands than before. It is my impression that the cases in which marriage was undertaken irresponsibly are no more numerous than in any other time, and that divorce is not often lightly resorted to but is a confession of failure in an undertaking in which both parties have usually tried very hard to succeed.[3]

I cite this example because it is a conspicuous special case of the more general considerations I wish to discuss. The first keynote here is the rising general level of expectations. The primary reference point, of course, is that of adult roles at their peak of responsibility in middle age. The most prominent example is that of the higher levels of masculine occupational roles, in which (in those with technical emphasis) the requisite levels of training and technical competence are continually rising. With respect to managerial roles, the size and complexity of organizations is increasing, and hence the requirements necessary for their successful management also. Similar things, however, are true in various other fields. Thus the whole range of associational affairs requires membership support for leadership as well as responsible leadership itself, both of which involve complicated responsibilities. These range from the many private associations and "good causes" through participation on boards and staffs (including university departments and faculties) to participation through voting and other forms of exercising public responsibility.

The family in this context is a further case. The feminine role is typically anchored in the first instance in the family. Family duties may not be more onerous in such senses as drudgery and hard work than they were, but they involve a higher level of competence and responsibility, particularly, though not exclusively, in the field of the psychological management of both children and husbands, as well as of selves—the latter because wives are now far more autonomous on the average than they were. What we may call the independence training of children is more delicate and difficult than was the older type of training in strict obedience—that is, if autonomy for the

3. See Talcott Parsons and Robert F. Bales, *Family, Socialization and Interaction Process,* New York, The Free Press of Glencoe, 1955, especially Ch. 1.

young is to be accompanied by high levels of self-discipline and responsibility. But in addition, the typical married woman participates far more extensively outside the home than she formerly did, and in particular she forms a rapidly increasing proportion in the labor force.

Perhaps the central repercussion of this general upgrading of expectations (and hence of the norms with which conformity is expected) on the situation of youth is in the field of formal education. Here, of course, there has been a steady process of lengthening the average period of schooling, with the minimum satisfactory norm for all approaching the completion of high school, while nearly forty percent of the total age cohort now enter college, and a steadily increasing percentage complete college. Finally, by far the most rapidly growing sector has been that of postgraduate professional education. Uneven as standards are, and unsatisfactory as they are at many points, there is no solid evidence of a general tendency to deterioration and much evidence of their improvement, especially in the best schools at all levels.[4]

It seems fair, then, to conclude that in getting a formal education the average young American is undertaking a more difficult, and certainly a longer, job than his father or mother did, and that it is very likely that he is working harder at it. A growing proportion is prolonging formal education into the early adult years, thus raising important problems about marriage, financial independence, and various other considerations.

Furthermore, he is doing this in a context in which, both within and outside the school, he must assume more autonomous responsibility than did his predecessors. In the school itself—and in college —the slow though gradual trend has been in the direction of a mildly "progressive" type of education, with a diminution of the amount of drill and learning by rote. In certain respects, parents have grown distinctly more permissive within the family and with regard to their children's activities outside. This throws an important stress on the child's relations to his age peers, one that becomes particularly important in adolescence. This is the area least under adult control, in which deviant tendencies can most readily be mutually reinforced, without being immediately checked by adult

4. For example, I am quite certain that the general level of academic achievement on the part of students of Harvard College and the Harvard Graduate School has substantially risen during my personal contact with them (more than thirty years).

intervention. This is to say that in general the educational process puts increased demands on the younger group.

Three other factors seem involved in this situation of strain from the combination of enhanced expectations and autonomy. They concern one aspect of the psychological preparation for the tasks of maturing, one aspect of the choices that are open, and one aspect of the situation with reference to normative regulation.

First, with respect to psychological preparation, there seems to have been a trend within the family to *increase* the dependency of the young pre-oedipal child, particularly on the mother, of course. This trend is the consequence of the structural isolation of the nuclear family. There is less likelihood of there being close relatives either directly in the home or having very intensive and continual contact with the family. For middle-class families, the virtual disappearance of the domestic servant has also left less room for a division of responsibility for child care. Further, the proportion of very large families with five or more children has been sharply decreasing, while those with three and four children have been increasing. All these factors contribute to a concentration of relationships within the family and of the parents' (especially the mother's) sanctioning powers—both disciplinary and rewarding.

Psychological theory, however, indicates that under the proper circumstances this enhanced dependency contributes to developing motivations for high levels of achievement. These circumstances include high levels of aspiration for the child on the part of the parents and the use of the proper types of discipline. The essential point is that high dependency provides a very strong motivation to please the parent. This in turn can be used to incite him to learn what the parent sets him, if he is suitably rewarded by parental approval. The general findings of studies on the types of discipline used in middle-class families—the use of the withdrawal of love and approval as the predominant type of negative sanction—seem to fit in this picture.

The dependency components of motivation, however, are seldom if ever fully extinguished. The balance is so delicate in their relation to the autonomous components that it is easily upset, and in many cases this is a source of considerable strain. Attempting to maintain this balance, for example, may very well contribute to the great increase in the practice of "going steady" and its relation to the trend to early marriages. Emerging in adolescence, the dyadic heterosexual relation is the main component of the relational system of youth that articulates most directly with the earlier dependency complex— though some of it may also be expressed in same-sex peer groups, and indeed in "crushes" on the teacher. It is striking that the main trend seems to be toward intensive, and not merely erotic but diffuse, dyadic relations, rather than to sexual libertinism. This is in turn reflected in the emotional intensity of the marriage relationship and hence in the elements of potential strain underlying the problem of divorce.

This brings me to the second of the factors mentioned above, the range of choices open. A progressive increase in this range is a consequence of the general process of social change sketched above, namely, differentiation in the structure of the society. As this process goes on, types of interest, motivation, and evaluation that were embedded in a less differentiated complex come to be separated out, to become more autonomous and more visible in that they are freed from more ascriptive types of control. Ties to class and family, to local community and region become more flexible and hence often "expendable" as more choices become available.

One of the most conspicuous cases in relation to the present interest is the erotic component of sex relations. In an earlier phase of our society, it was rather rigidly controlled even within marriage, indeed, not infrequently it was partially suppressed. The process by which it has become differentiated, allowing much greater freedom in this area, is closely related to the differentiation of function and the structural isolation of the nuclear family.[5] In a society in which autonomous freedom is so widespread, there is much greater freedom in this field as in many others, not only in practice but also in portrayals on the stage, in the movies and television, and in the press, magazines, and books.

In this connection, since much of the newer freedom is illegitimate in relation to the older standards (normative upgrading and value generalization take time), it is very difficult to draw lines between the areas of new freedom in process of being legitimated and the types which are sufficiently dysfunctional, even in the new state of society, so that the probability is they will be controlled or even suppressed. The adolescent in our society is faced with difficult

5. The emancipation of components that were previously rigidly controlled by ascription is of course a major feature of the general process of differentiation, which could not be detailed here for reasons of space.

problems of choice and evaluation in areas such as this, because an adequate codification of the norms governing many of these newly emancipated areas has not yet been developed.

The third factor, that of normative regulation, is essentially a generalization of the second factor. We have maintained (though of course without documentation) that, contrary to various current opinions, the basic pattern of American values has not changed. Value patterns, however, are only part of the normative culture of the society. At the lower levels, both at the more specific levels of values and of what we technically call norms, it is in the nature of the type of process of change we have been discussing that there should be a continual reorganization of the normative system. Unfortunately, this does not occur as an instantaneous adjustment to the major innovations, but is a slow, uneven, and often painful process. In its course, at any one time (as we have noted), there are important elements of indeterminacy in the structure of expectations—not simply in the sense that there are areas of freedom in which autonomous decision is expected, but also in the sense that, where people feel there ought to be guidance, it is either lacking altogether, or the individual is subject to conflicting expectations that are impossible to fulfill all at once. This is the condition that some sociologists, following Durkheim, call *anomie.*

There seems to be an important reason why this source of strain and disturbance bears rather more heavily on the younger generation than on others. This is owing to the fact that the major agents for initiating processes of change lie in other sectors of the society, above all, in large-scale organization, in the developments of science and technology, in the higher political processes, and in the higher ranges of culture. Their impact tends to spread, and there is a time lag in change between the locations of primary change and the other parts of the social structure.

Though there is of course much unevenness, it seems correct to say that, with one major exception, the social structures bearing most directly on youth are likely to be rather far down the line in the propagation of the effects of change. These are the family and the school, and they are anchored in the local residential community. The major exception is the college, and still more, the university, which is one of the major loci of innovation and which can involve its students in the process more directly.

By and large, it seems fair to suggest that adults are on the average probably more conservative in their parental roles than when their children are not involved, and that this is typical of most of their roles outside the family. Similarly, schools, especially elementary and secondary schools, are on the whole probably more conservative in most respects than are the organizations that employ the fathers of their children. In the present phase of social development, another important institution of the residential community, the parish church or synagogue, is probably distinctly on the conservative side as a rule.

This would suggest that, partly as a matter of generation lag, partly for more complex reasons of the sort indicated, the adult agencies on which the youth most depends tend to some extent to be "out of tune" with what he senses to be the most advanced developments of the time. He senses that he is put in an unfair dilemma by having to be so subject to their control.

If we are right in thinking that special pressures operate on the younger generation relative to the general pressures generated by social change, on the other side of the relationship there are factors which make for special sensitivities on their part. The residua of early dependency, as pointed out above, constitute one such factor. In addition, the impact on youth of the general process of social differentiation makes for greater differences between their position and that of children, on the one hand, and that of adults, on the other, than is true in less differentiated societies. Compared to our own past or to most other societies, there is a more pronounced, and above all (as noted) an increasingly long segregation of the younger groups, centered above all on the system of formal education. It may be argued especially that the impact of this process is particularly pronounced at the upper fringe of the youth period, for the rapidly increasing proportion of the age cohort engaged in higher education—in college, and, very importantly, in postgraduate work. These are people who are adults in all respects except for the element of dependency, since they have not yet attained full occupational independence.

THE YOUTH CULTURE

THE question may now be raised as to how young people react to this type of situation. Obviously, it is a highly variegated one and therefore occasions much diversity of behavior, but there are certain broad patterns which can be distinguished. These may be summed up under the conception, now familiar to social scientists, of a relatively differentiated "youth culture." Perhaps S. N. Eisenstadt is its most comprehensive student, certainly in its comparative perspective.[6]

It is Eisenstadt's contention that a distinctive pattern of values, relationships, and behavior for youth tends to appear and become more or less institutionalized in societies that develop a highly universalistic pattern of organization at the levels of adult role involvements. Since all lives start in the family, which is a highly particularistic type of structure, there is not only the difficulty of rising to higher levels within the same type of relationship system, but also of learning to adjust to a very different type. What has been discussed above as the enhancement of dependency in early childhood is a special case of this general proposition. Totalitarian societies attempt to bring this period under stringent centralized control through officially organized, adult-directed youth organizations such as the Soviet *Komsomols,* or earlier, the *Hitlerjugend.* In democratic societies, however, it tends to be relatively free, though in our own it is rather closely articulated with the system of formal education through a ramifying network of extracurricular activities.

As a consequence of youth's being exposed to such strains, it might be expected that youth culture would manifest signs of internal conflict and that it would incorporate elements of conformity as well as of alienation and revolt. In nonrational, psychological terms, rather than in terms of rational aims, youth culture attempts to balance its need for conforming to the expectations of the adult agencies most directly involved (parents and the local residential community) with some kind of outlet for tension and revolt and with some sensitivity to the winds of change above and beyond its local situation.

For two reasons, one would expect to find the fullest expression of these trends at the level of the peer group. For one thing, this group is the area of greatest immunity to adult control; indeed, the range of its freedom in this respect is particularly conspicuous in the American case. The other reason is that this is the area to which it is easiest to displace the elements of dependency generated in early experience in the family—on the one hand, because the strong

6. S. N. Eisenstadt, *From Generation to Generation,* New York, The Free Press of Glencoe, 1956. See also his paper "Archetypal Patterns of Youth," *Daedalus,* Vol. 91, no. 1 (Winter, 1962).

stress on autonomy precludes maintaining too great an overt dependence on parents or other adult agencies, and, on the other, because the competitive discipline of school achievement enforces autonomous responsibility in this area. The peer group then gradually differentiates into two components, one focusing on the cross-sex relationship and one focusing on "activities," some of which occur within the one-sex group, others, relatively nonerotic, in mixed groups.

In general, the most conspicuous feature of the youth peer group is a duality of orientation. On the one hand, there tends to be a compulsive independence in relation to certain adult expectations, a touchy sensitivity to control, which in certain cases is expressed in overt defiance. On the other hand, within the group, there tends to be a fiercely compulsive conformity, a sharp loyalty to the group, an insistence on the literal observance of its norms, and punishment of deviance. Along with this goes a strong romantic streak. This has been most conspicuous in the romantic love theme in the cross-sex relationship, but it is also more generalized, extending to youth-culture heroes such as athletes and group leaders of various sorts, and sometimes to objects of interest outside the youth situation.

It is my impression (not easy to document) that important shifts of emphasis in American youth culture have occurred in the last generation. For the main trend, notably the increasingly broad band we think of as middle class, there has been a considerable relaxation of tension in both the two essential reference directions, toward parents and toward school expectations—though this relaxation is distinctly uneven. In the case of the school, there is a markedly greater acceptance of the evaluation of good school work and its importance for the future. This, of course, is associated with the general process of educational upgrading, particularly with the competition to enter good colleges and, at the next level, especially for students at the better colleges, to be admitted to graduate schools. The essential point, however, is that this increased pressure has been largely met with a positive response rather than with rebellion or passive withdrawal. The main exception is in the lowest sector, where the pattern of delinquency is most prominent and truancy a major feature. This is partly understandable as a direct consequence of the upgrading of educational expectations, because it puts an increased pressure on those who are disadvantaged by a combination of low ability, a nonsupportive family or ethnic background.

As to youth's relation to the family, it seems probable that the institutionalizing of increased permissiveness for and understanding of youth-culture activities is a major factor. The newer generation of parents is more firmly committed to a policy of training serious independence. It tolerates more freedom, and it expects higher levels of performance and responsibility. Further, it is probably true that the development of the pattern of "going steady" has drained off some tension into semi-institutionalized channels—tension formerly expressed in wilder patterns of sexual behavior. To be sure, this creates a good many problems, not only as to how far the partners will go in their own erotic relations, but also possibly premature commitments affecting future marriage. It may be that the pendulum has swung too far and that adjustments are to be expected.

Within this broad framework, the question of the content of peer-group interests is important. What I have called the romantic trend can be broadly expressed in two directions; the tentative terms "regressive" and "progressive" are appropriate, if not taken too literally. Both components are normally involved in such a situation, but their proportions and content may vary. They derive specifically from the general paradigm of social change outlined above, the former, at social levels, tending to resist change, the latter to anticipate and promote it.

One of the most striking interests of American youth culture has been in masculine physical prowess, expressed in particular in athletics. It seems quite clear that there has been a declining curve in this respect, most conspicuous in the more elite schools and colleges, but on the whole it is a very general one, except for the cult of violence in the delinquent sector. The cult of physical prowess has clearly been a reflex of the pressure to occupational achievement in a society in which brains rather than brawn come increasingly to count. From this point of view, it is a regressive phenomenon.

The indication is that the lessened concentration on this cult is an index of greater acceptance of the general developmental trend. Alcohol and sex are both in a somewhat different category. For the individual, they are fields of emancipation from the restrictions of childhood, but they are definitely and primarily regressive in their significance for the adult personality. However, as noted above, the emancipation of youth in this respect has been connected with a general emancipation which is part of the process of differentiation in the adult society, which permits greater expressiveness in these areas. I have the impression that a significant change has occurred from the somewhat frenetic atmosphere of the "flaming youth" of the 1920's and to some extent of the 1930's. There is less rebellion in both respects, more moderation in the use of alcohol, and more "seriousness" in the field of sexual relations. Youth has become better integrated in the general culture.

On the other side, the progressive one, the most important phenomena are most conspicuous at the upper end of the range, both in terms of the sociocultural level and of the stage of the life cycle. This is the enormous development of serious cultural interests among students in the more elite colleges. The most important field of these interests seems to be that of the arts, including highbrow music, literature, drama, and painting.

The first essential point here is that this constitutes a very definite upgrading of cultural standards, compared with the philistinism of the most nearly corresponding circles in an earlier generation. Second, however, it is at least variant and selective (though not, I think, deviant) with respect to the main trends of the society, since the main developments in the latter are on the "instrumental" rather than the "expressive" side. As to the special involvement of elite youth in the arts, it may be said that youth has tended to become a kind of "loyal opposition" to the main trends of the culture, making a bid for leadership in a sphere important to a balanced society yet somewhat neglected by the principal innovating agencies.

The question of youth's relation to the political situation is of rather special interest and considerable complexity. The susceptibility of youth groups to radical political ideologies, both left and right, has often been remarked. It appears, however, that this is a widely variant phenomenon. It seems to be most conspicuous, on the one hand, in societies just entering a more "developed" state, in which intellectuals play a special role and in which students, as protential intellectuals, are specially placed. In a second type of case, major political transitions and instabilities are prominent, as in several European countries during this century, notably Germany.

Seen in this context, American youth has seemed to be apathetic politically. During the 1930's and 1940's, there was a certain amount of leftist activity, including a small Communist contingent, but the main trend has certainly been one of limited involvement. Recently, there seems to have been a kind of resurgence of political interest and activity. It has not, however, taken the form of any explicit, generalized, ideological commitment. Rather, it has tended to focus on specific issues in which moral problems are sharply defined, notably in race relations and the problems of nuclear war. It does not seem too much to say that the main trend has been in accord with the general political characteristics of the society, which has been a relatively stable system with a strong pluralistic character. The concomitant skepticism as to generalized ideological formulae is usually thought deplorable by the moralists among our intellectuals. In this broad respect, however, the main orientation of youth seems to be in tune with the society in which they are learning to take their places.

The elements in youth culture that express strain because of deviations from the main standards of the adult society are by no means absent. One such deviation is what we have called the "romantic," the devotion to expectations unrealistically simplified and idealized with respect to actual situations. A particularly clear example has been the romantic love complex. It is interesting, therefore, that a comparable pattern seems to have appeared recently in the political field, one that is connected with a pervasive theme of concern: the "meaningfulness" of current and future roles in modern industrial society.

As Kenneth Keniston has recently pointed out[7] in the field of politics, one not very explicit interpretation of a meaningful role for youth in general is to exert a major personal influence on determining the "big" political decisions of our time. The realistic problem, of course, is the organization of large-scale societies on bases that are not rigidly fixed in tradition, not authoritarian, and not unduly unstable. In this respect, public opinion (though in the long run extremely important) is necessarily diffuse and, with few exceptions, unable to dictate particular decisions. The main policy-making function is of necessity confined to relatively few and is the special responsibility of elected representatives who, in large-scale societies, become professionalized to a considerable degree. The average adult citizen, even if high in competence and responsibility, is excluded from these few. Yet this is not to say that in his role as citizen his responsibilities are meaningless or that his life in general can become

7. Kenneth Keniston, "Social Change and Youth in America," *Daedalus,* Vol. 91, no. 1 (Winter, 1962).

meaningful only if his principal concerns (*e.g.,* his nonpolitical job) are sacrificed to the attempt to become a top "influential" in national politics. If this were true, representative democracy as we know it would itself be meaningless. The alternative, however (if large-scale society is to exist at all), is not populistic direct democracy but dictatorship.

This particular syndrome, of course, is a part of a larger one: the general difficulty of accepting the constraints inherent in large-scale organizations—in particular, the "instrumental" aspect of roles other than those at the highest levels. We have already pointed out some of the features of our developing social system that make this a focus of strain. Equally, through the development of institutionalized individualism, there is a whole series of factors making for an increasing rather than a diminishing autonomy. The question, however, concerns the spheres in which the autonomy of various categories of individuals can operate. Differentiation inevitably entails mutual dependence: the more differentiation, the more dependence. In a system characterized by high levels of differentiation, it is to be expected that organizational policy making will also become differentiated. Hence, only a few will become very intimately concerned with it. The problem of what mechanism can control these few is indeed a complex one which cannot be analyzed here. The political role, however, seems to provide particularly striking evidence of a romantic element in current youth ideology.

Perhaps the most significant fact about current youth culture is its concern with meaningfulness. This preoccupation definitely lies on the serious and progressive side of the division I have outlined. Furthermore, it represents a rise in the level of concern from the earlier preoccupation with social justice—even though the problem of race relations is understandably a prominent one. Another prominent example is the much discussed concern with problems of "identity." This is wholly natural and to be expected in the light of *anomie.* In a society that is changing as rapidly as ours and in which there is so much mobility of status, it is only natural that the older generation cannot provide direct guidance and role models that would present the young person with a neatly structured definition of the situation. Rather, he must find his own way, because he is pushed out of the nest and expected to fly. Even the nature of the medium in which he is to fly is continually changing, so that, when he enters college, there are many uncertainties about the nature of opportunities in his chosen field on completing graduate school. His elders simply do not have the knowledge to guide him in detail.

It is highly significant that the primary concern has been shifting since early in the century from the field of social justice to that of meaningfulness, as exemplified by the problem of identity—except for the status of special groups such as the Negro. In terms of the social structure, this enhances the problem of integration, and focuses concern more on problems of meaning than on those of situation and opportunity in the simpler sense. It is a consequence of the process of social change we have outlined.

It is also understandable and significant that the components of anxiety that inevitably characterize this type of strained situation should find appropriate fields of displacement in the very serious, real dangers of the modern world, particularly those of war. It may also be suggested that the elite youth's resonance to the diagnosis of the current social situation in terms of conformity and mass culture should be expected.[8] Essentially, this diagnosis is an easy disparagement of the society, which youth can consider to be the source of difficulty and (so it seems to them) partially unmanageable problems.

CONCLUSION

THE above analysis suggests in the main that contemporary American society is of a type in which one would expect the situation of youth to involve (certainly, by the standards of the society from which it is emerging) rather special conditions of strain. As part of the more general process of differentiation to which we have alluded, youth groups themselves are coming to occupy an increasingly differentiated position, most conspicuously, in the field of formal education. Though an expanding educational system is vital in preparing for future function, it has the effect of segregating (more sharply and extensively than ever before) an increasing proportion of the younger age groups. The extension of education to increasingly older age levels is a striking example.

The other main focus of strain is the impact on youth of the pace and nature of the general process of social change. This is especially observable in the problem of *anomie*. In view of this change, youth's

8. For an analysis of this complex in the society, see Winston R. White, *Beyond Conformity*, New York, The Free Press of Glencoe, 1961.

expectations cannot be defined either very early or very precisely, and this results in considerable insecurity. Indeed, the situation is such that a marked degree of legitimate grievance is inevitable. Every young person is entitled in some respects to complain that he has been brought into "a world I never made."

To assess the situation of American youth within the present frame of reference presents an especially difficult problem of balance. This is an era that lays great stress, both internally and externally, on the urgencies of the times, precisely in the more sensitive and responsible quarters. Such a temper highlights what is felt to be wrong and emphasizes the need for change through active intervention. With reference to the actual state of society, therefore, the tendency is to lean toward a negative evaluation of the status quo, because both the concrete deficiencies and the obstacles to improvement are so great.

That this tendency should be particularly prominent in the younger age groups is natural. It is both to be expected and to be welcomed. The main feature of the youth situation is perhaps the combination of current dependence with the expectation of an early assumption of responsibility. I think that evidence has been presented above that this conflict is accentuated under present conditions. The current youthful indictments of the present state of our society may be interpreted as a kind of campaign position, which prepares the way for the definition of their role when they take over the primary responsibilities, as they inevitably will.

It seems highly probable that the more immediate situation is strongly influenced by the present phase of the society with respect to a certain cyclical pattern that is especially conspicuous in the political sphere. This is the cycle between periods of "activism" in developing and implementing a sense of the urgency of collective goals, and of "consolidation" in the sense of withdrawing from too active commitments and on the whole giving security and "soundness" the primary emphasis. There is little doubt that in this meaning, the most recent phase (the "Eisenhower era") has been one of consolidation, and that we are now involved in the transition to a more activistic phase.

Broadly speaking, youth in a developing society of the American type, in its deepest values and commitments, is likely to be favorable to the activistic side. It is inculcated with the major values of the society, and strongly impressed with the importance of its future responsibilities. At the same time, however, it is frustrated by being deprived of power and influence in the current situation, though it recognizes that such a deprivation is in certain respects essential, if its segregation for purposes of training is to be effective—a segregation which increases with each step in the process of differentiation. A certain impatience, however, is to be expected, and with it a certain discontent with the present situation. Since it is relatively difficult to challenge the basic structure of the youth situation in such respects (*e.g.,* as that one should not be permitted to start the full practice of medicine before graduating from college), this impatience tends to be displaced on the total society as a system, rather than on the younger generation in its specific situation. From this point of view, a generous measure of youthful dissatisfaction with the state of American society may be a sign of the healthy commitment of youth to the activist component of the value system. However good the current society may be from various points of view, *it is not good enough to meet their standards.* It goes almost without saying that a fallibility of empirical judgment in detail is to be expected.

The task of the social scientist, as a scientific observer of society, is to develop the closest possible approach to an objective account of the character and processes of the society. To him, therefore, this problem must appear in a slightly different light: he must try to see it in as broad a historical and comparative perspective as he can, and he must test his judgments as far as possible in terms of available empirical facts and logically precise and coherent theoretical analyses.

Viewed in this way (subject, of course, to the inevitable fallibilities of all cognitive undertakings), American society in a sense appears to be running a scheduled course. We find no cogent evidence of a major change in the essential patterns of its governing values. Nor do we find that—considering the expected strains and complications of such processes as rapid industrialization, the assimilation of many millions of immigrants, and a new order of change in the power structure, the social characteristics, and the balances of its relation to the outside world—American society is not doing reasonably well (as distinguished from outstandingly) in implementing these values. Our society on the whole seems to remain committed to its essential mandate.

The broad features of the situation of American youth seem to accord with this pattern. There are many elements of strain, but on the whole they may be considered normal for this type of society. Furthermore, the patterns of reaction on the part of American youth also seem well within normal limits. Given the American value system we have outlined, it seems fair to conclude that youth cannot help giving a *relative* sanction to the general outline of society as it has come to be institutionalized. On the other hand, it is impossible for youth to be satisfied with the status quo, which must be treated only as a point of departure for the far higher attainments that are not only desirable but also obligatory.

Clearly, American youth is in a ferment. On the whole, this ferment seems to accord relatively well with the sociologist's expectations. It expresses many dissatisfactions with the current state of society, some of which are fully justified, others are of a more dubious validity. Yet the general orientation appears to be, not a basic alienation, but an eagerness to learn, to accept higher orders of responsibility, and to "fit," not in the sense of passive conformity, but in the sense of their readiness to work within the system, rather than in basic opposition to it. The future of American society and the future place of that society in the larger world appear to present in the main a *challenge* to American youth. To cope with that challenge, an intensive psychological preparation is now taking place.

8

The Link Between Character

and Society

WITH Winston White

I. RIESMAN'S APPROACH AS WE SEE IT

AS INDICATED by the subtitle—*A Study of the Changing American Character*—Professor Riesman has addressed himself in *The Lonely Crowd* to major trends in American society, with particular reference to the relation between character and social structure. We find ourselves in general agreement that these major changes have had far-reaching implications for the socialization process and that they have significance for personality.

Our primary objective is to present an alternative interpretation of certain of these recent changes and their consequences. In an effort to clarify our areas of agreement as well as our points of departure, the first section of this essay will set forth our understanding of his main position without critical comment. We will reserve our own opinions for the second section, where we will present our alternative approach. A third section will then look into some of the empirical issues we have raised.

The central structural focus in Professor Riesman's work, it seems to us, is the "link between character and society . . . the way in which society ensures some degree of conformity from the individuals who

Reprinted from Seymour Martin Lipset and Leo Lowenthal, eds., Culture and Social Character, *New York, The Free Press of Glencoe, 1961, pp. 89–135.*

make it up"[1] and, reciprocally, the way in which individuals seek meaningful guidance from society. After pointing out the necessary abstractions one must make in talking about the "individual" and "society," Riesman sees this link as forged by three mechanisms, each one of which is characterized by a source of direction—tradition, inner, and other. Since these mechanisms link the individual and society, the typology of direction is at the same time applicable to either.[2]

Riesman explicitly points out that all three types are universal, with no society or person ever wholly dependent on one; but any particular individual or society can be characterized by the one mechanism on which principal reliance is placed.[3] With respect to society, he sees an historical process of development from tradition- to inner- to other-direction that permits a fundamental analysis of why these mechanisms have succeeded one another as primary sources of direction. We want to sort out what we think are the basic reference points in his conception of that process, in order to show how they lead quite logically to his empirical conclusions, particularly to the salient features of other-directed society.

Historical Process

In the tradition-directed society, there is a high degree of ascription; status and its consequent relations of power are largely determined by birth, with a fusion of political, economic, and religious functions within the kinship nexus. Because of this ascription, both goals and their implementation through specific acts are prescribed to a much greater degree than in the subsequent stages of societal development. Riesman speaks here of the focus on "securing external *behavioral* conformity."[4]

With inner-direction these ascriptive ties begin to break down, for reasons we need not go into here except to say that they are broadly included in what Max Weber meant by the process of ra-

1. *The Lonely Crowd,* Doubleday, p. 20. References to *The Lonely Crowd* will be made to both the hard-cover (New Haven, Yale University Press, 1950), and the paperback (New York, Doubleday Anchor, 1953) editions, in that order, unless the reference is to be found only in one (as in the above instance).
2. *Faces in the Crowd,* New Haven, Yale University Press, 1952, p. 4.
3. *Ibid.,* p. 7.
4. *The Lonely Crowd,* p. 15; 30.

tionalization. Increased personal mobility, expanding geographical frontiers, the development of market systems freed from particularistic relations, and rapid technological innovation, among other factors, necessitated greater freedom in the implementation of goals, an emancipation of goal-fulfillment from the specifications of a tradition that no longer proved adequate. But, although the goals changed, they remained inescapably destined—by the exigencies of an expanding society and economy—to acquire capital, master techniques, and the like. And such goals were implanted by parents and other adult authorities in the young, who—knowing their destination—had to arrive at it as best they could.

With the development of a highly industrialized society and its mature economy, the problems of production become relatively solved, the exigencies of financing and of technological advance routinized. What had previously been areas of daring innovation in an inner-directed society becomes institutionalized, "built into" society. The attainment of these goals by the society greatly diminishes them as a source of direction for the individual.

. . . on the whole, contemporary society, especially America, no longer requires and rewards the old enterprise and the old zeal. This does not mean that the economic system itself is slowing down: total production may continue to rise; but it can be achieved by institutionalizing technological and organizational advance. . . . The invention and adoption of new improvements can be routinized, built into the system, so to speak, rather than into the men who run the system.[5] In general, I think it can be said that many of the motives which were in earlier decades built into the character structure of individuals are now built into the institutional structure of corporate life.[6]

In this last stage, society becomes characterized by other-direction, wherein the individual looks to his peers—and those formidable peer-surrogates, the mass media—for his source of guidance. Here the goals are no longer set but ever shifting, and only the mechanism of direction itself remains.

The goals toward which the other-directed person strives shift with that guidance; it is only the process of striving itself and the process of paying close attention to the signals from others that remain unaltered throughout life.[7]

5. *Individualism Reconsidered*, New York, The Free Press of Glencoe, 1954, p. 104.
6. *Ibid.*, p. 231.
7. *The Lonely Crowd*, p. 22; 37.

Order and Agency

In analyzing Riesman's scheme, we want to introduce two central reference points—order and agency. From the point of view of the individual, his behavior can be looked at as a choice—as Rostow has put it—among perceived alternatives. But in making a choice, the individual necessarily applies some criteria of selection: why choose X when the choice of X necessarily means the rejection of Y and Z? Unless one wants to adopt the utilitarian position of assuming that such choices are made on the basis of individual criteria alone, a major source of criteria lies in the normative order of society, the shared expectations of what is considered desirable (*ought* to be desired). Indeed, Riesman's concept of direction takes cognizance of this aspect (although the other-directed case raises certain problems to be discussed later).

In addition, these societal criteria are transmitted by agents of socialization—by the extended kinship nexus, by parents, or by peers. Riesman's typology of mechanisms collapses these two reference points of order and agency into the single concept of source of direction. In sorting them out, we see a decrease in the specification of order and a shifting of primary agency as follows:

Source of Direction	Order	Agency
Tradition	Goals and their means	Kinship
Inner	Goals only	Parents
Other	Indeterminacy	Peers

This is not to say that with this decrease in specification there is less conformity, but rather to say that societal processes and ensuing shifts of direction have made the content of that conformity more fluid, to the point that in other-direction its shifting structure becomes indeterminate. We next want to look at the salient features of other-direction, using the underlying reference points we have suggested.

1. Indeterminacy of Order

In tradition-direction and inner-direction, societal criteria had a determinate structure in either traditional prescriptions or set goals. They had an order that was analytically independent of the agents who transmitted them. But in other-directed society, this order is said to be greatly reduced. The content of conformity becomes so fluid and the changes so rapid[8] that the other-directed person is hard-pressed to keep up with what it is he is supposed to conform to. His only guidance comes from signals from others like him, from the primary agents of socialization.

But this indeterminacy of structure in normative content also has the consequence of homogenizing the structure of the agents in the peer group, in that their role-relationships tend to be less functionally differentiated in terms of leadership and the like. Since conformity with a shifting content of expectations is problematical, the only reassurance that one is getting the proper guidance is approval "irrespective of content";[9] thus no one member of the group can go too far in giving direction to others for fear of losing their approval. The group, then, is characterized by marginal leadership, by competing for approval.

The other-directed situation becomes a caricature of Cooley's looking-glass self, where peers reflect each other in infinite regression like mirrors on barbershop walls. The other-directed person is an agent himself for the agent he looks to. Riesman characterizes this suggested lack of structure by noting that "the other-directed person grows up in a much more amorphous social system, where alternative destinations cannot be clearly chosen at an early age."[10] In the realm of consumption, he speaks of an *"objectless craving"* in which the craving itself "for the satisfactions others seem to have"[11] transcends the craving for specific objects.

Where in previous stages agents of direction (as in socialization) had been agents *for* a determinate structure of tradition or goals, they are now only agents for other agents. Order as an independent source of direction has disappeared, and other-direction relies on agency alone. Given this definition of the situation, Riesman quite rightly focuses on this aspect in the titles of Chapters 2 and 3: ". . . Changes in the Agents of Character Formation."[12]

The reliance on agency alone has an interesting parallel to the utilitarian conception of society, in which order was assumed to be random but a "natural identity of interests" was maintained by a metaphor of agency—"the invisible hand" (to which Riesman al-

8. *Ibid.*, p. 26; 42.
9. *Ibid.*, p. 49; 66.
10. *Individualism Reconsidered*, p. 105.
11. *The Lonely Crowd*, p. 80; 100. (Italics in original.)
12. *Ibid.*, pp. 36, 84; 54, 86.

ludes).[13] The conceptualization of other-direction implies, it seems to us, a recrudescence of utilitarianism, applied to the peer group. This is particularly evident in the realm of consumption.

2. Consumption, the Last Frontier

Riesman's analysis of the societal processes underlying the shift from inner- to other-direction focuses on production, specifically economic production. When the solution of the problems of production becomes built into the system, the goals of production cease to be problematical for the individual and he turns to consumption. Where the inner-directed person pioneered on the frontier of production, the other-directed is "moving to the frontiers of consumption"[14] —not just consumption of goods, but of words, images, and personal relationships themselves, particularly those aspects that deal with "the minutiae of taste or speech or emotion which are momentarily 'best.'"[15] Approval is bestowed on those who embrace the momentarily right consumption preferences, the "fandoms and lingoes" of the peer group.[16]

Since these preferences are momentary and not seen as structured —as was production by the goals of attaining it—they are dominated by swings of fashion.[17] "To escape the danger of a conviction for being different from the 'others' requires that one can be different— in look and talk and manner—from oneself as one was yesterday."[18]

Thus the only source of guidance that remains in other-direction is the approval by one's peers of shifting consumption preferences. Or, to put it in our terms, the only determinate reference point is the sanctioning by other agents of performances of an indeterminate nature. In the utilitarian conception, these sanctions become the "glad hand"[19] that replaces the invisible hand; the consumption preferences of the group replace individual wants as "givens."

This aspect of increasing indeterminacy in consumption is crucial in its bearing on future process; that is to say, how can the previous shifts of direction, seen in the context of societal process, be ex-

13. Ibid., p. 130; 151.
14. Individualism Reconsidered, p. 211.
15. Ibid., p. 105.
16. The Lonely Crowd, Doubleday, p. 94.
17. Ibid., p. 95.
18. Ibid.
19. The Lonely Crowd, pp. 130 ff; 151 ff.

trapolated to possible future situations? With the institutionalization of production goals, no further direction of the individual from society seems possible other than the sanctioning of peer-agents. The "end-of-the-line" seems to have been reached. "Today, in the advanced industrial countries, there is only one frontier left—that of consumption."[20] Where the individual formerly innovated on the frontier of production, he now *adjusts* to others on the *last* frontier —that of consumption.

Innovation has been routinized into the system and taken out of the hands of the men who run it. Institutionalization is thus interpreted as made at the expense of individuality, and the individual has suffered a "loss of function."

. . . it is difficult, as an empirical matter, to decide who is autonomous when we are looking at the seemingly easy and permissive life of a social class [upper socioeconomic levels] in which there are no "problems" left, except for persons striving for autonomy.[21]

Given this interpretation, the individual must rely on himself for future direction by means of his autonomy; ". . . the other-directed person cannot proceed toward autonomy by any other route than that of self-awareness."[22]

By this, we do not interpret Riesman as saying flatly that innovation is no longer possible at the societal level, for he explores such possibilities in the realms of city planning, educational experimentation, and the like. Nor does he fail to point out persistently the rich variety of models for personal exploration and innovation already existent in the society. But he does seem to be saying that these are not sources of direction for the individual without his assertion of autonomy, without his transcending the limitations of other-direction.

3. Personal Relationships

The heavy reliance on peers as agents of direction, on agency itself as the sole remaining source of direction, emphasizes the importance of personal relationships in other-direction. The "hardness of the material" of inner-direction (hard because of structured goals?) is replaced by the "softness of men."[23] This conceptual em-

20. *Individualism Reconsidered,* p. 103.
21. *The Lonely Crowd,* pp. 301–302; 294.
22. *Faces in the Crowd,* p. 736.
23. *Ibid.,* p. 131; 152.

phasis is strongly supported empirically by the increase, in general, of the division of labor launched in the inner-directed era, with the associated phenomena of urbanization, rise of bureaucratic structure, increase in the proportion of labor-intensive industries, and the like.

The necessity of coping with this proliferation of "others"—both at work and at play—and of seeking their approval is such that personal relationships in and of themselves become the main highway to self-definition, to identity; and in so doing, they tend to make other avenues seem like detours without guideposts. "The world of interpersonal relations almost obscures from view the world of physical nature and the supernatural as the setting for the human drama."[24] The peer-agents, engaged in socializing each other in consumption preferences, in the last analysis, consume their own membership.[25]

Socialization in the Other-Directed Society

A few more words will touch on the implications that these changes of direction in American society have for socialization, particularly the socializing agents—the family and the school and the peer group.

Other-directed parents, no longer able to instill in their child the unequivocal goals that an inner-directed society presented, "can only equip the child to do his best, whatever that may turn out to be. What is best is not in their control but in the hands of the school and peer group that will help locate the child eventually in the hierarchy."[26] Since, in a changing world, they can no longer "hold themselves up as exemplars—when both they and the child know better,"[27] they install something like a psychological radar set in him that will enable him to be sensitive to the guidance of others.

Thereafter, the parents influence the children's character only insofar as (a) their own signals mingle with others over the radar, (b) they can locate children in a certain social environment in order to alter to a very limited degree what signals they will receive, (c) they take the risks of a very partial and precarious censorship of incoming messages. Thus the parental role diminishes in importance as compared with the same role

24. *Faces in the Crowd*, p. 7.
25. *The Lonely Crowd*, p. 82; 102.
26. *Ibid.*, p. 48; 65.
27. *Ibid.*, p. 52; 70.

among the inner-directed.[28] The family is no longer a closely knit unit to which [the child] belongs but merely a part of a wider social environment to which he early becomes attentive.[29]

With the diminution of their authority, parents seek to retain what control they can by "manipulation in the form of reasoning,"[30] or they may seek to "force the pace . . . in the child's social life" as, for example, "stage managers for the meetings of three- and four-year-olds."[31] There is, too, less discontinuity between the parents' lives and those of the children. The children have less privacy as anxious parents supervise their affairs, at the same time confronting them with the uncertainty of their supervision. The mass media, as an all-inclusive peer surrogate, beam their messages at the entire family, so that parents and children alike can participate in the discourse of consumption preferences.

In school, too, the social distance between teacher and pupil dwindles, with the manipulation of emotions and the socialization of taste and interest replacing the inner-directed style of impersonal stress on accomplishment.[32] Teachers, increasingly, are taught "to be more concerned with the child's social and psychological adjustment than with his academic progress—indeed, to scan the intellectual performance for signs of social maladjustment."[33] They convey "to the children that what matters is not their industry or learning as such but their adjustment in the group, their cooperation, their (carefully stylized and limited) initiative and leadership."[34]

The curriculum tends to be more "realistic"—as in the emphasis on social studies—with consumption of current affairs diminishing the time spent on more abstract pursuits. And here the subject matter may be vitiated by the effect of community vigilantes on vulnerable teachers. "Thus the children are supposed to learn democracy by underplaying the skills of intellect and overplaying the skills of gregariousness and amiability."[35]

These agents of socialization—the parents and the school—have, then, virtually abdicated their authority to the peer group, for it and

28. *Ibid.*, p. 55; 74.
29. *Ibid.*, p. 26; 41.
30. *Ibid.*, p. 52; 70.
31. *Ibid.*, p. 70; 91.
32. *Ibid.*, pp. 60–64; 79–85.
33. *Ibid.*, p. 60; 80.
34. *Ibid.*, p. 62; 83.
35. *Ibid.*, p. 64; 84.

it alone can determine what is momentarily best and pass judgment on the child's ability to adjust. As agents for each other, the peers are now jury, now defendants; and the peer group becomes the primary and overwhelmingly significant agent of character formation. As it becomes increasingly uniform in age and class composition (because of ecological selection in suburban patterns of living), it increasingly demands submission of the individual to its criteria of taste and style of behavior. Individual performance, indeed, any manifestation of idiosyncratic variation is discouraged in favor of holding the correct preferences in common. The other-directed peer must keep solvent with "counters in a preferential method of relating oneself to others,"[36] with approval as a sort of favorable credit rating.

Three characteristics seem to be salient in such a group. First, since only marginal differentiation is tolerated or even dared, leaders —although powerful—do not lead too far ahead lest the fate of the prematurely streamlined Chrysler overtake them. Second, the group exerts a tyranny over the individual in such a way that other alternatives of direction are seen as an *escape* from it. Thus the peer-group role does not complement other roles as much as it conflicts with them. It is a case of "peer group or else."

. . . we can distinguish conceptually between the needs of society (as a system of social organization) and those of environing groups (as a system of psychological ties and expectations). As so defined, society, the larger territorial organization, often provides the mechanisms by which the individual can be protected against the group, both by formal legal procedures as bills of rights, and by the fact that large-scale organization may permit the social mobility by which individuals can escape from any particular group.[37]

But even in a large-scale organization, the individual may find himself in yet another group where he perforce must manipulate and conciliate others. Thus escape from any particular group is likely to be an appointment in Samarra (a happy metaphor that Riesman has used in another connection). The third characteristic, then, seems to be that such group-direction follows one throughout the stages of life, for occupational roles in labor-intensive industry are subject to the same exigencies of coping with the others. Riesman notes that even in consumption patterns the same mechanisms operate on adults and children alike. "The child may consume comics or toys

36. *The Lonely Crowd*, Doubleday, p. 99.
37. *Individualism Reconsidered*, p. 26.

while the adult consumes editorials and cars; more and more both consume in the same way."[38] The following passage sums up:

The other-directed child, however, faces not only the requirement that he make good but also the problem of defining what good means. He finds that both the definition and evaluation of himself depend on the company he keeps. Approval itself, irrespective of content, becomes almost the only unequivocal good in this situation: one makes good when one is approved of. Thus all power, not merely some power, is in the hands of the actual or imaginary approving group, and the child learns from his parents' reaction to him that nothing in his character, no possession he owns, no inheritance of name or talent, no work he has done is valued for itself but only for its effect on others. Making good becomes almost equivalent to making friends, or at any rate the right kind of friends.[39]

II. AN ALTERNATIVE APPROACH

IN the preceding section we have outlined our understanding of Professor Riesman's main position with reference to the relation between social structure and character in contemporary American society. We have indicated that there is an important area of agreement between us (*i.e.,* Riesman and the authors of this paper), but our specific task in the present paper is to present, and relate to that of Riesman, an alternative interpretation of some of the salient empirical and theoretical problems involved in his position, particularly those concerning the relevance of values to these problems. The present section is devoted to the exposition of our own alternative view, while the third and final one will attempt to bring the comparison of the two to a head in relation to some of the empirical issues involved.

We would like to put the problem in terms of the concept of values in its relation, in the first instance, to the structure and functioning of the society, but also as a factor in the personality of the individual. We will start with a delineation of what we conceive to be the paramount American value-system and will proceed to a discussion of the ways and levels in which it is institutionalized in the structure of the society, with special reference to the areas of Professor Riesman's main concern: work in occupational roles, the family and consumption, and the social context of the development

38. *The Lonely Crowd*, p. 80; pp. 100–101.
39. *Ibid.,* p. 49; 66.

of the individual personality, especially the role of the peer group in the latency and adolescent periods.

There is no clearly settled usage of the concept of value in sociology, anthropology, and psychology, and hence of the ways in which it is to be used in the analysis of social and personality systems. We cannot take space for an exegetical discussion of different usages here, so will confine ourselves to setting forth our own view as clearly as possible and juxtaposing this with that of Riesman.

First we follow Clyde Kluckhohn in defining values as "conceptions of the desirable." Such conceptions are, in the first instance, part of a culture; they may, on the one hand, be more or less fully shared by the human individuals participating in the culture; the degree to which they are *common* to the members of a society or subsystem of it is clearly highly important. Secondly, on the other hand, they may, as conceptions, be more or less explicitly stated in verbal pronouncements. Often values have to be inferred from more diffuse or particularized attitudes and from behavior.

Next, we would assume that values are conceptions of the desirable at the highest level of generality that is applicable to the system of action in question. As we conceive them, they are not concerned with the internal differentiation of the object of evaluation or with the specificities of the situation either for the system as a whole or for subunits within it. Thus to "contain" the expansion of Communist influence in the world is not, in this terminology, a *value* of American society, but a policy *goal* of its government, as is, say, to raise the standard of living of the lowest income groups in the society. Similarly, for a personality, to "get to the office on time today" is not a value, but a goal. Otherwise the concept of value would tend to be identified with the specific normative content in the regulation of behavior in general.

Values, we assume, are located in the first instance in the *culture*. The first-order differentiation of values then concerns the primary classes of objects with which human action is inherently concerned. On the one hand this differentiation would apply to the valuation of the cultural patterns themselves and of the "nonempirical" references in relation to which they are grounded, on the other to the four great categories of empirical objects with which human beings are inevitably implicated, namely social systems, personalities, organisms, and the physical world.

Values we define as conceptions of the desirable *type* of object in each of these categories. Social values, then, are conceptions of the desirable social system; personality values, of the desirable type of personality; and so on. They evaluate the type of society without reference either to its internal differentiation or to particularities of its situation; they are thus concerned only with the *generic* features of the relation of the system to the equally generic features of its situation.

A particularly important aspect of values for our present purposes concerns the *self*-valuation of a social object, *i.e.* a human individual or collectivity. In the case of a personality, this is his "ego-ideal" as a normative self-image. In the case of a social system it is the conception, held by members in common, of what is a *good* social system—in the most important case, a society good *for them,* whatever may be held to be good for others differently situated. In the personality case, we would speak of the values as internalized; in that of the social system, as institutionalized, which implies internalization as well, but not necessarily evenly over the population. The institutionalized values of a society thus constitute the conception of the good society as applied to their own society by its own members.

Using the concept of values for the social system in the above sense, we shall maintain two principal theses with respect to the American value system at the highest level of generality. The first is that there is, and for some time has been, a single relatively well integrated and fully institutionalized system of values in American society, and second, that at this most general level the value-system has not undergone a fundamental change in recent times.[40] Our immediate concern is not with the empirical defense of these two theses, but with the delineation of what we conceive to be the main outline of this value system. Following this delineation we will discuss, only in broad outline because of limitations of space, the main trend of structural differentiation within the society in the recent

40. Most of the distinguished foreign observers of American society emphasize patterns that are consistent with this statement. Their statements are fully reviewed by S. M. Lipset, who also presents important independent evidence in "A Changing American Character?" in *Culture and Social Character,* New York, The Free Press of Glencoe, 1961, Chap. 7. Kluckhohn maintains the same thesis down to the decade of the 1930's; hence it is only for the most recent period that we are forced to differ with him. Our evidence for the thesis of continuity down to the present and the immediately foreseeable future will be presented below.

period and the types of strain and the concomitant patterns of deviant behavior associated with this very large-scale process.

We have stated above that the primary roots of a system of social values lie in the cultural rather than the social system. In the American case this means, above all, in its religious heritage, centering on "ascetic" Protestantism—a proposition on which there seems now to be fairly wide agreement. Our task here is not, however, to attempt to analyze this heritage and its development, but rather, taking it for granted, to delineate the value-system at the social level and to test its fit with the facts of those areas of American social life that figure most prominently in Riesman's work.

The most general formula we would propose for the value-system is that it represents, for the society as a system, an orientation of *instrumental activism.* When we say "instrumental" we contrast it with "consummatory." The society is conceived to be not an "end in itself" but rather an instrumentality to ends that in some sense are outside or beyond it. In terms of the cultural heritage, these ends have been defined in religious terms, the most important conception being that man, including his social organization, was to be conceived as the instrument of God's will. In secular terms it generally takes the form of what may be called a secular "individualism." The society exists in order to "facilitate" the achievement of the good life for individuals. A crucial question then concerns the content of this good life for the individual: is it in some sense "self-indulgence" or is it in turn his dedication to values and goals that are "above and beyond" his purely "personal" needs or interests?

It is at this point that the relevance of the other component of the system, what we call its "activism," becomes relevant. This essentially is to say that the society is conceived to have a *moral mission* and that, relative to this mission though *not* relative to the interests of the society as such (*i.e.,* its "consummatory" interests), the individual in turn is also conceived to be an instrumentality. In religious background terms again, this refers to the Divine Will, which enjoins the building of a Kingdom of God on Earth. In secular terms, this becomes the building of a good society in which the primary obligation of the individual is *achievement.* Not every exhibition of "prowess," however, is valued; the achievement must be "worth while," and the criteria of worth-whileness must be found in some kind of "contribution" to the building (not merely the maintenance) of the good society.

The term "activism" as used above was meant, as a characterization of a set of values for a social system, to refer to an orientation to active mastery of its external situation in an empirical sense of situation. Though indirectly including the physical environment and other societies, in the most direct sense, in analytical terms, "situation" here means the motivations and behavior of the human individuals who are members of the society itself. We interpret active mastery to mean essentially the *mobilization* of resources, among which the commitments of individuals occupy the key place, in the interest of a mission for the society that is not defined as the "gratification" of individual wishes in the usual psychological sense.

But does this "mission" imply a *goal* for the society if not for the individual? This is in one sense a semantic issue. If the question refers to a source of leverage on the individual, who is expected instrumentally to serve an interest beyond himself, the answer is clearly yes. On the other hand, we prefer to reserve the term "goal," as applied to the society as a system, for a specific state of affairs, toward the attainment of which the system as such is conceived to be striving and which, when attained, is conceived as a definitive realization of the "desirable" for the society. Communist societies, for example, may be conceived as oriented toward such a goal: the achievement of the state of "communism." The American value-system, however, does not imply the primacy of such a goal. Its values place the *unit* of the system, in particular the individual, in an instrumental position. *His goal* cannot be self-indulgence or the maximization of the gratification of his personal wishes, but must be achievement in the interest of the good society. The society itself does not, however, tend toward a specific goal, but rather to a prospect of progressive improvement of the level of realization of its values.

What may be called instrumental or institutionalized individualism is therefore a very important keynote of the American value system. What we have in mind must, however, be clearly distinguished from the "utilitarian" version of individualism which has played such an important part in the intellectual history of the English-speaking peoples. Instrumental individualism differs from the latter on two counts. First, the utilitarian version, by postulating the givenness of the individual's wants, does not take account of the element of activism that we have emphasized; there is simply no basis of an obligation to achievement rather than an orientation to hedonistic enjoyment.

Secondly, there are no adequate criteria of the worth-whileness of individual goals and action; these are left to the theoretically arbitrary discretion of the individual. Instrumental individualism, on the other hand, imposes the obligation of contribution to the goodness of the society. For the individual this means, first, the obligation of commitment to an instrumental role and, second, that the criteria of what is worth while are *socially* given. Whereas the *implementation* of his obligation is left very largely within his own discretion, the normative criteria that define it are not; they are institutionalized. It is in this direction that we will have to look for the component of order in the most recent phases of American social development, which we think Riesman overlooks.

There is one further implication of our position on values which needs to be brought out before we take up some of the complexities of their institutionalization in the society. There is no question in our minds that the obligation of individual achievement is paramount at that level. But the criteria of worth-whileness involve contribution to the functioning of a certain kind of society. Hence there is no presumption that a particular contribution that can be identified as "purely individual" has any precedence over one that is on some level collective. In value terms, there is no basis of choice as to whether contribution through collective organization or "independently" of such organization is better; it is a pragmatic question depending on the more specific nature of the contribution and the situational circumstances. Thus if economic production is valued and if it is more effective in large organizations, we should have large organizations. It is, however, true that the absence of a specific definitive goal for the society as a system precludes the primacy of the over-all paramount collectivity in organizing all activity in the society. But this is a special case and does not imply that at many intermediate levels collective organization stands in opposition to the value-system; on the contrary it receives a powerful legitimation.

Structural Differentiation

We have noted above that the value-system for a society is couched on a level of generality such that it can define only the generic type of society in relation to a generic type of situation. As such it cannot, without further specification, serve as an adequate guide for the conduct of individuals or collectivities as units of the system. In dealing with the problem of normative specification we come to a central point of our argument; this is that the mode and level of specification required for normative integration of a society, for order in the regulation of the action of its units, is a function not only of its value-system, but of its more detailed structure, in particular of the kinds and levels of *differentiation* of that structure. Structural differentiation is, however, a function of several variables other than the value-system, and can change independently of any change in the value-system itself. One of our principal theses about American society is that, whereas the paramount value-system has (as we believe) remained stable, the structure of the society has been undergoing a major process of differentiation. We believe that a major part of the phenomena that form the center of the analyses of Riesman, Kluckhohn, and others are results of these structural changes and can be analyzed in terms, not of the breakdown or disappearance of the component of normative order, or of a new one at the general-value level, but of new *specifications* of the general value-system, in relation to new structural and situational conditions. Another component, about which we will also have something to say, is the malintegration which is a necessary concomitant of extensive and rapid structural change.

Here, both for reasons of space and because the levels of specification called for are a function of particular modes and levels of differentiation, we propose only to outline the most general principles according to which the analysis of specification should be carried out, then to move over directly to some problems of empirical interpretation of the relevant aspects of American society.

The Inner-Directed Case

It may be useful to couch the beginning of this discussion in terms of Riesman's own scheme of analysis as outlined above. It is our view that the specifications of expected conduct for units of the social structure in the tradition-directed case include, and indeed focus at, the lowest level of specification—namely that of the specific procedures that should be taken in the attainment of institutionalized unit goals. Every social system must institutionalize a normative order in this area, but we feel that the most important range of variability

is that of the level of generality at which this order is institutionalized. In the traditionalistic society, to a far higher degree than in
others, units, both collective and individual, must fulfill detailed
prescriptions of *what* they should do. In the course of the evolution
that Riesman outlines, these detailed prescriptions are suspended;
it is left up to the unit to decide the "what" in the sense of *how* to
proceed to a goal. But we think we differ from Riesman in interpreting what this means. If we interpret him correctly, he seems to suggest that the inner-directed unit is left without institutional guidance
in the area of procedures, of mobilization and utilization of facilities.
Our view is rather that he is still given guidance, but of a different
kind on a different level, one that increases the stress of his own
responsibility.

What come to be institutionalized are no longer the specific
procedures to be taken, but certain *more generalized criteria* for the
choice of specific procedures. The crucial case here is the criterion of
economic rationality, which states in general that value of yield
should be related to cost, so that a commitment involving excessive
cost in relation to probable yield should be avoided. There are many
complex questions concerning the relation of this pattern to social
structure, particularly respecting markets and the monetary system.
In our opinion, however, there is little doubt that, while the institutionalization of norms in this area has necessitated breakdown of
more specific normative prescriptions, this breakdown is only one
side of the coin. The other side is the new development of *positive*
institutionalization of generalized normative criteria that make it
possible to handle a situation in which both the resources and the
destinations of production are far more mobile than in a tradition-
directed situation.

Perhaps we are not far wrong in feeling that the prototype of
Riesman's inner-directed man is the nineteenth-century business
entrepreneur. By contrast with earlier forms of the organization of
economic production, the classic entrepreneur was precisely characterized by independence from the detailed prescriptions of earlier
tradition. He enjoyed a wider margin of freedom and concomitant responsibility. But this did not occur without positive institutionaliza-
ton of the more generalized criteria by which he was expected to
operate.

Our understanding of the nature of this new institutionalization fits with Riesman's formula for the case. It is that a set of *goals* had become institutionalized, and hence internalized in the personality of the individual. In the paradigmatic case of the entrepreneur, this is the *dual* goal of contribution to productivity of the economy and the measurement of success in this endeavor by the symbol of profit. Whatever the qualifications that must be made about the adequacy of the profit criterion in a free-enterprise economy, and they are many and serious, in the broadest sense we contend that this is precisely the core of the set of mechanisms that made possible a relative integration of a competitive market economy, in part through the institutionalization of the dual goal of production and profit. It is true that this could be metaphorically described by Adam Smith's famous figure of the "invisible hand." But since Durkheim, though the mechanisms are invisible to the ordinary person, we need not represent them as the operation of a "supernatural" agency; they are empirically understandable in terms of our general knowledge of social systems. They quite definitely include patterns of normative order defining not only goals, but acceptable ways of going about attaining them.

There is, however, an important sociological qualification that must be entered to the formula that it was "the individual" who was the primary focus of this internalized productive-achievement goal. The primarily structural context of this type of achievement was the family firm, which is still predominant in the small business sector of the economy today. Above all it was the commitment of family property and fortunes to the enterprise, in a sense structurally different from commitment to an occupational role today, which was the main focus of responsibility.

In our analytical terms the emergence of entrepreneurial free enterprise represented above all the differentiation of a major sector of the society, where economic primacy could have far wider scope than in earlier types of social organization. This has meant that the differentiated values of the economy as a subsystem of the society could predominate in this area and be more directly internalized in the personalities of those responsible for it. And one major aspect of this differentiation was in turn the emancipation of the entrepreneur from a whole range of the traditionalistic restrictions that bound his predecessors in leadership of productive functions, but another was the institutionalization of a more generalized normative order.

The Other-Directed Case

Let us now apply the same analytical logic to the next phase in Riesman's series, the shift from inner- to other-direction. Here our thesis is that in the main structure of the American economy, and with special reference to the bearing of this on the system of occupational roles more generally, the primary incidence of patterns of order has moved up still another step in the scale of levels of generality. This means that certain earlier bases of institutionalized prescription have dropped out; therefore it is quite correct to say that on one level previous institutionalized guides to conduct for the individual have been lost. At the individual level we think it is broadly correct to say that a very general goal of "success" has tended to become the predominant one. We would, however, insist that it has the same basic duality of structure that characterized the goal of the entrepreneur; it is a goal of achievement on the one hand, of symbolic recognition of that achievement on the other. Recognition of success or approval is the equivalent, for the new phase, of profit for the older one.

To interpret this statement it is essential to see the occupational role of the individual in its structural setting. On the one hand, in the pace-setting aspects of the social structure, the burden of full responsibility for producing a marketable[41] product is no longer typically taken by "the individual" but by an organization. The decisions are made by individuals, but in their capacities as officers of the organization. Business entrepreneurs, like many others, perform their functions predominantly in occupational roles. Their personal return is not "profit" in the older economic sense, but occupational remuneration, which is an individualized success-symbol as well as, of course, an essential facility for household maintenance.

This seems to be the context to which Riesman refers when he speaks of the productivity function having become institutionalized in the society. What we disagree with is simply the possible implication that somehow the new system can operate on a lower level of average individual responsibility than was the case before; we believe the exact opposite to be true.

It is also important to note that the rapidly increasing develop-

41. We mean this in a broader sense than that of economic primacy alone. Higher education is "marketed" to students, even though not financed on "business" principles.

ment of a system of occupational roles make possible the great extension of certain principles of social organization beyond the business sphere. This is to say that, in the business case, the "profit-orientation" no longer applies in the old sense to "the individual" but is transferred to the firm as a complex organization. Other organizations are not governed by a primacy of profit orientation in this sense, *e.g.* governmental agencies, educational organizations, hospitals, and clinics, to say nothing of churches and families. But *for the individual* it becomes increasingly indifferent what the "goal" of the employing organization may be, in the sense that the social structuring of his role can be treated as, to a substantial degree, independent of that goal.[42] Thus engineers are employed by business concerns, but also by various governmental, educational, and research organizations. Salary in all these cases is an important measure of past or expected achievement level, but this does not define expectations for the organization so much as for the *role*.

Essentially what has happened is that a level of social structure, the operating organization or collectivity, has developed between the basic social function, which defines what we interpret to be "goals" in Riesman's sense, and the role-expectations applying to the individual. It follows that this order of goals can no longer be directly the individual's responsibility, and cannot be directly specified to him as part of his preparation for his role.

A corresponding process of differentiation has gone on in the other aspect of the individual's role-participation. We stressed above that the classical entrepreneur was the head of a family business. Here neither the property interests nor the fortunes of the kinship unit were dissociated from the productive organization except at the lower, the "employee," level. In the phase of structural differentiation with which we are here concerned, the organization responsible for the primary functional contribution to the society becomes dissociated from the "consumption" interests of those involved in it. It is of course true that the institutionalization of occupational roles means that the family becomes overwhelmingly dependent on the occupational income of its employed members for its standard of living. But this is a very different matter from the kinship unit itself acting as a productive unit. The family does not stand or fall by the

42. By "goal" here we mean essentially what Barnard meant by "organization purpose" (cf. C. I. Barnard, *The Functions of the Executive*, Cambridge, Mass., Harvard University Press, 1938).

fortunes of *this particular* productive unit, but "labor" at these levels has become a mobile resource transferable from one unit to another. Hence not only is the typical employed individual not the focal center of a direct productive unit, but he must function in the occupational world in a role that is far more independent of the kinship base in which he occupies an ascribed position than had previously been the case. This applies above all from generation to generation; the imperatives of the organization preclude guaranteeing generational succession in particular roles, even though the same occupational categories may be acceptable. But it also means that the household must be structurally "segregated" from the occupational organization, in a much more radical sense, than was previously the case.

What are the implications of this for the element of order we have emphasized? In the first place the expectations of order most directly relevant to primary social function, such as economic production, no longer confront "the individual" so directly; his personal goals are not directly of this order. They have been transferred to the employing collectivity so that, even where an individual takes high responsibility for the operation of such a collectivity, it is on its behalf, not on his own behalf, that he takes it. This shift does not mean that operation ceases to be dependent on individuals, but that the mechanisms through which this dependence works out have changed. The sociological conclusion that the regulative functions of normative order are just as vital and just as definitely operative in the new society as in the old seems to us to be inescapable.

Conversely, a new order of structural differentiation between production and consumption has entered in. The household unit, even in the higher groups, is no longer in the same sense as before a productive unit, in the economic and certain other occupationally relevant senses. Consumption has, in this sense, been "set free" from a set of constraints previously operating upon it.

The individual is in a sense left "in the middle." On the one hand, his personal occupational goals have become structurally differentiated from the goals of the employing organization. He cannot in a one-to-one sense "identify" with them. On the other hand, these same occupational goals and interests have become differentiated from his household and kinship associations, so that they cannot in the old sense be identified with the goals of the family either.

Hence it is quite correct to say that two older elements of order that have defined expectations for a strategic class of individuals have been weakened in their direct impact on him. But this is not to say that the *functions* previously performed by these elements of order have ceased to be performed, or are today performed, if at all, only in terms of a radically different system of generalized values. One set of functions of order is, as we have suggested, to be found in the restructuring of the family, which we will discuss presently. But we feel also that there has been a new structure of order developing in the sphere of the occupational expectations of the individual, which has been filling the gap left by the changes Riesman has emphasized. To see the main outline of this new order, it is necessary to say something of the general trends of change of the American occupational and educational systems.

The Occupational System

We may say that three primary processes of change in the occupational system have been going on, which may be called, respectively, quantitative *expansion, differentiation,* and qualitative *upgrading.* By expansion we mean, *relative* to the population of working age, the increasing proportion performing structurally differentiated occupational roles in the above sense, not only "in the labor force" in the statistical sense, but in roles that are structurally segregated from nonoccupational contexts, particularly those of kinship. Perhaps the largest single contribution to this expansion has come from the immense relative decline in the proportion of the population engaged in agriculture; since the family farm is the basic unit of agricultural production, this case will illustrate our meaning.

The second fundamental process of change has been one of qualitative differentiation. If it was ever possible to say reasonably, as the Marxists have, that the only two important types of occupation besides agriculture were those of proprietor of a business enterprise and worker employed in one, that time has long passed for our type of society. Perhaps the most important single direction of differentiation has been in the immense proliferation of *technical* occupational roles. Though still quantitatively only a small proportion of the total labor force, strategically the most important of these have been the professional roles, which have been the fastest-growing category of all. Among these, in turn, the roles involved in scientific investigation, in training in the pure and applied sciences, and in the practical uses of science are the most prominent. As part of what we just referred to as "expansion" it is notable to what extent the study and the management of human relations and personality have become the object of differentiated occupational roles.

A close second to the technical roles in differentiation are those that may be called "executive" or in some sense "managerial," which have emerged in many different fields and of course at many different levels. Naturally, this type of differentiation is the consequence and concomitant of the immense proliferation of increasingly large-scale organization within the society. There are complex patterns of overlap between what we are calling technical and executive role-types, e.g., the person trained as an engineer or a lawyer functioning as a business or governmental administrator. But there cannot be any doubt that both the differentiation of executive from technical roles and the internal differentiation of the latter category have proceeded a very long way in even the last half-century.

The third most important aspect of differentiation has probably been the "occupationalizing" of many functions that previously were handled within functionally diffuse social structures, such as kinship and the local community. The whole field of social and personal relations, on which we will comment presently, is one of them; another very important one is the field of communications, perhaps particularly where content is only peripherally "utilitarian."

By "upgrading" we mean the process by which the general levels of competence and responsibility required for adequate occupational role-performance have been rising. For the case of responsibility the most important indices lie at two levels: first the scale of organization, and second the replacement of traditionalistic norms in interorganizational relations by generalized normative patterns that leave much determination to be reached by explicit decision-making processes. In the former context it is important to bear in mind that not only do large organizations require a very high level of responsibility on the part of their "top" executives, but that as they become more complex, the number of echelons requiring substantial levels of such responsibility increases. We feel confident that a careful analysis would reveal that in contemporary organizations not only larger absolute numbers, but larger *proportions* of those involved are carrying more complex decision-making responsibilities than was true fifty years ago. Then, in the interorganizational field, the very

fact that the automatisms of the ideal type of pure economic competition cannot be relied upon means that very complex processes of
adjustment and regulation must continually be going on.

In the technical fields the most tangible indices of the change are
the levels and spread of qualifications of training for occupational
functions. It is true both that higher levels than were ever before
required have become commonplace, and that the range of incidence
of such qualifications has immensely widened. The relevance of this
to the educational system is obvious and will be briefly discussed
presently.

The above shifts are most conspicuous at or near the top of the
occupational pyramid. An equally significant process has been going
on at and near the bottom. In broad terms, this is the elimination of
an immense proportion of the previous lowest-level occupational
functions and roles. One of the most notable phenomena in this field
is the fact that, after the 1920's, the proportion of the labor force
engaged as "workers" in manufacturing industry steadily declined in
spite of the immense increases in manufacturing production. This
shift and the corresponding ones in other areas have been the product
of mechanization, and now "automation," and also of improved
organization of the work process. Now, not only have most of the
older unskilled "pick-and-shovel" type jobs been eliminated, but an
increasing proportion of the "semiskilled" machine-tending and
assembly-line types of jobs have followed them.

It is our general contention, then, that an occupational system
that has generalized the occupational role-type farther than ever
before, that has become immensely differentiated and greatly upgraded in average levels of competence and responsibility, cannot
be making lower rather than higher demands on the individual
persons who participate in it. First, the performance of functions
within diffuse social structures is very generally accompanied by a
larger proportion of ascriptive specification of processes than in occupational contexts. Second, differentiation of the system automatically
produces more complex problems of integration of the highly differentiated parts than before; and third, the highest levels of functional requirement, in contexts both of technical and of organizational
responsibility, require independence, initiative, and responsibility on
higher levels than before.

If this be true, then we think it follows that such a system must
and does involve both institutionalization of determinate normative

culture in the society and internalization in personalities, at higher and on the whole firmer levels than before.

On the societal level, the relevant normative patterns are to be looked for in three main places. The first of these is in the standards of competence which operate predominantly in the technical aspects of occupational role-functions. Increasingly these standards are rooted in the sciences and applied from this source to the various fields of operation. Not only have the older sciences been rapidly developing, but the range of science has been expanding so that a larger and larger proportion of the field of social action has been covered by such standards. The second area is that most directly involved in organizational responsibility, the normative structure relevant to the "good"—good in the sense both of effectiveness and of compatibility with the social interest—conduct of organizations. Because of the general process of differentiation, this organizational responsibility is a special concern of a smaller proportion of the labor force, but in the society it has become a more rather than less prominent area of concern. Finally, the third primary point of incidence of this normative culture is that at which these many functions have to be integrated in the interest of the society as a whole. We feel that the law as a system is very crucial on this level, and it surely cannot be said that concern with law is atrophying in our society. Law, however, does not exhaust this category. Other examples that fit in the same general category are important areas of political functioning and of the operation of "fiduciary" functions.

If, then, we contend that a restructured, more generalized normative order has become an increasing instead of diminishing source of "direction" to individuals' action, how do we conceive its relation to that "direction"? With Riesman, we think it is fruitful to treat the problem in the context of the process of socialization. The best introduction to the structural setting of this process is, we feel, a brief sketch of some highlights of the educational system in the United States and of the altered structural position of the family, since, in our opinion, these are the two primary agencies of the socialization function.

Some Highlights of American Education

The same general classification of processes that we used in connection with the occupational system is also applicable to education. There have been processes of expansion, of differentiation, and of upgrading.

Since something approaching universal primary education, at least in the earlier grades, was achieved more than half a century ago in this country, the most conspicuous expansion has occurred at the higher educational levels—and here we mean expansion relative to the size of the age-cohorts, not the component resulting from increase of population as such. This expansion has gone on all along the line. Whereas in the last quarter of the nineteenth century it was still a minority, about 35 per cent, who had any secondary education at all, recently it can be said that over 80 per cent have completed a high-school course. It seems that we are approaching a situation where only a residual minority, who are essentially "defectives" of some sort, will do without a high-school education.

In the meantime, the proportion going on from high school to some kind of college has also steadily increased, now having reached the neighborhood of 35 per cent. And though, of course, the percentages are much smaller, the same general trend is not only conspicuous, but most rapid, at the highest level of all, namely postgraduate training of some professional or semiprofessional character.

This process of expansion is quite clearly at the same time a very notable process of upgrading. Whereas up to about the end of World War I it could be said that there was still a considerable problem of illiteracy in this country, this has almost disappeared. As noted, the normal minimum is approaching completion of high school, and the college sector, already about one third of the cohort, is rising steadily,[43] to say nothing of the postcollege level.

It is in the nature of formal education that in the earlier stages it should be relatively undifferentiated. The common foundation of the three R's has to be shared by all. But by essentially the same token, the process of expansion and upgrading is almost by definition at the same time a process of differentiation. As the scale is pushed upward

43. It has frequently been alleged that this immense quantitative expansion of the educational system has been accompanied by a serious decline of qualitative standards. This is a complex question. Recently, however, Lipset (*op. cit.*) has surveyed the available evidence, which is admittedly fragmentary, and finds no support for this view. Even if there were a moderate average decline of standards, the net result would be an impressive upgrading of the average educational level of the population. The burden of the proof would seem clearly to be on the side of those who claim, not only that there has been a decline, but that it has been so great as to cancel out the quantitative gains.

there are not only on the average higher levels of educational attainment, but an increasingly wide variety of kinds. It is no accident that, at the same period when the university rather than the college came to constitute the upper layer of the educational system, the traditional rigid language-mathematics curriculum broke down. Perhaps President Eliot's elective system represented an extreme reaction, but the varieties of human learning were by that time too diverse to to be successfully contained in the older strait jacket of predominantly classical studies, particularly the rote-learning of dead languages. The counterpart of this is the immense development of postgraduate university studies, the bringing of medical and legal education into the university setting, and the enormous proliferation of the sciences and the many professions associated with them. The immense variety presented today by the offering of a "university college," like Harvard, Chicago, or the University of California at Berkeley, illustrates the point.

What then of the connection between education and future occupational role? Again there would seem to be no doubt about one major trend: that entrance to the higher occupational role-levels has been becoming increasingly dependent on educational qualifications. The myth about the superior virtues of the "school of hard knocks" attended by the man without "book-learning" still lingers and will doubtless be with us for a long time, but the facts of the realistic structure of opportunity do not bear the myth out.

Even in the business world, at least college attendance, distinctly preferably a bachelor's degree, is certainly an important if not yet essential prerequisite of a career. Indeed an increasingly important group of business executives now have postgraduate training, both in schools of business administration and in other professional fields, above all engineering and law. What is true to this degree for business goes without saying for the proliferating technical specialties, where a career is clearly out of the question with only a high-school education.

This development on the positive side of the connection between education and occupational status is clearly complemented by the decreasing importance of ascriptive bases of higher occupational status, at least standing alone. It is of course true that children of the higher groups have important differential advantages in access to higher occupational and educational opportunity. But they must now go through the educational channel, whereas this was previously unnecessary, and they must measure up to the educational standards. And the universalization of the principles of educational achievement means that the same facilities also, with certain qualifications, become accessible to persons born without the advantages of ascriptive status. Otherwise how account for such phenomena as the extraordinary success story of the American Jew?

Not only is there, thus, a very close, indeed increasingly close, connection between educational attainment and future occupational career status, but there is solid evidence that *academic* attainment within the educational system is the principal selective mechanism that operates. Let us cite two kinds of evidence. First, a study of four thousand high-school boys in the Metropolitan Boston area, by Samuel Stouffer, Florence R. Kluckhohn, and Talcott Parsons, has shown unmistakably that the overwhelmingly predominant criterion of selection between those who do and do not go to college is the academic record of the pupil in school performance. It is interesting that the decision focuses primarily on entrance into the college preparatory course in senior high school (under New England conditions), and that it is made on the basis of *achievement in primary school* and the first year of junior high school. The influence of family socioeconomic status, which was carefully studied, does not operate independently of school record, but as a factor predisposing to good school records,[44] and through this to occupational success.

The second type of evidence we have in mind concerns the process of selection operating between the college and the various graduate and professional schools. Here it seems to be abundantly clear that academic achievement counts very heavily indeed. The proportion of college graduates going on to postgraduate work has,

44. It is important also to point out that the results of this study do not bear out the common view, particularly put forward by Prof. Allison Davis of the University of Chicago, that school achievement is determined by middle-class values through the mechanism of systematic discrimination by teachers against lower-class children. The relation between ability (as measured by I.Q.) and school performance (as measured by grade records) remains essentially constant from the first grade through the high school. Hence unless the I.Q. tests themselves, as administered in the first grade, are the source of the bias, we have no evidence for its existence. It may be further noted that in this study approximately 50 per cent of the high-ability, lower-class boys in fact did go to college. It remains true that the *low-*ability lower-class boy has a far smaller chance of going to college than does the low-ability higher-class boy. Thus it may be said that high status predisposes *both* to good school work and to occupational success, not to occupational success without good school work.

as noted, been continually increasing. A general atmosphere of increasingly serious attention to studies in the colleges has been widely noted, particularly in the years since World War II. In our opinion this is very directly related to the problem faced, in terms of their own ambitions, by an increasing proportion of students of securing admission to the graduate school of their choice.[45]

In general, therefore, corresponding to the occupational picture, we have an educational picture of rapid expansion, upgrading, and differentiation. In our view this picture is not consistent with the interpretation that internalized norms, values, and indeed goals have lessened in average importance for the typical individual going through the system. Above all, the educational picture is not consistent with the conception that normative patterns, inculcated by teachers and by the faculties of colleges and universities, are playing a smaller part than they did earlier in the orientation of the oncoming generation.

Trends in the American Family

Before approaching the problem of the role of the peer group in socialization, which is so central to Riesman's ideas, we must say something about the family. Our general view is that, in the time period under consideration, the American family has been undergoing an important process of restructuring, which is part of the more general process of differentiation we have been stressing. It has first become a much more differentiated unit than before, and hence its functions relative to those of other units have become more specialized. In the process, as always and necessarily happens, there has been a "loss of function" to other units, which include, at the childhood level, the school and peer group and to some extent the mass media, and at the adult level, above all economic organization and

45. Perhaps one example from personal experience is in order. When the senior author of this paper came to Harvard in 1927, any honors graduate of any reputable college could be admitted to the Graduate School of Arts and Sciences in the social sciences without question. In the postwar years the Department of Social Relations has rejected approximately four out of five applicants who, on the older basis, would readily have gained admission. For graduates of Harvard College, not attaining the A.B. degree *magna cum laude* is almost fatal to chances of admission. See Talcott Parsons, *Report to the Dean of the Faculty of Arts and Sciences on the First Ten Years of the Department of Social Relations,* Cambridge, Mass., Harvard University, 1957.

other occupationally organized types of units, such as hospitals, but also certain voluntary associations.

The most conspicuous change is the one already alluded to, where functions of economic production have been transferred to other units. Also, however, through private and social insurance and other agencies, even important parts of the older responsibility for financial security have been transferred. The broad result has been to concentrate family functions on what, in certain respects, may be called the highly personal relations of its members to each other.

Associated with this is the increasing structural "isolation" of the nuclear family. Seen in comparative terms, this is particularly conspicuous in the setting of kinship as such—relative, that is, to "extended" kinship relations. The new marriage establishes a unit, which in residence, economic support, and a wide variety of relationships, is independent of the families of orientation of both partners. This isolation is strongly reinforced by geographical mobility, since in a decreasing proportion of cases are the parents of either marriage partner resident in the same local community, especially at the neighborhood level. Isolation, however, in this sense, has the further aspect that there is far less continuity of neighborhood relations over long periods, to say nothing of that of generations, than in other societies or in our own past. It is the nuclear family that is the primary unit of our processes of social mobility in both the geographical and status senses.

These changes, which we interpret as primarily processes of structural differentiation, have not led to any general tendency to "dissolution" of the family; rather, we think, the contrary. Of this there are such evidences as, first, that the proportion of the population married and living with their spouses has increased rather than decreased; it now stands at the highest level in the history of census data. Second, the divorce rate, after reaching a peak after the war, has considerably receded. Third, home ownership of single-family dwellings is at an all-time high, with an immense relative as well as absolute increase since the war. Finally, fourth, the postdepression revival of the birth rate has persisted, so that it is no longer possible to interpret it as simply an economic recovery phenomenon. Indeed, the general "familistic" trend has gone so far that some of our ideological bellwethers are coming to view it with alarm, as evidence that interest in occupational concerns in declining. In this connection, whatever the masculine role, it is interesting, and in line with our general view, that this process of reinforcement of the nuclear family has coincided with a very large increase in the participation of married women in the labor force.[46]

Our view, then, is that the family has become substantially further differentiated from other agencies in the social structure than previously. Its primary societal functions are now much more sharply defined than before: the socialization of children and the psychological or personality "tension-management" of its adult members. On this new structural basis, after a considerable period of crisis, it has now begun at least to be stabilized.

This restructuring of the relation of the family to the wider society has been accompanied by important internal changes, which involve the fundamental roles of the sexes and the generations in relation to each other and have an important bearing on the socialization function. The first of these is a shift in the balance of the sex roles, which is often, with only partial accuracy, described as a decline of masculine "authority." Our interpretation of the shift is that, broadly speaking, as the family has become a more specialized agency in terms of societal function, the "managerial" responsibility for the implementation of its functions has tended to become increasingly concentrated in the wife-mother role, whereas the husband-father has tended to assume more of a "fiduciary"—"chairman of the board"—type of role, concentrating his primary commitments more in the field of extrafamilial functions, particularly through his occupational role. This shift naturally appears to some as an "abdication" of masculine prerogative, but we think of it rather as an aspect of the "loss of function" which *always* accompanies processes of structural differentiation. Essentially, this is to say that the "average" woman is trained to be more of a specialist in "human relations" and the management of motivationally subtle psychological problems than is the average man (discounting of course the senses in which men on occupational bases can become higher-level experts in certain of these fields). The more that functions other than this type of management are dissociated from the family, the more a differentiated specifically feminine role comes into its own, and the more it is emancipated from an authority that was grounded

46. Cf. Manpower Commission Report. The broad data on the family situation were summarized in Talcott Parsons and R. F. Bales, *Family, Socialization and Interaction Process,* New York, The Free Press of Glencoe, 1955, Chap. 1. The trend since these data were brought together has been somewhat further in the same direction.

in other functional imperatives, such as the maintenance of family property through business enterprise.

The related shift in the generation roles is, we feel, intimately connected with this. Essentially it is that the child is no longer to the same extent placed in a situation to which he has to "adapt" in the sense of "conforming"; but *his* "problems" are more explicitly taken into account and made the object of more or less deliberate management. This is connected with the sex-role shift in that the average woman, both by virtue of her own socialization and by virtue of her actual role-responsibilities in the family, which include far more continual and intimate contact with the children, is better fitted than her husband to undertake the active management of these problems, so far as it is undertaken at all.

One aspect of the generation shift is, necessarily, greater permissiveness to children, more concern with them as persons. The crucial question is whether the essential feature of this aspect is the abdication of parental authority, and still more of responsibility, in the interest of letting children do anything they want, or is rather a new way of "leading" the child, rather than "forcing" him, to higher levels of growth through the internalization of social object-systems and patterns of normative culture. It is definitely our view that the latter is the main trend, though of course on the way there are many actual failures of responsibility.

If our interpretation is correct, then a very important apparent paradox must be faced. As a condition of building up motivation to the higher levels of autonomous and independent achievement, it is necessary to cultivate *dependency* in the relation of child to parent, at the appropriate stage. We feel that the greater and more explicit emotional intensity of American family relations, particularly between mother and pre-oedipal child, is directly linked with the greater requirements that the child has to face later on in developing capacity for independent achievement without the guidance of specific parental role-models that could be presumed, in an earlier type of social situation, to be more nearly adequate.

Thus on the one hand, by cultivating intense attachments, the American family deprives the young child of the emotionally "cool" early independence conspicuous above all in the English family. But this dependency in turn is the psychological foundation on which is built a later autonomy that helps to equip him for facing situations that are specifically *unstructured* by comparison with our own earlier and other social systems. What seems to many foreigners to be the incredible leeway given to American latency-period and adolescent children is thus linked with the intensive concern of parents, particularly mothers, with the children's attachment to them, especially in the earlier periods. To us this is an instance of the increasing mobility of resources constituting one of the central conditions of the development of an industrial society.

Look, now, at the structural situation facing the child in these terms. In the pre-oedipal period within his own family he has been very intensively "enveloped" in a "close emotional corporation." The condition of such envelopment is the existence of a group, the members of which are bound to each other by essentially ascriptive ties, and who do not compete with one another. Then, first in the immediate neighborhood, the child is exposed to relations to others, with whom his parents have no ascriptive ties at all—most definitely his playmates are not cousins, or even the children of close family friends, but are likely to be the children of relative strangers. Then, on entering school, he is exposed to a highly formalized process in which, regardless of sex and family relation, he must strive to achieve in a context where the judge is an impersonal teacher. It is crucial here that his achievement in the first few years of schooling will become the primary basis of his occupational future, which, in the American system, is *the* primary aspect of his total future as a person.[47]

Seen in this perspective, the recent changes in the American family may be said to be adjustments to the requirements of the type of society we have sketched above, as those requirements apply to the earlier stages of the socialization process for adult roles in that

47. Seen in this context, the nursery school is an interesting phenomenon. It may be regarded as a response primarily to two complementary pressures. One is the difficulty faced by the child in unregulated peer relations in the neighborhood. The other is the parents', above all the mother's, drive to get him started on independence, which we believe is only secondarily motivated by her understandable desire to "get him off her hands" for part of the time. Essentially what the nursery school does is to provide an opportunity for working out relationships to age-mates to whom the ascribed relation of siblings does not apply, but under adult supervision and without the process of formal evaluation of performance that is the critical feature of the regular school. It fits very directly into the analysis put forward by S. N. Eisenstadt (*From Generation to Generation*, New York, The Free Press of Glencoe, 1956) concerning the mechanisms that must operate in mediating between the particularism of family involvements and the universalism of an achievement-oriented adult status system.

society. There has indeed been quantitative expansion in the newer type of family function—witness the proportion married and with children. But most important for our purposes, there has been both differentiation and upgrading. Differentiation in the present context applies above all to the functions of the family relative to other agencies in the socialization process, notably after the early period: the school and the peer group. This we will take up presently. But the most important point to make here is that, in relation to its function in the socialization process, the American family has been subject to a quite definite upgrading process, not, as is so frequently suggested, a downgrading process. The requirement of preparing the child for high levels of independence, competence, and responsibility means that as socializing agent the family cannot do its job unless it emancipates its children from dependence on the parents, an emancipation that precludes parents from being too definite role-models for the child's own life course. What Riesman interprets as the abdictation of the parents from their socializing responsibility can therefore be interpreted in exactly the opposite way. If parents attempted to impose their role-patterns in a detailed way on their children, they would be failing in their responsibilities in the light of the American value system.

The Continuity of the American Socialization Pattern

Particular attention should be called to the *continuity* of the main features of the socialization situation, from the pre-oedipal stages within the nuclear family to postgraduate professional training. The central keynote is training for achievement, conceived, as we have suggested above, in the first instance as contribution to the good society in the sense we have outlined. This contribution is to be made within an occupational system that has been coming to be progressively more widely expanded, more highly differentiated, and in general upgraded. Furthermore, as a result of this process, and of the attendant social mobility, the average time-interval between the laying of the motivational foundations of this achievement-orientation in the family and the actual commitment to occupational roles has been increasing, thereby decreasing the detailed and specific influence of parents in determining the commitment pattern.

We have maintained that the primary keynotes of the adult occupational role, so far as these can be generalized relative to the immensely differentiated variety, are, besides the commitment to achievement as such, "independence," responsibility, and competence. Independence in the present sense refers above all to capacity to "alienate" the orientation of labor from undue attachment to functionally diffuse contexts of attachment, in the first instance delineating commitment to the job context independently of family, friendship, and the like. The meaning of competence would seem to be clear enough without further elaboration. By responsibility we mean, in the occupational context itself, psychological capacity to make decisions in accord with the relevant normative criteria as distinguished from undue vulnerability to the various internal and external pressures to evasion by the "easy" way.[48]

As we have noted, the development of the personality structure in which these motivational patterns are highly developed requires the temporary cultivation of high levels of emotional dependency. The most conspicuous and best-documented case of this is the early dependency on the mother. This is associated with the motivational capacity necessary for the earlier phases of performance-learning, in the pre-oedipal period starting with the very basic motor and communication skills exemplified by walking and talking and their subsequent elaborations. The "dialectical" relation between dependency on the one hand, independence and achievement on the other, we believe does not cease with the oedipal period.

To be sure, the child becomes "emancipated" from his parents, through several stages, but most conspicuously in the early latency period and again in adolescence. We suggest that the very compulsiveness of his attachments to his peer groups at those stages is an

48. We have chosen to stress the occupational role as the goal of the socialization process because of its strategic place in our social structure. Clearly not even for the most committed male is this exhaustive of his role-obligations, and it does not explicitly take account of the predominant factor in the feminine role. With respect to the latter it is undoubtedly significant that a larger and larger proportion of women in increasing proportions of the life cycle are indeed assuming occupational roles—as well as becoming more highly educated. But in addition to this, as an aspect of the differentiation of the family from other structures, there has been a change in the direction of "occupationalizing" familial roles, particularly for the adult woman. We feel that the concern for psychology, the "rationalizing" of child training and the like, fit into this pattern, as do the more "material" aspects of home management. Similar considerations apply to other roles that have not become formally occupational, such as much "volunteer" community service.

indirect expression of the severe psychological strains that the process entails. More broadly, we suggest that the school, with the performance-learning expectations associated with it, is the primary focus—in the structure of socialization agencies—of the pressure to learn independence and achievement; whereas the peer group tends to replace the parents, or more broadly the family of orientation, as the primary focus of the emotional support that is necessary if the effort exerted in competitive achievement is not to be too severely disorganizing to the developing personality.

On these grounds we would expect that, as a consequence of the general process of differentiation and upgrading in the occupational and education spheres, there would appear, in addition to the phenomena of those spheres we have reviewed, a more prominent and more differentiated set of peer-group expectations and interactions than was characteristic of an earlier type of social system. Broadly, from the psychological point of view, this peer-group structure tends to fulfill one set of needs that are prominently involved in the socialization process, and is in this respect the primary successor of the more supportive and nurturant aspects of the family functions, which of course tend to be centered primarily in the maternal role. Furthermore, as noted, we think that these phenomena are most prominent at two different phases. The first is the early latency period, in which the crucial phenomenon is the one-sex peer group. This may be regarded as a mechanism of reinforcement of the ascription of sex-role, the primary structuring of which was a central aspect of the oedipal period itself; one might say it was a mechanism for carrying over this structure from the familial to the extrafamilial context, thereby generalizing sex-role commitment. The second is the adolescent peer group, where the primary pattern of independence from the family has already become established, and the "problem" is that of mobilization of motivational resources for the decisive phase in which both occupational role and marriage commitment are to be worked out, notably, by contrast both with our own past and with most other societies, *independently* of the family of orientation.

It is our main contention that the phenomena of peer groups in our society should not be treated in isolation but should be seen in the context of their relation to the educational and occupational systems on the one hand, to the family on the other. In interpreting them it should be remembered that the child who is a peer-group member is at the same time in school as well as typically living at home and economically dependent on his family; and that he is, with increasing self-consciousness, looking forward to a place in the adult world—for the boy, above all his own position, for the girl, partly her own but more decisively that of her prospective husband. Furthermore the family lies not only *behind* him in the form of his family of orientation but also *ahead* of him as his own prospective family of procreation. His "job" is not only to internalize the values and orientations of his family of orientation, but to adapt himself to the exigencies of the educational system and to treat these, by both conscious and unconscious mechanisms, in relation to his future in both occupational and familiar terms. Seen in this way, we do not think that the phenomena of peer-group behavior and orientation, which Riesman emphasizes so strongly, are—with certain empirical corrections, which we will discuss presently—in conflict with the interpretation of American social development we have sketched in this section; but that they find their place as an important part of that development, which can be "retrospectively predicted" on the basis of sociological analysis.

III. SOME EMPIRICAL ISSUES

LET us turn now to a few of the issues of the interpretation of empirical phenomena of American society highlighting the similarities and differences between Riesman's interpretations and our own. These are deliberately selected as issues where the empirical consequences of our respective conceptual analyses come to focus. They are hence, with respect to the society as a whole, selective rather than broadly representative. For this purpose we have chosen three interconnected issues. The first of these is the problem of the nature and place of the peer group in American society, particularly the adolescent peer group. The second is the place of consumption relative to production, not only in the structure of the economy as such, but in the articulation of the economy with the rest of the society. Finally, the third is the broader problem of the relation of the capacities, values, and attitudes of the individual personality—his "character"—to the pattern of functioning of our type of society, which is involved in Riesman's emphasis on the growing importance of "personal relations."

The Place of the Adolescent Peer Group

We have already given the main points of reference for our interpretation of this problem. Our main thesis is that the emergence of youth culture and peer groups is part of the general process of structural differentiation that has been going on in American society under the relatively stable general system of values we have sketched, and that within this framework the peer group has assumed a place that is *complementary* to that of the school on the one hand, the family on the other, in the differentiated subsystem of the society having to do with the socialization process. Within this subsystem, in turn, we feel that broadly the peer group represents patterns of orientation that are secondary to the main patterns, which are those of the system of formal education. In this context, we feel that the main difficulty with Riesman's position is that he tends to "reify" the peer group, as if it were the overwhelmingly predominant factor in socialization and constituted a kind of microcosm of the emerging adult "other-directed" society.

Within this more general framework, we would like further to suggest that internally the typical peer group is more definitely structured about a normative culture of its own than Riesman's formulations imply, and that its members mutually control one another in terms of these values and norms. Secondly, we suggest that this structure of the peer group is typically more closely integrated both with school norms and with parental expectations than he indicates. Finally, third, we would like to suggest a formulation of certain broad social mechanisms by which peer groups, more broadly the youth culture, operate to facilitate the process of socialization and the allocation of new members within the status system of the society.

Internal Structure. Riley, Riley, and Moore,[49] in a study of 2500 high-school adolescents, gathered data about their subjects' attitudes toward a variety of youth situations—peer relations, school work, and outside interests. They found that their adolescent peer groups were relatively determinately structured with respect to institutionalized norms; the peers' attitudes revealed a clear differentiation between approved and disapproved patterns of behavior. While such "other-directed" traits as popularity and friendliness were prominent

49. See Matilda White Riley, John W. Riley, Jr., and Mary E. Moore, "Adolescent Values and the Riesman Typology," in S. M. Lipset and L. Lowenthal, *op. cit.,* Chap. 16.

among approved traits, so also were other traits of a less *ad hoc* nature (to be discussed later).

Another study of the same subjects by Riley and Cohn[50] gives strong evidence that the peer groups studied are also determinately structured with respect to differentiated roles, particularly with respect to social control. The subjects were asked whom among their peers they liked and whom they disliked, and then to describe those named in terms of conformist and/or deviant traits.

As might be expected, the attribution of conformist traits was more likely to go with liking, of deviant with disliking—even with respect to the same person when named by both likers and dislikers. Further, there is important evidence of the existence of consensus on norms in the fact that the more widely a group member is liked, the more likely he is to be described as having conformist traits; the more widely disliked, the more deviant. Conformity with group norms did indeed elicit approval, as others—Jennings and Blau, for example—have shown.

But Riley and Cohn went on to show that the relation between approval and conformity was no simple matter, for their data also revealed that those who were widely liked by many of their peers were also relatively widely disliked by others. Likability and dislikability were not merely poles on a single continuum, nor were peers perceived with unalloyed consensus. There was a definite status hierarchy (supported in addition by independent variables) in terms of the combination of being liked and disliked, being considered conformist and deviant.

All group members were differentially perceived by others, and these differentiated perceptions served the complementary functions of rewarding conformity and punishing deviance. Social control in the group operated through a determinate system of role-differentiations, oriented to the shared normative culture.

These findings should be sufficient to suggest that these peer groups are not unstructured in either the role-differentiation or the normative senses. They possess a relatively definite set of patterns of institutionalized norms, which are upheld by a complex set of sanctioning mechanisms. The individual member is not left without criteria to guide him as to what behavior is and is not approved in the

50. Matilda White Riley and Richard Cohn, "Control Networks in Informal Groups," *Sociometry*, 21 (March, 1958), 30–49.

group. And though the group is fairly permissive in permitting a considerable range of tolerated behavior, there are definite rewards for conforming and punishments for deviant behavior. The essential point is that "approval" is not left completely "free-floating," but is bound down to fairly definite normative criteria.

Articulation with Norms outside the Peer Group. If the peer group is organized about a fairly definite normative culture, how does the content of this normative culture relate to that of the wider society? Because, as we contend, the peer performs differentiated functions in the socialization system, we would expect that it would not be a microcosm of the general value and normative system we have sketched, but its norms would be differentiated in the direction of stressing the personality needs of its members with special reference to "dependency," which at this level we may say takes the form above all of the need for "social acceptance."

We do indeed find this to be true according to the findings of the Rutgers study by Riley, Riley and Moore reported above. The most highly valued orientations of all are those referred to as "popularity" and "friendliness." Other important ones that are prominent, though perhaps less potentially useful for adult life, are interest in "fun with the gang," athletics, and popular music. These are all familiar aspects of "youth culture."

There is, however, another significant finding. This is that, whereas popularity and friendliness retain their prominence broadly across the board the desirability of being a good student and the valuation of achievement also come in a position of almost equal prominence for a substantial proportion of the sample. Broadly, the authors distinguish two main types of peer group, one which stresses these youth-culture values and plays down studentship and achievement, and a second which gives almost equal value to both complexes at once. We may regard this second type of peer-group orientation as a direct point of articulation between the youth-culture values on the one hand and those of the adult society on the other.

It should be further emphasized, as noted above, that there is definite social control in the form of negative attitudes toward radically deviant behavior of the too hedonistic and "wild" kind, of radical isolation or retreatism, and of radical rebellion against school work.

Further evidence of the linkage between the youth culture and adult values is given in the data concerning the subjects' perception of their parents' expectations, and their own evaluations of the significance of these traits for their own futures after they finish school. It is perhaps not surprising that these adolescents perceive their parents as valuing school work and achievement, for the "other-directed" cases, more highly than they themselves do. It is, however, more surprising that parents share the combined popularity-friendliness and achievement pattern of expectations, though with substantially more emphasis on achievement than the predominantly youth-culture-oriented younger generation. Then, with regard to self-assessment of what counts for the future, even the extremer youth-culture groups value achievement much more highly than the evaluation they attribute to their peers in the peer situation itself.

We have cited from the Rutgers study in this connection only sufficient data to give empirical substance to our view that the values of the peer group are, to be sure, differentiated from those predominant in the larger society, particularly in the occupational system, but are sufficiently in contact with those values so that the degree of divergence is consistent with the conception of a differentiated functional subsystem in the system of agencies of socialization. The peer group, particularly the more other-directed subtype, is neither a radically dissociated "sport" phenomenon within the society nor a microcosm of a wider society in which achievement values are minimized; nor, we think, is it a prototype of the direction of the development of the society.

We attribute considerable significance to the coincidence of the values of one wing of the peer-group structure and of parents on the *combination* of the other-directed valuation of popularity and friendliness, *and* studentship and achievement. The significance of this pattern may, we think, be dual. On the one hand, as we noted in the last section, an increasing proportion of occupational roles in the society are performed within the context of organization, in which ability to "get along with people" has in fact become an increasingly important condition of successful achievement. (Similar considerations apply to the shift in family structure.) On the other hand, the prominence of the pattern may also be a function of a later stage in the process of institutionalization of achievement values for the individual. This is to say that, with progressively fuller institutionalization, the values have come to be more symmetrically implemented on both the performance and the sanction sides of the interaction process. They are, therefore, *incorporated in* the norms on which approval is contingent, and not so exclusively localized in the internalized orientations of a limited class of performers. This we conceive to be an aspect of the processes of expansion and upgrading in the educational and occupational systems we have outlined. It seems to underlie what Riesman refers to as the institutionalizing of the productive functions.

Allocation of Persons among Peer Groups. Still another aspect of the situation is suggested by the Rutgers finding of the tendency to bifurcation of the peer-group system, as between the contingent in which the popularity-friendliness element is clearly dominant and that in which it is combined with the studentship-achievement element. The study does not have direct evidence on the matter, but it is the impression of the authors of the study[51] that there is a broad relation between the first type and the prospect of not going to college; between the second and college-orientation.

In connection with the Stouffer-Kluckhohn-Parsons study referred to above, we were struck by the salient importance of the bifurcation of the age-cohort in terms of whether they were to go on from high school to college, or to go directly into the labor force. As noted, this "decision" (for the individual) has a clear relation to his probable future status in the occupational system and hence in the stratification system generally. From the point of view of the society as a system this is a focal point in the process of allocation of its resources.

There are clearly, seen in terms of social structure, in turn two correlated but independent focuses of the organization of those resources. One is the fact that families that can, by virtue of cultural level, income, and other factors, provide their children with "advantages" constitute a favorable point of departure for children seeking to attain not only high status but high achievement levels. The other is the fact that the distribution of "ability," whatever its more ultimate determinants, is in important degree independent of the family status of the individual. Therefore, along with the process of "training" as such, there must be a process of selection through which a balance is struck between these two essential components of the "performance capacity" input into the adult role-system of the society.

We suggest, along lines sketched by the senior author in a previous publication,[52] that the functions of the peer group are in this

51. Oral communication.
52. Robert K. Merton *et al.* (eds.), *Sociology Today,* New York, Basic Books, Inc., 1959.

respect closely analogous to those of political parties on the national scene. Some groups of candidates for higher occupational status are anchored primarily in the expectations of family status, while others are anchored more in the ability of the individual. Thus the high-ability, low-family-status boy is under "cross-pressure" in the sense of the Berelson-Lazarsfeld studies of voting behavior.

From both the Rutgers study and our own we infer that there is not just one type of peer group, but that peer groups in most communities constitute a differentiated system. They range all the way from those composed of members who, on ascriptive bases, are definitely slated for high occupational status to those that overwhelmingly reinforce what are, in this respect, the "low" expectations of their members (the delinquent gang is at the extreme in this respect). But somewhere in the middle there is a set of peer groups in which the potentially conflicting elements of the cross pressure system meet, where those of higher family status but indifferent ability and those of lower family status but higher ability are together present. The peer group in this area is a mechanism for fixating the "independent vote." It helps to test out the qualifications, *other* than academic achievement as such, of the candidate for higher status; and hence its acceptance or rejection can, along with the evaluating processes of the school, contribute to the general allocative process.

Peer-group membership is a resultant of the preference of the individual within the available range on the one hand, acceptance by the other members on the other. Broadly, then, we suggest that the individual headed for higher occupational status will choose peer groups that tend on the whole to facilitate his progress in this direction. But his success in this respect is not only his own doing. He may find it easy or hard to gain acceptance. Though of course there are many complex problems in this area, we suggest that, *statistically* viewed, the rejections by peer groups of otherwise "qualified" persons are not likely to be too grossly dysfunctional; and, on the other side, the retention, by peer groups oriented to lower eventual status, of persons of relatively high ability may, again statistically, be related to motivational weaknesses that eventually, in spite of current indications of ability, would impede success when tougher tests were applied.

The broad bifurcation of the peer-group structure revealed by the Rutgers study thus seems to us to be analogous to the two-party system in politics. The latter may be viewed as a mechanism for allocating a fundamental societal resource, namely generalized support for political leadership, between groups oriented to more activistic or "liberal" political policies and those with more conservative policies.[53] The parties mediate between the focused responsibility of office on the one hand and the diversity of "interest groups" on the other.

Similarly, with all the importance of qualitative differentiation, the educational system has a definite hierarchical structure in terms of educational level attained, and the attainment of college entrance is the most significant single "cutting point" in this hierarchy. Those who reach the higher level are of diverse social origin, with a substantial contingent exposed to the cross-pressures of conflicting predisposing factors. The schools, by virtue of their commitments to universalistic standards of the evaluation of achievement and to the specificity of academic work, cannot serve as mediating integrating mechanisms except so far as types of schools themselves are differentiated. This seems to us to be an important aspect of the positive functional significance of the peer-group structure. It stands, as it were, "behind" the school, in that it can test out the strength of motivation and other factors in the capacity of individuals (in the diffuser contexts) for making the commitments that are essential for successful educational, and later occupational, performance.

In relation to lower-status families, we suspect that there is a dual function. On the one hand, acceptance in the "right" kind of achievement-oriented peer group can be a major factor in reinforcing the child's predispositions, in terms of his own ability and its encouragement in the school, to transcend the expectations of his class origin. In such cases the peer group takes over a supportive function, which the family, by virtue of its status, cannot effectively perform and which the school, because it is the immediate agency of evaluation, also cannot perform. On the other hand, in a society where upward mobility is so highly valued, it is inevitable that many lower-status families will have unrealistic expectations for their children. We suspect that in a statistically significant proportion of these cases the peer group performs the function of damping these unrealistic expectations by providing for the child a network of associations that do not encourage his ambitions to go beyond the levels his abilities

53. Cf. Talcott Parsons, " 'Voting' and the Equilibrium of the American Political System" in E. L. Burdick and A. J. Brodbeck (eds.), *American Voting Behavior,* New York, The Free Press of Glencoe, 1959.

would justify. In all such connections, however, it must be strongly emphasized that there are many *individual* cases in which the connections we suggest fail to work out; our generalization is statistical.

We have now suggested three different contexts in which we think the available information about adolescent peer groups in American society fits with our view that it is a society with a strongly institutionalized normative culture oriented in terms of the values of instrumental activism. The crucial points are, first, that the peer group itself is not a system in which the individual is left without normative guidance to seek a merely arbitrary approval, but is a normatively structured social system; second, that the norms of this system are not unrelated to the general value structure of the society as we have outlined it, but can be interpreted as a differentiated subsystem of this normative structure in the context of socialization; finally, third, the peer-group system is itself differentiated in ways that seem to be functionally related to the exigencies of the selection process in a highly differentiated yet mobile society.

With these considerations in mind, let us now turn back to the family. Its place in the picture will provide an advantageous point of departure for taking up the problem of consumption raised in the first section.

Like the peer group, the family also fills similar functions complementary to the educational system. Since children are socialized by other agencies earlier and oftener, and since the father's occupational role is largely distinct from ascriptive ties to the family, instrumental norms of achievement become increasingly independent of the familial context. The family itself becomes more than ever an area of controlled expressive gratification (but also of motivational management) where children may be heard as well as seen, where fathers may participate in domestic activities that would formerly have been incongruent with their previously fused roles as head of family *and* of family firm (or farm).

It is central to our thesis of structural differentiation to see the implications of the consequent functional specialization. When two functions, previously embedded in the same structure, are subsequently performed by two newly differentiated structures, they can *both* be fulfilled more intensively and with a greater degree of freedom, of mobility. The particularities of either one no longer act as ascriptive limitations on the other. Thus, on the one hand, parents not only push their fledglings from the nest earlier and oftener through independence training, but—conversely—they can allow them greater permissiveness on their return from flight.

Insofar as the management of the individual personality is concerned, the upgrading of achievement and the maintenance of discipline in certain areas thus becomes linked with the relaxation of that discipline in others. In this sense, both the family and the peer group may be seen as cases of the latter, focuses of "socialized regression" where an emotionally supportive floor is required under the demands of achievement in other contexts. If our position is correct that a general process of upgrading has made these demands greater in one direction, then it is possible to contend that greater permissiveness is a concomitant in another.

Kluckhohn, among others, comments on the current expansion in America of aesthetic and expressive activities "greatly beyond mere 'comfort.' "[54] Riesman calls attention to the concern with taste in the widespread sophistication about food and dress. We suggest that this rise in aesthetic appreciation, in hedonism, if you will, is not merely an effort to establish new criteria of status through marginal differentiation[55] but mainly a heightened expressiveness—complementary to, rather than conflicting with, a rise in instrumental demands for achievement. In addition to its being an instance of further differentiation, this phenomenon is also one of extension, in that it is manifested by a larger proportion of the population.

Consumption and the Noneconomic Resource

The distinction between what is instrumental and what is expressive (or consummatory, to use the more inclusive term) should not, however, be equated with the distinction between production and consumption, in the conventional sense of economics. In economic parlance, only those resources generated within structural units in the society having economic primacy (broadly speaking, the business sector) are customarily regarded as production. Their utilization outside the "economy," and particularly in the household, is seen as consumption.

From the economist's point of view, such terminology is of course

54. Clyde Kluckhohn, "The Evolution of Contemporary American Values," *Daedalus*, Spring, 1958, p. 96.
55. *The Lonely Crowd*, p. 153; pp. 171–172.

justifiable, but a functional approach to the total social system requires that production and consumption be analyzed in terms of their specific relevance to each type of unit under consideration. Food, the consumable *par excellence,* is an essential resource for the human organism. What may be consumption from one point of view may not be from another. Take, for example, the so-called hard goods —such things as washing machines and dryers, dishwashers and power mowers. While in terms of economic production these are considered consumers' goods, they are, for the household, factors of production, and otherwise serve as instrumental facilities that in part replace labor-input. Members of the household have, so to speak, made a decision to plow back a portion of their income into plant equipment; their "consumption" of these goods is, analytically speaking, actually an input of resources to the household.

It may be fruitful to trace through some of the implications of such household capitalization in order to assess the consequences of what is ordinarily thought of as consumption. Members of the household, in sloughing off the drudgery of routine tasks on machines, are upgraded from such unskilled labor and "set free" for the further pursuit—on the one hand—of more constructive work (*e.g.,* do-it-yourself improvements in the home, civic participation outside the home), or—on the other hand—of gratifying expressive needs (which, as we have maintained, is essential to personality-management and not just hedonism). Again, one must look on such a process of specialization as affecting complementary functions at the same time. Not to be overlooked is the concomitant emancipation of the labor force previously employed (by those who could afford it) in domestic service—a substantial reduction not solely due to the increased cost of such service.

To use economic terms in a noneconomic context, as the household become more capital-intensive, the labor-input into household tasks is emancipated for higher-level activities. Thus to equate resources held by noneconomic structural units with consumption may be misleading in analyzing a total society. At times Riesman seems to adopt this approach. In characterizing the shift from inner- to other-direction, among other factors, by a solution of the problem of production, he tends to generalize the strictly economic interpretation to the total society and so equate consumption with everything "noneconomic."

[Other-directed people] move around . . . in search of frontiers of consumption as well as of production. That is, they look for nice neighborhoods in which their children will meet nice people. Although much of the moving about in America today, within and between cities, is in search of better jobs, it is also in search of better neighborhoods and the better schools that go with them.[56]

If better neighborhoods and schools are to be viewed primarily as preferred markets for exchanging the currency of approval alone, then they are indeed frontiers of consumption, although how long even the rapid fluctuations of such markets, or the constant moving about required to escape those declining, can keep the frontier open is another question.

As an alternative approach, we suggest that there are many noneconomic resources that are generated by processes quite outside the structurally defined economic sphere, generated by a plowing-back of income diverted *from* consumption. Our illustration of household capitalization is one example, not to mention the home itself (including the marginal utilities beyond having "a roof over one's head"), schools, and many public facilities, but—most crucial of all—the personalities of members of the society.

We should try to make as clear as possible the analytical complexity of the problem involved here. We have taken the position that in the analytical economic sense a very important component of household consumption is properly to be regarded as investment in the greater effectiveness of the operation of the household. In *this* respect the household may be regarded as analogous to a firm. But a firm is an organized social unit with primacy of economic production as its definition of function, symbolized by profit as the measure of its effectiveness. The household, on the other hand, is definitely *not* a firm; its primary functions in the society are noneconomic, belonging in the area which, technically, we call "pattern-maintenance." In this particular case the primary output is motivational commitment to the type of achievement valued in the society, a commitment which in turn is one major component of "capacity for role-performance."

This capacity in turn constitutes *one* of the primary factors of production in the economist's sense, namely labor. It therefore enters into the economy, analytically considered, in the first instance (though not solely) through the medium of the labor force, part of

56. *Ibid.*, p. 66; pp. 87–88.

which is employed in business enterprises, but an important and probably increasing part in organizations that have primacies in other directions than production. The essential point here is that the *generation of these factors* of production is not itself a process of production in the economist's sense, but nevertheless the process of generation involves an economic—in this sense, a "productive"—component.

Personality as Resource

In *The Affluent Society*, Galbraith draws attention to the importance of what we call noneconomic resources, particularly to those generated by means of governmental expenditures.[57] His theory of social balance stresses their current deficiency and ascribes it to the aversion to public expenditures and the difficulties of justifying costs and benefits. But he stresses, above all, the importance of the human individual as a resource to the society as a whole and of building up the capacities of that resource through investment in education. In doing so, he points out how the concept of consumption is linked with earlier conditions:

A century ago, when educational outlays were not intimately related to production, men sensibly confined the word investment to the increase in capital which brought a later increase in product. Education was a consumer outlay. The popular usage has never been revised.[58]

Human development, in other words, is what economists have long termed an external economy.[59]

He also points out how societal development, through what we have called upgrading, has increased the importance of human resources:

However, with the development of a great and complex industrial plant, and even more with the development of a great and sophisticated body of basic science and of experience in its application, all this has been changed . . . modern economic activity requires a great number of trained and qualified people. Investment in human beings, is *prima facie*, as important as investment in material capital.[60]

57. J. K. Galbraith, *The Affluent Society,* Boston, Houghton Mifflin Co., 1958.
58. *Ibid.,* p. 274.
59. *Ibid.,* p. 275.
60. *Ibid.,* pp. 271–272.

Thus the process of generating societal resources does not stop with the attainment of a mature economy as an end-of-the-line. Indeed, this stage, by progressively emancipating personality resources from lower-level resources, is antecedent to bringing a really crucial focus to bear on their full development. In the earlier stages of societal development, not only property but human services have tended to be ascriptively bound. For personal capacities to become a fully fluid resource for societal functions, these ascriptive bonds must dissolve and be replaced by other allocative mechanisms. We interpret the process under analysis here as the latest major stage in this development toward greater mobility of human resources.

We think Durkheim was aware of this when he affirmed that as the complexity of society increases through the division of labor, individuals face demands for "greater specialization, harder work, and intensification of their faculties."[61] He goes on to say that these demands need not imply social regimentation of the individual, for specialization of functions brings about flexibility and individual variety by giving the individual progressive independence from ascribed ties.

. . . independence is not a pristine fact in societies, since originally the individual is absorbed in the group. But we have seen that independence later appears and progresses regularly with the division of labor.[62]
It is none the less true that individualism has developed in absolute value by penetrating into regions which originally were closed to it.[63]

The development of individualism and the intensification of the faculties of individuals, then, are dependent on the development of society. Further, such development does not reach the point where the individual must (or can) proceed entirely on his own. The link between character and society does not break. Thus we agree with Riesman when he says that *the product now in demand is neither a staple nor a machine; it is a personality.*[64] But, we add, a product in the sense of a highly developed resource, not a product marketed for peer consumption alone.

In this connection, a study by Miriam Johnson[65] of a sample of

61. Emile Durkheim, *The Division of Labor in Society,* New York, The Free Press of Glencoe, 1947, pp. 336–337.
62. *Ibid.,* p. 287.
63. *Ibid.,* p. 198.
64. *The Lonely Crowd,* p. 46; 64. (Italics in original.)
65. Miriam Johnson, "Instrumental and Expressive Components in the Personalities of Women," Ph.D. dissertation, Radcliffe College, 1955.

college women reveals some interesting evidence about the attitudes of prospective mothers toward children. On the basis of responses from her subjects, she classified them on a Guttman scale as being either instrumental or expressive. She found that the former were more likely to want an occupation outside of the home—to be teachers at more advanced levels, or social workers or technicians of various sorts. The latter, if they planned to work at all, tended to want to teach very young children or to be private secretaries.

In addition, the instrumental girls wanted *more* children than did the expressive girls and expected to get gratification from training them for adulthood; they were already looking ahead to the time when their as yet unborn children would enter society as full-fledged members. The expressive girls expected to "enjoy" their children in and for themselves. The correlation between wanting larger families and thinking in terms of their mature development is significant. We consider socialization, including the agencies of family, school, and peer group, as the process by which personality as a resource is generated. In addition, we would include the necessary "plant equipment" to implement this process. The increased activity of parents, particularly mothers, in civic affairs as well as P.T.A. and church activities, is a manifestation of concern over maintaining and developing those facilities.

Personal Relations

We have, up to this point, stressed personality as a resource in performing increasingly upgraded and specialized functions. In the attainment of collective goals, such functions have of necessity to be integrated; the proliferation of roles must be organized in highly complex collectivities. As Riesman says, "People, therefore, become the central problem of industry."[66]

It is easy, perhaps a pardonable error, to write off the efforts to solve the problem of coordination as manipulation, groupism, or "togetherness," and to lump them all together under the rubric of the "social ethic," as Whyte has done. But it is another matter to come up with effective organization—a resource in itself. No doubt some of the efforts have backfired or been characterized by crudity, and the adverse criticism they have elicited may prove to be salutary. But inadequacy in solving a problem does not mean that the problem

66. *The Lonely Crowd*, p. 132; 152.

does not exist or is not worth solving. The division of labor necessitates group coordination and demands that individuals acquire the necessary role-skills to make coordination possible.

Problems of social organization are, of course, not limited to occupational contexts, but apply to human relationships generally. The activism that has characterized American mastery of production applies equally to mastery of personal relationships (this does not mean "domination" of other people). In extending the development of resources to a more organized and differentiated set of mechanisms for developing and regulating personality, the constellation of role-relationships that constitute it becomes, in the last analysis, the crucial link between character and society. It seems to us, for example, that it is this particular emphasis that lies behind the American psychoanalytic stress on the ego—a product of social interaction—as opposed to the more European interest in the id—a given. Kluckhohn observes a "rise in 'psychological values' related to mental health, the education and training of children, and the like."[67] We interpret this rise as an increasing concern with the production of personality through socialization.

In presenting our alternative interpretation, we by no means intend to overlook empirical instances where, as Riesman observes, there are low occupational commitments, where standards of achievement have declined, where the socialization process has turned out passive approval-seekers. But we believe that the empirical issues we have raised indicate that the other side of the picture deserves serious attention. If our interpretation is correct, the developmental trends we have outlined—not the failures—define the main stream.

67. Kluckhohn, *op. cit.*, p. 105.

9
Toward a Healthy Maturity

THE problem of health and illness generally lies at a major cross-roads between the biological and the social reference points for the study of human affairs, with the psychological aspect strategically situated somewhere in the middle. If this be true generally, perhaps it is even more so where the older age groups are concerned. In this connection, the biological reference must be extended from the consideration of the relatively short-run state of the individual organism to that of the life cycle as a whole.

On the biological side, then, it seems to be an essential basic assumption that the life cycle as a whole must be considered to be a base-line of "normality." Death itself is clearly among the biologically normal phenomena, and the changes which are inseparably connected with the passage of time are equally so. Only premature death and the disabilities of later life which, relative to the main pattern of the cycle are "adventitious," can be considered to be pathological, and, hence, appropriately categorized in the domain of illness. Thus, a person clearly approaching death "from old age" is, properly speaking, no more "sick" than is a pregnant woman approaching the end of her term, however much both may have special requirements of care and however much the proper care may be defined, in part at least, as "medical." However vague this criterion of distinction between the normal and the abnormal may be, it will

Reprinted from the Journal of Health and Human Behavior, *Vol. 1, Fall, 1960, pp. 163–173. This paper was presented originally at the Opening Session of the National Health Forum on "Positive Health of Older People," conducted by the National Health Council, March 13–17, 1960, at Miami Beach, Florida.*

be taken as a base-line for this discussion; its filling in must be a problem for the biological sciences and the health professions, not for the sociologist.

Certain more specific facts, however, are so important that they must be made explicit. First, it is well known that, though the average length of human life has greatly increased, for example, during the present century, its maximum span has increased very little, if at all, within the period for which reliable information has been available; and much the largest decreases of death rates have been in infancy and childhood. Nevertheless, once past these early critical periods, there is a greatly enhanced probability that the individual will survive until a "normal old age." As a result of factors such as these, the proportion of our population in the older age groups, taking for instance the conventional cutting point of 65, has been steadily increasing for a considerable period, and can be expected to do so further for a considerable period of time. In 1900, only 4.1 per cent were 65 and older. In 1955, the proportion had grown to 8.5 per cent. If anticipated trends hold, in 1975 it will be 9.7 per cent, or nearly one-tenth. Hence, by sheer weight of numbers, if nothing else, the older groups are becoming increasingly important in our society, as in all others where the demographic revolution is taking place.

THE OLDER AGE GROUPS IN TWO CONTEXTS

IN discussing the implications of these facts for our society, and for the health problem in particular, it is important to emphasize two main contexts. The first of these is the American value system in its implications for our fundamental attitudes in this field, while the second is the trend of change in our society, with special reference to the process of structural differentiation which it is undergoing.

The American Value System

In spite of the complexity of our contemporary society and the heterogeneity of its population by ethnic origin, region, class, religion and other variables, it can be said that there is a relatively coherent, unified and, on the whole, stable set of values institutionalized in America. By the values of the society is meant conceptions of the desirable *type of society*, not of other things the valuations of which may or may not be shared by its members.

The American value system may be characterized as one of *instrumental activism*. *Instrumental*, in this connection, means that neither the society as a whole nor any aspect of it, like the state, is elevated into an "end in itself," but it is considered to be an instrumentality for "worth while" things, with a very widely open range of conceptions of what things in particular may be considered to be worth while. The element of activism, however, narrows this range. For the unit of the society, whether it be a collectivity or an individual, it means the *achievement* of something important. So far, in turn, as these achievements are contributions to the society, they must consist in maintenance or, still better, improvement of the society as a base and environment for achievement.

The spelling out of this abstract formula brings up a number of familiar themes. Valuing achievement, we must value the conditions which are essential to it. From the point of view of the achieving unit, we may speak of freedom and opportunity as the essential parts of the environment. Freedom here implies absence of unnecessarily hampering restraints, while opportunity is a structuring of positive possibilities. Indeed, we may go a step further and suggest the importance of positive rewards for achievement which are in some respects involved in the somewhat maligned "success" complex. This essentially is to say that, if achievement is valued, not only should people be given freedom and opportunity, but if they in fact achieve admirably, this achievement should be recognized in some way.

A strong emphasis on achievement, however, raises inevitably the problem of equality; because an inherent unevenness of achievement and its rewards creates positions of differential power and privilege. Hence, we not only value achievement as such and the freedoms, opportunities and rewards that go with it, but also *access* to these good things. The basic formula in this respect is equality of opportunity. Opportunity in turn is, however, a relative concept. What is an opportunity for one trained, or financially able, to take advantage of it may not be an opportunity at all for others. What is realistically an opportunity in particular depends on the capacity of the individual to do what the opportunity in turn makes possible. Capacity is the potentiality for achievement which, in turn, is partly a matter of innate ability, but probably even more of the "advantages," or their reverse, which the individual has experienced in his earlier life history.

The activism of our values makes clear that we do not value a static, unchanging society. Rather, we value one which is continually changing in a "progressive" direction, which is to say in accord with the central values. Above all, it may be said that this direction is defined as a progressive increase in capacities and opportunities for achievement, not only on the same, but on progressively higher levels, and in the freedoms necessary to use them. The maintenance of certain equalities—or improvement of them—goes without saying. We value stability, but a stability *in* change, not a stagnant total absence of change.

The Importance of the Value-Complex

What is the bearing of this value-complex on our problem? One would very readily associate this value-complex with the much discussed "accent on youth" of American Society. The most important resources of a society are the capacities and commitments to achievement of its people and, in the nature of the case, the longer the prospective time available to an individual, the greater his potential contribution. Hence, the capacities of the young above all, through the two fundamental channels of health and education, have formed a major focus of concern in our society, as has the level of opportunity open to young people in the educational system and in what it leads to. It is therefore not surprising that we have had a very grave concern for the young, particularly in the period of our very rapid territorial, population and economic expansion of the last century. What many European observers have seen as the "child-centered" character of American society is perhaps less to be interpreted as "indulgence" of children than as the centering of concern on them and the investment of resources, economic and other, in their futures.

This tendency is reinforced by another important structural fact, namely that the succession of the generations tends to focus responsibility for the young on the parental generation. The younger generation then eventually achieves its independence; but it is not so obviously a problem what is to happen to the elders after their main responsibilities for their children have been discharged. As the formerly self-sufficient ones from whom independence had to be gained, it is perhaps not surprising that it should be assumed they should "take care of themselves."

Pursuing this line of thought, it seems logical that the first major basis of concern with the older groups should be a manifestation of the more humanitarian aspect of our values—our concern with the more elementary bases of need, namely, the fundamentals of economic subsistence and health. Indeed, concern with the older groups as a resource could very well be inhibited by a certain prodigality of a young and expanding society which has coincided with certain types of structural change.

These changes include the immense process of urbanization and industrialization which we have been through. In the simpler rural society of our past, where most productive activity was carried on in household units, the problem of retirement, as it has developed with the growth of large employing organizations, was not nearly so acute. Much more generally, as is true of such conditions today, a person's capacities were more likely to be utilized as long as he was physically able to be useful.

Provision for the elderly in a situation where their relative numbers were increasing and where, for a variety of reasons other than sheer economic capacity, it was becoming progressively more difficult to integrate them in the households of their children, tended to leave increasing proportions more or less stranded and created an emergency situation the first major reaction to which was the social security legislation of the 1930's.

With increasing maturity of the society, however, it is natural that attention should turn to the fuller utilization of its less obvious resources; just as after a somewhat prodigal exploitation of natural resources a major conservationist movement developed in the early part of this century, so in the far more important field of human resources we are moving into an era of major concern with those resources we have not been adequately utilizing.[1] This concern and

1. In the field of race relations which is so acute just now, for understandable reasons the primary accent at this stage is on the simple matter of social justice in terms of the values embodied in constitutional rights. Underlying this, however, in a society with our type of values, is the fundamental fact that the attempt to hold the Negro to a menial status is also a fundamental waste of human resources. For the type of value system sketched above, justice and equality are inseparable from capacity and opportunity to achieve.

the directions it can take will be the principal subject of the remainder of this discussion.

By way of transition, however, from the subject of general
American values to that of the special problem of the older groups,
it is apropos to discuss briefly the problem of biological "decline"
and our attitudes toward it, including first of all the implications of
American values for the problem of death.

American Values and the Denial of Death

It has sometimes been said that we Americans do our best to
deny the reality of death. We dislike to think or talk about it, or to
face up to its inevitability; and, when it does occur, we try to get the
necessary observances over as quickly as possible and go back to
living as nearly as possible as if nothing had happened. In other
cultures there is something like this picture, but it is not so extreme
as this, except in certain deviant manifestations.

The most important point seems to be that we (as Americans)
cannot glorify death simply because we value achievement in this
life, and death necessarily puts an end to that achievement. Its
acceptance within the context of our values rests, in part, on the
general realistic recognition of the "facts of life" which is one major
cultural imperative and, in part, on a sense of the self-limiting
features of the individual's "task in life"—the sense that the time
comes when *his* job is done—though for the society the job is in
principle never done. Whatever the philosophical and religious views
involved, death may be thought of as a natural marking of the
completion of an inherently self-limited—and increasingly self-
assigned—task. In certain respects, the metaphor of the well-earned
rest, with its release from pressing responsibilities, is an appropriate
one. Though there is a "projection" beyond earthly limits, there
certainly tends to be no trend in the predominant Protestant tradition
to glorify an after-life, if the latter term is used to mean primarily a
"release" from the "bondage" of the flesh. The very religious sanction of conscientious living in this world precludes a certain order of
evaluative contrast which, in the great cultures of the world, is perhaps most marked in India. Indeed, Indian society seems to involve
almost a glorification of death as that for which life is really lived.

Broadly this interpretation seems to be confirmed by medical
and other experience—for example, from the New England Age

Center.[2] This is to the effect that the primary anxieties of older people do not tend to center on the expectation of death as such; persons who are knowingly approaching death, in general, do so relatively without fear. Anxiety focuses rather on the definition of the individual's role for the remainder of his life, on his own capacities to do the things he thinks worth while or obligatory to do, the welfare of those he loves, and the fulfillment of what he feels to be his obligations. The same basic interlocking of considerations of task or obligation with those of self-interest which applies at other age-levels seems also to be present here. Of course, people's needs have to be met; but, given a reasonably adequate situation in this respect, they will continue to do what they can that they feel to be "worth while" until called to leave the field. The essential question is: *What* things are to be considered most worth while?

Changing Culture and Capacity for What?

This brings up the question of the relations between capacity and disability with respect both to health and to other aspects of the problem. Here, it is well known that the content of the concept *health* includes certain elements of relativity. This point has been most thoroughly explored with reference to cross-cultural perspectives, but here it is relevant in two other contexts, namely within the population of one society, our own, as a function of age, and in terms of the changing definition and relative importance of its different components over time.

The most important consideration, here, is the relativity of "capacity," the maintenance of which is focused in our meanings of health. The central question is, then, capacity for what? In the more pioneering phases of the development of a country there tends to be a high premium on physical prowess, on sheer strength, agility and endurance. Quite clearly the high points of these capacities are reached quite early in life, perhaps in the early twenties; and, while maintenance of good levels is possible for many years after that, the process is still one of "decline." The symbolic importance of this complex in our culture is clearly shown in the virtual cult of

2. A study under the direction of Hugh Cabot, on "Prejudices and Older People" cf. Natalie Cabot, *You Can't Count on Dying,* Boston, Houghton Mifflin, 1961.

athletics and its relation to the whole complex of the valuation of youth.

With increasing differentiation of the society and higher cultural levels, however, a different set of capacities comes to be increasingly salient—accumulated and organized knowledge, technical competence and sophisticated skills, capacity to plan and carry sustained responsibilities, and balanced judgment. Though much is unknown in these areas, the major trend is unmistakable, namely, that the age-peak of such capacities comes very much later than is the case with physical prowess. Furthermore, it seems probable that the course of medical development leads in this direction, rather than in simply allowing more people to live longer and without the grosser disabilities. The ground for this suggestion is that such capacities seem to be dependent on the maintenance of relatively good states of the most important organ systems and not on the highest peaks, in particular, of the perceptual and motor systems. The main organic base seems to lie in the central nervous system which does not seem, except probably for vascular conditions, to be subject to an early physiological "decline" that leads to an impairment of "mental capacity" which closely resembles the much advertised impairment of capacity for physical prowess after the early twenties.

There is naturally a limit, the ultimate one being death. But the basic emphasis is on the point that, the more sophisticated the culture, the higher the levels of intellectually defined technical competence, of responsibility and the like, the more it seems likely that people past their physical "prime" will have capacities of the first importance for the society.

In sociological terms, the importance of these capacities may be related to the *upgrading* aspect of the development of the society. With its general process of social growth and differentiation, bigger and more difficult things are continually being undertaken which, for increasing numbers of individuals, call into play their higher capacities along the lines which have been indicated. The problem is that of the basis of these capacities in the biological equipment of the individual and in his personality structure. The very broad hypothesis is that, with some exceptions, the higher the capacity, the later is its maturing, and perhaps, though not as certainly, the less is it subject to the kind of decline of which the decline of physical prowess has become the prototype.

This problem of the different types of capacity in relation to social role performance, and their relations to the stages of the life cycle certainly should be a major object of research interest, one in which the disciplines converging on the health problem need to cooperate very closely with those associated with education and the analysis of social problems generally. It is now time to take up the second main theme of the relation of these questions to the process of differentiation in the society.

THE IMPLICATIONS OF THE PROCESS OF STRUCTURAL DIFFERENTIATION

IT is characteristic of a society, which is involved in a major process of growth, that its internal structure will be continually differentiating. There are many complex features of such a process, but the ones which concern us here are those that impinge directly on the individual through the structure of his roles. The most obvious of these is the development of mutually independent *multiple* participations for increasing proportions of the population. We have jobs and family memberships which, though articulated, are not ascriptively bound to each other. We have memberships in the families into which we were born and those we establish by our marriages, which again are importantly independent. We have religious group memberships, roles as citizens at the various community levels, and we are likely to participate in a number of more specialized associational groups. All of this, of course, occurs simultaneously at any given point in the life of a particular person.

The aspect of immediate concern, however, is differentiation with respect to the life cycle. The same person, that is to say, not only participates in more different kinds of relational contexts at the same time, he does more different kinds of things at different periods of his life. We may follow this theme through in a broad way.

Implications for Education

It goes without saying that all human beings must start as helpless infants and go through the combined process of biological maturation and psychosocial training which leads to adulthood. But we can see that a particularly important reference point in this connection is given by formal education which, as including the whole population, is barely over a century old. Its more elementary phases may be interpreted as mainly different ways of treating the "immature" who, in any case, are not yet ready for adult responsibilities. The history of education has, however, been not only one of extension to increasingly larger proportions of the age cohort, but, also, its prolongation to later periods of the life cycle.

If we take the eighth grade as the termination of "elementary" education and the average of its completion as fourteen, those who have completed it, in the more routine work-contribution senses, very generally have been ready for assumption of adult roles, though, in most of the Western world, marriage as early as that has been rare. Hence, even secondary education may be taken to be a case of an "investment" in the future through the "segregation" of an age group, on grounds other than their biological capacity, to perform the simpler sorts of adult functions, in the sense that, if this age group is withheld from functional performance and subjected to training, its future contributions will be far greater than they otherwise would have been. American society now has reached the point where completion of secondary education has become the nearly universal norm for satisfactory preparation for adult role-performance.

On top of this, there has emerged a vastly extended resort to still further formal education. Now about one-third of the total age-cohort go on to some college education. This proportion is steadily growing, and can be expected to do so for the foreseeable future. Finally, at the educational top, post-graduate training in the professional fields still takes only a small proportion. But it has become appreciable and is by far the most rapidly growing sector of the educational system.[3]

This is to say that, today, an increasing proportion of every age cohort is spending an increasing proportion of the period of what, from the older point of view, is that of adult capacity in pursuits which are clearly differentiated from their principal adult "contributions." Moreover, the stages of formal education have become clearly differentiated from each other. After the elementary grades, and certainly after the secondary, it seems improbable that biological maturation is the primary factor in the differentiation. Its main basis is rather that of the stages in which a cumulative development of *learned* capacity has to take place.

Let us now turn to the occupational side. A kind of base line may

---

3. To take one atypical example, in the 1920's about 20 per cent of a graduating class of Harvard College went on to any type of postgraduate formal education. In the 1950's, it had become about 75 per cent.

be said to be the performance of the ancient work-jobs of maintaining households, the more elementary types of cultivation of the soil, and the traditional handicrafts—rough carpentry and the like. The necessary skills could be adequately learned by a child in the early teens. A peak of competence could be reached within a short time, and nothing left to change or "advance" until physical disabilities set in in advanced old age. The whole structure of the educational system just sketched introduces a different set of dimensions. It is preparation for functions which must be elaborately prepared for, with respect to which anything like peak proficiency can be attained only much later and after longer preparation.

The structure of careers is another example of the same basic principle. The simplest "worker" role is almost undifferentiated over time. But the higher the level of performance the more likely it is that the peak will have to be attained by way of a series of stages of "gaining experience" through the performance of easier and less demanding tasks. It will be only after a considerable period of years that a person, even after he is "trained," will be performing at the very highest level of which he is capable. This seems to be particularly true of the functions in which responsibility and judgment play a central part.

Quite obviously, "capacity'" is only one factor in the structuring of careers. Opportunity, or the "demand" factor, is equally essential. Thus, a man is not likely to be called upon to carry the highest responsibilties until he has established a reputation on the basis of which others have a high level of "confidence" in him. He may be capable of carrying the responsibility long before this confidence is established. Nevertheless, with due allowance for these factors, the central proposition certainly holds, namely that the differentiation of appropriate kinds of things to do through the stages of the career line continues on bases which are independent of formal "preparation." The pattern is not that one is "prepared" and, then, functions on a fixed "plateau" until decline sets in.

The central question, then, is how the limits of this process of differentiation in relation to upgrading are to be defined. It should be noted, in approaching the question, that upgrading is accompanied with differentiation of *kinds* of performance and function. The student is doing a different kind of work from the man on the job; even professional training is only very partially apprenticeship, important as this component is. Similarly, the junior executive, even though he is likely to become the "top boss" in time, is as a junior executive doing something very different from his top superior.

The thesis is that we are only beginning to explore the possibilities of extension of this pattern of differentiation beyond what has come to be institutionalized as the peaks of careers. Above all, we may question the ready assumption that the appropriate conception for everything beyond that institutionalized peak is "decline" and that the problem is one of accepting the limitations imposed by "disability" and learning to live within these limitations, rather than one of having an opportunity for new and different kinds of achievement and contribution.

Implications for the Feminine Role

One very important aspect of the problem concerns the family rather than the occupational sphere, and its special relation to the feminine role. Perhaps some attention to it will help clarify the problem for the occupational sphere. The family and the feminine role in American society have, in the past half century or so, been undergoing a notable process of differentiation. First, the family itself has become a far more specialized agency and, by virtue of that fact, has lost many of its previous functions, notably in the field of economic production. Above all, the household, as a place to "live" and a group with whom one shares this living, has become structurally segregated from the organizations in which occupational work is carried on, and has turned over many of its previous functions to such organizations. In connection with this development, however, the place of woman has come to be decreasingly confined to "the home." One major development is the enormously increased participation of women in formal education at the higher levels as well as the lower. Another is involvement in many kinds of community interests outside the home, while not least is the increased participation of women in the labor force. The proportion of healthy single women under 65 not employed (except widows) has come to be minimal, but the most striking recent development is that of the employment of married women living with their husbands.

Overwhelmingly, the central specifically feminine function is the rearing of children. There has been an important resurgence of devotion to this function in our generation through the famous "baby boom," which is all the more significant because it has occurred in a population where knowledge of contraceptive measures is certainly more widely spread than ever before. But another interesting thing has happened. This is the concentration of childbearing within a substantially shorter time period than before. As of the most recent information,[4] women are on the average likely to bear their *last* child at the age of 26 or 27; and so parents, by the time their youngest child has left home, are likely to be under fifty, with, on the average, about a third of their married life still ahead of them.

This phenomenon is associated with the very rapid recent increase in the employment of married women who are in their forties, fifties, or older. This has, indeed, been the largest single factor in the recent growth of the labor force relative to the total population of working age. It thus appears that special devotion to child-rearing, notably of course of younger children, is becoming a more differentiated role in the life-cycle of the mother as well as in other respects. Thus, she is freed for other functions, partly by living longer in a better state of health and partly by concentrating her primary attention to motherhood within a shorter time-span.

This seems to be associated, in turn, with another set of phenomena. We do not have to go back farther than the early years of this century to find a time when the average woman in her mid-forties was, by current standards, definitely "old." It was as if her child-rearing function had virtually exhausted her capacities and she had relatively little left to do. The preservation of feminine "attractiveness" into much more advanced ages is an important symptom of a major change in this respect.

One aspect of this problem concerns the continuity of kinship relations and responsibilities. The older type woman, as grandmother, exercised more responsibility and authority for the families of her children than does her current opposite number. It is, however, perhaps not illegitimate to suggest that the lessened responsibility of the older woman in this respect has been balanced by the upgrading of the role of mother; the younger woman takes a larger share of the total responsibility for her children than did her forebears. This frees *her* mother, and, later, herself, for other functions. With all the strains and difficulties symbolized by the famous Helen Hokinson cartoons, it can be said fairly that an enormous upgrading in the utilization of feminine capacities has resulted from this general

4. Paul C. Glick, *American Families,* New York, John Wiley & Sons, 1957, p. 66.

process of differentiation. Furthermore, a particularly conspicuous part of it has been better utilization of the capacities of the woman past the child-bearing ages. The menopause is no longer, in any comparable sense, the sign of a termination of important usefulness and status.

The principle involved here can be generalized. If child-rearing has been the primary center of the feminine role, occupational achievement has been that of the masculine. There are very important reasons why the "job" should have come to be such an important focus in the role-organization of our type of society, and within this more general category, why the career and its peak should be so important. These are, above all, the central symbols of the masculine "contribution" to social welfare; they have, above all, provided the standards by which the utilization of masculine capacity has been judged. If, given the overwhelming importance of this category of contribution, the individual is no longer wanted or needed, or if his capacity declines, the obvious conclusion seems to be that he should be placed in a lower category of social worth.

Implications for Patterns of Retirement

Seen in this context, the development of the age 65 as the canonical age of retirement is an interesting social phenomenon. Obviously, the changes of relevant capacity, whatever the part played by biological-genetic and by experimental factors, are in the nature of the case gradual, except for suddenly drastic changes which do not often conveniently fall on the 65th birthday. There is enormous individual variation as to whether there will or will not be a social loss from dispensing with the services of the particular individual in his particular job at this point of time. Clearly, a system based on evaluation of particular capacities would, in an abstract sense, be far more rational.

Very generally, however, the main lines of differentiation in social structure cannot be so neatly tailored to the needs and capacities of the individual as this would require. Clearly, the emergence of this pattern was a product of the rise in employment by large-scale organizations and the necessity to establish general policies in their conduct. Furthermore, it is understandable that, in its first phase, the negative uses of such a policy should be stressed, namely the relieving of the organization from being burdened with responsibility for workers so old that often their capacities were not up to the demands of the job, and with this, the hastening of the opening of opportunities for younger people.

The retirement pattern may, however, be looked upon as not simply a protection of standards of efficiency and of openness of opportunity, but a focus for a process of differentiation, by drawing a clearer line than had obtained and otherwise would obtain between phases of the life cycle. We are entering now the process of redefining the content of the later phase; as this process meets with success, it is likely to turn out that the earlier rigidity of the retirement line will be substantially mitigated.

There is still, however, a good deal of pressure for earlier retirement, so long as financial security is reasonably assured; there is also a good deal of anticipation of the finally compulsory retirement age. Furthermore, it has been pointed out that there are, from the point of view of the person retiring, as well as the employer, certain advantages in the general rule. This, above all, has to do with protection of the autonomous dignity of the individual. If permission to stay on the job beyond the regular age limit is dependent on the judgment of the "boss" from month to month or whatever, then the security of expectation, which we have come to regard as normal even without formal tenure, is undermined and the individual may often come to feel that his fate is in the hands of the arbitrary judgment or whim of another. The impersonal rule at least avoids any such invidious implications.[5]

SUMMARY OF FORCES MAKING FOR A REDEFINITION OF THE ROLE OF THE OLDER PERSON

IN the nature of our society at the present phase of its devlopment, there is a powerful set of forces leading to a positive redefinition of the role-expectation of the older person who has passed the normal occupational career peak, as that has been defined. The first factor to mention again is that of the direction of pressure exerted by the value system. As previously contended, it seems that this direction will have to be compatible with the idea of instrumental ac-

5. This point was underlined in particular by Mr. Hugh Cabot of the Age Center of New England (in a personal discussion).

tivism; it will have to define opportunities and expectations to *do* things that in these terms are worth while. This need not be in the least incompatible, however, with withdrawal from many of the activities and involvements which are considered normal for younger groups.

The second major factor is the increase in numbers and in proportion of the total population of people in these categories; and the third is the actual, and still more, the prospective improvement in their average levels of capacity. Health is one major component of this capacity; but other capacities are certainly equally important. A very central complex of these is that associated with education; and it is another cardinal fact that, as a result of the general educational upgrading of the population, after the requisite time-lag, this older group will, on the average, be far more highly educated than any of their predecessors. This may be expected to make them more, rather than less, demanding of a satisfactory place in the society.

There is a most intimate connection between this educational trend and the direction in which the solution of our problem is to be sought. The general tendency of the upgrading process, at one pole, leads to the downgrading of physical prowess; at the other, it leads toward increasing emphasis on cultural concerns. This, in turn, is associated with capacity to think abstractly and generally and to take the long view. For a long time there has been something like general agreement that certain types of functions could be particularly well performed by older persons. One of the most conspicuous of these is that of judge. Informally, judicial type functions are often performed by people with a kind of "elder statesman" status. Certainly, in many fields of scholarship, distinguished contributions are made in later years. That eminently successful organization, the Roman Catholic church, has for centuries been governed mainly by old men, a fact which is associated with its trusteeship of very long-run interests.

It has often been suggested that influence in the hands of the old, almost by definition, leads to a bias toward conservatism in an undesirable sense. That this sometimes happens is undoubtedly true, but it seems to be far from inevitable. Above all, the issue here is not so much about the exercise of power over current organizational decision-making; the trend is, and rightly so, away from putting more of that power in the hands of the old. It is rather concern for the highest institutional interests of the society and the culture in the longest perspective. The very fact that the older person no longer has a career to make, that his basic position in the society has already been decided, and that his time is running out, means that under favorable conditions he can afford to be more "disinterested," to see things not in terms of what he personally can gain or lose, but from a larger point of view.[6]

A research group engaged in study of aging has put forward the interesting formula of "disengagement" as a pattern for describing the main tendency of older people.[7] Relative to the concerns of middle life, the main theme may legitimately be included under this formula. It should, however, be interpreted not only in terms of disengagement *from* previous obligations, but also a disengagement *for* new tasks. It may be thought of as one more case of the freeing of the individual from ascriptive ties, which is such a central theme in the general development of advanced societies. It involves, as the authors say, a relative freeing from the more intensely affective attachments to persons and causes.[8]

Finally, a set of reasons why the problem of health occupies such a central place in the whole range of problems may be presented. In spite of the conception of the normality of aging and death here put forward, it is obvious what a very close connection there is, realistically and symbolically, between illness, disability and aging. The significance of this needs to be seen on the background of the more general significance of the problems of health and illness in American society.[9] Illness, that is to say, is to a very high degree a pattern of *deviant behavior*. Health is valued as capacity for achievement. The enormous American effort to improve health is legitimized above

6. The most obvious examples are from high social statuses, but the point is meant to apply to all levels. Who among us cannot cite examples of the special disinterestedness of old people in all walks of life?

7. Cf. *Growing Old: The Process of Disengagement* Elaine Cumming and William E. Henry, Foreword by Talcott Parsons, New York, Basic Books, 1961.

8. Certainly, one major feature of the experience of aging is that of the deaths of a considerable proportion of other individuals who have been the most important "significant others" in the individual's life experience. If the traumatic effects of these experiences are to be surmounted, we can say on psychological grounds that it must be through the internalization of the "lost objects"; and perhaps it can be said that the process of disengagement in this sense goes back to the first emancipation from infantile dependency on the mother.

9. Cf. The following chapter, "Definitions of Health and Illness in the Light of American Values and Social Structure."

all in terms of our achievement values and of the equalizing of opportunity for achievement.

At the same time, however, since it is conditionally legitimized, sickness provides for the individual, perhaps, the most important single escape hatch from the pressure of obligations to achieve; pressures which, because of the upgrading process which has been stressed here, are becoming, for the average individual, more rather than less intense. Seen in this light, illness is far from being an exclusive and unmitigated evil; it is also an important "safety valve" for the society.

The most obvious field in which such considerations operate is that of so-called mental illness. The evidence, however, is overwhelming that it is not possible to draw a rigid line, that the "psychosomatic" area is of cardinal importance to most of the problems of health and illness. However efficacious our methods of somatic control may be, it is very doubtful if a stable situation can be achieved independently of the social and cultural structuring of the group whose health is the object of concern.

This seems to be preeminently true of the aging groups. It seems almost obvious that illness is a *particularly* important form of deviant behavior for them. Its basic meaning in this connection is very clear. If it is the broad societal verdict upon older people that they are "useless," then the obvious way to legitimize their status is to *be* useless through the incapacitation of illness. The channels through which such influences operate are still understood only in the most fragmentary fashion, but *that* they operate in this direction seems to be beyond doubt.

The most fundamental task in our society in "caring for" (itself a pejorative expression) the aged, therefore, seems to be that of giving positive *meaning* to their place in the society. To be an *authentic meaning,* it must be in accord with our general value system. It not only need not, but by and large should not, however, mean pretending that there is no important difference between capacities and, above all potential contributions, at different age levels. Our greatest deficiency has been in this area of defining positive opportunity for the persons of advanced age. That there should have been a lag in this respect is understandable, but this does not lessen the urgency of the task. The medical and public health aspects of the care of illness and disability, in this even more than other connections, depends on providing such opportunity as its most fundamental precondition. For why should a person recover from an illness or take good care of his health, if there is nothing worth while for him to live for? He cannot be "forced to be free" unless freedom is the condition of something beyond it, which *both* he and the others whom he respects, really want, and value.

PART Three

HEALTH

AND ILLNESS

IO

Definitions of Health and Illness in the Light of American Values and Social Structure

THE aim of the present paper is to try to consider the socio-cultural definition of health and illness in the United States in the light, in the first instance, of American values, but also in terms of the ways in which the relevant aspects of the value system have come to be institutionalized in the social structure. I shall give primary attention to mental health, but will also attempt to define its relation to somatic health and illness as carefully as possible. I shall also try to place the American case in comparative perspective.

First, it is important to try to define the respects in which health and illness can be considered to be universal categories applying to all human beings in all societies and to distinguish them from the respects in which they may be treated as socially and culturally relative. It will be possible here to say only a few rather general things, but the development of social science does, I think, permit us to be somewhat more definite than it has been possible to be until rather recently.

There is clearly a set of common human features of health and illness; indeed more broadly there is probably a set of components

Reprinted from E. Gartly Jaco (Ed.), Patients, Physicians and Illness, New York, The Free Press of Glencoe, 1958.

which apply perhaps to all mammalian species. There is no general reason to believe that these common components are confined to somatic illness; my view would be that there are also such components for mental illness. It does, however, seem to be a tenable view that there is a range, roughly, from the "purely somatic" to the "purely mental"—both of course, being limiting concepts—and that as one progresses along that range the prominence of the factors of relativity as a function of culture and social structure increases. The importance of the "interpenetration" between somatic and mental aspects is so great, however, that it would be a mistake to draw a rigid line, in any empirical terms, between them.

One point is relatively clear. This is that the primary criteria for mental illness must be defined with reference to the social *role-performance* of the individual.[1] Since it is at the level of role-structure that the principal direct interpenetration of social systems and personalities come to focus, it is as an incapacity to meet the expectations of social roles, that mental illness becomes a problem in social relationships and that criteria of its presence or absence should be formulated. This is of course not at all to say that the state which we refer to as mental, as of somatic, illness is not a state of the individual; of course it is. But that state is manifest to and presents problems for both the sick person and others with whom he associates in the context of social relationships, and it is with reference to this problem that I am making the point about role-performance.

At the same time I would not like to treat mental health as involving a state of commitment to the performance of *particular* roles. Such a commitment would involve specific memberships in specific relational systems, *i.e.,* collectivities. Mental health is rather concerned with *capacity* to enter into such relationships and to fulfill the expectations of such memberships. In terms of the organization of the motivational system of the individual, it therefore stands at a more "general level" than do the more specific social commitments.

1. Both health and illness, in general, I would like to treat as states of the individual person; the "pathology" of social systems, real and important as it is, should not be called "illness" nor the absence of it, "health." Cf. Talcott Parsons, "The Mental Hospital as a Type of Organization," in *The Patient and the Mental Hospital,* edited by Milton Greenblatt, Daniel J. Levinson, and Richard H. Williams, New York, The Free Press of Glencoe, 1957.

There is a set of mechanisms in the operation of which social system and personality aspects are interwoven, which make possible the many complex adjustments to changing situations which always occur continually in the course of social processes. It is when the mechanisms involved in these adjustive processes break down ("adjustive" as between personalities involved in social interaction with each other) that mental illness becomes a possibility, that is, it constitutes one way in which the individual can react to the "strains" imposed upon him in the course of social process. This can, of course, occur at any point in his own life cycle from the earliest infancy on. Also, I take for granted that mental illness is only one of several alternative forms which "deviance" can take, again at every stage. Mental illness, then, including its therapies, is a kind of "second line of defense" of the social system vis-à-vis the problems of the "control" of the behavior of its members. It involves a set of mechanisms which take over when the primary ones prove inadequate. In this connection it can also be readily seen that there are two main aspects of the operation of the mechanisms involved. First, the individual who is incapacitated from performing his role-functions would be a disturbing element in the system if he still attempted to perform them. Hence we may say that it is important to have some way of preventing him from attempting to do so, both in his own interest and in that of the system itself. Secondly, however, there is the therapeutic problem, namely of how it is possible to restore him to full capacity and return him to role-performance after an interval.

So far, I have been speaking of mental health with special reference to its place in the articulation between social system and personality. Mental health—and illness—are states of the personality defined in terms of their relevance to the capacity of the personality to perform institutionalized roles. For analytical purposes, however, I have found it necessary to make a distinction, which a good many psychologists do not make, between the personality and the organism. They are, of course, not concretely separable entities, but they are analytically distinguishable systems. There would be various ways of making the distinction, but for present purposes I think it is best to put it that the personality is that part of the mechanisms involved in the control of concrete behavior which genetically goes back to the internalization of social objects and cultural patterns in the course of the process of socialization. The organism, as distinguished from this, consists of that part of the concrete living individual which is attributable to hereditary constitution and to the conditioning processes of the physical environment. Hence, from the point of view of its relation to the personality, it is that aspect of the mechanisms controlling behavior which is not attributable to the experience of socialization in and through processes of social interaction.[2]

It will be noted that I have been careful not to say that the mechanisms through which the personality component of the concrete individual functions are not "physiological." In my opinion, it is not the distinction between physiological and in some sense "mental" processes which is the significant one here. Indeed, I think that *all* processes of behavior on whatever level are mediated through physiological mechanisms. The physiological mechanisms which are most significant in relation to the more complex forms of behavior are, however, mainly of the nature of systems of "communication" where the physiological mechanisms are similar to the physical media and channels of communication. Hence, in both cases the content of "messages" cannot be deduced from the physical properties of the media. In the higher organisms, including man, it seems clear that the focus of these mechanisms rests in the central nervous system, particularly the brain, and that the next level down in the order of systems of control, has to do with the hormones which circulate through the blood stream.

It is important to stress this "interpenetration" of personality and organism, because, without it, the complex phenomena usually referred to as "psychosomatic" are not understandable. Correspondingly, I do not think that the way in which *both* somatic and mental health and illness can fit into a common sociological framework are understandable without both the distinction between personality and organism and the extreme intimacy of their interpenetrating relationship.

Coming back to the relation of both to the social system, I should

2. I have put forward this general type of view on two previous occasions. For the general conception of the relation of personality to the internalization of social and cultural objects, see Parsons and Bales, *Family, Socialization and Interaction Process,* New York, The Free Press of Glencoe, 1955. A more extended discussion of the relation of personality and organism will be found in Parsons, "An Approach to Psychological Theory in Terms of the Theory of Action," American Psychological Association, *Studies in General Theory,* ed. Sigmund Koch, New York, McGraw-Hill, 1958.

like to introduce a distinction which has not been consistently made by sociologists either in this or in other connections, but which I think is very important for present purposes. This is the distinction between *role* and *task*. There are many different definitions of the concept role in the sociological literature. For my present purpose, however, I think one very simple one is adequate, namely a role is the organized system of participation of an individual in a social system, with special reference to the organization of that social system as a collectivity.[3] Roles, looked at in this way, constitute the primary focus of the articulation and hence interpenetration between personalities and social systems. Tasks, on the other hand, are both more differentiated and more highly specified than roles; one role is capable of being analyzed into a plurality of different tasks.

Seen in these terms I think it is legitimate to consider the task to define the level at which the action of the individual articulates with the *physical* world, *i.e.,* the level at which the organism in the above analytical sense is involved in interaction with its environment in the usual sense of biological theory. A task, then, may be regarded as that subsystem of a role which is defined by a definite set of *physical* operations which perform some function or functions in relation to a role and/or the personality of the individual performing it. It is very important that processes of communication, the *meanings* of which are by no means adequately defined by the physical processes involved at the task level, are not only included in the concept of task, but constitute at least one of the most important, if not *the* most important, categories of tasks, or of components of them.[4]

3. This definition clearly matches that put forward by Merton as the "role-set." See R. K. Merton "The Role-Set," *British Journal of Sociology,* June 1957.

4. Thus I am at present engaged in the task of "writing" a paper on the institutionalization of the patterns of health and illness in American society. The "technique" I have chosen for this task is manipulating the keyboard and other parts of a typewriter. This process clearly engages the hands and fingers, eyes, and other parts of the physical organism; internally above all, the brain. The physical result is the arrangement on a number of sheets of paper, previously blank, of a very large number of what we call linguistic symbols; letters arranged in words, sentences and paragraphs. I could have chosen alternative techniques, such as writing longhand with a pen, or possibly dictating to a machine. In these cases the physical result might well have been different. But in any case the "significance" of the task is only partly "physical," it lies more in the "meanings" of what has been physically "written." Finally, the task of writing this paper is only one rather clearly defined subsystem of my *role* as sociologist.

Coming back to the problem of health and illness, I should now like to suggest that somatic illness may be defined in terms of incapacity for relevant task-performance in a sense parallel to that in which mental illness was thought of as incapacity for role-performance. In the somatic case the reference is not to any particular task, but rather to categories of tasks, though of course, sudden illness may force abandonment of level rather than any particular task.[5] Put the other way around, *somatic health is, sociologically defined, the state of optimum capacity for the effective performance of valued tasks.*

The relation between somatic and mental health, and correspondingly, illness, seen in this way, bears directly on the problem of levels of organization of the control of behavior. It implies that the "mind" is not a separate "substance" but essentially a level of organization, the components of which are "nonmental," in the same basic sense in which for example, the hypothetical isolated individual is "nonsocial." It further implies that the mental level "controls" the somatic, or in this sense, physical, aspect of the individual, the "organism." Somatic states are therefore necessary, but in general *not* sufficient conditions of effective mental functioning.[6]

THE PROBLEM OF "CULTURAL RELATIVITY" IN HEALTH AND ILLNESS

OUR present concern is with the relation of personality and organism on the one hand, the social system and its culture on the other. It is now possible to say something on the question of the relations between the universal human elements and the sociocultural variable ones in health and illness on both levels. Clearly,

5. Referring to the writing task, a paralysis of both arms would obviously incapacitate me for writing this and other papers on the typewriter, and for all other manual tasks, but not necessarily for dictating them to a secretary.

6. This view of the relation of mind and body and in turn, their relations to the two great categories of health and disease with which we are here concerned, does not imply that all "somatic" phenomena can be analyzed as standing on one level. For various reasons it seems to me that at least one comparably basic distinction needs to be made within the organism, as defined above, namely, between the "behavioral" system and what might be called the "homeostatic" system (what Franz Alexander calls the "vegetative" system—cf. his *Psychosomatic Medicine: Its Principles and Applications*, New York, W. W. Norton and Co., Inc., 1950). For present purposes, however, it is not necessary to go into these further refinements.

by the above definition, *all* human groups have highly organized personalities which must be built up by complex processes of the sort we call socialization and which are subject to various sorts of malfunctioning at the level of social adjustment which has been referred to. All human societies have language, a relatively complex social organization, complex systems of cultural symbols and the like. The individual in such a society, however "primitive," is always involved in a plurality of different roles which are the organizing matrix of the various tasks he performs.

Clearly this personality element of the structure of the individual person is closely interpenetrating and interdependent with the organic-somatic aspect. Hence, there are clearly "problems" of both somatic and mental illness and health for all human groups. Furthermore, all of them are deeply involved with the structures of the social system and the culture.

That there are uniformities in the constitutions of all human groups at the organic level goes without saying, and hence that many of the problems of somatic medicine are independent of social and cultural variability. Thus such things as the consequences and possibilities of control of infection by specific bacterial agents, the consequences of and liability to cancerous growths and many other things are clearly general across the board. This is not, however, to say that the *incidence* and probably degrees of severity of many somatic diseases are not functions of social and cultural conditions, through many different channels. But within considerable ranges, independent of the part played by such factors etiologically, the medical problems presented are essentially the same, though of course, how to implement medical techniques effectively is again partly a socio-cultural problem.

It follows from the conception of personality put forward here, that constancies in the field of mental health are intimately related to uniformities in the character of culture and social structure. Here it is particularly important that, after a period in which a rather undiscriminating version of the doctrine of "cultural relativity" was in the ascendant, much greater attention has recently come to be paid to the universals which are identifiable on these levels. It is not possible here to enter into any sort of detail in this field, but a few highlights may be mentioned.

Most fundamental, I think, is the fact that every known human society possesses a culture which reaches quite high levels of generalization in terms of symbolic systems, including particularly values and cognitive patterns, and that its social structure is sufficiently complex so that it comprises collectivities at several different levels of scope and differentiation. Even though, as is the case with most of the more "primitive" societies known, there is scarcely any important social structure which is not, on a concrete level, a kinship structure, such kinship systems are clearly highly differentiated from each other.

With minimal exceptions, the nuclear family of parents and still dependent children is a constant unit in all kinship systems, though structural emphases within it vary.[7] It is clearly the focal starting point for the process of socialization and the source of the primary bases of human personality organization. But the nuclear family *never* stands alone as a social structure, it is always articulated in complex ways with other structures which are both outside it and stand on a higher level of organization than it does. This involvement of the nuclear family with the wider social structure is, from the structural point of view, the primary basis of the importance of the incest taboo, which, as applying to the nuclear family, is known to be a near universal.[8] Put in psychological terms, this means that the internalization of the object systems and the values of the nuclear family and its subsystems, starting with the mother-child relation, constitutes the *foundation* of personality structure in all human societies. There are, of course, very important variations, but they are all variations on a single set of themes. Because the internalization of the nuclear family is the foundation of personality structure, I suggest that *all mental* pathology roots in disturbances of the relationship structure of the nuclear family as impinging on the child. This is not in the least to say that there are not somatic factors in mental pathology; some children may well be constitutionally impossible to socialize adequately. But the *structure* of pathological syndromes which can legitimately be called mental will always involve responses to family relationships.

It is, however, equally true and important that in no society is the socialization of an adult exhausted by his experience in the nuclear family, and hence in his personality *only* a function of the familial

7. Cf. M. Zelditch, Jr., "Role Differentiation in the Nuclear Family," Chapter VI of Parsons and Bales, *Family, Socialization and Interaction Process,* New York, The Free Press of Glencoe, 1955.

8. For a general discussion of the significance of the incest taboo, cf. chapter 3 of this volume, "The Incest Taboo in Relation to Social Structure and the Socialization of the Child."

object systems he has internalized. Correspondingly, mental pathology will always involve elements in addition to disturbances of the nuclear family relations, especially perhaps those centering about peer-group relations in the latency period and in adolescence. These other factors involve his relations to social groups other than the nuclear family and to higher levels of cultural generalization and social responsibility than any of those involved in the family.

It is thus, I think, fully justified to think of both mental and somatic pathology as involving common elements for all human groups. But at the same time both of them would be expected to vary as a function of social and cultural conditions, in important ways, and probably the more so as one progresses from the more "vegetative" aspects of organic function and its disturbances to the more behavioral aspects and then from the "deeper" layers of personality structure to the "higher" more "ego-structured" layers. It is also probable that the lower in this range, the more the variation is one of incidence rather than character of pathology, the higher the more it penetrates into the "constitution" of the illness itself.

HEALTH AMONG THE PROBLEMS OF SOCIAL CONTROL

HEALTH and illness, however, are not only "conditions" or "states" of the human individual viewed on both personality and organic levels. They are also states evaluated and institutionally recognized in the culture and social structure of societies. Can anything be said about the ways in which the constancy-variability problem works out at these levels?

Clearly the institutionalization of expectations with respect both to role and to task performance is fundamental in all human societies. There must, therefore, always be standards of "adequacy" of such performance and of the "capacities" underlying it which must be taken into account, and hence, a corresponding set of distinctions between states of individuals which are and are not "satisfactory" from the point of view of these standards. But by no means all types of "conformity" with performance-standards can be called "health" nor all types or modes of deviation from such conformity "illness." Are the categories health and illness, as we conceive them, altogether "culture-bound" or is there something about them which can be generalized on the social role-definition level? To answer this question, it will be necessary to enter a little more fully into the sociological problems presented by these definitions.

Since I am attempting to deal with illness in the context of "social control," I should like to approach the problem in terms of an attempt to classify ways in which individuals can deviate from the expectations for statuses and roles which have been institutionalized in the structure of their societies. In spite of the fact that it will complicate matters, it seems unavoidable to deal with the problem on two different levels.

The first of these two levels concerns the relation of the problem of health and illness to the whole range of categories of deviant behavior. In this connection, I shall attempt to assess the relative importance given to the health complex in different types of society and to show that it is particularly important in the American case. The second level will take up the problem of selectivity and variation *within* the health-illness complex itself. Here, I shall discuss how this relates to selective emphasis on the different components of the role of illness and of the therapeutic process, and will attempt to show that, not only does American society put greater stress on the problem of illness than do other societies, but that its emphases in defining the role and in therapy are also characteristically different.

I shall outline the classification I have in mind on the first level in terms of the way it looks in our own society and then raise the question of how universally it may be assumed that the relevant categories are in fact, differentiated from each other in different societies. The first category is that of the control of the capacities of units in the social structure in the sense in which this conception has been discussed above in connection with the definition of health and illness. Every society must have important concern for the level of these capacities. The present context, however, is that of social control, not socialization, so it is not a question of how these capacities come to be developed in the first place, but rather how tendencies to their disturbance can be forestalled, or, once having occurred, can be rectified.

Though comparable considerations apply to collectivities as units, in the present context the relevant unit is the human individual, and with reference to him we must consider both of the two aspects which have been distinguished, namely, somatic and mental health. Capacity, it will be remembered, is thought of as standing on a more "general" level than commitment to any particular role or task obligations. It does, however, include the motivation to accept such obligations given suitable situation and opportunity.

There is a second category of problem of social control in relation to the individual which in another sense also stands on a more general level than any particular action-commitments. This may be called the problem of *morality*. This concerns the state of the individual person, but not with respect to his capacities in the same sense as these are involved in the problem of health, but with respect to his commitment to the *values* of the society. This is the area of social control which has traditionally been most closely associated with religion, especially when the reference is to the person, rather than to any collective unit of the society. When I associate the problem with religion, I do not wish to imply that every attachment to a religion or religious movement automatically implies reinforcement of commitment to the values of a *society*. This is by no means necessarily the case. The point is, rather, that it is in the sphere of religious orientation, or its functional equivalents at the level of what Tillich calls "ultimate concern," that the individual must work out the problem of how far he is or is not committed to the values of his society.

There is, of course, a great deal of historical and cross-cultural variation in the ways in which individuals may be treated as standing in religious states which need to be remedied or rectified. It seems, however, to be sound to distinguish two very broad types, namely, those involving "ritual impurity" of some sort, and those involving the problem of "salvation" or "state of grace" in a sense comparable to the meanings of these terms within the Christian tradition. In speaking of religion in this connection, I also do not wish to rule out cases which do not include an explicitly "supernatural" reference in the meaning we would tend to give that term. Thus from a "humanistic" point of view the problem still exists of ensuring commitment to the humanistic values. Perhaps the best single example of this reference is the ritualistic aspect of classical Chinese culture with its "secular" ideal of the "superior man."

Both the above two contexts of the problem of social control of individuals refer to rather generalized states of individuals which may be conceived to "lie behind" their commitments to more differentiated and particularized role-obligations and norms. If both of these latter categories be interpreted in the context of social system involvement, then it is a problem in every society how far different elements in its population maintain operative commitments on both these levels which are compatible with the social interest.

The reference to norms, which I have in mind in the first instance in a society as a whole, focuses on the legal system. Any going society must cultivate a rather generalized "respect for law," and this must be specified in several directions to come down to the level of particular legal obligations.

It is important to note that commitment to law-observance stands on a level more general than that involved in any particular role. Such principles as honesty in the sense of respect for the property rights of others, "responsibility" in the sense of the obligation to fulfill contractual obligations once entered into, or recognition of the general legitimacy of political authority; none of these is specific to any particular role in a particular collectivity. In a highly differentiated society like our own, the practicing legal profession may be said to carry out functions of social control in this field which are in some ways parallel to those of the medical profession in the field of health.[9]

Of course, commitment to norms is by no means confined to the norms which in a modern type of society are given the "force of law." But the law first may serve as a prototype, and second is, in a well-integrated society, necessarily the paramount system of norms with respect to the society as a system, though norms of "morality" may as noted above, take precedence on a religious or purely "ethical" level. "Below" the legal level, however, every collectivity in the society has some set of rules, more or less formalized, to which it is essential to secure some order of commitment on the part of its members.

The last of the four contexts in which the problem of social control in the present sense arises is that of commitment to role-obligations in particular collectivities. This also is a broad category running all the way from the obligations of marriage, to a particular spouse, and of occupational commitment in a particular "job" to the obligations of the citizen of loyalty to his national government. One would expect mechanisms of social control to cluster about this area. In our own society, this is the least differentiated of the four, but cer-

9. Cf. Talcott Parsons, "A Sociologist Looks at the Legal Profession," in *Essays in Sociological Theory,* Revised Edition, New York, The Free Press of Glencoe, 1954.

tain relatively specialized agencies have begun to emerge. On the "lower" levels, social work is one of the more prominent. "Industrial sociology," so far as it is oriented to the problem of the individual worker as a member of a formal organization, is another. This is the area of which Chester Barnard spoke[10] as that of "efficiency" in the technical meaning he gave to that term.

I have taken the space to review these four different contexts of the problem of social control, because I think it is essential to have such a classification as a basis for placing the treatment of any of these problems in a comparative setting. In a highly differentiated society like our own, these four functions have become relatively clearly differentiated from each other, and the operative processes of social control are, with certain indefinite border-lines, of course, to be found in the hands of different organizational agencies. The last of the four I outlined is by a good deal the least firmly institutionalized as a distinct function and it is probably significant that, in our society, it is most fully worked out, through social work, for the lower status-levels of the society.

The present situation with respect to differentiation cannot, however, be said to be typical of all societies; indeed, I doubt whether any case can be found where a comparably close approach to completeness in this differentiation can be found.

Two major "axes" of differentiation were implicit in the classification I have just presented. Both need to be taken into account in placing the problem of health and illness relative to the others. The first of these may be called the differentiation in terms of orientation, on the one hand, to the exigencies of the *situation* in which the person must act; on the other hand, orientation to or through *normative patterns.* The second axis concerns not this problem, but that of whether the "problem" lies in the state of the person as a whole, at a level deeper than the problem of his acceptance of particular obligations, or whether it lies in the question of his "willingness" to accept certain more specific obligations, to particular norms and classes of norms, and to particular roles in particular collectivities.

The first of these two axes differentiates the types of deviance involved in illness and disturbance of commitments to collectivities on the one hand from those involved in disturbance of commitments to norms and to values on the other. The second axis differentiates the

10. C. I. Barnard, *The Functions of the Executive,* Harvard University Press, 1938.

problems of illness and of disturbance of commitment to values on the one hand from the problems of commitment to collectivities and to normative patterns (rules and law) on the other. The following tabular arrangement may be helpful to the reader.

	Disturbance of Total Person	Disturbance of Particular Expectations
"Situational" Focus	Problem of "capacities" for task and role performance Illness as deviance Health as "conformity"	Problem of commitments to collectivities (Barnard's "efficiency") Disloyalty as deviance Loyalty as conformity
"Normative" Focus	Problem of commitments to values, or of "morality" "Sin" and "immorality" as deviance State of grace or "good character" as conformity	Problem of commitments to norms, or of "legality" "Crime" and "illegality" as deviance Law-observance as conformity

It is in terms of the first axis that one fundamental type of differentiation involving health can be made, that which treats health as a "naturalistic" state which is not to be explained by or treated through religio-magical media. It is of course a commonplace that in all nonliterate societies, with relatively minor exceptions such as fractures, this differentiation has not yet taken place, and much the same can be said about the high civilizations of the Orient such as India and China until touched by Western medicine. This of course, is in no way to say that "therapies" which are couched in magico-religious terms are necessarily ineffective. On the contrary, there is much evidence that they have been very effective in certain cases. It would, however, hardly be denied that with the clear differentiation of roles in this area which has taken place in the modern world, much greater effectiveness has been made possible over at least a very large part of the range.

Though differentiation on the first axis discriminates the problem of health from that of the "ritual" state of the individual, or his state of grace or, more generally, commitment to values, it fails to discriminate between the more general level of his state "as a person" and his commitment to the more specific obligations of societal membership and activity. Here a problem which has been very central in the modern world in drawing the line between problems of mental health and of law seems to be a major one. This is the question of whether and how far the "deviance" of the individual from conformity with social expectations can be considered to be "intentional" *i.e.*, the question of how far he may legitimately be held *responsible* for his actions. In one area, at least, this has in fact come to be accepted as a main differentiating criterion and, I think, rightly so.

Let me try to elucidate a little some of its implications in the present context. It has long been one of the principal criteria of illness that the sick person "couldn't help it." Even though he may have become ill or disabled through some sort of carelessness or negligence, he cannot legitimately be expected to get well simply by deciding to be well, or by "pulling himself together." Some kind of underlying reorganizing process has to take place, biological or "mental," which can be guided or controlled in various ways, but cannot simply be eliminated by an "act of will." In this sense the state of illness is involuntary. On the other hand, both obedience to norms and fulfillment of obligations to collectivities in roles are ordinarily treated as involving "voluntary" decisions; the normal individual can legitimately be "held responsible."

Certainly both in fields such as law and in that of collectivity obligations, there are many cases where failure to live up fully to "formal" obligations is not "blamed on" the individual. But the distinction is, on the whole, clear; if he is not "ill" (or in a state of ritual impurity, or "sin"), or willfully recalcitrant, it must be the fault of somebody else or of "the system." The essential basis of this possibility of "holding responsible" is the particularity of specific norms and role-obligations. A normal person has the capacity to accept or reject particular obligations without involving a reorganization of the major structures of his personality or of his body. It is only when there is a "disturbance" which goes beyond these particularities that we can speak of illness, or of disturbed commitment to values.[11]

11. An interesting case of difficulty with respect to the line of discrimination discussed above is presented by Mark Field in his study of Soviet

This same problem occurs in the relation to the commitment to values as operating through religion and cognate mechanisms. It is very clear that among many nonliterate peoples, states of ritual impurity are treated as outside the control of the individual victim. They are states for which he may not legitimately be held responsible, except, and this is a most important exception which applies to illness as well, for subjecting himself to the proper treatment institutionally prescribed for those in such a state. In general, some ritual performance is called for, which may even sometimes be self-administered, to "rectify" his state.

Without attempting to discuss the situation in other major religions, it is a very important fact that the conception of original sin in the Christian tradition defines the situation in a cognate way. Though retroactively and mythologically Adam is held to have sinned "voluntarily," the burden of original sin on mankind is held not to be the responsibility of the individual, but something which is inherent in the human condition. Conversely, it cannot be escaped from without outside help.

Here it is important to distinguish original sin from the infraction of the norms and role-obligations of a religious collectivity. I think it can fairly be said that that aspect of "sin" which is treated by religious authorities as *within* the responsibility of the individual is strictly analogous to the civil responsibility for law-observance and/or the responsibility for living up to the obligations of a particular role, in this case of church-membership. Christianity thus has institutionalized the differentiation of these two aspects of the problem of social control. Original sin belongs, with respect to *this* axis of differentiation, on the same side as does illness.

With respect to the major categories I have been discussing for the last few pages, societies may be expected to differ in two major respects. The first I have already been stressing, namely with respect to the *degree* to which these major types of deviance are *differentiated from each other* and the functions of social control with respect to them institutionalized in differentiated agencies. In an evolutionary sense (with societal, not organic reference) they may be said all to

medical practice, where pressure has been put on physicians, more than in our own system, to provide excuses for avoiding extremely onerous and rigorously enforced role-obligations. Cf. his *Doctor and Patient in Soviet Russia*, Cambridge, Harvard University Press, 1957.

have originated in religion.[12] Priests and magicians have thus been the "original" agents of social control everywhere. The roles of physician, of lawyer and, if you will, of "administrator" and social worker have only gradually and unevenly differentiated off from the religious roles.

The second range of variation concerns the relative stress put on conformity with social expectations in each of these categories and hence the seriousness with which deviance in each is viewed, and the importance given to building up effective mechanisms of social control in the area in question as distinguished from others. Thus in a society like that of Hindu caste in India, the overwhelming emphasis seems to have been religious, with ritual purity on one level, the problem of control of and emancipation from the Hindu counterpart of Christian original sin on another as the primary preoccupations. The neglect of health as Westerners understand it in India (until very recently) is too well-known to need emphasizing. Soviet society may be said to be a type which puts primary emphasis on effective role-performance in the socialist state and hence to bend its primary efforts to controlling the commitments of the population (above all through "propaganda" and "agitation")[13] to exerting the utmost effort, especially in production. Finally, with differences, of course, it may be suggested that both classical Rome and modern England have laid more stress on law and integration through the legal system than any other of the major features with which this discussion has been concerned.

Seen in this perspective, contemporary American Society is, with respect to institutionalization of mechanisms of social control, probably as highly differentiated as any known, certainly as any outside the modern Western world. But among those which are highly differentiated, it is also one which places a very heavy emphasis on the field and problems of health and illness relative to the others, probably as high as any. It is also clear that our concern with problems of health has increased greatly since about the turn of the present century, and furthermore, that the emergence of the problem of mental health into a position of salience, on anything like the scale which has actually developed, is a new phenomenon.

12. This is a major thesis of Durkheim in *The Elementary Forms of the Religious Life,* New York, The Free Press of Glencoe, 1957.

13. Cf. Alex Inkeles, *Public Opinion in Soviet Russia,* Cambridge, Harvard University Press, 1950.

A RESTATEMENT OF THE CRITERIA
OF HEALTH AND ILLNESS

BEFORE attempting to relate this emphasis systematically to American values and social structure, it would be well to attempt to state somewhat more precisely what seem to be the principal general characteristics of health and illness seen in the context of social role structure and social control.

Health may be defined as the state of optimum *capacity* of an individual for the effective performance of the roles and tasks for which he has been socialized. It is thus defined with reference to the individual's participation in the social system. It is also defined as *relative* to his "status" in the society, *i.e.,* to differentiated type of role and corresponding task structure, *e.g.,* by sex or age, and by level of education which he has attained and the like. Naturally, also there are qualitative ranges in the differentiation of capacities, within sex groups and at given levels of education. Finally, let me repeat that I am defining health as concerned with capacity, not with commitment to *particular* roles, tasks, norms or even values as such. The question of whether a man wants to remain with his wife or likes his particular job or even feels committed to refrain from highway robbery is not *as such* a health problem, though a health problem may underlie and be interwoven with problems of this sort.

Illness, then, is also a socially institutionalized role-type. It is most generally characterized by some imputed generalized disturbance of the capacity of the individual for normally expected task or role-performance, which is not specific to his commitments to any particular task, role, collectivity, norm or value. Under this general heading of the recognition of a state of disturbance of capacity, there are then the following four more specific features of the *role* of the sick person: (1) This incapacity is interpreted as beyond his powers to overcome by the process of decision-making alone; in this sense he cannot be "held responsible" for the incapacity. Some kind of "therapeutic" process, spontaneous or aided, is conceived to be necessary to recovery. (2) Incapacity defined as illness is interpreted as a legitimate basis for the *exemption* of the sick individual, to varying degrees, in varying ways and for varying periods according to the nature of the illness, from his normal role and task obligations. (3) To be ill is thus to be in a partially and conditionally *legitimated* state. The essential condition of its legitimation, however, is the recognition by the sick person that to be ill is inherently *undesirable,* that he therefore has an obligation to try to "get well" and to cooperate with others to this end. (4) So far as spontaneous forces, the *vis medicatrix naturae,* cannot be expected to operate adequately and quickly, the sick person and those with responsibility for his welfare, above all, members of his family, have an obligation to *seek competent help* and to cooperate with competent agencies in their attempts to help him get well; in our society, of course, principally medical agencies. The valuation of health, of course, also implies that it is an obligation to try to *prevent* threatened illness where this is possible.

These criteria seem very nearly obvious on a common sense level in our society, but some aspects of their subtler significance become evident when we consider the way in which, through the channels of mental and psychosomatic illness, the balance of health and illness comes to be bound up with the balance of control of the motivation of individuals in their relation to the society as a system. This is what I had in mind in discussing illness in the context of the problems of deviance and social control in the first place. I shall not take space to go into this set of problems here, since they have been dealt with elsewhere, but will only call attention to them, and draw a few inferences.[14]

The most important inferences for present purposes concern the importance of *two* related but distinct functions for the society of the health-illness role structure. The first of these is the *insulation* of the sick person from certain types of mutual influence with those who are not sick, and from association with each other. The essential reason for this insulation being important in the present context is not the need of the sick person for special "care" so much as it is that, motivationally as well as bacteriologically, illness may well be "contagious." The motives which enter into illness as deviant behavior are partially identical with those entering into other types of devi-

14. I have dealt with them primarily in the following places: *The Social System,* Chapter X, New York, The Free Press of Glencoe, 1951; the paper "Illness and the Role of the Physician," *American Journal of Orthopsychiatry,* July 1951, pp. 452–460, also printed in Kluckhohn, Murray, and Schneider, *Personality in Nature, Society and Culture,* 2nd Edition, New York, Alfred A. Knopf, 1953, and in somewhat more specialized context in Parsons and Fox, "Illness, Therapy and the Modern Urban American Family," *Journal of Social Issues,* Vol. 8, pp. 31–44.

ance, such as crime and the breakdown of commitment to the values of the society, partly they are dynamically interrelated with these so that stimulation of one set of motives may tend to stimulate others as well.

In the light of the motivational problem the important feature of insulation is the deprivation, for the sick person, of any claim to a more general legitimacy for his pattern of deviance. As noted above, the conditional legitimation which he enjoys is bought at a "price," namely, the recognition that illness itself is an undesirable state, to be recovered from as expeditiously as possible. It is at this price that he is permitted to enjoy the often very powerful gratifications of secondary gain. But the importance of the institutionalization of the role of illness is not confined to its bearing on the motivational balance of the sick person. As Durkheim pointed out for the case of crime, the designation of illness as illegitimate is of the greatest importance to the healthy, in that it reinforces their own motivation *not* to fall ill, thus to avoid falling into a pattern of deviant behavior. The stigmatizing of illness as undesirable, and the mobilization of considerable resources of the community to combat illness is a reaffirmation of the valuation of health and a countervailing influence against the temptation for illness, and hence the various components which go into its motivation, to grow and spread. Thus, the sick person is prevented from setting an example which others might be tempted to follow.

The second important implication of institutionalization of the roles is that being categorized as ill puts the individual in the position of being defined as "needing help" and as obligated to accept help and to cooperate actively with the agency which proffers it. The role of illness is not confined to its bearing on the motivational in it into contact with therapeutic agencies. It is therefore involved in both negative and positive mechanisms of social control, negative in that the spread of certain types of deviance is inhibited, positive in that remedial processes are facilitated.

An interesting and important intermediate aspect may also be noted. By defining the sick person as in need of help and tending to bring him into relation to therapeutic agencies, the role of illness tends to place him in a position of *dependency on* persons who are *not* sick. The structural alignment, hence, is of each sick person with certain categories of nonsick, not of groups of sick persons with each other.[15]

AMERICAN VALUES AND THE HEALTH PROBLEM

NOW let us turn to the question of the way in which American values and social structure may be said to operate selectively with reference both to the place of the health-illness complex among other mechanisms of social control and with respect to emphases within the health-illness complex itself. To start with it will be necessary to sketch the main outline of the American value system in the relevant respects.

I would like to suggest that even so complex and highly differentiated a society as our own can be said to have a relatively well-integrated system of institutionalized common values at the societal level. Ours I shall characterize as a pattern emphasizing "activism" in a certain particular sense, "worldliness" and "instrumentalism." Let me try, briefly, to explain these terms.

In the first place, a societal value system concerns the orientations of members to conceptions of what is desirable for the society itself and as a whole as a system or object of evaluation. Only derivatively, does it provide patterns of evaluation of the individual. When I refer to activism, I mean that in relation to *its* situation or environment, the society should be oriented to mastery over that environment in the name of ideals and goals which are transcendental with reference to it. The relevant environment may be either physical or social, but because of our relative isolation from other societies until the last generation or so, the physical environment has been particularly prominent in our case. The reference point for exerting "leverage" on the environment has been, historically, in the first instance religious. It will not be possible here to go into the question of the sense in which, or degree to which this is still the case; nevertheless, the main orientation clearly is one of maintaining the pattern of

15. The latter does of course happen in hospital situations. It has been clearly shown (Cf. Ivan Belknap, *Human Problems of a State Mental Hospital*, New York, McGraw-Hill, 1956, and Barbara Burt Arnason, unpublished Ph.D. Dissertation, Radcliffe College, 1958) that in mental hospital settings the social group of chronic patients, particularly in a kind of symbiosis with attendants, can, under certain circumstances, come to constitute a seriously *anti*-therapeutic social community.

mastery, not of "adjustment" to the inevitable. In no field has this been more conspicuous than that of health where illness has presented a challenge to be met by mobilizing the resources of research, science, etc., to the full.

When I speak of the "worldliness" of the American value system, I mean that, in spite of its religious roots, the *field* of primarily valued activity is in practical secular pursuits, not in contemplation or devotions, or aesthetic gratifications. In its societal application this means a conception of an ideal *society,* originally the Kingdom of God *on Earth,* in a secularized version a good society in which such ideals as liberty, justice, welfare and equality of opportunity prevail.

Finally, when I speak of "instrumentalism," I refer to the fact that, in the first instance for the society as a system, there is no definitive "consummatory" state which is idealized, no definitive societal goal state which is either attained or not—as in the case of "communism." There is rather an indefinite perspective of possible improvement, of "progress" which fulfills by degrees the ideal by moving in the right *direction.*

The absence of a definitive goal for the system as a whole, places the primary active achievement emphasis on the level of the goals of *units* and measures their achievements in appropriate terms. There is a kind of "liberal" pluralism in that any unit in the society, individual or collective, has liberty to pursue goals which to it may seem worthwhile, but more importantly, there are standards of *contribution* to the progress of the society. Perhaps the most obvious (though not the only) field of such contribution is that of economic productivity, for it is the productivity of the economy which is the basis of the availability of facilities for attaining *whatever* goals may seem most worthwhile, since income as generalized purchasing power is nonspecific with respect to particular uses. This is the most generalized basis of opportunity to do "good things." But equally important is the provision of the society with units which have the *capacity* for valued achievement.

I may note that collective units and their achievements are of the utmost importance in the American system, for example, the business firm. But their achievements are fundamentally dependent on the capacities and commitments of the human individuals who perform roles and tasks within them. It is in this connection that the relevance of the valuation of health appears. For the individual, the primary focus of evaluation is universalistically judged *achievement*. The possibility of achievement is, of course, a function of opportunity at any given point in his life cycle, which in turn is a function of the economic level of the community, because openings both for self-employment, *e.g.,* in independent business, and for employment by others, are a function of markets and of funds available through whatever channels. But on a "deeper" and in a sense more generalized level, this achievement is dependent on two basic sets of prior conditions which underlie his capacities, namely, on education in the broadest sense, and on health. It is in the first instance as an essential condition of valued achievement, that the health of the individual is itself valued.

There is another very central strand in the pattern of our evaluation in both respects. This is the relation of both education and health to the valuation of *equality* of opportunity. For reasons which cannot be gone into here, but which bear above all on the high level of structural differentiation of our society, it is one which shows a great deal of mobility of resources. Ascribed status is relatively minimized. The "pluralism of goals" which has to do with the instrumental emphasis in our value system raises the problem of "justice" with great acuteness. One aspect of this is distributive justice with references to the allocation of rewards. But with the emphasis on active achievement, even more crucial than justice of reward distribution is that of *opportunity* for valued achievement. But education and health are clearly more fundamental conditions of achievement than is access to investment funds or to employment, since they condition capacity to exploit opportunity in this narrower sense. Hence, *access* to education and to health services becomes, in a society like our own, a peculiarly central focus of the problem of justice in the society.

On technical grounds I do not classify education as a function of social control in a society.[16] Within the field of problems of social control, as discussed above, the problem of health clearly constitutes the "rock bottom" of the series. There seem, when the problem is seen in this light, to be a number of reasons which I may review briefly, why it has emerged into a position of special prominence in contemporary America.

First, and of course a very important point, the development of

16. In my own technical terms, it is a "pattern-maintenance" function.

medicine and of the health sciences underlying and associated with it, has made possible an entirely new level of control of illness, both preventive and therapeutic, far higher than has ever existed before in history. There is, of course, interdependence. American medicine did not just take over a medical science ready-made, but has developed the European beginnings with an energy and resourcefulness probably matched only in the field of industrial technology. There is, hence, interdependence between the development, on the one hand, of medical science and technology, and on the other, of interest in, and concern for, effective handling of health problems.

Secondly, the order of significance of the problems of social control, starting with commitment to paramount values themselves, running through commitment to norms, then to roles and tasks, is probably, in a very broad sense, of evolutionary significance. This is to say that there is a tendency for a problem area to emerge into salience only when, to a degree, the ones ahead of it in the priority list have in some sense been "solved." This is not to say that any of them ever are definitively solved, but in a relative sense one can speak of solution.

It is not possible to discuss this question here in detail. But it may be suggested that by the mid-nineteenth century, with the very important exception of the problem of the South, a certain national unity had been achieved in terms of values and norms.[17] It can then be further suggested that in the latter half of the nineteenth century there was concentration on the problems of setting up the new industrial system with the institutionalization of the principal role-categories which have to go into that, notably, of course, an occupational role system which was structurally quite different from that of the earlier society of "farmers and mechanics." Not least important in this connection was the institutionalization of the repercussions of these changes on the family, because of the drastic nature of the differentiation of occupational from familial roles. From the point of view of the individual, it may be said that the development of the industrial economy provided, in terms of structural type congruent with American values, a new level of solution of the problem of opportunity.

From this point of view, one might say that after the turn of the

17. Dr. R. N. Bellah, in an unpublished paper, has suggested the great importance of revivalist religion in the former of these contests.

century the stage was set for a new level of concern with the problems of education and health, which have indeed figured very prominently in this period, though not by any means to the exclusion of
the others. Their importance is, I think, further accentuated by another
feature of the development of the society. This is the fact that, with
the development of industrialization, urbanism, high technology,
mass communications and many other features of our society, there
has been a general *upgrading* to higher levels of responsibility. Life
has necessarily become more complex and has made greater demands
on the typical individual, though different ones at different levels.
The sheer problem of capacity to meet these demands has, therefore,
become more urgent. The motivation to retreat into ill-health
through mental or psychosomatic channels, has become accentuated
and with it the importance of effective mechanisms for coping with
those who do so retreat.

Seen in terms of this kind of historical perspective, it makes sense,
I think, that *the first major wave of development of the health institutions was in the field of somatic illness and the techniques of
dealing with it, and that this has been followed by a wave of interest
in problems of mental health.* This is partly, but by no means
wholly, because the scientific basis for handling somatic illness has
developed earlier and farther. In addition to this, it is well known
that the resistances to recognizing the existence of health problems
are stronger in the field of mental than of somatic health. Furthermore, a larger component of the phenomena of mental illness presumably operates through motivation and is hence related to the
problems and mechanisms of social control. Social changes, however,
have not only increased the strain on individuals, thus accentuating
the need for mechanisms in this area, but some of the older mechanisms have been destroyed or weakened and a restructuring has been
necessary.

For one thing, levels of mental pathology which could be tolerated under pre-industrial conditions, have become intolerable under
the more stringent pressures of modern life; this probably includes
the pushing of many types of personality over the borderline into
overt psychosis, who otherwise would have been able to "get along."
Furthermore, the family, for example, has undertaken a greatly increased burden in the socialization and personality-management
fields, and new institutional arrangements for dealing with the health

problems of its members are required. This seems, for example, to be one major factor in the rapid spread of hospitalization.[18]

I may sum up this aspect of the discussion by saying that both by virtue of its value system, and by virtue of the high level of differentiation of its social structure, American society has been one in which it could be expected that the problem of health, and within this more particularly of mental health, would become particularly salient. Its "liberal" cast which militates against highly stringent integration with reference to a system goal tends to emphasize the problem of getting units to "come along." The human individual is the end of the series of units on which the functioning of the society depends, and is hence the "last resort" in this connection. At the same time, the activistic orientation of the society militates against any orientation which would be inclined to let individuals "rest on their oars," but puts very much of a premium on the protection and development of capacity in the sense in which I have discussed it here.

The same factors, particularly seen in the context of the stage of development of the society, tend to prevent too strong an emphasis on any of the other primary problems and modes of social control. Generally, I think, contrary to much opinion, it can be said that the American society is very firmly attached to its primary values, so much so that they tend to be placed outside the field of serious concern. There is, to be sure, much controversy about what are alleged to be changes in values. But a careful analysis, which cannot be entered into here, will reveal that very much, at least, of this does not lie at this level, but rather at ideological levels.

A very good example of this is the amount of concern displayed over the developing salience of problems of mental health, and the scope given to the permissive and supportive elements in the orientation to the mentally ill. But people who show this concern often forget to emphasize the other side of the coin, namely, the equally prominent concern with therapy, with bringing the mentally ill back into full social participation, which above all, means into full capacity for achievement. Particularly revealing, I think, is the conception that the therapeutic process involves active *work* on the part of the patient, his seriously *trying* to get well. He is conceived of as anything but a passive object of the manipulations of the therapeutic personnel.

18. Cf. Parsons and Fox, *op. cit.*, for a further analysis of this problem.

AMERICAN SELECTIVITY WITHIN THE
PATTERNS OF HEALTH AND ILLNESS

I HAVE argued above, that among the problems and mechanisms of social control, both the values and the social structure of American society will tend to place emphasis on the problems of health and illness which concern commitment to roles, as compared with those of commitment to collectivities, to normative rules, or to the values themselves. This essentially is to say that it is *capacity* which is the primary focus of the problem of social control for us. With the increasing complexity and "maturity" of the society in turn, the problem of motivation to adequate role-performance and hence, to mental health becomes a salient one.

The problem now arises of what kind of selectivity we may expect, on the basis of the above analysis, *within* the complex of illness, and the corresponding attitudes toward therapy, relative to other ways of treating the problem of illness as such. In order to approach this question, I would like to use the formulation of the main components of the definition of illness, as stated previously herein, as my main point of reference. The first point, namely, a disturbance of capacity, is general, and is the link with the foregoing discussion of selectivity among the problems of social control. This is to say that in the United States we are more likely to interpret a difficulty in an individual's fufilling social role-expectations as a disturbance in capacity, *i.e.*, as illness, than is true in other types of society with other types of value systems.

The other four criteria, it will be remembered, were exemption from role-obligations, holding the patient not responsible for his state, conditional legitimation of the state, and acceptance of the need for help and of the obligation to cooperate with the source of the help.

My suggestion is that, compared with other societies in which other value systems have been institutionalized, in the American case the heaviest emphasis among these tends to go to the last. Essentially, this derives from the element in the American value system which I have called "activism" above. The implication of that element, in the context of the others to which it relates, is for the personality of the individual, the valuation of *achievement*. This in turn, as was developed above, implies a strong valuation of the capacities which under-

lie achievement, capacities which are primarily developed through
education or socialization and protected and restored through health
services. But in the American case, this does not imply that the primary stress is on the dependency aspect of the "need for help"—I
shall return to the question of the role of dependency presently. It is
rather, from the point of view of the society, the attitude which as-
serts the desirability of *mastery* of the problems of health, and from
that for the individual sick person, the obligation to cooperate
fully with the therapeutic agency, that is to *work* to achieve his own
recovery. The rationale of this is plainly that, if he is not motivated
to work to attain the conditions of effective achievement, he cannot
very well be considered to be motivated to the achievements which
require good health as a condition.

It might then be said that the other three components of the role
of illness are institutionalized as subsidiary to, and instrumental to,
this one. With respect to legitimation there is a particularly strong
emphasis on its *conditional* aspect, that illness is only legitimized
so long as it is clearly recognized that it is intrinsically an undesirable state, to be recovered from as expeditiously as possible.
Similarly, with the factor of exemption from role-performance and
the "admission" that the patient cannot be held responsible in the
sense discussed above. In this connection, there is a very important
relation to the scientific aspect of our cultural tradition. That the
patient "can't help it" is simply one of the facts of life, demonstrated
by medical science. Where scientific evidence is not available, the
tendency is to give the benefit of the doubt to the possibility that he
can help it. Thus, we tend to be relatively suspicious of plans for
"free" health care because of the readiness to impute malingering
wherever objective possibility for it exists.

I shall wish to suggest very tentatively how this American
emphasis on active therapy differs from emphases in other societies,
but before taking this up, I would like to try broadly to answer two
other sets of questions about the American case. The first of these is
how the patterning of illness in our society relates to the problem
of the *directions* of deviant behavior, the second to selective emphases
among the social components involved in the therapeutic process.

In a previous publication, I attempted to classify the directions
which deviant orientations might take in terms of three major
dimensions, two of which were very close to, if not identical with,

those set forth by Merton.[19] These were first the variation between *alienation* from social expectations and *compulsive conformity* with them, second between *activity* and *passivity,* and third between *object*-primacy and *pattern*-primacy. The first two of these are the ones also selected by Merton.

In terms of these first two dimensions, illness clearly belongs in the general category of a type of deviance categorized by alienation and by passivity. This general type I have designated as withdrawal whereas Merton calls it "retreatism." This tendency to withdrawal as the most prominent type of deviance is typical of American society generally. But some of the dynamics of it are relevant to the questions of selectivity within the components of the pattern of illness.

Before entering into these, however, it may be noted that with respect to the American pattern of illness, I think it can be said that the primary focus is object-oriented rather than pattern-oriented. This is above all because illness focuses at the level of capacity for role and task performance, not at the level of norms or values and conformity with them. This would also be true of illness generally but for reasons which will be discussed presently. I think it likely that it is more accentuated in the American case than others.[20]

What then, can be said to be some of the main patterns of motivational dynamics relevant to the problem of illness in American society and their relation in turn to these features of the role of illness as an institutionalized role? I may start by suggesting that all patterns of deviant behavior, as distinguished from creative alteration of the cultural or normative tradition, involves the primacy of elements of *regressive* motivational structure in the psychological sense.[21] But for different types of deviance and within the category of illness as a type of deviance there will be selective emphases on different phases of psychological regression.

19. Cf. *The Social System, op. cit.,* Chapter VII, and R. K. Merton, *Social Theory and Social Structure,* New York, The Free Press of Glencoe, 1957, rev. ed., Chapter IV.

20. By the three critera, then, of alienation, passivity, and object-orientation, the pattern of illness should be considered a case of "compulsive independence" (*Social System, op. cit.,* p. 259). Compulsive independence in this case may be interpreted to involve reaction-formation against underlying dependency needs, as I shall note.

21. A fuller discussion of the nature of the "regression scale" will be found in *Family, Socialization and Interaction Process, op. cit.,* especially Chapter II.

It is not possible to enter into all the complications here, but I suggest that in the American case, the primary focus lies in the residues of the pre-oedipal mother-child relationship, that phase of which Freud spoke as involving the "first true object-attachment." The basis on which this develops goes back to the very great, and increasing prominence in socialization of the relatively *isolated* nuclear family. The "American dilemma" in this case is that the child is, typically, encouraged to form an extremely intense attachment to the mother at this time, while at the same time he is required later to break more radically with this early dependency because the process of emancipation from the family of orientation is pushed farther and faster than in other systems. Independence training, that is to say, forms a particularly prominent part of our socialization process and the strength of the mother attachment is an essential condition of its successful carrying out.

The alienation involved in the motivation to illness may then be interpreted to involve alienation from a set of expectations which put particular stress on independent achievement. Because of this complex, the importance of the passivity component of the deviance expressed in illness is particularly great, because the ambivalent motivational structure about the dependency-independence problem is particularly prominent. Therapy then focuses on the strengthening of the motivation to independence relative to dependency and on overcoming the alienation, focussing on the expectations of independence and, through it, achievement.[22]

I suggest, then, that the American pattern of illness is focussed on the problem of capacity for achievement for the individual person. Therapeutically, recovery is defined for him as a *job* to be done in cooperation with those who are technically qualified to help him. This focus then operates to polarize the components of the "problem" in such a way that *the primary threat to his achievement capacity which must be overcome is dependency.* The element of exemption from ordinary role-obligations may then be interpreted as permissiveness for temporary relief from the strains of trying hard to achieve. The patient is permitted to indulge his dependency needs under strictly regulated conditions, notably his recognition of the condi-

22. In this light the motivation to illness may, with only apparent paradox, be characterized as a case of "compulsive independence from the requirement to be independent." It is a kind of "to hell with it all" pattern of withdrawal.

tional nature of the legitimacy of his state, and exposure to the therapeutic task.[23]

These elements of the situation relate in turn to the components of the therapeutic process. I have elsewhere[24] designated these, in terms of role-pattern, as permissiveness, support, selective rewarding and reinforcement. An essential point is that the dependency component of the deviance of illness is used constructively in the therapeutic pattern, essentially through what is in certain respects a recapitulation of the socializing experience. This is to say that through permissiveness to express dependency, both in exemption from role-obligations and in supportive relations to others, the patient is encouraged to form a dependent attachment to others. The permissive and supportive treatment of the sick person, by giving him what he wants, undercuts the alienative component of the motivational structure of his illness. He finds it much more difficult to feel alienated toward social objects who treat him with kindness and consideration than he would otherwise be disposed to feel—though, of course, there may be a problem, particularly with some types of mental illness of getting him to accept such kindness and consideration, even to accept his need for the exemptions permitted by virtue of illness.

At the same time the element of dependency, through "transference," is the basis of a strong attachment to therapeutic personnel, which can then be used as a basis of leverage to motivate the therapeutic "work" which eventually should result in overcoming the dependency itself, or mitigating it sufficiently so that it no longer interferes so seriously with his capacities. Building on this, then, the

23. Unfortunately, there will be no opportunity in this paper to take up the empirical problem of how far the available data on illness bear out this interpretation of the central importance of the dependency-independency axis. Not only do I suggest that this is more important in the American case than in others but also that it applies to somatic as well as mental illness. The ulcer complex is widely believed to relate especially to this problem. It may also be suggested that the special concern with polio in America relates to our horror of the dependency which the permanent cripple must bear. Almost better death than not to be able to do one's part, but remain dependent on others.

24. Cf. *The Social System, op. cit.,* Chapter VII and Parsons, Bales, and Shils, *Working Papers in the Theory of Action,* New York, The Free Press of Glencoe, 1953, Chapter V. In earlier versions, what I am now calling selective rewarding was called "denial of reciprocity" (this term emphasized only the negative aspect) and what I now call reinforcement was called "manipulation of rewards." The new term for the latter emphasizes the continuity of a *pattern* of rewards over time.

active work of therapy, adapting to the fundamental conditions of
the biological and psychological states of the patient, can take hold
and operate to propel toward recovery.[25]

I should finally like to turn to a brief and very tentative sugges-
tion of the main differences between the orientations to illness in the
United States and in two other modern societies, namely Soviet
Russia and Great Britain. Let us take the Soviet case first.[26]

Whereas in the American case I suggested that our concern with
capacity for role-achievement put the primary emphasis on the
restoration of that capacity through therapeutic work, the general
orientation of Soviet society is different; it is to the attainment of a
collective goal for the society as a whole, the "building of socialism."
With reference to the problem of illness this tends to shift the
emphasis from obligation to cooperate in therapy to the problem of
responsibility and non-responsibility. This is most conspicuous in the
field of mental illness where the Soviet attitude is an extreme antithesis of our own precisely on this point.[27] One very telling expression of it is the complete prohibition of psychoanalysis, whereas
psychoanalysis has had greater success in the United States than in
any other country. My interpretation of this would be that psychoanalysis is a threat from the Soviet point of view, because through
the theory of the unconscious, it so strongly emphasizes the elements
in the personality of the individual which are outside his voluntary
control. It would give too plausible excuses for too many for the evasion of responsibility. In the American case, on the other hand,

25. In Parsons and Fox, *op. cit.*, it was suggested that the trend toward
hospitalization, again in cases of both mental and somatic illness, was related to these factors. On the one hand, it is related to technological exigencies of modern medicine. Also it is a way of relieving the family of
burdens of "care." But at the same time it is both a way of protecting the
family from the patient, that is above all the impact of his dependency
needs on other members, and the point of primary present importance, of
protecting the patient from his family. The family, that is to say, is very
likely to be "over-protective" and over-supportive. Because of the tempta-
tions of "seduction" of the patient into more or less permanent dependency,
it lacks the basis of effective leverage which a more "impersonal" agency
may be in a position to exert. Also, it was noted above, there is reason to
believe that the acuteness of the dependency problem has been increasing
with recent developments in family structure.

26. My most important sources on Soviet medicine are Field, *op. cit.*,
and R. A. Bauer, *The New Man in Soviet Psychology.* I am also indebted
to Dr. Field for suggestions made in personal discussion which go beyond
his book.

27. Cf Bauer, *op. cit.*

psychoanalysis is defined more as offering *opportunity* for constructive therapeutic work, to the patient as well as the therapist.[28]

The same general strain seems to be conspicuous, from Field's account, in the field of somatic medicine. The attitude seems to be one of reluctant concession to human frailties. Of course, it is part of socialism to have a national medical service, but at the same time party and administrative personnel keep strict watch on the medical people to be sure that they do not connive in malingering which—because of the great severity of labor discipline—they have been under strong pressure to do. To American eyes the Soviet treatment of illness seems to be marked by a certain perfunctoriness, as if it were up to the patient to prove that he is "really" sick rather than it being the physician's role to investigate the possibilities on his own. I suggest that this may be more than a matter of scarcity of personnel and resources; it is probably at least in part an authentic expression of Soviet values.

Reinforcing this conclusion is the probability that illness is not the primary type of deviance for Soviet society in the sense that I have argued it is in the American case. I think it probable that what I have called "compulsive acquiescence in status-expectations" is the most prominent type. This, of course, very generally does not appear overtly as deviance at all and hence is difficult to detect.[29]

There is, however, another side of the Soviet picture, just as there is in the American case of polarity between the emphasis on active mastery and the problem of dependency. This is that in medical care, especially in the hospital, there seems to be a particularly strong supportive emphasis. This is to say that, once the status of being sick is granted, there is not nearly so strong an emphasis on the conditional character of its legitimacy as in the American case, and patients are encouraged to relax and to enjoy being taken care of.[30]

This suggests a permissiveness for regression, but one which is differently structured from the American. It is less the need to express dependency on particular social objects which does not threaten essential acceptance or belongingness. Psychologically it suggests

28. The extent to which the ego as distinct from the id has come to be emphasized in American versions of psychoanalysis seems to fit with this interpretation.

29. Cf. *Social System, op. cit.* This is Merton's "ritualism."

30. On this point I am directly indebted to Dr. Field (personal discussion).

primacy of oral components rather than of the mother-child love-attachment.

Thus, on the one hand, the role of illness is not given nearly so wide a scope in Soviet Russia as in the United States, particularly in the direction of mental illness. At the same time, it is also differently structured in that the primary focus is the problem of the responsibility of the individual rather than his capacity in our sense to achieve and to cooperate in recovery. The permissive element is more for "rest," for relaxation from responsibility, than it is for the direct expression of object-oriented dependency.

The British case does not seem to be quite so clear, but I think it is different in important ways from either the American or the Soviet. By contrast, with the other two, British society has a particularly strong integrative emphasis. From this point of view, illness is not so much a threat to the achievement of the individual or to his responsibility as it is a threat to his *status* as an acceptable member of the society and its various relevant subgroupings. The main emphasis in treatment then would be on reintegration, an element which is always present, but is more strongly stressed in the British case than in others.

One important type of evidence is the particularly strong British feeling that the sick individual has a *right* to care in case of illness. The whole welfare state is related to the integrative emphasis in the society, but the particularly full coverage provided by the National Health Service for the whole population is one very salient aspect of this general orientation. On the part of the nation and its health agencies then, it is strongly declared that illness, far from jeopardizing the individual's status, gives him special claims on the collectivity. The burden of proof is not nearly so much on him that he is "really" sick as in either the American or the Soviet cases. One might speak of a scale of decreasing "tolerance of the possibility of malingering" in the order, British, American, Soviet.

Another interesting point is that, with respect to the scope given to the recognition of mental illness, the British case is intermediate between the American and the Soviet; this includes the position of psychoanalysis. I suggest that this has to do with the very strong British emphasis on the importance of self-control in social relations. Somatic illness is generally clearly beyond the responsibility of the individual, and generally the legitimacy of illness is not made so highly conditional as in the American case. But capacity is not so highly valued and mental disturbance is not to the same extent seen as an opportunity for therapeutic achievement. The deliberately encouraged regression which, with all the differences, is shared by the Soviet and American cases, is substantially less conspicuous in the British.

The above are, as I have emphasized, extremely tentative and sketchy impressions of relatively systematic differences between American, Soviet, and British selectivities in the definition of health and illness, and in the roles of patient and of therapeutic agencies. I have introduced them and carried the analysis as far as I have, only to try to give some empirical substance to the general view of the nature of variability from one society to another in those respects that have been presented herein.

I I

Mental Illness and "Spiritual Malaise": THE ROLE OF THE PSYCHIATRIST AND OF THE MINISTER OF RELIGION

THE recent period in the development of Western society generally, and of the United States in particular, has posed with increasing urgency the problem of this paper. Whatever the situation with respect to whether or not mental illness has increased notably in our time, there is no question that *concern* with the problem of mental illness has become very much more salient than it was, for instance, in the nineteenth century. Furthermore, a growing intellectual tradition of psychology and psychoanalysis which is concerned with the diagnosis of mental illness, and with the definition of appropriate therapeutic measures, has become an increasingly prominent feature of the cultural scene. The relation of this development to the traditional religious basis of concern for the individual is undoubtedly close, so close indeed that assertions that the psychiatrist has taken over the functions of the minister of religion have been common. It has also been asserted that movements in the mental health field, notably psychoanalysis, are themselves new "religions."

Reprinted from Hans Hofmann (ed.), The Ministry and Mental Health, *New York, Association Press, 1960.*

From the religious side there has also been much concern with the situation of the times, with what seems to be a relatively widespread state of "spiritual malaise." There is the same order of doubt as to how far, if at all, this is a new or more serious problem now than in previous periods. There is, furthermore, a marked concentration of concern in this area, as in that of mental illness, on the problems of the individual. How is he to achieve a sense of meaning, to be capable of faith in an uncertain, skeptical, and, many say, a "materialistic" age?

In such a situation it seems to be highly important that attempts should be made to sort out some of the different factors which bear on the "plight" of the individual in our time, in a context which is concerned with the question of whether and on what basis a meaningful line of differentiation between these two problem areas can be drawn, how they are related to each other and what areas of overlap or at least joint concern may exist.

A good starting point is the well-known fact that treatment of problems of health with religious (including magical) techniques is, for practical purposes, a universal feature of "primitive" societies and cultures. Essentially this is to say that the health problem is "fused in with" the area of religion; the two are not differentiated. There are, however, very important variations in the extent to which primitive religions are oriented to problems of health. To take a well-known example, in the American Southwest the Navajos have a very strong religious emphasis on health whereas the immediately neighboring Zuñi are much less concerned in this direction.

Within a broader context—that is, in relation to Judaism—it can be maintained that the most distinctive feature of early Christianity was its religious "individualism," its concern with the fate of the individual soul. Since the problem of health is also—however much it is socially conditioned—a problem of the state of the individual, it is not surprising that early Christianity was permeated wth concern with health, and that religious healing was one of its central bases of validation. The impact of the Gospels would certainly have been greatly diminished had this element been removed.

Perhaps the main starting point of a differentiation between the "cure of souls" in the religious sense and what we think of as the problem of health came from the juxtaposition of the Christian and the Greek traditions. Whatever may have been, in Greek terms, the religious elements in the "cult of Aesculapius," Hippocratic medicine was a genuinely scientific tradition and, if it remained alive at all, could never be completely reabsorbed into a tradition of purely religious healing. The basic fact that Christianity grew out of a synthesis of Hebraic and Greek cultural traditions, with a very distinctive contribution of its own of course, meant that the scientific strain was an essential one which could not be eliminated.

With all the qualifications which must be made in terms of a sociology of knowledge, I should interpret the emergence of modern psychopathology as, in its *main* trend and meaning, a development of modern science. It represents the gradual, difficult, and socio-culturally speaking, often painful extension of scientific knowledge and the scientific point of view into areas of concern from which it has tended in other cultures and in our own past to be excluded. It is, in this perspective, by no means to be wondered at that scientific medicine was first introduced in the somatic field and has only gradually spread to the "mental."

In this connection it should not be forgotten how very recent a development genuinely scientific medicine over a wide front is. I have suggested that the Hippocratic tradition is genuinely scientific. But, given its presence in classical Greece, perhaps the salient fact about its history is the extreme slowness of progress from its brilliant beginnings until quite recent times; it is indeed only since the middle of the nineteenth century that it can be said that a broadly scientific medicine was coming to be established. And even the beginnings of a scientific psychopathology belong to the present century. Clearly the field is still in a very elementary stage of its development.

The fundamentals of the religious aspect of the picture of course go much further back. They are found, in various forms and combinations, in many different religions, and the specifically Christian patterns go back to the earliest phases of its history. However, the whole process of development and differentiation which has occurred in societies with a predominantly Christian religious tradition, and which in its recent phases underlies the emergence of scientific medicine, has involved important changes in the religious definition of the situation as well as that of other phases of social life, and so a review of some highlights of the American situation in this respect will be called for. Before introducing that, however, a general analytical approach to the relation of the two main foci of reference in our problem will need to be worked out.

RELIGION, SOCIETY, AND THE PERSONALITY OF THE INDIVIDUAL

LET us start at the religious end. As I conceive it, religion roots in the most general cultural orientations of human action— orientations which underlie the structuring both of social systems and of the personalities of individuals. These orientations, following Max Weber, I should think of as orientations in terms of the ultimate "problems of meaning" which are involved in the human situation as such.

Not only must such orientations be grounded at the level of what Tillich calls "ultimate concern," but they must somehow define meaningful orientations *to* all the main areas of inevitable involvement of human beings. These may conveniently be classified as the physical world as such (one meaning of "material") including the human organism; the world of personality of the individual human being (and in some degree nonhuman living things) as an acting, evaluating sensitive (including suffering) entity, of the social world in which numbers of persons are involved in relations of mutual solidarity and/or obstructiveness, and in which they share a common fate; and, finally, the world of cultural orientations and meanings themselves, including not only the religious aspects but the fields of secular cognitive culture, of art and other forms of expressive symbolization, and of values. All these areas of human concern and of the structuring of human action and relationships are closely interdependent and in many areas interpenetrating.

Any adequate analytical treatment must, however, start with their *conceptual* discrimination from one another. Our concern is with two principal contexts of relationship in which religious orientations are involved. On the one hand, there is the relation to the social system which I conceive above all as centering on the problem of values in their relation to the normative aspects of the structure of societies. On the other hand, there is the problem of the relation to the individual personality, which concerns the cultural level of values also, but this time in relation to the definition of the goals of the life of the individual by their relations to what Weber called his "religious interests," and the bearing of his inevitable involvements in social relationships, and with the organic basis of his own life, on these.

I conceive religious orientation as inherently independent of any of these other contexts of action. But it is the kind of independence which also implies interdependence; it is not "lack of relationship to. . . ." However, this independence implies an inherent possibility of *tension* as between a religious orientation and the exigencies imposed by involvement in nonreligious aspects of the culture, in society, in other aspects of the personality, and in the physical world. But by the same token, since human life is inherently involved in all these sets of exigencies, no religious system can cut loose from them too drastically if it is long to survive as a mode of shaping actual life, and there are certainly inherent tendencies to try to establish bases of working integration between them so that the tension, though not necessarily eliminated, is still kept within moderate bounds. Finally, the conception of interdependence implies that the adjustments which are involved in integration may in principle be mutual; there is no a priori reason why they must come in any particular degree from one side or the other. Furthermore, we must allow for ranges of difference in intensity of influence from either side.

In the social direction the most fundamental relationship is the religious grounding of the institutionalized values of a society. What I call the societal value system is in turn the apex of the structure of its "normative culture," which in turn is the primary constitutive element of its structure as a system. But a societal value system is never a simple function of religious orientations. It is rather a result of the specification of the implications of these orientations through several steps in relation to a variety of exigencies and factors having at most only secondarily a religious reference.

Among the most important of these is first the involvement of the social system with the cognitive culture—above all, in the fields of science and philosophy. The two areas of cognitive culture most directly independent of religion are, first, science, extending all the way from the physical world, through the aspects of medical science which closely involve the personality of the individual, to that dealing with the society itself as an object. Second, merging into science is what we call ideology. This is the empirically oriented but evaluative set of conceptions of a system of social action, notably a society itself or its parts, in which the holders of the beliefs in question are themselves involved. It is the area in which their values are integrated, more or less successfully, with their cognitive conceptions of the objects evaluated. The same considerations apply to the personality as a system.

A next category of factors and exigencies involved in social systems which are independent of religion are of course those concerned with the structural differentiation and conditions of functioning of a society itself as a system. Here, above all, political organization and its relation to phenomena of authority, power, coercion, and at some point the use of force come in. Another primary focus is the institutionalization of economic production and the attendant relationships: the existence of monetary systems, markets, productive organization, and, underlying it all, the necessity for the average human being to make his living by the "sweat of his brow." Still another focus is in the phenomena of social stratification. Most sociologists would argue the inevitability, particularly in complex societies, of substantial ranges of inequality, though of course the bases on which they are structured vary greatly.

Last, but in the present context perhaps not least among these specifically social exigencies, is that of religious organization itself. A church, sect, denomination, or religious movement is, among other things, a social organization. If it has special functions, they must be staffed; there must be problems of how to structure internal authority; and indeed the activities of the organization must be financed. Successful meeting of the exigencies of running churches as organizations is *never* a simple function of the religious orientations which govern them, alone.

Finally, the human personality is certainly subject to exigencies which are both independent of the religious and other components of the cultural tradition and of those of the society in which the individual has been brought up and lives. I shall return to certain of these later.

There is a crucial sense in which the structure of the society stands between the cultural system including its religious components on the one hand, the personality system on the other. And the focus of the set of interconnections is the set of values institutionalized in the society and internalized in the personality. Crucial as social values are in the dynamics of the social system, in the nature of the case they cannot be the sole determinants of processes in the society. These also are a function of the resources which are available for the implementing of values and goals, including the organizational resources. They are a function of many processes of internal adjustment within the society by which various strains and tensions can be handled. And, it goes without saying, every society is subject to varying exigencies outside itself.

Furthermore, let us remember that what I have called societal values do not themselves stand at the religious level of human values. The former can be reached only by a process of specification from the latter, in the course of which the *relative* valuational significance of interests in effective implementation of the values of his society and of the subsystems of it in which he may be involved (which is never quite the same thing), of the interests of personalities including both his own and others, of organic welfare, again both his own and others, and of course the preservation of his conception of the imperatives of religious ultimate concern itself.

It follows from these considerations that as Max Weber was so acutely aware, the bearing of religious orientations on the values institutionalized in a society is *always* and in the nature of the case problematical; there can never be an assumption that religious imperatives require either acceptance or rejection of particular values institutionalized in the society, or at what level. Furthermore, actual situations in the society are never fully in conformity with institutionalized values and always vary independently of them. Thus, we may say that leaving out the problems of personality as such, the relation between religious orientation and imperatives of action in society is inherently complex, and that this complexity tends to come to a focus on moral problems. The fundamental form the question takes is that of whether my obligation as a responsible member of my society is compatible with my religious commitment, and on occasion the conflict may be very acute indeed. Putting the question in this broad way, however, clearly does not get very far, since it provides only the most general framework. Anything like the resolution of tension which might bring something like a feeling of "good conscience" requires a very much more detailed working through of the almost endlessly ramifying particularities of the problem.

Naturally also the problem is the more complex, on the one hand the more complex the society is in which the individual is placed; and, on the other hand, the more it has been and is involved in a process of change so that traditional formulae prove to be inadequate.

In the discussion above I have stressed the factors by virtue of which a clear and simple relation, either of conformity or of opposition between the values institutionalized in a society and the imperatives of religious obligation, cannot be assumed. This position should not be allowed to obscure the fact, for which I believe there is overwhelming evidence, that in the very long run religious orientations and the values associated with them constitute crucially important factors in determination of the major patterns worked out in the organization of societies. This fact should be enough to caution those who tend to assume that there is always an inherently unbridgeable gap, that the "world" in its social aspect is always in the most fundamental sense in radical conflict with religious values. Such positions appear from time to time in religion, but certainly cannot be ascribed to religion in general. At the same time the process of religious influence is slow and halting, and is cross-cut by many factors independent of it. Hence, however much the positive side may be stressed, at any given time the moral complexity of the relation I have been outlining is always a very real problem.

From the point of view of the relation of religion to the social system this problem comes to a head in the question of the nature of religious collectivities and their relation to the rest of the structure of the society. Two major types may be distinguished, though they may on occasion be combined. One is the collectivity organized around the conception of a specifically "religious life," participation in which is dependent on conditions incompatible with the ordinary lives of people embedded in any type of secular society and, not least important, those who are obligated to important responsibilities in the operation of the secular society, such as political responsibilities, those of economic production, and not least the socialization of children through the family and the educational system.

The second type is an organization primarily of the "laity," of persons who are basically anchored in the life of a society and whose secular obligations, if not taking precedence over their religious commitments, must in some sense be treated as compatible with them to the extent that remaining in a secular status and performing the obligations attached to it is not declared to be radically unacceptable from the religious point of view.

The first type is of course above all illustrated by the religious order, organized about a segregated monastic life. The Protestant denomination of contemporary society is an almost pure case of the second type. The Catholic church of course combines the two. Subsequent discussion in this paper will be confined to the second, and the prototype of the role of the clergy will be the Protestant minister whose primary responsibility is the leadership of a congregation, the membership of which consists overwhelmingly of people who are not devoted to the religious life in the sense of withdrawing from worldly participations. Clearly the problem of moral complexity as just outlined is most acute for this group.

PERSONALITY AND THE SOCIAL STRUCTURE

LET us now turn to the side of the personality of the individual. This of course is rooted in the physical organism with its genetic constitution and its metabolic needs for food, respiration, elimination, and so forth. But more importantly for our purposes, the main structure of the personality is built up through the processes of social interaction. It develops through the internalization of social objects and of the normative patterns governing the child's interaction in social situations.

Of course the primary agency of early socialization is the family in which the child is brought up—very centrally in our society, and with some important qualifications over the whole of humanity. The process in general starts with the development of a deep, in some senses an indelible, attachment to the mother. This in due course is used as a basis of leverage to motivate and reward the autonomous behavior, within the framework of a basic security of acceptance. Erotic components, as we know since Freud, play a central role in these early relationships, particularly as a bridge between the needs of the organism and the generalization of motivation to the level of socially organized patterns of behavior.

With the oedipal transition the child emerges from a life primarily contained within the family. His sex role has become emotionally consolidated to a considerable degree; and he enters upon a new and rapid process of instrumental learning especially concerned, in our society, with the school and with informal relations to his age peers. Then, as he enters adolescence, he becomes capable of a much more differentiated set of commitments, not only to the continuance of formal education, but to responsible participation in associational activity, to a re-emerging basis of concern with his relations to the opposite sex, leading eventually up to marriage, and, on a new level, with the problem of his personal moral commitments and their backing with reference to an orientation to the problems of meaning.

Any individual person is inescapably bound within the framework not only of the genetic constitution of the organism and the condition of its healthy functioning, but of his personal life history, which is never exactly like that of any other, and its bearing on his interests, goals, and capacities for dealing with the problems of adult life. And these involve all his roots in the biological, social, and cultural soil of his experience. He is what and who he is by virtue of the time and status of his birth, his sex, his parentage, his many associations. In this sense every human life starts from an ascriptive origin and can depart from the fixities of this origin only by the paths of structured "opportunity" provided by the structure of the culture and society in which he is embedded and by the exigencies of his own personality.

Whatever its origins and constraints along the way, however, this personality always comes to be a system with its own distinctive constitution, its own goals and imperatives of internal integration, its own characteristic ways of dealing with life situations. These were developed in the closest involvement with *one* part of the society and the culture, through a widening series of circles from his relation to his own particular mother, through the family of orientation, to the school system and local community of his latency and adolescent periods. But he is never socialized into "the" society so that he becomes just a standardized cog in the machinery. Mothers, families, schools, and communities are all widely and subtly variant, as are the initial constitutions of individuals. It is a striking case of interdependence and interpenetration, but most emphatically not of the sort which implies the extinction of independent distinctiveness.

I have made the relation to the values of the social system the main axis of the present discussion of religious orientation on the one hand, personality structure on the other. This is indeed a crucial common factor, but it should now be clear that it enters in a very different way and on very different levels in the two cases. In the religious case, as noted above, the religious anchorage of societal values stands at a higher level of cultural generality than do the societal values themselves. At the valuational level they involve the basis of relative valuation of societal obligations, personal obligations and those independent of either, for example, to scientific "truth" or to religious salvation. On religious levels these very highest valuational choices are "grounded" in the highest-order orientations of meaning.

Nothing could be more important than the proposition that the personality of the individual is organized about internalized values. But these are not, in any simple sense, "religious values." The initial reference point of personal values is at the opposite extreme of a scale of generality to specificity of values from the religious level. It is the value system which can come to be shared in common in social interaction by a helpless, unformed small child and *one* adult, his mother, in a two-person relationship system. This value-pattern must be very specifically tailored to the capacities and exigencies of a very small child acting only with a very specific, limited and controlled environment. It is highly dependent on the idiosyncratic characteristics of the mother as a person and her relation to her child. Only on this foundation are successive layers of value-internalization painfully built up step by step in the socialization of the child.

Looked at from the point of view of a societal, to say nothing of a religious, value-system, this relationship seems to be a slender reed indeed on which to build the main foundations of a personal character. The essential point, however, is that the crucial problem of personality development in its earliest stages is not how to get commitment to the "right" values, but how to get commitment to *any* values. It is the persistent fallacy of "emanationist" theories of human behavior to hold explicitly, or to imply, that if you have the "right" orientations, their implementation in action follows automatically. This could not be farther from the truth. From its very nature the process of building up a personality structure is one in which preparation of the "soil" for the growth of value-commitments must take precedence over concern with the content of those commitments. The basis of this view is the conviction of how very precarious a truly human level of personality development in any sense is. And the safeguarding of minimum conditions of this development concerns factors which are at the furthest range of independence from religious orientations, the ineluctable needs of organisms, and the exigencies of successful development of any sort of personality. The role of erotic factors in personality development constitutes a particularly important focus of this problem.

The erotic-need system of the individual, which has caused so much concern and conflict in religious connections, is only in a relative sense the focus of "bodily" needs. It is, for instance, not at all on the same level as the need for nutrition. It is rather, in the genetic development of the individual, the most important *bridge* between the biological and the social levels. It is an essential component in the first genuine *attachment* to another human being and hence in the building up of capacities for higher levels of attachment, of love, including eventually the religious levels of love and devotion. It is of the first importance that the erotic attachments of childhood must be transcended if these higher levels are to be attained. But it now seems entirely clear that they must be genuinely transcended, not bypassed altogether or, once developed, merely repressed again.

In the normal process of "socialization," as sociologists call it, this transcending occurs in two most important stages. The first of these takes place within the family in which the child grows up, his family of orientation. Freud made the famous statement that the infant is "polymorph perverse." This is to say that the form his erotic motivational structure will take is not determined in advance by genetic factors (in the hereditary sense), either with reference to the object choice, that is, whether he is heterosexual or homosexual, or with reference to zonal primacies, that is, whether he is oral, anal, or genital in primary focus of erotic need. A process of developing learned organization takes place in the early years, which can be profoundly disturbed if the relationship structure of his family situation is abnormal.

At the end of this period, in the oedipal transition, childhood erotic interests are normally more or less fully abandoned (in a certain sense repressed) and during the next few years the child is in what Freud called a state of "latency." This is a period of tremendous advance in instrumental learning, and in the development of emotional capacities in nonerotic connections. His relations to his parents are greatly altered in the direction of affection and respect rather than erotic attachment. He must also develop a respectful attachment to teachers and loyalty to peers of his own age. Then, in adolescence, the erotic component begins to emerge again, but this time with two crucial differences. In the first place, the normal object is a person of opposite sex outside his family and belonging to his own generation. And second, this component no longer dominates his whole personality in the old sense, but is built into and controlled by a structure of values and interests which far transcend the scope of this component. In his adult life only one of his principal role complexes, that of his family and his devotion to cultural commitments, including those of religion, will have other primary bases of anchorage in his personality system. In a *genetic* sense, however, the system in which the erotic component is central remains at the "root" of his whole personality system. It is this circumstance which underlies the element of truth in Freud's conception of the "sexual" —I prefer to say erotic—basis of all the neuroses.

From one point of view the process of transcending childhood erotic needs may be regarded as, at the same time, the process of internalizing higher levels of value. The first major step here is the internalization of what Freud called the *superego,* which essentially is the level of internalized control that makes the renunciations of childhood eroticism in the latency period possible. This, however, is far from being the end of the road. Every major step in achieving greater maturity involves the internalization of still higher levels of value-commitment, up to the level of full adulthood.

If, as was noted above, religious collectivities constitute the primary social context in which the religious commitments of the individual are directly expressed and in certain respects regulated, for his personality as a system the corresponding area of social involvement is clearly the family. Here, however, a very special duality of structural relation of the individual to kinship collectivities becomes of central importance. This is to say that the normal individual is, in his lifetime, a member not of one family, but of two, that into which he is born and grows up as a child and that formed by his marriage in which he functions in the role of spouse and parent.

There is a very fundamental dynamic relation between the two in which the personality of the individual constitutes the primary link. For the adult his family of procreation is clearly the most important focus of his personal "security" as an individual person. It is the motivational foundation on which the stability of his capacities for participation in what—from the point of view of the society— are the "higher level" functions of adult life, is built. These include of course contribution through occupational performance, through community responsibility in various associational forms, and through cultural concerns.

For the living individual the stability of this foundation is not to be taken for granted. It may be suggested that the most important set of mechanisms of its regulation consists in the fact that the basic motivational themes and components of childhood are directly involved in the life of the family for the adult. It is well known that in the process of socialization the reciprocal role relation of interacting partners is internalized. From this point of view performance of the parental role is, for the individual, the acting out of the obverse role pattern to that which he in fact played as a child. Functioning as a parent, then, constitutes a long succession of recapitulations in reverse roles of the individual's own childhood experience, reaching from early infancy to the final emancipation from the family of orientation. Then, in a subtler and in some ways deeper sense, the relation of marriage partners is not only a living out of the relationships of their own parents to each other, but in its erotic phase, involves deep symbolic references to the direct eroticism of early childhood. Very broadly it may be said that the act of heterosexual intercourse is a symbolic recapitulation of the erotic ties between mother and pre-oedipal child.

The crucial point here is that these symbolic recapitulations are carried out within the context of socially responsible adult life situations. The primary tests and rewards come, particularly for the adult male, in these situations. But the motivational commitments which make socially acceptable achievements, and those acceptable to the higher-level consciences of individuals, possible are deeply regulated by the subtle emotional interchanges of family life.

FAMILY AND CHURCH AS "BOUNDARY" STRUCTURES

IT has been suggested that however fragmented in particular cases, a religious tradition is inherently part of a culture and that this in turn is in the first instance integrated with a society rather than the personality of an individual. With reference to the theme of values, it is closest to the level of value-commitment which is institutionalized in the society—it is the highest level in the general scale of "ultimacy."

Given this very fundamental difference between the involvement of values in the personality of the individual in the genetic sequence on the one hand, in the culture and from it the society on the other, can there be said to be any analogy between the duality of involvement in the individual in two families, and his involvement in religious organization? I should like to suggest that there is, but that the sense in which this is the case must be very carefully formulated.

There is a critical sense in which the pre-oedipal child is not yet "in the society"; he is in his family. The family is the borderline structure between the roots of the personality of the individual and his beginning participation in the society. As an adult he is a full

participant in the society, but through his family of procreation he
still participates in this "presocietal soil" of his being as a human
personality. There is an analogous sense in which, in all the higher
religions, but notably Christianity, the religious collectivity is not
fully "in the society." It is in an important sense "set apart," a field
of participation which, to use the old phrase, is "in the world but not
of it." The ways in which this is the case may of course vary immensely, but I should like to postulate an essential element of constancy in this respect.

In the case of a church or denomination in the modern sense,
however, its typical member is, in his other roles, very much a member of society. But the church is a partially segregated area where
the concerns of secular life can, within limits, be held in abeyance.
This would seem to be an important aspect of the more general
phenomenon of the "set-apartness" of the realm of the sacred.

Churches, in their symbolic and ritualistic traditions, utilize a set
of references of meaning which are particularly "set apart" even from
intelligibility in the context of secular life. My general hypothesis
here is that these references are to what may be called metaphorically
the "childhood of the culture." They do not refer primarily to stages
in the life history of the individual, but to the "foundations" on
which the present stage of religious commitment, particularly with
reference to "the world," have been built up. In the Christian case,
this reference is to the basic constitution of the early Christian
church. There are four basic references, involved in all Christian
ritual from this point of view, to God the Father as the transcendental reference of the ultimate ground of meaning; to the Christ figure
as the mediator between Divinity and humanity and hence as the
symbolic head of the church; to the church itself as the brotherhood
of Christians imbued with the Holy Spirit, and to the individual
Christian as participant in the church and, through it, in Divine
grace.

From the point of view of adequate adjustment to and involvement in a society of the modern type, the early church was clearly
"archaic." It was quite literally not "of" this world, particularly a
modern world. Modern churches are the product of a complex
process of evolution from the early church, but they of course still
perpetuate this same fundamental complex of belief and symbolism
and make it the focus not only of their ritualistic practices but in
some sense of their organization as collectivities. In the "middle"

period of this evolution the church became a very elaborate organization, which in a sense commanded jurisdiction over something approaching a half of life in society. Since the Reformation there has been a process of social differentiation in the course of which the church has become a more specialized agency to the point where, in the modern Protestant denomination, it has become predominantly a private association which has "lost" many of the functions of the earlier, particularly the mediaeval, church, notably with respect to jurisdiction over secular culture, education, and family life, whereas the political and economic spheres had earlier been predominantly institutionalized in secular terms. The pattern of the denomination has, particularly in the United States, profoundly influenced the religious organization of Judaism, and even considerably that of the Catholic church in that through its minority position and the separation of church and state the religious collectivity is deprived of many of the prerogatives it had traditionally enjoyed and still does where it is the established church.

The most important point for present purposes is that churches as social organizations constitute only a small fraction of the framework of organization of a complex modern society while the rest of the society is specifically categorized as secular. There is a certain parallelism to the fact that the family has, in the course of recent social evolution, also become a more differentiated, specialized agency, less diffusely embedded in larger social structures, such as the nexuses of extended kinship and local community.

This differentiation does not, as it is often contended, imply that either or both have lost most of their "importance" in modern society. It means that the influence they do exert is not through organizational jurisdiction over certain spheres of life now structurally differentiated from them, but through the value-commitments and motivational commitments of individuals. In spheres outside their families and their churches, then, individuals have come to be by and large free of organizational control and in this sense to act *autonomously,* on their own responsibility. But this is by no means to say that their behavior in these "external" spheres is uninfluenced by their participation in the family and the church respectively.

In modern society, then, the family and the church are "boundary-structures" vis-à-vis, respectively, the motivational and the value components of the individual personality. Let us try to sum up how these are related to each other. The axis on which I have tried to relate them is that defined on the one hand by the series of steps in the specification of orientation of value, from the highest religiously grounded level, down through the value system institutionalized in the society, to the levels which can become meaningful in the orientation of the particular individual, faced with a particular life situation within the society. The other series is grounded in the most general exigencies of the organization of the motivational system of the personality, starting in the earliest attachment to the mother, going up through the oedipal stage, through latency and adolescence to adulthood.

The latter series may, from one point of view, be regarded as a series of internalizations of value-patterns, of their "combination" with motivational components. But it starts with highly specific values, and only gradually works up to more and more generalized levels. Conversely the "religious" series is in the first instance one of the specification of values. It, however, starts at the *most* general level and must work "down" from there. Moreover, this process also, to be effective in conduct, must include the *institutionalization* of the values, and one major component of this process of institutionalization is the motivational commitment of individual personalities to them.[1] The church or churches have been the primary social agencies of this process of *institutionalization*.

For the given individual there must of course be a process by which the religious values are internalized in his personality; various aspects of religious education are involved here, but we cannot take space to go into them. Once internalized, however, their reinforcement and maintenance operate through mechanisms which are analogous to those operating in the family of procreation. This is universally the process of religious observance and teaching, perhaps notably observance, on the ritualistic level. The most important point is that in both cases the stabilization functions operate mainly through institutionalized mechanisms which do not require any elaborately specific attention to the problems of the particular individual. It is rather that he normally participates in a nexus of social relationships and the attendant activities, and this participation normally regulates his pattern of commitments.

1. On the general nature of this process see "Christianity and Modern Industrial Society," by Talcott Parsons, in *Sociological Theory, Values, and Sociocultural Change,* Edward A. Tiryakian, ed., New York, The Free Press of Glencoe, 1963.

Now we may raise the question of where and how these two series meet in the structure of the society and the life-pattern of the individual. Looking at the problem from the life-cycle point of view the evidence seems to be that a specially crucial point is adolescence. There are certainly normally what we would call religious components in the orientations internalized throughout the life cycle, and certainly in the pre-oedipal and latency periods. But it is in adolescence that the child first comes to play a more highly differentiated set of roles in a variety of different contexts of participation. Furthermore it is here that he first, in a sense implying real commitment, faces the formation of the basic pattern of his adult life, notably with respect to choice of occupation and of marriage partner. Late adolescence brings both these commitments and also the first formal admission to participation in community responsibility, in modern societies especially symbolized by the right to vote. Finally, most modern religious groups institutionalize full religious participation through ceremonies such as confirmation sometime during this period.[2]

We may thus say that it is typically in adolescence that the individual enters into full participation in his society; that he becomes a contributor through occupational performance to its functioning, and thereby economically self-supporting; that he assumes his share of collective responsibility; and that he begins to participate in the socialization function through marriage. Here for the first time he is really confronted with the problem of the nature and extent of his value-commitments as an adult member of the society.[3]

2. Particularly illuminating observations on the significance of adolescence for the religious orientations of the individual are presented in Robert N. Bellah, "The Place of Religion in Human Action," *Review of Religion*, March, 1958.

3. An important, relatively new factor seems to have entered into this situation, the implications of which are far from clear. This is the increasing participation of the population in higher education even beyond the college level through advanced professional training. Just what are the limits of adolescence is a moot question, but certainly the middle twenties are beyond them. Anyway the effect is to postpone the full assumption of occupational roles and the attendant responsibilities and rewards to a much later point than has been typical of most of the population for most periods. It may well be that this is an important factor in the ferment about problems of meaning in our own time, since there is a certain conflict between the general emphasis on early independence and responsibility on the one hand, and the kind of tutelage in which persons in the system of formal education generally, and of professional training in particular, tend to be kept. One possible tendency may be to treat the higher commitments of

We have emphasized that this extent and nature of societal commitment is in the nature of the case problematical on cultural—that is, eventually religious—levels. Somehow societal interests must be balanced against others, notably those of the individual's own personality itself, and the balance grounded in some orientation defining the meaning of *his* life.

Our very broad conclusion is that the problems of the groundwork of the motivational structure of the personality come to a head in relation to the oedipal stage of personality development, and to the relation between the individual's participation in his family of procreation, as spouse and parent, as an adult. The problems of value-commitment and its grounding in the individual's relation to the deeper layers of the cultural tradition of his society come to a head in his life history in adolescence, and in principle in terms of the current social structure, in his relation to the organized religion in which he was brought up or toward which he may be drawn.

SOCIAL DIFFERENTIATION AS AFFECTING THE STATUSES OF FAMILY AND CHURCH

LET us now attempt to look at the problem from the point of view of the social structure. Here the salient fact about modern society is the high development of structural differentiation, and the rapidity with which processes of structural change at the requisite levels have gone on. It has already been noted how the family has become a substantially more specialized agency, more fully differentiated from other agencies. By virtue of this fact its members are placed in a position of far greater autonomy in their relations outside the family, and these spheres constitute an increasingly large share of their life-interests. For the child of course this increasing autonomy centers in his schooling, and the relations to his age peers which are closely associated with the school, but are also in important respects independent of it.

At the other end of our scale, the church in the denominational pattern has also become a more specialized agency and by virtue of this fact has lost many of its former functions. Its organizational in-

meaning as even more tentative than before, since only the fully "mature" person should enter into them. But if this is the tendency, one would expect much conflict in the process of the working out of the new pattern, and that certain groups should feel a particularly urgent need to have firm "answers" almost immediately.

volvement in the "things of this world" has in one important sense steadily receded. It has certainly lost notably in political power, relative to the situation in which established churches existed. It takes far less of a role in the control of economic production, and most notably perhaps it has renounced much of its formal jurisdiction over secular culture and education, and over family relations. By the same token as the family, it has tended to come to exert influence increasingly through its "moral" hold on individuals rather than through the more "massive" societal means of exerting influence.

Like marriage for the adult, church affiliation has become a voluntary matter. This is closely associated with the system of religious toleration, separation of church and state, and denominational pluralism. Religious adherence has become "privatized."

The fact that both institutional complexes have been so involved in the process of differentiation means that a gap has been created between them, which did not previously exist to the same extent. The "wedge" which symbolizes and has in part created this gap is, above all, secular education—in the United States, the public school system. But it is also clearly signalized by the tendency to deny to *organized* religion even directly moral, to say nothing of legal jurisdiction over marriage and divorce and many of the problems of private morality, particularly those associated with the family.

It is in our opinion this process of structural differentiation in the society which underlies the emerging salience of the problem with which the discussion of this paper started. Our general thesis here is that the problems of mental health and illness root in the motivational organization of the personality of the individual. This in turn genetically is primarily concerned with the process of socialization down through the oedipal period, and in terms of the problem of adjustment of the individual, in the first instance with his roles in marriage and cognate relations and his role as a parent. Since mental illness ramifies into the personality as a whole, it affects all the behavioral contexts in which he is involved, but its structural core rests in the areas designated.

What has been referred to above as "spiritual malaise" is empirically often associated with psychopathology, but must be considered to be analytically independent of it. It concerns above all the individual's commitments to the values of his society and the various subsectors of it with which he is or potentially might be associated, and, from this point of departure, his involvements in problems of meaning. This is in turn genetically associated with his experience in the religious groups with which he and his parents and associates have been affiliated, an experience the personal significance of which has very generally come to a head in adolescence. It leads over into acute problems of the meaning of his life commitments.

Both sets of problems are closely related to strains which are inherent in the structure of a rapidly developing and differentiating society. The family itself has been rapidly changing its character. It is furthermore an important "residual legatee" of strains generated in other parts of the society and hence may often become disorganized under the impact of these strains. On the other side of the picture the religious organization is necessarily deeply involved in the structure of the society as a whole. Hence any major changes of the latter have a strong impact on organized religion. For these reasons, attitudes toward organized religion and its symbol-systems understandably play a major part in the impact on personalities of all the strains which are operative in a changing society.

Perhaps the most generalized formulation of the common factor in these two problem areas which is current in sociological thinking is the concept of *anomie*. This may be said to be the disturbance of the state of internalized expectations of persons occasioned by the processes of change in the normative components of the institutionalized culture, and hence in the definition of what can legitimately be expected of individuals and classes of them. The most essential point is that in the process of such change, what is expected often over wide areas becomes seriously indeterminate. Anomic components of the situation may, we feel, be propagated in both directions. On the one hand, they may raise questions on the more religiously based level of meaning. Where the normative structure involves serious anomic elements in particular, the balances between performance and sanction, between what is felt to be earned and the actual available rewards in fact forthcoming, will be upset. (The upset, it may be noted, may result from excessive as well as from inadequate reward.) In the other direction, looking to the motivation of the personality, life simply becomes more complex and there are problems of how far individuals are capable of "taking it" from the point of view of their own characters, particularly with respect to their "tolerance of ambiguity" and their capacity to handle risks.

This discussion has stressed the differentiation between the personality and religious contexts, between family and church. Before closing this structural analysis something should be said about one very important context of connection between them. Both the problem of mental health and that of religious commitment involve matters of intimate personal significance to individuals, what in a certain sense are highly "private" affairs. It is not fortuitous, therefore, that both center in the life of the local residential community and that by and large it is as family members that people are associated in churches. Both are hence somewhat withdrawn from the larger economic and political affairs of the society, and are associated together in this withdrawal. This situation has much to do with the sense in which the church has tended to maintain, and even develop further, a set of functions as a diffuse center of association at the first level beyond the household. It is a kind of substitute for the undifferentiated neighborhood, a place where "like-minded" people can get to know each other and be made to "feel at home" in contexts not specifically connected with religion.

It is not uncommon to suggest that this set of functions has in fact become primary, that modern churchgoers are "not really" religious at all, but are only interested in sociability. In my opinion this is a misinterpretation. This associational aspect of the modern denominational parish is a predictable feature of the general pattern of the development of modern society when the fact is taken into account that family and church have such intimate intrinsic relations to each other. The sociability pattern is the primary mechanism by which family and church are brought together with each other. Each, in its own specialized way, involves the "whole person." Unless they are to be, not merely differentiated, but *dissociated,* there must be some adequate mechanism of linkage. My hypothesis is that the church as a "social center" provides this mechanism, and that, as a result of the structural differentiation of modern society, this has become more rather than less important.

FAMILY STRUCTURE AND THE PROFESSION OF PSYCHIATRY

WE may now return to our problem of the relation between mental illness and spiritual malaise and the structure of the social agencies oriented to them. It has been pointed out that in earlier societies the problems of illness and of the religious states of the individual have tended to be fused, and that a process of differentiation has occurred from there.

Very broadly it may be said that the first major complex to become differentiated (from the fusion, in earlier societies, of the problems of illness and of the religious states of the individual) was that having to do with somatic illness. The long history of the problem cannot be gone into here. Suffice it to say that a crucial stage was reached with the great scientific developments of the late nineteenth century and the full institutionalization of "scientific medicine" in this period. Generally this development posed few problems for religion since it was almost a dogma that only "the body" was involved in such illness. This relative insulation of the problems of the state of the body from those of "the mind" proved to be unstable and shortlived, however. Our own century has seen, particularly in this country, a progressively increasing salience of the conception of illness precisely in the area of the personality (mental illness) and its complex interrelations with the organism (the so-called "psychosomatic" field).

This development was certain to have a major impact on religion since it is a matter of the mechanisms by which human behavior is controlled. On one level mental illness could be defined as a Divine punishment; on another as a way in which the individual could evade his moral responsibilities. But whatever the difficulties, it is, as noted, clear that the main trend in the definition of mental as of somatic illness, and of the possible therapeutic measures for coping with it, has been in terms of the development of *science,* of its extension into spheres where its possibility and significance have in previous cultures been questionable. Certainly the scientific underpinning of the diagnoses and treatment of mental illness is still in a very early stage of development, but a relatively firm institutional pattern of this definition has become established, and it is one which specifically differentiates a problem of applied science from anything legitimately falling within the jurisdiction of religion. However indeterminate the boundaries between the two jurisdictions, and they are certainly far from having been settled, this is a firmly established fact of modern society which is extremely unlikely to be reversed by a return to an across-the-board conception of the primacy of "religious healing."

The function of dealing with mental illness has become, at least tentatively, institutionalized in the profession of psychiatry as a branch of the medical profession. There are many unresolved problems about the exact status of psychiatry, the ingredients which should go into psychiatric competence, and its relation to other possible therapeutic agencies. But, however these questions may stand, the broad location of this function in the social structure is certainly "appropriate." In its recent development medicine has centered in the bodily welfare of the individual, and the main residual locus of care for this welfare has of course been the family household. Hence there is an ancient and honorable tradition of the central importance of the "family physician" as the guardian of this welfare in the sense of "backing up" the more routine and common-sense operations of the family. Medicine has, seen in this light, been a "second line of defense" of the somatic welfare of the individual, tending to step in where the difficulties exceeded the capacities of the family to cope with them. As the conception of incapacitation through illness has broadened into the "mental" areas this same basic reference point has continued to be the central one, namely that of a professional agent who could treat the individual for the problems particular to him, in close collaboration with his family.

This is of course far from telling more than a fraction of the story, since the development of the hospital and various complex patterns of medical, including psychiatric, care, have greatly modified this simple pattern of an individual professional practitioner serving as a backstop to the family.

Nevertheless, I do not think that the significance of this pattern can be ignored. It certainly fits with the view put forward above that the personality of the individual is rooted in his experience in his family of orientation and is most intimately regulated, in his adult life, in his relationships within the family of procreation. It is an expectable development that there should be mechanisms in the society which backstop the family in this set of functions as well, and do so by and large in the tradition of "classical" medical practice.

However far hospitalization, group therapy, and various other arrangements have gone, for the present context it is important to note that in the field of mental health the main pattern has been that there should be, at the disposal of the individual in intimate relation to this family, an *individual* person, qualified by scientifically based competence, to deal with his individual problems. This person is, in his therapeutic role, to be sure, anchored both in the scientific culture of the society and in its moral standards, which define health and hence the respects in which a "sick" person deviates from those standards. The medical profession as a social entity is of course the primary institutionalized guardian of this definition of the role of psychiatrist. But the medical profession is not a collectivity which as a collectivity undertakes responsibility for the health of the community as a whole. It is rather an *association* of practitioners whose institutionalized roles as individuals are organized about their responsibilities—assuming the requisite competence, of course—for caring for the needs of particular patients. This, after all, is the primary basis of the difference between the medical and the public health professions in modern society.

THE CHURCHES AND THE PROBLEM OF SPIRITUAL COUNSELING

I BRING out this last point because it presents a notable asymmetry between the therapeutic function in the medical-psychiatric function and that of the trusteeship of the religious interests of the individual. The organ of this latter trusteeship has, historically, been the church. However much the character of the church has been modified in the course of its evolution, particularly in the recent denominational phase, the church has always been defined as primarily a *collectivity* which *combined* the trusteeship of the great religious tradition—in relation to the society of its primary values —with a concern for the spiritual welfare of individual persons. Thus, as has been suggested, the church is far more closely analogous to the family than to the psychiatric profession. The family and the church have both served as *collective* trustees, responsible to be sure for their individual members' welfare and development, but depending in this respect mainly on mechanisms which operated "nonrationally" in that the persons implementing them were not in a scientific sense aware of "what they were doing." As noted, the basic religious mechanism in this respect has been the ritualistic function.

Seen from this point of view the minister of religion is not parallel to the psychiatrist in his relation to individuals.[4] If we look at the problem in terms of structural parallels he is in a certain sense parallel to the "father" of the family. What I mean here is that he is, in certain respects which need careful defining, the responsible

4. On this difference cf. Kaspar D. Naegele, "Clergymen, Teachers, and Psychiatrists," *Canadian Journal of Economics and Political Science,* February, 1956.

leader of a collectivity, a collectivity to which the welfare of individuals in very crucial respects has been entrusted, but where his primary function is responsible leadership *of* the collectivity, not individualized attention to individuals. In religious terms these functions have centered on the administration of the ritualistic cult, and on the teaching function with reference to maintenance of the cultural tradition itself. These are both contexts in which the maintenance of uniformity takes clear precedence over individuation.

The problem of the "cure of souls" has of course by no means been absent from Christian tradition. Its most massive institutionalization has perhaps been in the Catholic confessional, and of course very generally in the "pastoral" function of the clergy. In a few variant, if not deviant, cases like Christian Science, it has been elevated to a primary level, but, in this case, in terms directly competing with the medical treatment of illness—a role which most religious groups have understandably avoided.

Our general line of argument is that this pastoral component of the role of the minister of religion is, structurally speaking, far more closely analogous to the sense in which good parents take an individualized interest in and responsibility for the psychological welfare of their children than it is to the role of psychiatrist. In both cases, however, this must in the nature of the case be an "auxiliary" function since their primary responsibilities in both cases are inherently focused on the collectivities in question.

I take it that the important feature of the development of psychiatry for present purposes is the emergence of a professional role which is structurally differentiated and hence in a sense segregated from that of parent or spouse in the family, but which is adapted to the task of dealing with problems of the personality of the individual which root in the family, but which, precisely because of the nature of the family as a collectivity, cannot be effectively dealt with simply as a function ascribed to familial roles. This structural segregation can be shown to provide an essential condition of the permissiveness which is central to the psychotherapeutic process, and for exercising the leverage necessary for getting out of vicious circles of involvement with familial problems which are often both symptoms and determinants of psychopathological conditions.

Hence it seems logical to suggest that a corresponding problem exists in the religious context. The minister is in the first instance the responsible leader and administrator of a congregation and a parish. He is the guardian of the cult tradition and of the church's responsibility for the morality of its members. In this connection he is subject to the same order of handicaps in dealing with his parishioners' intimately personal problems of religious orientation, as are family members in dealing with each other's psychological problems; in both cases of course the problems become acute when they get beyond a certain level of complication, above all when they involve irrational mechanisms of defense which are not accessible to the ordinary appeals at the "rational" level of belief and teaching which is taken for granted in most Christian and Jewish denominations.

I have argued that perhaps the most important keynote of the process of social change in modern society is structural differentiation. This have been very much involved in the changing status of religion and the pattern of its social organization. The present American system of denominational pluralism is a product of such a process of differentiation. But there is no reason to believe that the process has reached a limit.

Clearly Christian ministers and their Jewish counterparts have come into a difficult and in some respects anomalous position with respect to their functions as "spiritual advisers" to individuals. On the one hand, there is the tendency to encroach on the functions of psychiatry as a branch of science-based medicine and thus not to differentiate the problems of the individual's commitments to values, and to solutions of the problems of meaning, from the problems of the underlying organization of his personality as a motivational system. On the other hand, there is the set of problems concerned with the conflict between the minister's primary responsibilities as leader of a congregation and the kinds of permissiveness and support which are indicated in a role that is trying to deal with the complex interweaving of religious problems with the personality structure of the individual.

My suggestion is that it is in the logic of the present situation that there should soon emerge a distinct, differentiated professional role which might be called that of "spiritual counselor," differentiated, that is, both from the role of psychiatrist on the one hand, and from that of minister in his capacity of leader of a congregation, on the other.

The essential bases of the differentiation vis-à-vis the psychiatrist should be clear from the discussion above. It is probably a fact that psychiatry has tended to take over certain of the functions which probably belong in this area, and that it is likely it will tend to retreat in certain respects to a more restricted area. As I see it, the primary focus of the psychiatric role should be on the problem of the *capacity* of the individual to *implement* the values and other commitments which he may come to regard as legitimized for his life.[5] The complexity of borderline relations is such that such capacity can seldom if ever be improved without attempted clarification of *what* it is that the patient most fundamentally wants. But however important this interpenetration, it is not the psychiatric function to consider the bases of the legitimation of this "what," above all to confront the individual with the underlying problem in choice-and-meaning terms. This is not to say that psychiatric clarification does not or should not extend to consideration of the consequences of the individual's value-commitments to himself and to others; this it necessarily does, but this is not the same problem as that of legitimation.

In drawing the line vis-à-vis the traditional ministerial role, the distinction outlined above between familial and psychiatric roles can, if properly qualified, provide a model. Just as the family is the primary locus of the regulation and stabilization of the motivational structures of the individual, so it may be argued that the church is the primary locus of the regulation and stabilization of his spiritual commitments. Seen in terms of its relation to the institutionalized value-system of the society this is indeed the primary function of the church. But, just as in the case of the family certain problems of the personality come to be beyond its capacity to cope with, so for the church, certain of the value- and meaning-problems of its members become too acute to be coped with within the traditional framework of church organization. If not adequately handled, in both cases there is a tendency to the establishment of vicious circles, involving "alienation" of different types.

The conditions necessary for coping with such vicious-circle tendencies are known in a broad way. These include a sphere of institutionalized "permissiveness" within which the individual may freely express his attitudes and sentiments without being exposed to the normal negative sanctions in case they deviate from those accepted in the relevant collectivities. They include a "floor" of supportiveness so that a generally accepting attitude is not jeopardized

5. Cf. the preceding essay, "Definitions of Health and Illness in the Light of American Values and Social Structure."

by these deviant expressions. At the same time, however, they include only selective rewarding of specific overtures toward new "definitions of the situation," the standards being their conformity with a higher-level conception of the relevant values and beliefs. Finally, they include the availability of a consistently reinforcing pattern of sanctions which will consolidate a renewed orientation in terms of the values and beliefs to which the agent of this "therapy" is himself committed.

A slightly different way of putting it is to say that any therapeutic agency in this sense must be capable of operating at two levels in relation to the internalization and institutionalization of the relevant cultural components. On the one hand, it must be firmly anchored in the higher institutionalized level—in the psychiatric case, in that considered normal to the "mature" personality. The therapist must not let himself be drawn into the "pathological" expectations of his patient in such a way as to reciprocate them. He must firmly "stand for" the values of health. At the same time, however, he must also be able to "empathize" with his patients' "deviant" preoccupations, which in the psychiatric case are psychologically regressive. He must give a properly controlled opportunity for their expression, and not let this expression undermine the generally supportive attitude indicated.

Turning back to the case of the minister, I should suggest that the leader of the congregation is handicapped in performing this role in a sense directly parallel to that in which a family member is handicapped in performing a psychiatric role. In the nature of the case he is the primary focus of the sanction system on which the functioning of the collectivity he leads is dependent. He is responsible for exhorting to proper participation in ritual, proper affirmation of belief and proper moral conduct. At the very least he must show disapproval of acts and attitudes which are deviant from these standards. Furthermore, by and large his implementation of these sanctions is public within the collectivity, though some modification of this is possible.

The exigencies of this collective leadership role constitute a formidable barrier to effective implementation of the permissive and supportive components of the "therapeutic" role, and indeed of the element of tentativeness which is necessarily involved in what I have called "selective rewarding." Experience in the psychological field has shown clearly that these functions are greatly facilitated if the agency responsible for them is clearly differentiated from that of the "normal" implementation of sanctions, and if these two agencies are mutually insulated from each other by a pattern like the privileged communication which is so deeply rooted in the traditions of the medical profession. It is precisely crucial that the patient's deviant phantasies should *not* be communicated to the members of his family. My suggestion is here that the minister is a "parental" figure in his psychological significance, and that it is important for the individual in religious quandaries to have a forum of expression of religious atttitudes, which will be guaranteed against communication to his minister since the latter is inevitably put, by such knowledge, in the dilemma of how far to exert pressure to "correct" the deviance.

That a profession of spiritual conselors in this sense should be a specialized group clearly separated from the parish ministry, and that the function should not be treated as an auxiliary function of the minister himself, seems to me to be strongly indicated. I would even suggest the possibility of going a step beyond this, namely to the point where such a group should be independent of at least formal denominational affiliation. It is of course a very serious question how far different denominational groups could tolerate entrusting their members to intimate religious counselors who were not committed to the particular denominational position. But it seems to me that the existence of the substratum of religious and moral consensus which is to me the necessary condition for the functioning of a system of denominational pluralism indicates the feasibility of such a separation. It would certainly greatly facilitate the impression of the genuineness of the "disinterestedness" of the counselor, namely, by removing the suspicion that he was simply an agent of the denominational authorities, not sincerely concerned with his client's personal religious problems, but only commissioned to bring him back into the fold by whatever pressures were necessary. Just as the conception of mental health in our society permits of leading a healthy life within a wide range of social statuses, occupations, and indeed family situations, so it would seem to be logical that a life of approved spiritual commitment could be lived within any one of a range of denominational affiliations, or indeed independently of any, and that a profession of spiritual counselors might well hold themselves formally free of commitment to any of them within an institutionalized range.

This of course is not to say that the members of such a group should be empirically independent of closer ties to some denominational groups than to others. The same set of forces which make our particular denominations in fact more closely connected with some parts of the social structure than others would operate in this direction. It is not considered deviant for some psychiatrists to have mainly a Jewish clientele, or mainly an academic one. But this is a very different thing from the profession being broken up into sectors which are formally committed to the service of particular social groups and these only.

The main tenor of this paper has been to emphasize the importance of the *differentiation* between the focus on the motivational foundations of the personality as these root in the process of socialization and in the family and, on the other hand, the involvement of the individual in religious and value-commitments at the more mature levels, as these are institutionalized in churches and in the value-patterns of the society at the more generalized levels. But this emphasis should not distract attention too much from the fact that these two levels are in fact intimately connected as well. Were this not so, the early fusion of the problems of health and of religious "purity" which is of such great historic significance would not be understandable. Both spheres involve the "deeper" and often unconscious layers of the personality of the individual. They are, moreover, deeply and subtly intertwined so that at many points they are only analytically distinguishable. This circumstance does not cancel out the importance of the process of differentiation which has been analyzed here, but it does make clear that it is a differentiation of deeply interconnected elements and that, since it is not a dissociation, their relations to each other remain of the first importance. Nothing said in this paper should be construed to minimize the importance of these interconnections.[6]

CONCLUSION

There is, by something like common consent, much spiritual malaise in our time. Diagnoses of the situation differ widely. My own

6. An exceptionally fine and perceptive analysis of these relations has recently been made by Erik H. Erikson in *Young Man Luther* (New York, W. W. Norton & Co., Inc., 1958). Contrary to the tendency of many psychoanalytically inclined writers to attempt to "reduce" the religious components of the problem to what we have here called "motivational" terms, Erikson consistently keeps the distinction clear, yet noting the highly intimate nature of their interdependence.

inclination is to put considerably more emphasis on the process of social and cultural change, including growth, which have gone on in recent times and which certainly have not ceased to go on, rather than, as is so commonly done, on factors of spiritual decline or moral collapse.[7] In my opinion the severity of the adjustments that have to be made in the processes of change which we know to occur are quite sufficient to account for the order of magnitude of the phenomenon.

In the nature of the case a major part of these adjustments must take place at levels entirely out of reach of the suggestions put forward in this paper. They must involve the major symbol-systems and ritualistic practices of churches, their organization as social collectivities and their place in the societies of which they are parts. No individualized measures can take the place of such readjustments. By exactly the same kind of reasoning much of the psychopathology of our time is a function of these same processes of social and cultural change, and certainly the psychiatric treatment of individuals cannot by itself control these processes or prevent them from having all deleterious impact on individuals.

At the same time, when due account is taken of these considerations, certainly the therapy of individuals at the psychiatric level can save many of the casualties of the social maladjustments and malintegrations with which we are so familiar and can mitigate their impact. In so doing it can greatly lessen the spread of personality breakdowns which make the stabilization of social situations and the assimilation of structural changes more difficult. By the same token, though individualized handling of spiritual malaise cannot hope to eliminate it, it can in principle have the same order of effect in raising the levels of commitment of large numbers of individuals, and in softening the severity of the phenomena of religious and to some extent moral crises on a societal level. It can, that is to say, mitigate the cost of religious changes, and certainly in individual instances, if not on some collective levels, it can avert some acute crises and possible shipwrecks.

It should be clear from the preceding argument that the prospects of success of any such institution as a profession of spiritual counseling rest on the existence of a sufficiently institutionalized consensus, above all with respect to what constitutes "moral integrity" in our

7. I have stated the main case for the growth rather than the decline-hypothesis in "Christianity and Modern Industrial Society," in Tiryakian, ed., *op. cit.,* and cannot take space to repeat it here.

society. This is parallel to the sense in which psychiatry rests on a consensus with respect to what constitutes mental health. This consensus need not be explicit in detail nor very tangible, but it must exist. It is my own view that it does in fact exist, that without it the degree of stability which our type of society has shown could not be understood. This is perhaps the main point at which issue must be joined with the prophets of spiritual doom who are so prominent in our time.

I 2

Some Theoretical
Considerations Bearing on the
Field of Medical Sociology

IT has been suggested that as, in one sense, a pioneer in the field of medical sociology, it would be appropriate for me to write a semi-autobiographical account of some of the problems and circumstances which lay in the background of the very striking growth of the field in recent years insofar as they bore on my own interests and experiences. In doing so it must be frankly recognized that I have only a very partial perspective on the total development. I shall hence recount some of the considerations which have been involved in the place of medical sociology in my own development as a sociological theorist and an interpreter of American society.

It is perhaps not irrelevant to remark that at the time I became interested (in the middle 1930's), the principal link between medicine and the social sciences was by way of "medical economics," not medical sociology. The focus of this was the immense project of study of the costs of medical care, which was a rather typical foundation-supported economic study in its attempt to bridge considerations of academic economics and of public policy. In the latter connection its

Written for a book by Robert N. Rapaport and Robert Wilson tentatively entitled The Worlds of Medicine in Social Perspective *to be published by the Russell Sage Foundation.*

report set off a storm in the relations between its proponents and the American Medical Association, being stigmatized by the latter's Journal as socialistic, though by present standards it was very mildly so, if indeed at all. In any case the primary concern was with the economic aspects of the welfare of the underprivileged sector of the American population, and the appropriate types of administrative organization called for to meet the needs. The whole basic controversy was of a piece with the general discussions of public policy in the New Deal era. The role of sociologists was entirely peripheral.

Of course, these problems have continued to reverberate, and have by no means lost their importance, but at that time it would have been difficult to predict the extent to which sociology, anthropology, and psychology would so soon become involved in the health fields and, in the case of the first of these in particular, the extent of dissociation from the interests of the medical economics of thirty years ago.

This shift is of particular interest to me, because my initial interest in the field was, at least overtly, in terms of an economic frame of reference. In this case, however, it was a theoretical one, rather than one oriented to immediate concerns of public policy with reference to health services. The psychologically oriented among readers may wish, however, to take into account the facts that I myself had, early in my college career, seriously considered studying medicine, and had become diverted, first into economics, then into sociology, and that a much admired older brother had in fact gone into medicine. Since the present essay is autobiographical at the intellectual rather than the personal level, I shall not now pursue further the motivational implications of these facts.

THE PROBLEM OF SELF-INTEREST

IN about 1936, I was in the last stages of finishing my first major work, the *Structure of Social Action,* and naturally concerned with a next step in scholarly and research work. On the empirical side, my main though not exclusive interest was macrosocial as distinct from the microsocial interest of so much subsequent sociological work, particularly in the medical field, but still it concerned imputations of motivation even to the level of the individual. The focus had been the problem of the nature of "capitalism," first as this had been analyzed in German sociological literature.[1] This had in turn led to certain problems of the general status of economic theory, in particular the status in that body of thought of the doctrine or postulate of "self-interest." Though in the Anglo-American discussion this problem had been very sketchily handled, it became increasingly clear that this could not be a simple empirical generalization about a "propensity of human nature," but must be treated as either—or both—a postulate of an abstract theoretical scheme or a culturally variant set of institutionalized expectations of behavior.

It gradually became clear to me that the principal theorists of capitalism, notably Marx and those in his tradition, tended to characterize the whole of modern industrial society in terms of this conception and to treat the business firm as *the* typical unit of its organization, beyond the family. In doing so they tended to ignore the existence of another major component of the social structure of the same society precisely at the relevant occupational level; namely, the professions, a category the members of which explicitly repudiated the allegation that orientation primarily in terms of economic self-interest was legitimate for them, or that empirically it characterized the typical orientation of the incumbent of a professional role. Moreover, from the point of view of the theorists of capitalism, it seemed paradoxical that the professions should have been growing in importance in the same society in which private business enterprise had prospered, while at the same time they belonged mainly to the private sector; they were not, as elements of government, a "socialistic" element.

This complex of empirical-theoretical problems constituted the point of departure for my interest in the medical profession—though doubtless the fact that among the modern professions the medical was first chosen for study led back to more personal reasons. However that may be, it was a prominent slogan of medical men that the "welfare of the patient" should be the dominating concern of the physician and that his own self-interest, financial and otherwise, should be systematically subordinated to this. My original goal was to investigate what underlay this difference from business by interviewing physicians about this conceptions of their professional roles and, so far as possible, by observing them at work.

1. My doctoral thesis submitted at Heidelberg in 1927 had been on this topic.

PATTERN-VARIABLES

THE theoretical conceptualization of the problem of self-interest with which I worked had reference to the main traditions of economic theory, but also, given my study in Germany, to the well-known dichotomy of Toennies between *Gemeinschaft* and *Gesellschaft*. Here the orientation of self-interest obviously belonged on the *Gesellschaft* side, was indeed its prototype. This is so much the case that it can almost be said that *Gemeinschaft* was a residual category. In view of the variety of institutional patternings which Weber and others had discussed, it was perhaps not surprising that I approached this entire problem in a sceptical frame of mind, one which on the political level was disinclined to accept the current dichotomy between capitalism and socialism—the professions did not seem to fit—and more theoretically was equally disinclined to accept the dichotomy between *Gemeinschaft* and *Gesellschaft*—again the professions did not seem to fit. Could there perhaps be something wrong with this dichotomous thinking at both levels? Could these dichotomies suppress consideration of the independent variation of components which were not inexorably tied to each other?

On the theoretical level at an early phase of the investigation I began to experiment with breaking down the Toennies dichotomy into independent components. Above all it seemed that the self-interest problem could not be properly assimilated to the one which had so often been tied in with it, namely "rationality" of orientation, as distinguished either from "traditionalism," as Weber used that term, or from various types of "emotional" attitudes. The crucial point here was that the professions were not, apparently, in the requisite sense "self-interested," but on the other hand they constituted the most important medium for the application of science to practical affairs. To say that practice in the framework of "scientific medicine" was in principle nonrational, did not make sense. Yet Toennies had built very heavily on this association.

This was the context in which the beginnings of what later took shape as the scheme of "pattern variables" were worked out. The initial starting point was the discrimination between the antithesis of self-interest, which at that time was called "disinterestedness," and the basis of scientifically oriented rationality. For technical reasons "rationality" was not as such included—as a pattern variable component I still believe it belongs on another level—but the scheme attempted to formulate the institutional patterns favorable to "rational action" in both the economic and the technological sense. The categories of universalism and specificity of function turned out to be the most immediately important in this context. In both cases I owed a great deal to Weber's discussions, particularly of bureaucracy (for reasons I shall return to), but also empirically to my observations of medical practice and of the attitudes of physicians.

Universalism here referred in the first instance to the generalized "impartiality" which was necessitated by treating a sick patient as presenting a problem for applied science. The imperative of scientific objectivity required abstracting from considerations of personal relationship or group belongingness in favor of diagnosis and treatment as a "case" of whatever the disease category happened to be. It soon appeared, however, that in addition to this there were certain more strictly social aspects of the relevance of universalism. The basic criteria of eligibility to enter a relationship to a physician had to do with an objective condition of the patient, with a state of illness, which "could happen to anyone" and was thus not a function of prior social status.

Functional specificity was the concept used to designate an independently variable component of the medical situation. This concerned the basis of the relation of physician to patient in the sense of the scope of mutual concern. The essential point was its limitation to matters relevant to the health of the patient. Thus physicians must often have access to confidential information about their patients' private lives; on what basis is such a claim justified? Clearly the relevance of the information to the health problem at issue—there is, for instance, no claim to information about the patient's financial affairs if they are not relevant to his state of health. Specificity in this sense is to be contrasted with the diffuseness of relations of kinship and friendship where the burden of proof of claims to information, to take this one case, is on the other side; thus a husband must positively justify refusal to answer his wife's question about his financial affairs; he cannot just say "this has nothing to do with our marriage," as the patient can say the question has nothing to do with health—of course in all such matters there are borderline questions.

The choice of medical practice for this study of a profession turned out, however, to open up another line of consideration in a way in which this would not have happened—to the same extent at least—if law or teaching had been chosen. The starting point here was the element of "intimacy" which was involved in the doctor-patient relationship and its bearing on the motivational state of the patient. Here, along with confidential information, a particularly important point is that the physician must often have access to the body of his patient for physical examination and various treatment purposes, access which is very generally inhibited in other relations. One important exception is sexual relations, and in some situations exposure and touch, especially where physician and patient are of opposite sex, could easily remind both parties of a sexual relation. This type of consideration, generalized to a wider attitudinal complex, was the primary source of definition of the pattern variable, affectivity vs. affective neutrality. One of the features which characterizes definition of the physician's role in this type of connection is a "neutral" attitude in the sense that he inhibits what would otherwise be "normal" emotional reactions. Attitudinally this point can be traced into the general field of the discrimination between attitudes appropriate to personal intimacies of various sorts and the "professional" attitude. Where the same persons are involved in both it is possible to trace a clear discrimination as a function of context.

In some cases there is reciprocity in this affectively neutral attitude between physician and patient; the patient wants "a job done" and cooperates in what is objectively necessary. In many cases, however, it became evident that patients are characterized by a very marked sensitivity to the emotional attitudes of their physicians and that a very subtle, often unconscious, interplay goes on. On the medical side this seemed to be a major aspect of what was often called the "art" as distinguished from the "science" of medicine. It seemed likely that the attitude of affective neutrality then had something to do with important processes of social control.

THE "PSYCHIC FACTOR" IN DISEASE AND THERAPY

THOUGH firmly convinced of the importance of this art of medicine, many of my physician-subjects were almost totally insensitive to any deeper implications. However, because of my Harvard Medical School connection, I did a good deal of my work at the Massachusetts General Hospital, and this was a time when, among internists in particular, influenced by such psychiatrists as Dr. Stanley Cobb and Dr. Erich Lindemann, a substantial interest in the phenomena often called "psycho-somatic" was beginning to build up, was indeed, in intellectually sophisticated medical circles, coming to be a major field of interest—not only in Boston of course. It then began to appear that there was a growing scientific basis for believing that these "attitudinal" aspects of the physician's role, in addition to his role as a manipulator of biological and chemical techniques, might have an important bearing on the therapeutic functions of the profession.

These impressions coincided with a growing interest in personality psychology, which was fostered by certain relationships, notably with L. J. Henderson and Elton Mayo. About this time Henderson, with whom I had been associated in connection with his work on Pareto, and my own book, noted above, wrote a notable paper entitled "Physician and Patient as a Social System," [2] and he was one of my principal consultants on the whole study of medical practice. It was Mayo, however, to whom I turned in connection with the problem of psychology, and it was at his urging that I first undertook an intensive reading of Freud's works, beyond the level of acquaintance which a good many social scientists had acquired by that time.

Though this topic by no means stood alone, I was particularly fascinated by Freud's account of the psychoanalytic procedure, including his discovery of the phenomenon of transference. It was, I think, a little later that psychoanalysts came to be much concerned with countertransference and thus were able to fill out the paradigm to which I referred of a "subtle emotional interplay" between doctor and patient.

Not only did these considerations bear directly on the nature of the doctor-patient relationship. They showed that a most intimate connection must exist between its sociological character and the structure of the human personality generally. They also strongly suggested that there was a complete continuum between the most completely "mental" of mental illnesses and the corresponding processes of psychotherapy, through the various ranges of psychosomatic phenomena to the category of the completely "somatic," or however it might be termed, where illness was simply a "condition" with which human techniques had to cope.

Short of this, however, it became clear that there was a component of motivatedness in almost all of illness, and that the social structur-

2. Lawrence J. Henderson, "Physician and Patient as a Social System," *New England Journal of Medicine*, Vol. 212, May 2, 1935, pp. 19–23.

ing of the doctor-patient relationship had a great deal to do with the therapeutic control of these components—they had "latent functions" in these connections. From this point of view Freud's own functioning as a physician, and the predilection of psychoanalysts for the physician's role, did not seem to be matters of chance. Indeed, an important part of their work had already been done for them, by processes analogous to natural selection, in structuring a role-type which was to some significant degree adapted to the therapeutic function within the range of motivational relevance.

From here it was not a very great step to the insight that illness itself could probably be considered, at least over a very considerable range, to be more than an objective "condition" which came about independently of the motivational balances of the social system, and which was merely "acted upon" by a "technology" in the therapeutic process. It was itself integrally involved in the motivational balance and hence *institutionally* defined. To be "sick" was not only to be in a biological state which suggested remedial measures, but required exemptions from obligations, conditional legitimation, and motivation to accept therapeutic help. It could thus, in part at least, be classed as a type of deviant behavior which was socially categorized in a kind of role.

Still another major line of considerations opened out from this nexus. One could not become very deeply absorbed in Freud's work without being sensitized to the intimate connections between psychopathology and the process of genetic development of the personality. However, whereas Freud himself was ambivalent about the roles of biological or "instinctual" maturation and social, or "object" relations in the process, and most of Freud's followers have chosen the former emphasis, it was natural for a sociologist to pick up the latter thread of analysis and be particularly concerned with the impact of the social structure of the child's environment—in Freud's terms his "object-relations"—on the development of his personality. With Freud's own emphasis on the early phases, this naturally leads to consideration of the structure of the family in its relation to socialization, but the later phases may also be of considerable significance. Very particularly Freud's own emphasis on the Oedipal complex is of course most intimately connected with the structure of the family.

These various themes were developed only over a considerable period of years, often not in direct connection with the study of medical practice. However, they first acquired salient theoretical significance for me in this context and it has been a continuing point of reference for later work. Certainly all of these factors must feed into a consideration of the sociological significance of health and illness and of the institutional arrangements oriented to them.

THE INSTITUTIONAL PATTERNING
OF THE THERAPEUTIC ROLE

IN one particularly important respect the analysis came full circle. At an early stage there seemed to be cogent reasons why the "self-interested" orientation of business would at the least be dysfunctional in the care of illness. The most obvious line of argument concerned the facts that on the one hand a major feature of illness is helplessness and therefore sick people are peculiarly open to exploitation. On the other hand the medical profession is characterized by a special technical competence which is not open to the layman, who is incompetent not only to perform medical functions but even to judge whether they are being properly performed. If the "rational pursuit of self-interest" is an inherent "propensity of human nature" as has been so generally alleged, then surely its fully free operation in the medical setting could be expected to result in far more extreme exploitation than for instance in the famous employer-employee relationship—the power differential is certainly very great. Unless, then, a society is ready to abandon its sick to "natural selection" in the most drastic sense, there must be some mechanisms which protect the sick person. For sociologists it is not very far to seek to say that it is unlikely that such mechanisms consist entirely in governmental intervention in favor of the weak; there must be some "informal" mechanisms which operate in this direction. It seems likely that the "disinterestedness" of the medical profession could be put in this category.

The same reasoning could of course be extended to the other three pattern variable components which have been mentioned. First, a universalistic orientation could be conceived to be functionally necessary in order to bring the resources of scientific knowledge to bear on the therapeutic problem. Second, functional specificity could be conceived to be important in order to differentiate the physician's function from the other components which could readily become associated in a "personal" relationship of the type existing between physician and patient. Third, the affective neutrality of the expected professional orientation could be hypothesized to relate to another aspect of the "insulation" of the professional role from involvements to which the requisite situation would expose it, involvements which for example would not be expected to operate importantly in an ordinary commercial relationship but, on the other hand, would be altogether appropriate in a relationship within the family.

These four pattern variable components, then, taken together, seemed to characterize a role-pattern appropriate to the medical version of professional function (at the time, the fifth, quality-performance—a generalization of Linton's achievement-ascription, had not yet been identified as a pattern variable). Seen in terms of the *Gemeinschaft-Gesellschaft* dichotomy, the striking thing was that only the self-interest-disinterestedness component fitted the *Gemeinschaft* type, the three others were "typical" aspects of the rational, impersonal, etc., patterning of an "industrial" order, a "contractual" or indeed a "bureaucratic" social system. At this level this was sufficient to show the independent variability of the category of self-interest—only later did it become clear and important that bureaucracy also was "disinterested" in precisely the sense of this analysis. This seemed sufficient to break the "monolithic" unity of the alleged pattern of a "capitalistic society" if one granted that the functions of the professions were in fact crucial to it.

Of course, it will be recognized, if not insisted upon, that such functional considerations are not, by themselves, very decisive. They served, however, very much to clarify the *statement of a problem* and hence to point the direction in which *to look* for the relevant processes and mechanisms which could carry one from the statement of the initial problem of why professional roles existed in such a society at all to the question of *how* their alleged functions were performed.

It goes almost without saying that the problem could not be stated in this way without comparative perspective. One very obvious question in this connection is whether therapeutic functions can be found anywhere which are performed in a strictly business, *i.e.,* in our sense self-interested, context of role-definition. The answer is clearly no. The other comparative perspective concerns the conditions under which patterns of self-interested orientation *can* be found in a society, including their viability and functional effectiveness over a sufficiently wide range and long period. Furthermore, as will appear later, the level of differentiation of the systems in which therapy occurs needs to be taken into account.

The approach to the problem of mechanism is in one context given in the analysis of therapy as a *process.* In order to bring out this significance, however, two distinctions have to be made. One of them is that already sketched, between the motivated and the "conditional" components of the state of illness which in turn must be operated upon by therapeutic agency. With respect to the latter components, medical practice utilizes a complex technology, whereas with respect to the former, it involves processes of *social control, i.e.,* acting upon the "intentions" of patients, as Freud above others has taught us, at unconscious levels. The second distinction is between the therapeutic process itself and the conditions of its effective operation. The sociologist is concerned of course with the latter components of therapy, but in order to understand the problems presented he must have some understanding of the former.

A particularly salient illustration is provided by the problem of the importance of affective neutrality in the definition of the physician's role. One important line of reasoning runs as follows: Insofar as illness is motivated it can be assumed that patients will typically manifest defenses against recovery, because this threatens their "secondary gains." In entering into a relationship with a therapist, then, it can be expected that an attempt will be made to draw the therapist into a community of defense of the sick position, in this sense to "seduce" him. The pattern of affective neutrality can then be seen to be part of a mechanism which protects the physician against this seductive pressure (including his own unconscious motives) and enables him to maintain his position of "leverage" against the motivated elements of illness. The most explicit formulation of this is Freud's doctrine of the importance of avoiding—it later became controlling—the tendencies to countertransference, *e.g.,* through eliminating face-to-face interstimulation in psychoanalytic procedure.

The connection with the problems associated with access to the body of the patient is made clear in relation to the potential of sexuality. Sexuality is again, as interpreted in terms of psychoanalytic theory, basically regressive. The seduction of the physician into an erotic relationship is to put his relation to the patient onto what, *relative* to the level of professional orientation, is a more regressive basis. This then essentially is to say that by avoiding this, the physician's *rewards* are the patient's motives to act on the level of health, which in turn means that he must renounce at least certain of his regressive needs. The physician's function is to define the situation in these terms and to act as an agent of reward for more "mature" orientation and behavior.

This type of basic relationship between the structure of the physician's role and the therapeutic function became clear at quite an early stage of my work. Furthermore, there was a patent relationship between this and the element of "disinterestedness," namely, that this type of control of unconscious motivation could not operate without a relation of "trust" which was expressed ideologically in the medical doctrine that a patient must be able to have "confidence" in his physician. The essential point is that the physician is asking for a sacrifice, in the psychic case of primary interest to us, that of his secondary gains—in other cases, such as surgery, it may be exposure to risk of life—and the agent of imposition of a sacrifice must have the "welfare" of the "victim" at heart, if exposure to the deprivation is to be *voluntarily* assumed.

There was, however, a further ramification which took longer to work out. This concerned the fact that, whereas, over-all, the orientation of affective neutrality should be considered to be predominant, it did not stand alone. Indeed, in the "art of medicine" there was included a component of "empathy," of feeling for the predicaments of the sick which could amount to partial identification. Gradually this factor was clarified to the point of coming to understand that there is, in this respect, a duality in the role of the physician, namely, that whereas the orientation of affective neutrality is paramount, at certain stages and under carefully controlled conditions, certain types of affectivity are not only permitted, but expected. This concerns, in the earlier stages of a therapeutic process, the establishment of the basis of "solidarity" from which a positive transference can grow, which does in fact mean a kind of partial identification which includes a definite resonance to the pathological-regressive motives of the patient. If it is not to block the therapeutic process, this empathy must be practiced under controlled conditions, *e.g.*, within the framework of the professional role, and it is entered into only in order eventually to be overcome.[3]

With regard to the relation of the therapeutic role to the pattern variable scheme, there is one further problem which merits attention. This concerns the relation of the pattern variable ascription-achieve-

3. This aspect of the physician's role was worked out in particular on the basis of suggestions from two graduate students, now Dr. Renée C. Fox and Dr. Miriam Massey Johnson.

ment to the professional role. An important aspect of it was, as so often happens, empirically built in before it was theoretically clarified. This concerned the observation, so prominent in comparative perspective, of the *activistic* element in the orientation of Western medicine, backed by the values of the society as a whole, toward the problems of illness. This is to say that, by contrast with many other cases, we tended to accept illness not as a given aspect of the human condition but rather as something which was, within very wide limits, intrinsically manageable and controllable. There has been much talk about the "conquest of disease." Once this distinction, between the ascriptively given and the state to be achieved, or between existent qualities and performances, is given a salient theoretical significance, it becomes clear that the physician's role, like most other occupational roles in Western society, is characterized by a clear preference on the performance side.

THE DOCTOR-PATIENT RELATIONSHIP
AS A COLLECTIVITY

IT was much later that I came to realize that similar things could be said about the role of patient. One of the empirical clues to this aspect was the frequency with which psychiatrists referred to their expectations that patients should *work* with them on the latter's problems. The role of patient was not conceived passively as being "operated upon"—except, perhaps significantly, in surgery—but as actively striving for recovery through "cooperating" with the physician.[4]

These various factors eventually combined to introduce a new stage in theoretical significance. It will be clear from the formulations stated so far that the problem had been conceived from the point of view of role as reference point. This is to say, the therapeutic function was conceived as performed by a type of person-in-role, a physician, acting vis-à-vis another person-in-role, a patient defined as

4. This point was documented in the paper "Definitions of Health and Illness in Relation to American Values and Social Structure," in Chapter 10. It was, however, only subsequent to its writing that, through observations of Dr. Joseph Ben-David, I became aware that the clearest modern case of treating the patient as an object with an ascribed condition was to be found in certain patterns of nineteenth-century German medicine. Among other things the insight resulted from paying increased attention to illness as a social role, complementary to that of therapy. Cf. reference in Introduction, p. 11.

sick. It was partly for this reason of perspective that the nature and importance of the contribution of the complementary role performance, that of patient, was obscured and did not become of salient importance until a late stage.

It gradually became clear that the relevant antithesis to self-interest could best be formulated as "collectivity-orientation" and that what in the respects which had figured in the previous analysis were the important characteristics of the physician's role, could be taken account of by considering him as performing a function as a member of a collectivity. The classic "doctor-patient relationship" should then be considered to be the minimal relevant collectivity. It is the solidarity of this collectivity which constitutes the basis of mutual "trust" between physician and patient.

It seemed to follow that the primary *function* of medical practice, what we ordinarily call therapy, should be regarded as the goal not simply of the physician but of the collectivity constituted by physician and patient taken together. Looked at from this point of view, the contribution of the patient becomes immediately meaningful; the case of his being treated "purely" as an object, rather than as a partner, however "junior," becomes a limiting case, the point where his contribution is zero. Short of this he is not, for instance, just a "consumer" but to some degree a "producer" of health service.

From this point of view the element of solidarity falls readily into place. If there are to be at least two clearly differentiated roles in the same collectivity—in this case one sick and the other not, one technically competent in medicine, the other not—then there must be normative patterns at both the value and the norm levels which "bind" them together, which on the one hand legitimize the collective goal, on the other designate proper procedures in its carrying out, including specifying the terms of the division of labor between the roles. They must have a *common* commitment to the goal of therapy which "applies" only to the state of the patient, since by definition in the relevant situation and respects, the physician is not sick. But because of differentiation with respect both to illness and to the relevant competence, this common value-commitment does not prescribe identical courses of action—on the contrary. The factor of "disinterestedness," or better collectivity-orientation, is, however, common to both roles; it is this which defines their common membership in the same collectivity.

The problem of self-interest, as first approached, was conceived essentially as a problem of *the attitudes of individuals.* This component remains as an essential part of it, but the line of development which has been traced highlights the importance of another aspect; namely, that the problem involves a very direct relation to the structure of the social system, not only at the level of roles but of collectivities as well. What, then, are the implications of this for the self- rather than the collectivity-oriented case?

First let it be noted that the pattern just sketched can be generalized to the more usual type of collectivity characterized by plurality rather than duality of members. In the medical field, of course, the most familiar example is the hospital, and here the significant point is that patients must be regarded as "members of the hospital" regarded as a collectivity. This, for example, is symbolized by speaking of "admission" to the hospital; one does not as it were "automatically" belong by virtue of being or "feeling" sick, but has to be admitted by some sort of more or less formal procedure. In this respect, of course, the hospital belongs to a much larger class of collectivities which include both the purveyors and the recipients of services. One of the most familiar cases in other fields is the school, including colleges and universities. For example, the not uncommon term "members of the university" (or college) clearly includes not only faculty but also students. Similarly in the case of a church, the category of membership clearly includes both laity and clergy.

Among cases of the division of labor which differentiate providers and recipients of a functionally significant service, the question arises of the conditions which determine whether the two categories will tend to be included in a common membership or whether they will be separated. It seems that the case primarily considered in economic analysis is an extreme if not the limiting case in which a direct tie of solidarity between the two parties to the relationship need not exist; indeed if it did exist it could readily be regarded as hampering efficiency. If then the producer of economic theory was regarded as an "individual" it would seem natural to think of "him" as acting in terms of a self-interested orientation to the "market." His "customers" then could equally be thought of as acting in terms of self-interested seeking for the best possible bargain.[5]

5. A particularly revealing clue to the difference of the medical case even in the dyadic relation from the paradigmatic economic market is the objection of physicians to their patients' "shopping around," *i.e.*, seeking the best available medical care at the lowest cost, by sampling what a number

This paradigm of thought is so deeply ingrained in our cultural heritage that it is not surprising that it should be generalized to the professional relationship, and "the doctor" as an individual thought of as set over against "the patient."

It is also of interest to point out that the economic paradigm tends to treat the "other party," the customer, as not positively involved in the function of "production"—he is a "consumer." Among other things this point of view is related to the economist's primary concern with exchange of *commodities*. The typical consumer is a consumer of "goods," though the formula often takes care of the further extension by adding "and services." Economists, however, have generally not been very sensitive to the possibly profound differences between an exchange transaction which does and which does not involve the "human factor." There are, to be sure, cases of services—including some by members of the medical profession—which entail only the most fleeting of personal contact. There are also sales of commodities, including many durable goods, which entail a continuing and important "servicing" relationship between seller and buyer. Nevertheless, the distinction is clear in principle, and the doctor-patient relationship is far removed from the ideal type of commodity market.

Another way of looking at the difference between goods and services, to use the economists' formula again, is to point out that, though not usually looked at this way, the purchaser of a service is, functionally speaking, the *employer* of the performer of the service. Because we think of employees as "workers" and of professional men even as small "entrepreneurs," it is a bit jarring to think of the average patient as an employer. Analytically, however, the "private" case of the doctor-patient relationship is an undifferentiated one in which the relation of employer-employee and of seller-buyer are fused with each other. In clinic or hospital practice, on the other hand, they have become differentiated. Then the relevant patients, in the aggregate, have transferred the role of employer not to the physician but to the hospital or clinic as a collectivity, which in turn employs physicians.

---

of physicians have to offer and making up their own minds. This is not the place to enter into the reasons for the attitude, but clearly it is considered unethical by most physicians. A patient is "the patient" of one physician until or unless the relation is explicitly terminated, by the patient's "resignation" as it were, or much less frequently, by the physician refusing to continue to serve.

In the fully developed case this collectivity is a corporation, so that *no* individual person technically either employs physicians or sells medical services. The collectivity is a "third party" intervening in the relationship—which to be sure the American Medical Association deplores, but this is one of the facts of life. It is, however, typical of medical service that both physician and patient are members of the collectivity which both employs and sells.

Among other things, this perspective on the traditional doctor-patient relationship can help to throw light on the structure of the market for medical services in the matter of pricing. The classical market structure of the main traditions of economic theory is the "competitive" one. However, many modifications of it have had to be made, a basic conception has been for a given market that of a uniform price per unit of a uniform commodity or service—only "discriminating monopoly" removes this postulate. The striking feature of the professional case is the sliding scale, the graduation of charges for essentially the same service, according to capacity of the patient to pay.[6]

The legitimacy of the sliding scale is based on the conception of *contribution*. This in turn relates, as noted, to the conception that doctor and patient constitute a collectivity oriented to a common goal and function. The patient is in the nature of the case low in special knowledge and skill. Of course, so far as the physician is dependent on his profession for his living he must have some source of income, and the patient is generally in a position to contribute financially to the common enterprise. The justice of the level of contribution is partly a matter of tradition, partly of *ad hoc* judgments of "just price" by the physician. But clearly such judgments must be legitimized, they are not determined solely by the "play of market forces."

There is, indeed, a sense in which the sliding-scale method of payment is analogous to a budgetary allocation; it is giving a "department" of the organization the facilities it needs to perform its functions effectively—always remembering that budget funds are quite normally used to pay salaries as well as other expenses of operation. The difference from the normal case of budgeting lies in the factor of agency. In the medical case the recipient of budgetary funds

6. There are, of course, many further complications in this field, but for present purposes I shall confine myself to the undoubtedly central phenomenon of the sliding scale.

is also the "executive" who makes the decisions—and still further he is the "fund-raiser" for the common enterprise. This state of affairs clearly is possible only in a social system in which the more complex differentiations of function have not yet taken place. Furthermore, it places—as among others the late Hugh Cabot often pointed out—the physician in a particularly delicate and vulnerable fiduciary position, since as executive and fund-raiser he, as the member of the dyadic collectivity who was in the strongest power-position,—an interesting reversal of the classical conception of the power-position of the "employer"—has been expected to make the decisions on which his own personal financial self-interest depended.

So far as it was tenable at all, this system clearly depended on a particularly firm set of normative controls, however informal. Essentially, we may say, the classical private physician was—and to some degree still is—a kind of "aristocrat" of the occupational world. His *technical* functions had become specialized around the application of scientific knowledge, but his *social status* was a typically diffuse *fiduciary status*. In terms of the general process of structural differentiation which must be regarded as central to the development of industrial societies, this classical private physician must be regarded as a special, probably transitional, role-type. It seems inconceivable that this structural type could resist the pressures to further differentiation which have operated throughout the society.

SUMMARY OF THEORETICAL REORIENTATION

BEFORE attempting to sketch a few aspects of the kinds of trends in this direction which I think have been doing on, it will be well to summarize a few main theoretical considerations about the problem of self-interest and its relation to collectivity-orientation. My own initial orientation to the problem was, as I noted above, quite explicitly couched in terms of the traditional frame of reference of economic theory, which, as it were, regarded the physician as a producer and the patient as a customer. The initial problem was that of the nature and causes of the deviations existing in the case of the professions, medicine in particular, from the type of relationship which not only "capitalists" but socialists considered normal for the division of labor in this sense.

The most conspicuous deviation, the one taken as the original point of reference, was this one concerning self-interest. This path led first into a wider complex of factors impinging on the relationship on both sides; namely, the implications of the "competence gap" between physician and patient and the dependency involved in the sick role, then also the factors involved in the "personal" character of the relationship. All this was analyzed in terms of the pattern variable scheme in its earlier phases of development, treating what then was called "disinterestedness" as independently variable relative to the other factors of universalism, functional specificity, and affective neutrality. The outcome was a paradigm of the professional type of *role* which on a provisional level "explained" the difference between the role of the physician and of the "business man"—using reference to the individual and his orientation in both cases. Throughout this development the involvement of the medical role with the subtler aspects of personality psychology, especially as illuminated by psychoanalytic theory, played a prominent part. It was mainly these aspects of the medical function which underlay the eventual conception that it must be undertaken in the social context of a collectivity of which the patient is a member.

Before this new conception crystallized, however, a process of development in the pattern variable scheme itself took place which provided a considerably more favorable framework for working it out. This was the development documented in *Toward a General Theory of Action* (1951). One primary feature of it was the addition of quality-performance as a pattern variable. The other principal one was a grouping of the variables so that they no longer constituted merely a list, but took a step in the direction of a system.

The grouping consisted in two "sets," those of orientation and of object-categorization, the first comprising specificity-diffuseness and neutrality-affectivity, and the second universalism-particularism and quality-performance. This left the fifth pair, self vs. collectivity orientation in a special position. What this meant was gradually clarified as concerning the relation between two different levels of organization of systems of action. The case of interest to us here is that of the difference, in social systems, between the role and the collectivity levels. Self-orientation for this case is orientation independent of membership-commitments in any particular collectivity, whereas collectivity-orientation means expectations defined in terms of these commitments. The classical economic conception of the market is precisely one where contracting parties do not belong to a common collectivity with respect to the content of their transactions. They are, however, as Durkheim made so clear, subject to common norms, and these in turn are sanctioned in a collectivity of a higher order—the politically organized society. But this is a different story. The market is, as one type of "communication," one major mechanism of articulation *between* not *within* collectivities.

There are still further developments of the pattern variable scheme out of which the scheme of four basic functional categories came (*Working Papers in the Theory of Action,* 1953) and certain very recent developments (*Pattern Variables Revisited,* 1961) which need not explicitly concern us here.

Suffice it to say that if this view of the special status of the self-collectivity variable was correct, the problem could not be handled satisfactorily at the role level even for the dyadic case. Once this proposition and its spelling out, as that has been outlined above, has been stated, it seems almost obvious. But the economic schema has been so deeply ingrained in our traditions of social thought that it took a long and complicated process to arrive at this point. It seems to me this is a particularly good example of the importance of theoretical frames of reference for the development of social science. In this case the critical facts were by and large ready at hand, though firsthand observation made the significance of many of them salient in a way which would not otherwise have been possible. There were, however, certain fundamental biases in the interpretation of these facts which could not be overcome until a major revision in the underlying conceptual scheme had been worked out.

CHANGES IN THE SOCIAL STRUCTURE OF HEALTH SERVICES

THESE considerations make it possible to formulate a line of interpretation of some of the main processes of change which have been going on in the structure of the organization of health services. As has already been suggested, the main trend can be characterized as one of differentiation. Differentiation, however, should be regarded as part of a wider structural complex some of the other components of which will have to be discussed, and in addition there are several types of differentiation involved.

1. *"Bureaucratization"*

The most familiar line of differentiation is that of the increasing "division of labor" which moves from the one-man performance of function by the "individual" artisan or professional practitioner, to the specific-function organization as the agency of output of a commodity or service. This is a line which of course has specific relevance to general ideas of the development of industrial society—the prototypical outcome is the "bureaucratic" organization which is characterized above all by two main features. One of these is hierarchical ordering in terms of executive and administrative authority. The other is specialization of function at any given level in the hierarchical scale, in the "line" as it is often put. Both of these aspects have had their place in the structure of health services, but there have been certain special characteristics which distinguish these cases from the more familiar ones of governmental administrative bureaucracy or the business firm, particularly in manufacturing. These derive mainly from two clusters of factors; namely, those involved in the role of scientific levels of technical competence in medicine and those involved in the character of illness, with its personalness, its intimacies and the like.

With respect to the first, Max Weber's famous model of bureaucratic organization simply did not take adequate account of the fact that, even though technically an administrative "subordinate," a scientifically trained professional man cannot be "directed" by a superior who is less competent than himself in his specific technical field. In this connection it should be remembered that medicine itself has been differentiating into an increasingly complex cluster of specialties so that even if the superior is himself a physician there is no guarantee of his competence in the particular branches of medicine involved. If he is a generalist, his knowledge of all specialties is necessarily superficial; if he is a specialist, he can be competent over only a small part of the range covered, for example, in a general hospital. The problem of the hospital administrator, for example, is different only in degree from that of the university administrator.

This means that medical organization must take a form which is closer to that of the university faculty than it is to the classical paradigm of bureaucracy. The organization must be broken into a series of subunits, "departments" or "services," which enjoy a great deal of autonomy with respect to the performance of their respective technical functions. The professional staff are not "subordinates" in the usual bureaucratic sense, but themselves, usually with an important degree of "collegiality," carry the main technical responsibilities. The "administration" has more facilitating than directing functions.

Nevertheless, the differences from private practice in the classical sense are profound. Typically, three central functions are largely, though not necessarily, taken over from the professional staff by the administration. The first of these is the provision of facilities, which in turn subdivides into two main categories. Premises and the increasingly complicated and expensive equipment such as not only wards and clinics, but operating rooms, laboratories, drugs and many other items, constitute one obvious category. But hardly if at all less important are a myriad of auxiliary services, of nurses, technicians, orderlies, people responsible for the feeding of patients and the like. These, of course, are typical of any organization with complex functions, but nonetheless important in the health service case.

A second aspect of facilitation, however, is financing. This includes the often very complicated problem of paying for physical facilities and auxiliary services. It includes also, in an overlapping way, an area which has traditionally been very touchy from the medical point of view, namely, the problem of financial arrangements with patients. It is highly important that most medical organizations are financially subsidized, in three important ways, namely, by support from public funds, by voluntary financial contributions of various sorts—including some personal service by the laity—and by free or underpaid service by members of the profession. Nevertheless, there is a tradition and continuing tendency, to try to cover a substantial portion of expense by fees for service. The essential point here is that an organization cannot permit its own members to determine these questions individually without being subject to any general policies for the organization as a whole. There are many sorts of such arrangements, but there is an increasing tendency to take the problem out of the hands of the professional staff and treat it as an organizational matter. An important parallel is the university where the basic financial obligations of students are never determined by arrangement with the individual teacher, and certainly he does not either personally "give" financial support or receive tuition income, though there are various kinds of faculty participation in making scholarship awards and the like.

This context of functions shades over into the second particularly important one, which in the hospital and clinic case is that of "admissions." This has already been commented upon as the intervention of a collective agency between doctor and patient in setting the terms of their mutual solidarity. In the case of the hospital, for instance, it includes the procedures not only of admission in the first place, but of the "routing" of patients to various departments and services, and eventually the determination of what patient will be examined or treated by what physician or combination of them in the particular case. This is indeed the abdication of one of the most cherished aspects of the "sovereignty" of the traditional practitioner, but one which could scarcely be avoided unless the advantages of large-scale organization are to be abandoned altogether.

The third essential function is what may be called the *fiduciary* function, having to do, we may say, with the implementation of medical ethics in a complex society. In this even the storied private practitioner never stood entirely alone, though legend tends to maximize his personal responsibility. He has, however, always been a member of a profession which collectively has been conceived to be responsible for the welfare of the patient population. From an early date this has involved professional organization and even the formal codification of professional standards. Along the line, however, a variety of other agencies have come to assume important shares of this fiduciary responsibility. Clearly one of the most important has been focused on medical education. The steps in this development are highly significant in our context. One might say that the arrangement symbolically most appropriate to ideal typical private practice is apprenticeship—learning almost exclusively by doing under the supervision of an experienced practitioner. With increasing technicality, however, this no longer sufficed. The crucial step has been the establishment of the principle that only the *university* medical school was an adequate agency of basic medical education. University medical schools, of course, enjoy a great deal of autonomy within the university, but it is of the type enjoyed by departments within a faculty. Not only does the university take major financial responsibilities, but above all the continuity between the basic sciences in the medical school and their representation in other parts of the university clearly means that the medical group is not fully autonomous any more. The *scientific* standards of medical education are not specifically medical, they are basically those of university science generally. This consideration has become of even greater importance with the growth of research in medical contexts.

The second primary institutional arrangement has been the development of trusteeship, whether it be that of lay citizens of the community or, for example, of various types of government agencies. The essential point is that the responsibility, not merely for *operating* a medical installation, but for its major character and place of importance in the relevant sector of the society is not purely a responsibility of the medical profession, but this is shared with important nonmedical groups. In the earlier phases these tended to be mainly religious groups—this phase, however, is long past.

In this whole connection it should not be forgotten that medicine is an inherently risky business. For those who purport to care for the sick, the responsibilities are serious indeed. Many of the deepest of human concerns are very directly involved, most seriously risk to life, and the knowledge and techniques available are still very seriously inadequate to the task. It was truly an "aristocracy" which could shoulder this responsibility alone, saying in effect, if health is concerned in any way, both the credit and the blame go exclusively to members of the medical profession and to no one else. It is not surprising that, in a society which generally tends to "spread risks," other agencies come into this problem. Thus, though the university in no way takes responsibility for the treatment of particular patients, it takes a major responsibility for the scientific standards involved in medical training and research. Similarly, the lay trustee of a hospital obviously does not presume to treat patients. But not only is he responsible for helping to provide technically adequate facilities to the staff, he is very basically in part responsible for the medical standards of the organization. Any imputation of either unethical or technically substandard practice in his hospital should properly come home to him and his colleagues on the board.

Along with the development of specialized organizations dispensing medical services, of which the hospital and the clinic are prototypes, we have, of course, seen a very important development of specialized organizations and associations concerned with some part of the total complex of health care, but not themselves performing the operative functions. The most important of these have been in the financial field, the various types of disability insurance which the private insurance companies have introduced, but on the largest scale, the Blue Cross and Blue Shield organizations. This is not the place to attempt to supply figures, but surely now the proportion of payments for medical care coming from the immediate personal resources of the patient or his family has been diminishing greatly, and is by now probably of the order of 20 to 25 per cent at the most. When the various types of governmental provision—the largest being state mental hospitals and the Veterans Administration—are added together, and to them are added the many kinds of private collective provision, the total is already very large, and it is certain to grow.

An interesting and important consequence is the shrinkage of the population of pure "charity" patients. For example, the supply of "clinical material" for medical training formerly consisted mainly of these charity patients in the teaching hospitals and their availability for teaching purposes was interpreted as a kind of "price" they had to pay for the financially free care they were receiving. Now the great majority of patients are in some sense paying their way, even though out of various funded arrangements, so their role in teaching becomes much more of a voluntary contribution on their part.

It is, of course, interesting in the American case that this progressive involvement in organizational setting has proved compatible to a degree with the retention of partial private practice. At the very least, the general practitioner must have some sort of access to a general hospital when his patients require hospitalization, and most of them spend a rather large proportion of their professional time in the hospital, even though it would not be quite correct to say they are "employed" by it. From this situation there is a gradual shading to the situation where full-time hospital men take a few private patients. The important point is that the progressively increasing involvement in the nexus of formal organization has by no means eliminated the pattern of private practice, though it has modified it greatly.

2. Research and the Structure of Medicine

These aspects of structural change are in a certain sense obvious. There is, however, another set which is even more important, but of a type which has been less adequately handled by social scientists. These concern the involvement of medicine with the sciences and particularly the enormous recent proliferation of the research function. It should be remembered that the old pattern of medical practice was established before the era of "scientific medicine," following particularly on the discoveries of Pasteur and Koch. To be sure, since Hippocrates, Western medicine has in some sense been "scientific," but the mid- to later nineteeth century saw a new era. It was this which led to the establishment of the University medical school as standard, and to the teaching hospital as the focus of the very best of medical care to be found anywhere. The outside private practitioner applied what he had learned there; he was not the fountainhead.

The focus of the biggest change since then has been the general upgrading of the level of science involved in medicine, and with it the rapidly increasing participation of scientists who are not themselves medical men. The line, of course, has been indefinite, thus a W. B. Cannon, though a medical man working in a medical school laboratory, was functionally a general physiologist rather than a physician. Indeed, Pasteur himself was not even an M.D., but a chemist, which was one of the main sources of medical opposition to him. However, in the earlier phases, a larger proportion of "medical research" was carried on by physicians in the clinic. Gradually, however, as the scientific problems have become more technical, the proportion of laboratory as distinguished from strictly clinical research has increased, and above all the proportion of scientists whose qualifications are not clinical has increased, as has their strategic importance.

In Western society generally, American in particular, the world of science has, of course, been developing very rapidly, socially as well as culturally. Its organizational focus has been the modern university. The era of the early phase of scientific medicine was the first step of integration of medicine into this developing complex, which has since proceeded much farther, especially in terms of interpenetration between medical and other faculties, and of the increasing differentiation between research and clinical services as such. It is perhaps not too much to say that now the keystone of the medical arch has become the university-hospital research complex. This is the fountainhead of the *technical* standards of medicine as distinguished from its fiduciary standards.[7]

7. It is interesting that frequently it is asserted that the connection with good research is an essential prerequisite of good *patient care*. A significant example is the Department of Medicine and Surgery of the Veteran's Administration. In its first generation the V.A. system operated autonomously, and its medical standards left much to be desired. Following World War II, as a measure to raise standards of patient care, the basic decision was taken to seek affiliation for as many V.A. hospitals as possible with university

In the hospital and clinic, the physician has had to learn to co-operate on a daily basis with, if not laymen, at least fellow physicians who were not in fact practicing medicine. Indeed, the physician-administrator has been a transitional type and recently an increasing proportion of hospital administrators have been laymen.[8] Of course, this is much more generally, and early, true for the fiduciary level of boards of trustees.

At the training level, relatively early in the era of scientific medicine, physicians had to become accustomed to working with a class of nonphysicians at the level of equal colleagues; namely, the teachers of the "basic sciences" in medical schools, an increasing proportion of whom have been laymen in the medical sense. This situation, however, has been very greatly accentuated by the burgeoning of research. The *tendency*—though not without qualification—is clearly for the research scientist in this respect to become "top dog," and whether or not he holds a medical degree is irrelevant, and an increasing proportion do not. It is in the relatively restricted field of responsibility for the welfare of patients, who are being treated as subjects for research purposes, that the qualifications of the physician as such are essential. Of course, in turn, when the results of research reach the stage of clinical application, physicians as such naturally take over.[9]

It is particularly important here that in the earlier phases of the development away from the predominance of the completely isolated physician alone in relation to his patient, cooperation in the physician's function involved mainly what I have called "auxiliary" personnel, of whom the nurse is perhaps the prototype, followed by the

medical schools, so in effect they became teaching hospitals. Recently a further step has been taken, namely, it has been asserted, again in the interests of the quality of *patient care,* that it is essential that V.A. installations be actively involved in medical research.

8. This is not altogether new. In 1936, I visited the famous Mayo Clinic. To be sure, it was founded and in some sense controlled by physicians, the elder Mayo and his two sons. When it got large, however, it became necessary to employ a business manager, who was a layman. The Mayo Clinic has been famous for its use of the sliding scale. In an interview with him, the Manager told me that of course *he,* not the physician in charge of the case, made the final decision of what the patient should pay, though he was "interested" in the physician's opinion.

9. What is still, to me, the classical statement of this situation in medical research was made by Dr. Sidney Farber of the Harvard Medical School in a communication to the American Academy of Arts and Sciences, May 1957. This view is summarized in the *Bulletin* of the Academy.

laboratory technician, the social worker, and various others. The point is that such auxiliary personnel are in no professional sense the equals of the physician, they are there to "help" him, but very definitely under his direction. But the hospital trustee or administrator—particularly the latter because of his close involvement with day-to-day operations, and even more the scientist in "medical" research, cannot be treated as "helpers" of the physician. They are clearly his equals in general status, and his superiors with respect to certain essential functions. There is specialization not only *within* the medical profession itself but also *between* its members and the performers of other functions essential to the total complex of health care.

3. The Behavioral Sciences

A complicated special case involved in this process has been that of the surprisingly rapid, but still elementary, involvement of the behavioral sciences in the health situation. For reasons understandable in terms of their relative maturity at the time, the concept "scientific" medicine in the crucial period, clearly referred to natural science. Such relevance as psychology and sociology might have clearly belonged to the "art" not the "science" of medicine. Only gradually has this begun to change, not least because of the advances which have been taking place in the behavioral sciences themselves. But perhaps equally important has been the series of changing circumstances which have meant that the art of medicine in its traditional sense could no longer be taken for granted.

One direction of contribution from them has not impinged very directly on traditional medical concerns, namely, as medicine became more involved in larger-scale organization, naturally many problems arose as to the functioning of such organizations. The fields of study of bureaucracy and of "industrial sociology" had provided a certain set of points of reference for application to medical organizations, and a good deal of research has of course been carried out by social scientists in this field. In the field of mental health, however, the question arises relatively directly of the effects of organization directly on the state of the patient—though clearly this problem area ramifies into most fields of medicine. Thus the well-known Stanton and Schwartz study set a tone for the importance of these problems.[10]

10. Alfred Stanton and Morris Schwartz, *The Mental Hospital,* 1st edition, New York, Basic Books, 1954.

The other main line, however, ran from direct concern with the doctor-patient relationship itself, to its relevance not only to mental illness and its therapy, but to the whole psychosomatic field as well. Here the impingement of psychology, in the first instance, psychoanalysis, but then increasingly of sociology and anthropology, has borne very directly on the constitutive concerns of medicine itself. The relation of this theme to one of the main themes of this paper is clear, and will not be further pursued here.

A few points may, however, be made about the relevance of the status of the behavioral sciences from a sociological viewpoint in relation to medicine. First, two closely related phenomena should be called to attention and interpreted in the present context. The first is the gradual, but in this country nearly complete, drawing of the psychoanalytic movement into the medical orbit, so that today only physicians are authorized to conduct psychoanalytic therapy. It is, of course, well known that this occurred contrary to the wishes of Freud himself (cf. *The Problem of Lay Analysis*). Clearly, this has very much to do with the problem of legitimation of a new and widely disturbing set of innovations in the mental health field.

The second phenomenon is the special pattern of the involvement of "academic" psychology in the "clinical" field. It is perhaps to oversimplify, but not too seriously, to say that lacking the prestige of the older natural sciences which might have established psychology as a basic science relative to medicine, the psychologists, greatly aided by the severe shortage of psychiatrists relative to the demand for treatment, unfortunately accepted the status of an auxiliary profession in the medical setting, that is, of members of the "psychiatric team," but with the understanding that the psychiatrist was unequivocally captain of the team. This was clearly anomalous if there was a genuine component of basic science involved, in which the psychologist was presumably trained, whereas his professional superior, the clinical psychiatrist, was typically not—indeed before the broad reception of psychoanalysis, the psychiatrist's competence was based almost wholly on empirical clinical experience. The situation was then further exacerbated by the drive of psychologists to be allowed to take responsibility for psychotherapy in direct competition with psychiatry, which has among other things led them into the labyrinth of certification legislation.

Sociologists and anthropologists have been spared these difficulties for two main reasons, along perhaps with a somewhat lower position in the order of the academic disciplines, at least from the "natural science" point of view. One reason is that sociologists and anthropologists are not nearly so close to a competitive position in relation to therapy in any branch of medicine—they do not presume to replace the physician with respect to any of his primary traditional responsibilities. Unavoidably they sometimes have to tell him that what he fondly believed is often not so, but this is not so difficult a position as the psychologist's. A second reason, applying particularly to sociology, was its early dissociation from social work, precisely at a time when the latter had become integrated with medicine as an auxiliary profession. Since social work was not defined as "applied sociology" at that time, there was, even apart from the lesser demand, little temptation for sociologists to assume the role of auxiliary profession relative to medicine.

The entry of sociology and anthropology into the medical orbit has hence come about mainly in the research context. It was favored both by the more general development of the research interest in medicine and by the maturation of these fields themselves, as well as by the increasing consciousness of need in medical circles. Indeed, the increasing involvement in research instead of merely diagnostic testing and therapy has helped greatly to redress the balance of the relations of psychologists to medicine.

CONCLUSION

IN conclusion, the demand for the services of behavioral scientists in the medical context, should be fitted into the general process of structural differentiation and its concomitants. It is only with the breakdown of the "omnicompetence" of the traditional medical practitioner that occasion could arise for him to call on the services of specialists in certain phases of the previous art of medicine, which at one time and to some degree was believed not to be susceptible to scientific treatment at all. The opening for the behavioral scientist is thus a consequence of the differentiation of the cultural subject-matter itself.

This, however, has been associated with a wider process of the upgrading and generalization of the cultural basis of medicine. Not only have the previous basic sciences become much more "advanced" and their ramifications into medicine much more complex, but there has been a process of extension of the scientific base into new fields, notably the "behavioral." These fields were previously thought either to have no bearing at all on health, or not to be susceptible of scientific treatment, because they belonged to the field of "art."

This process in turn has been associated with an extension of the focus of ultimate "responsibility" for the health problems of the society. There was once a sense in which the medical profession shouldered that responsibility virtually unaided except for the basic legitimation of its position in the community. Now it clearly must be shared with administrators and trustees, governmental and private, and with universities as organizations. Perhaps above all it is now shared with the various relevant scientific professions, the most recent additions to which are the behavioral.

This, of course, is, from the point of view of traditional medical function, a fiduciary rather than an operative responsibility. The biochemist working in the field of cancer research does not treat a single patient, but the fates of many thousands of future patients may depend on the success of his work. Similar considerations apply to the contributions of administrative and fiduciary personnel.

A further highly significant feature of the general process of change which has been going on is the generalization of the value-complex involving health problems. This is a relatively intangible matter to which little explicit research attention has been devoted. The central phenomenon here seems to be the application of the basic concept of health, and hence illness, to progressively higher levels and broader ranges in the organization of human action systems. The earlier phase of scientific medicine treated illness as a result of highly specific invading bacterial agents, and the specific internal lesions were the prototypes. On the organic levels the direction of change has been toward increasing relevance of considerations of the general equilibrium of the organism.

The second direction of change has concerned the levels of organization of action involved. In the earlier period mental illness was treated as an anomalous item which either did or did not belong to medicine at all or was in some simple though unknown way a manifestation of organic disturbances—preferably in the genetic constitution. First there developed, pre-eminently through psychoanalysis, the beginnings of genuinely scientific understanding of mental pathology. From there, there has occurred the gradual building of a bridge to the somatic, in the clinical field of psychosomatic illness, lately very much backed up by rapidly developing understanding of the functioning of the brain.

Still a further and highly significant process has been the increasing extensity of the systems taken into account in the understanding of various levels of illness. At all levels these systems now transcend the individual. On the more organic ones, of course, the epidemiology of infectious disease established an important prototype, one response to which was the establishment of the new profession of public health. Similar phenomena are beginning to occur in the field of mental health and the psychic factors in somatic illness through increasing knowledge of the interdependencies of the states of health and illness in these respects of different individuals, hence the dependence for the particular case, on the states of the social and cultural systems in which he is involved.

Finally, particularly where the psychic components are involved, there has undoubtedly been an extension of the range of inclusion of phenomena which are defined as illness. In particular, as is well known, this extension has invaded the previous area allocated to the category of crime, and also to an important degree of "error" (cf. J. R. Pitts in *Theories of Society,* Introduction to Part III, 1961). This, after all, is to be expected if, as I have long contended, illness is to a high degree not only a "condition" but also an institutionally defined role-state in the social system. There is, on this basis, no reason to assume that either its content is fully determined by factors outside the social system or that this content will remain unchanged through important processes of change in the larger social system of which it is a part.

The above considerations focus on the criteria of categorization of an individual as sick and the various components which can be brought to bear in such a diagnosis. The relevance to values lies in the fact that this definition of illness is a part of the definition of a subsystem of the society, the category of its members who at any given time are defined as sick in relation to the therapeutic agencies which bear responsibility for their treatment. The value system is the pattern of instrumental activism, specified to the level of this subsystem of the society. This involves not only the negative valuation of the state of illness, but commitment to the attempt to control it —applying as we have noted to patients as well as to therapeutic agencies. It also implies the "therapeutic" method of control, which takes full account of the sense in which illness is not a matter of the personal responsibility of the sick person, that is, he cannot be expected simply to "pull himself together" and stop being sick, as a person can be expected to resist the temptation to commit a criminal act.

In terms of this definition of the situation, then, the values of medical practice, and other agencies involved in the health-illness complex, constitute the *commitments,* independent of particular situation or particular subfunction of those involved—again, let it be clear, including patients—to both effectiveness and integrity in the handling of these problems. As I see it the *pattern* of this value-complex has not changed in the relevant time-period, but the *content* has become more inclusive and more generalized, so that those committed to the value-pattern, and so situated in the social system that they must take an important share of responsibility for its implementation, must consider a wider range of conditions to fall within their sphere than before, and must be open to the relevance of a wider range and higher level of facilities—notably knowledge and skill—than before.

To come back to the main theoretical starting point: On the one hand it has become very clear indeed why the pattern of economic self-interest both does not and cannot dominate the institutional expectation system of the health field. It is also clear that with the general process of development even of the predominantly "free enterprise" type of industrial society, the range and importance of this complex has been increasing rather than decreasing, not because in the usual sense social change has generated an increasing burden of illness, but because the extension and upgrading of therapeutic functions is an integral part of the main process of development of the social system. Above all there had been increasing, not decreasing, integration into the main cultural process of the development of science and its applications.

The internal development of the health complex, has, moreover, been one of essential continuity, from the classical physician-patient relationship of private practice as a reference point. All of the main analytical components which have played essential parts in the later development were identifiable for this case. In order to interpret them properly, however, it was necessary to transcend the older paradigm of the patterns of "orientation" of two types of individual persons in roles, and to treat even this dyad *as a total social system,* above all as a collectivity with common norms and values. Once this has

been worked out it is possible to trace and interpret a continuous
series of steps of differentiation of this system, of increasing inclusiveness of collectivity organization, of normative upgrading in a number
of contexts and of generalization of the value system, all of which
are essential features of the present complex and rapidly changing
situation.

Bibliography of Talcott Parsons

1928

"Capitalism" in Recent German Literature: Sombart and Weber, I. *Journal Political Economy*, 36:641–661.

1929

"Capitalism" in Recent German Literature: Sombart and Weber, II. *Journal Political Economy*, 37:31–51.

1930

Translation of Weber, Max. *The Protestant Ethic and the Spirit of Capitalism*. London, Allen and Unwin; and New York, Scribners.

1931

Wants and Activities in Marshall. *Quarterly J. Economics*, 46:101–140.

1932

Economics and Sociology: Marshall in Relation to the Thought of his Time. *Quarterly J. Economics*, 46:316–347.

* Also in *Essays in Sociological Theory: Pure and Applied*, New York, The Free Press of Glencoe, 1st ed., 1949.
† Also in *Essays in Sociological Theory, op. cit.*, revised ed., 1954.
‡ Also in *Structure and Process in Modern Societies*, New York, The Free Press of Glencoe, 1960.
§ Also in this volume.

1933

Malthus. *Encyclopedia of the Social Sciences,* 10:68–69.
Pareto. *Encyclopedia of the Social Sciences,* 11:576–578.

1934

Some Reflections on "The Nature and Significance of Economics."
Quarterly J. Economics, 48:511–545.
Society. *Encyclopedia of the Social Sciences,* 14:225–231.
Sociological Elements in Economic Thought. I. *Quarterly J. Economics,*
49:414–453.

1935

Sociological Elements in Economic Thought. II. *Quarterly J. Economics,*
49:645–667.
The Place of Ultimate Values in Sociological Theory. *International J.
Ethics,* 45:282–316.
H. M. Robertson on Max Weber and His School. *Journal Political Econ-
omy,* 43:688–696.

1936

Pareto's Central Analytical Scheme. *J. Social Philos.,* 1:244–262.
On Certain Sociological Elements in Professor Taussig's Thought. In
*Explorations in Economics: Notes and Essays contributed in honor
of F. W. Taussig,* Jacob Viner (ed.), New York, McGraw-Hill, pp.
358–379.

1937

The Structure of Social Action. New York, McGraw-Hill. Reprinted by
The Free Press of Glencoe, New York, 1949.
Education and the Professions. *International J. Ethics,* 47:365–369.

1938

The Role of Theory in Social Research. *American Sociological Review,*
3:13–20. (An address delivered before the Annual Institute of the
Society for Social Research, at the University of Chicago, Summer,
1937.

*† The Role of Ideas in Social Action. *American Sociological Review,* 3:653–664. (Written for a meeting on the problem of ideologies at the American Sociological Society's annual meeting, Atlantic City, N.J., December, 1937.)

1939

*† The Professions and Social Structure. *Social Forces,* 17:457–467. Written to be read at the annual meeting of the American Sociological Society in Detroit, December, 1938.)
Comte. *J. Unified Sci.,* 9:77–83.

1940

*† Analytical Approach to the Theory of Social Stratification. *American Journal of Sociology,* 45:841–862.
*† Motivation of Economic Activities. *Canadian Journal of Economics and Political Science,* 6:187–203. (Originally given as a public lecture at the University of Toronto.) Also published in *Essays in Sociology,* C. W. M. Hart (ed.), Toronto, U. of Toronto Press, 1940; and in *Human Relations in Administration: The Sociology of Organization,* Robert Dubin (ed.), New York, Prentice-Hall, 1st ed., 1951.

1942

Max Weber and the Contemporary Political Crisis. *Rev. Politics,* 4:61–76, 155–172.
The Sociology of Modern Anti-Semitism. In *Jews in a Gentile World,* J. Graeber and Steuart Henderson Britt (eds.), New York, Macmillan, pp. 101–122.
*† Age and Sex in the Social Structure of the United States. *American Sociological Review,* 7: 604–616. (Read at the annual meeting of the American Sociological Society in New York, December 1941.) Republished in several sources, notably Logan Wilson and William Kolb, *Sociological Analysis,* New York, Harcourt, 1949; and Clyde Kluckhohn and Henry Murray (eds.), *Personality in Nature, Society and Culture,* New York, Alfred A. Knopf, 1st and 2nd editions.
*† Propaganda and Social Control. *Psychiatry,* 5:551–572.
* Democracy and the Social Structure in Pre-Nazi Germany. *J. Legal and Political Sociology,* 1:96–114.

* Some Sociological Aspects of the Fascist Movements. *Social Forces,* 21:138–147. (Written as the presidential address to the Eastern Sociological Society, 1942.)

1943

*† The Kinship System of the Contemporary United States. *American Anthropologist,* 45:22–38.

1944

*† The Theoretical Development of the Sociology of Religion. *Journal of the History of Ideas,* 5:176–190. (Originally written to be read at the Conference on Methods in Science and Philosophy in New York, November 1942.) Reprinted in *Ideas in Cultural Perspective,* Philip Wiener and Aaron Noland (eds.), New Brunswick, N.J., Rutgers University Press, 1962.

1945

*† The Present Position and Prospects of Systematic Theory in Sociology. In *Twentieth Century Sociology, A Symposium,* Georges Gurvitch and Wilbert E. Moore (eds.), New York, Philosophical Library.
*† The Problem of Controlled Institutional Change: An Essay on Applied Social Science. *Psychiatry,* 8:79–101. (Prepared as an appendix to the report of the Conference On Germany after World War II.)
Racial and Religious Differences as Factors in Group Tensions. In *Unity and Difference in the Modern World, A Symposium,* Louis Finkelstein, *et al.* (eds.), New York, The Conference on Science, Philosophy and Religion in Their Relation to the Democratic Way of Life, Inc.

1946

The Science Legislation and the Role of the Social Sciences. *American Sociological Review,* 11:653–666.
* Population and Social Structure (of Japan). In *Japan's Prospect,* Douglas G. Haring (ed.), Cambridge, Harvard University Press, pp. 87–114. (This book was published by the staff of the Harvard School for Overseas Administration.)
*† Certain Primary Sources and Patterns of Aggression in the Social Structure of the Western World. *Psychiatry,* 10:167–181. (Prepared for the Conference on Science, Philosophy, and Religion at

its September, 1946 meeting in Chicago; also published in the volume issued by the Conference.)

Some Aspects of the Relations Between Social Science and Ethics. *Social Science,* 22:213–217. (Read at the Annual Meeting of the American Association for the Advancement of Science in Boston, December, 1946.)

Science Legislation and the Social Sciences. *Political Science Quarterly,* Vol. LXII, No. 2 (June, 1947); *Bulletin of Atomic Scientists,* January, 1947.

Max Weber: The Theory of Social and Economic Organization. (co-translator with A. M. Henderson.) Oxford University Press, 1947. Edited, with an introduction, by Talcott Parsons. Reprinted by The Free Press of Glencoe, New York, 1957.

1948

Sociology, 1941–46 (Co-author with Bernard Barber). *American Journal of Sociology,* 53:245–257.

† The Position of Sociological Theory. *American Sociological Review,* 13:156–171. (Paper read before the annual meeting of the American Sociological Society, New York City, December, 1947.)

1949

Essays in Sociological Theory Pure and Applied. New York, The Free Press of Glencoe, 1st ed.

The Rise and Decline of Economic Man. *Journal of General Education,* 4:47–53.

* Social Classes and Class Conflict in the Light of Recent Sociological Theory. *American Economic Review,* 39:16–26. (Read at meeting of the American Economic Association, December, 1948.)

1950

* The Prospects of Sociological Theory. *American Sociological Review,* 15:3–16. (Presidential address read before the meeting of the American Sociological Society in New York City, December, 1949.)

* Psychoanalysis and the Social Structure. *The Psychoanalytic Quarterly,* 19:371–384. (The substance of this paper was presented at the meeting of the American Psychoanalytic Association, Washington, D.C., May, 1948.)

The Social Environment of the Educational Process. *Centennial,* Washington, D.C., American Association for the Advancement of Science, pp. 36–40. (Read at the AAAS Centennial Celebration, September, 1948.)

1951

The Social System. New York, The Free Press of Glencoe.

Toward a General Theory of Action. Editor and contributor with Edward A. Shils, *et al.,* Cambridge, Harvard University Press. Reprinted by Harper Torchbooks, New York, 1962.

Graduate Training in Social Relations at Harvard. *Journal of General Education,* 5:149–157.

Illness and the Role of the Physician: A Sociological Perspective. *American Journal of Orthopsychiatry,* 21:452–460. (Presented at the 1951 annual meeting of the American Orthopsychiatric Association in Detroit.) Reprinted in *Personality in Nature, Society and Culture,* Clyde Kluckhohn and Henry Murray (eds.), New York, Alfred A. Knopf.

1952

§ The Superego and the Theory of Social Systems. *Psychiatry,* 15:15–25. (The substance of this paper was read at the meeting of the Psychoanalytic Section of the American Psychiatric Association in Cincinnati, May 1951.) Reprinted in Parsons, *et al., Working Papers in the Theory of Action,* New York, The Free Press of Glencoe, 1953.

Religious Perspectives in College Teaching: Sociology and Social Psychology. In *Religious Perspectives in College Teaching,* Hoxie N. Fairchild (ed.), New York, The Ronald Press Company, pp. 286–337.

* A Sociologist Looks at the Legal Profession. *Conference on the Profession of Law and Legal Education,* Conference Series Number II, The Law School, University of Chicago, pp. 49–63. (This paper was presented at the first symposium on the occasion of the Fiftieth Anniversary Celebration of the University of Chicago Law School, December, 1952.)

1953

Working Papers in the Theory of Action (In collaboration with Robert F. Bales and Edward A. Shils). New York, The Free Press of Glencoe.

Psychoanalysis and Social Science with Special Reference to the Oedipus Problem. In *Twenty Years of Psychoanalysis,* Franz Alexander and Helen Ross (eds.), New York, W. W. Norton and Company, pp. 186–215. (The substance of this paper was read at the Twentieth

Anniversary Celebration of the Institute for Psychoanalysis, in Chicago, October 1952.)

* A Revised Analytical Approach to the Theory of Social Stratification. In *Class, Status, and Power: A Reader in Social Stratification*, Reinhard Bendix and Seymour M. Lipset (eds.), New York, The Free Press of Glencoe, pp. 92–129.

Illness, Therapy and the Modern Urban American Family (Co-author with Renée Fox). *Journal of Social Issues*, 8:31–44. Reprinted in *Patients, Physicians, and Illness*, E. Gartly Jaco (ed.), New York, The Free Press of Glencoe, 1958.

Some Comments on the State of the General Theory of Action. *American Sociological Review*, Vol. 18, No. 6 (December, 1953), pp. 618–631.

1954

§ The Father Symbol: An Appraisal in the Light of Psychoanalytic and Sociological Theory. In *Symbols and Values: An Initial Study*, 13th Symposium of the Conference on Science, Philosophy and Religion, Lyman Bryson, *et al.* (eds.), New York, Harper & Row, pp. 523–544. (The substance of this paper was read at the meeting of the American Psychological Association at Washington, D.C., September, 1952.)

Essays in Sociological Theory. New York, The Free Press of Glencoe, revis. ed.

Psychology and Sociology. In *For A Science of Social Man*, John P. Gillin (ed.), New York, Macmillan, pp. 67–102.

§ The Incest Taboo in Relation to Social Structure and the Socialization of the Child. *British Journal of Sociology*, Vol. V, No. 2 (June, 1954), 101–117.

1955

Family, Socialization and Interaction Process (With Robert F. Bales, James Olds, Morris Zelditch, and Philip E. Slater). New York, The Free Press of Glencoe.

"McCarthyism" and American Social Tension: A Sociologist's View. *Yale Review* (Winter, 1955), 226–245. Reprinted as "Social Strains in America" in *The New American Right*, Daniel Bell (ed.), New York, Criterion Books, 1955.

1956

A Sociological Model for Economic Development (Co-author with Neil J. Smelser). In *Explorations in Entrepreneurial History*, Harvard University.

Economy and Society. Co-author with Neil J. Smelser. London, Routledge and Kegan Paul; and New York, The Free Press of Glencoe.

Élements pour une théorie de l'action. With an introduction by François Bourricaud. Paris, Plon.

A Sociological Approach to the Theory of Organizations. *Administrative Science Quarterly,* I (June, 1956), 63–85; II (September, 1956), 225–239.

1957

‡ The Distribution of Power in American Society. *World Politics,* X (October, 1957), 123–143.

Malinowski and the Theory of Social Systems. In *Man and Culture,* Raymond Firth (ed.), London, Routledge and Kegan Paul.

Man in His Social Environment—As Viewed by Modern Social Science. *Centennial Review of Arts and Science,* Michigan State University (Winter, 1957), 50–69.

The Mental Hospital as a Type of Organization. In *The Patient and the Mental Hospital,* Milton Greenblatt, Daniel J. Levinson, and Richard H. Williams (eds.), New York, The Free Press of Glencoe.

Réflexions sur les Organisations Religieuses aux États-Unis. *Archives de Sociologie des Religions* (January–June), 21–36.

Sociologia di dittatura. Bologne, Il Molino.

1958

† Authority, Legitimation, and Political Action. In *Authority,* C. J. Friedrich (ed.), Cambridge, Harvard University Press.

§ The Definitions of Health and Illness in the Light of American Values and Social Structure. In *Patients, Physicians, and Illness,* E. Gartly Jaco (ed.), New York, The Free Press of Glencoe.

§ Social Structure and the Development of Personality. *Psychiatry* (November, 1958), 321–340.

General Theory in Sociology. In *Sociology Today,* Robert K. Merton, Leonard Broom, and Leonard S. Cottrell, Jr. (eds.), New York, Basic Books, 1959.

‡ Some Ingredients of a General Theory of Formal Organization. In *Administrative Theory in Education,* Andrew W. Halpin (ed.), Chicago, Midwest Administration Center, University of Chicago.

‡ Some Reflections on the Institutional Framework of Economic Development. *The Challenge of Development: A Symposium,* Jerusalem, The Hebrew University.

‡ Some Trends of Change in American Society: Their Bearing on Medical Education. *Journal of the American Medical Association* (May, 1958), 31–36.

‡ The Pattern of Religious Organization in the United States. *Daedalus* (Summer, 1958), 65–85.

The Concepts of Culture and of Social System. With A. L. Kroeber. *American Sociological Review* (October, 1958), 582.

Some Highlights of the General Theory of Action. In *Approaches to the Study of Politics,* Roland Young (ed.), Evanston, Northwestern University Press.

1959

An Approach to Psychological Theory in Terms of the Theory of Action. In *Psychology: A Science,* Vol. III, Sigmund Koch (ed.), New York, McGraw-Hill, pp. 612–711.

‡ The Principal Structures of Community: A Sociological View. In *Community,* C. J. Friedrich (ed.), New York, The Liberal Arts Press.

"Voting" and the Equilibrium of the American Political System. In *American Voting Behavior,* Eugene Burdick and Arthur Brodbeck (eds.), New York, The Free Press of Glencoe.

Implications of the Study (on Marjorie Fiske's study, "Book Selection and Retention in California Public and School Libraries"). *The Climate of Book Selection,* a symposium of the University of California School of Librarianship, Berkeley, University of California Press.

Some Problems Confronting Sociology as a Profession. *American Sociological Review,* Vol. 24, No. 4 (August, 1959).

§ The School Class as a Social System. *Harvard Educational Review* (Fall, 1959). Reprinted in *Education, Economy and Society,* A. H. Halsey, Jean Floud, Arnold C. Anderson (eds.), New York, The Free Press of Glencoe, 1961.

An Approach to the Sociology of Knowledge. *Proceedings,* Vol. IV Fourth World Congress of Sociology at Milan, Italy (September, 1959).

1960

§ Mental Illness and "Spiritual Malaise": the Roles of the Psychiatrist and of the Minister of Religion. In *The Ministry and Mental Health,* Hans Hofmann (ed.), New York, Association Press.

Structure and Process in Modern Societies. New York, The Free Press of Glencoe.

In memoriam, "Clyde Kluckhohn, 1905–1960," *American Sociological Review* (December, 1960).

The Mass Media and the Structure of American Society. Co-author with Winston White. *Journal of Social Issues,* Vol. XVI, No. 3 (1960).

Durkheim's Contribution to the Theory of Integration of Social Systems. In *Emile Durkheim, 1858–1917: A Collection of Essays, with Translations and a Bibliography,* Kurt H. Wolff (ed.), Columbus, Ohio State University Press.

Some Principal Characteristics of Industrial Societies. In *The Transformation of Russian Society Since 1861,* C. E. Black (ed.), Cambridge, Harvard University Press.

Pattern Variables Revisited: A Response to Professor Dubin's Stimulus. *American Sociological Review* (August, 1960).

§ Toward a Healthy Maturity. *J. Health and Human Behavior* (Fall, 1960).

Social Structure and Political Orientation (A review of S. M. Lipset, *Political Man,* and William Kornhauser, *The Politics of Mass Society*). *World Politics* (October, 1960).

A Review of *Max Weber: An Intellectual Portrait,* by Reinhard Bendix. *American Sociological Review* (October, 1960).

1961

Theories of Society (Co-editor with Edward Shils, Kaspar D. Naegele, and Jesse R. Pitts). 2 vols., New York, The Free Press of Glencoe.

§ The Link Between Character and Society (Co-author with Winston White). In *Culture and Social Character,* S. M. Lipset and Leo Lowenthal (eds.), New York, The Free Press of Glencoe.

The Cultural Background of American Religious Organization. The Proceedings of the Conference on Science, Philosophy and Religion, 1960.

The Point of View of the Author. In *The Social Theories of Talcott Parsons,* Max Black (ed.), Englewood Cliffs, N.J., Prentice-Hall.

The Problem of International Community. In *International Politics and Foreign Policy,* James N. Rosenau (ed.), New York, The Free Press of Glencoe.

Polarization of the World and International Order. *Berkeley Journal of Sociology* (1961). Reprinted in *Preventing World War III,* Quincy Wright, William M. Evan, and Morton Deutsch (eds.), New York, Simon and Schuster, 1962.

§ Youth in the Context of American Society. *Daedalus* (Winter, 1961). Reprinted in *Youth: Change and Challenge,* Erik Erikson (ed.), New York, Basic Books, 1963.

Some Considerations on the Theory of Social Change. *Rural Sociology,* Vol. 26, No. 3 (September, 1961).

A Sociologist's View. In *Values and Ideals of American Youth,* Eli Ginzberg (ed.), New York, Columbia University Press.

The Cultural Background of Today's Aged. In *Politics of Age,* Wilma Donahue and Clark Tibbitts (eds.). The proceedings of the Michigan University Conference on Aging (June, 1961).

Comment on Llewellyn Gross, "Preface to a Metatheoretical Framework for Sociology." *American Journal of Sociology* (September, 1961).

In memoriam "Alfred L. Kroeber, 1876–1960." *American Journal of Sociology,* Vol. LXVI, No. 6 (May, 1961).

Comment on William Kolb, "Images of Man and the Sociology of Religion," *Journal for the Scientific Study of Religion* (October, 1961).

Discussion of Trends Revealed by the 1960 Census of Population. *Proceedings of the Section on Social Statistics,* American Statistical Association.

1962

Polarization and the Problem of International Order (first published in 1961). See above: *Preventing World War III.*

Foreword to *Herbert Spencer: The Study of Sociology,* Ann Arbor, University of Michigan Press, Ann Arbor Paperback Series.

In memoriam "Clyde Kluckhohn, 1905–1960." With Evon Z. Vogt. *American Anthropologist* (February, 1962). Reprinted as "Introduction" in Clyde Kluckhohn, *Navajo Witchcraft,* Boston, Beacon Press.

Comment on Dennis Wrong, "The Oversocialized Conception of Man." *Psychoanalysis and Psychoanalytic Review* (Summer, 1962).

Review of Hurst, *Law and Social Process. Journal of History and Ideas* (October–December, 1962).

The Aging in American Society. *Law and Contemporary Problems* (Winter, 1962).

The Law and Social Control. In *Law and Sociology,* William M. Evan (ed.), New York, The Free Press of Glencoe, pp. 56–72.

In memoriam "Richard Henry Tawney, 1880–1962." *American Sociological Review* (December, 1962).

Review of Paul Diesing, *Reason in Society. Industrial and Labor Relations Review,* Cornell University, Ithaca, N.Y., 1962.

La struttura dell'azione sociale. Introduzione di Granfranco Poggi. Bologna, Il Molino, 1962.

1963

Introduction to Max Weber, *The Sociology of Religion.* Translated by Ephraim Fischo from *Wirtschaft und Gesellschaft.* Boston, Beacon Press.

Social Strains in America: A Postscript (1962). In *The Radical Right,* Daniel Bell (ed.), Garden City, N.Y., Doubleday and Company.

Christianity and Modern Industrial Society. In *Sociological Theory, Values, and Sociocultural Change: Essays in Honor of Pitirim A. Sorokin,* Edward A. Tiryakian (ed.), New York, The Free Press of Glencoe.

Social Change and Medical Organization in the United States. *Annals of the American Academy of Political and Social Science* (March, 1963).

On the Concept of Influence, with rejoinder to comments. *Public Opinion Quarterly* (Spring, 1963).

On the Concept of Political Power. *Proceedings of the American Philosophical Society,* Vol. 107, No. 3 (June, 1963).

Death in American Society. *The American Behavioral Scientist* (May, 1963).

To Be Published

§ Some Theoretical Considerations Bearing on the Field of Medical Sociology. For a book by Robert N. Rapoport and Robert Wilson, tentative title: *The Worlds of Medicine in Social Perspective,* probably to be published by the Russell Sage Foundation.

The Intellectual: A Social Role Category. In *The Intellectuals: Basic Readings,* Philip Rieff (ed.), to be published by Doubleday in 1964, and later in an Anchor edition.

The Ideas of Systems, Causal Explanation and Cybernetic Control in Social Science. *Cause and Effect,* Daniel Lerner (ed.), New York, The Free Press of Glencoe. (Compilation of papers given at MIT symposium on Cause and Effect.)

Some Reflections on the Place of Force in Social Process. In *Internal War: Basic Problems and Approaches,* Harry Eckstein (ed.), New York, The Free Press of Glencoe, 1964.

Evolutionary Universals. *American Sociological Review,* Spring, 1964.

Societies: Evolutionary and Comparative Perspectives. In *Foundations of Modern Sociology Series,* Alex Inkeles (ed.), Englewood Cliffs, N.J., Prentice-Hall, 1964.

Sociological Theory. *Encyclopaedia Britannica,* tentatively 1963.

Index*

* I am indebted to Walter Corson for compiling this index.

Lindemann, Erich, 330
Linton, Ralph, 334
Lipset, Seymour Martin, 9 n, 151 n, 184 n, 195 n, 209 n, 221 n
Lowenthal, Leo, 9 n, 151 n, 184 n, 221 n
Love attachment, 39, 44, 51, 93–94, 290
Love dependency, 4, 90
    transition from pleasure dependency to, 27

MacIver, R. M., 3 n, 34 n
Market, 339–341, 344
Marriage, 38–39, 58, 61, 64, 75, 105, 152–153, 213, 268, 300, 304–305, 309, 311, 329
    cross-cousin, 63 n, 65
    increased strain in, 166, 170
    See also Oedipal crisis
Marx, Karl, 327
Masculine role, 54–55, 60, 65, 98, 167, 213–214, 249
Massachusetts General Hospital, 330
Mayo Clinic, 351 n
Mayo, Elton, 13, 331
McClelland, David C., 138 n
McPhee, W. N., 146 n
Mead, George Herbert, 2 n, 80
Mead, Margaret, 44 n
Mechanism, 6, 13–14, 333, 335
Mechanism, control, 6, 121–124, 259–260, 273, 276–277, 304
    hierarchy of, 6, 114–115, 125–126
    See also Direction; Money; Pleasure; Reward
Mechanism, stabilizing, 22, 37
Medical economics, 325–326
Medical insurance, 348–349
Medical profession, 11, 13, 123, 268, 270, 280, 288–291, 315–316, 325–358
Medical research, 349–352
Medicine, and behavioral science, 352–358
Mendel, Gregor, 19, 80
Merton, Robert K., 97 n, 165 n, 225, 261 n, 285, 289 n
Minister, 12, 292, 299, 316–322
Mobility, 157, 228
Money
    as communication medium, 115
    as generalized exchange medium, 5–6, 116–119, 122
Moore, M. E., 151 n, 221, 223
Moral authority, 19
Moral standards, 22
    See also Norms; Values
Mother as social object, 89, 92
Mother role, 3, 60 n, 73–74, 95, 142–143, 153, 214, 219, 247–249, 308
Motivation, 17, 33, 45, 72, 85, 92, 103, 110, 218, 258, 284–287, 304–312, 322, 328–332, 335–336
    See also Achievement motivation; Internalization; Personality
Murdock, G. P., 58, 65
Murray, Henry A., 275 n

Naegele, Kaspar D., 316 n
Need gratification, see Gratification
Neurosis, 40, 51, 55, 102–103, 304
Neutrality, 343
Normative order, 21, 160, 171, 186, 199, 201, 204–205, 208, 268, 342
Normative pattern, 91, 96, 208, 212, 215, 221–222, 269–270, 300, 312, 338

Norms, 18, 80, 88, 163, 221, 267–268, 269–270, 280, 344, 357
    commitment to, 268, 270, 280
    See also Upgrading, normative

Object categorization, 343
Object cathexis, 5, 21–24, 29–30, 38–39, 45, 70, 80, 83, 85, 92–98, 103, 105–109, 120, 286
    See also Eroticism
Object choice, see Object cathexis
Object cognition, and culture, 23
Object relations, 4, 79–83, 92–99, 102–108, 118, 143, 332
Occupation of father, and college plans of child, 132
Occupational role, 7, 48–51, 64, 167, 193, 201–207, 210–211, 217–219, 224, 228, 245–247, 309
    and affective neutrality, 64
Occupational system, change in, 205
Oedipal crisis, 4, 7, 9, 30, 34, 39, 41, 51, 53, 79, 92 n, 95, 97–103, 218–219, 300, 303, 308–311, 332
    ambivalence in, 54
    erotic component in, 40
    source of strain in, 100
    See also Aggression; Marriage
Olds, James, 4, 5, 70 n, 84, 85 n, 91 n, 117 n, 126 n
Opportunity, 239, 279, 280
Oral dependency, 3
    See also Dependency
Oral phase, 93, 99, 108
Order, indeterminant in "other direction" (Riesman), 186–189
    See also Law; Normative order; Norms
Organism, see Personality
Organization of motivational system, 30, 85–88, 93, 109, 119, 258, 303, 308
    See also Ego
Organizations, 8, 64, 156–158, 167, 171, 178, 192, 198, 202–203, 206, 208, 234, 240, 249, 251, 269, 345–349, 352, 355
Orientation, modes of, 21, 36, 42, 45, 50, 269, 343, 357
    See also Collectivity; Self-interest

Parent role, 43, 45, 141, 171, 190 n, 215, 304, 311
Pareto, Vilfredo, 331
Particularism, 8, 47, 48, 136, 143, 343
Pasteur, Louis, 350
Patient role, 337–342
    See also Physician
Pattern variables, 328, 330, 333–334, 336, 343–344
    See also Achievement; Ascription; Collectivity orientation; Particularism; Universalism
Pattern maintenance function, 231, 279 n
Peer group, 10, 49, 75, 104–105, 130, 136, 139–140, 144, 150, 168, 173, 175, 185, 189, 190–192, 212, 217–228, 234, 265, 300, 310
    characteristics of, 139
    psychological functions of, 139
    relation to school class, 138–140
Performance, 47–48, 334, 343
Personality, 1–2, 8–10, 13–14, 32–35, 67, 75, 79, 84, 92, 94, 106, 115, 125, 143, 152, 159, 183, 230, 243, 259, 263–265, 271,